Contents

SOCIOLOGY IN PRACTICE

An introduction to sociology and social science

Mike O'Donnell
Joan Garrod

To Tara and Enid With Love

Thomas Nelson and Sons Ltd
Nelson House   Mayfield Road
Walton-on-Thames   Surrey
KT12 5PL   UK

51 York Place
Edinburgh
EH1 3JD   UK

Thomas Nelson (Hong Kong) Ltd
Toppan Building 10/F
22A Westlands Road
Quarry Bay   Hong Kong

Thomas Nelson Australia
102 Dodds Street
South Melbourne   Victoria 3205
Australia

Nelson Canada
1120 Birchmount Road
Scarborough   Ontario
M1K 5G4   Canada

© Mike O'Donnell and Joan Garrod 1990

First published by Thomas Nelson and Sons Ltd 1990

ISBN 0-17-448173-X
NPN 9 8 7 6

Printed in Hong Kong.

Preface

This book is intended as an introduction to sociology and social science at GCSE level. It differs from purely sociological introductory texts in that it provides very full sections on economics and politics, and also raises economic and political issues throughout the chapters.

As a GCSE text, this book seeks to be accessible to the full ability range of students preparing for that examination. The main way in which we have tried to achieve this is by keeping the vocabulary of the text straightforward (or giving explanations where it is not) and by defining all the main sociological terms both in the text and in a glossary. Main stimulus questions are 'stepped' in ascending order of difficulty, as is the case with most GCSE examination questions.

We have tried to appeal particularly to mature and adult students. This has been done by using material likely to be of interest to them as well as to fourteen to sixteen year olds, and by trying to avoid a simplistic approach. In addition, the strongly issue-oriented, questioning approach of the text and many of the activities should particularly stimulate students who have some relevant experiences to draw on.

The title, *Sociology in Practice*, indicates the practical emphasis of the book. Firstly, students will be doing much more thinking, discussing and working on activities than in pre-GCSE days. There is also full guidance on project and assignments work, and each chapter concludes with several suggestions for these. Secondly, sociological concepts and analysis are illustrated more by reference to current issues and trends than to sociological works. We hope that teachers will be sufficiently sympathetic to this approach to want to keep updating the material by the use of their own data and examples.

Most chapters are divided into two or three sections, each of which ends with a major stimulus and/or structured question and an activity. However, we have departed from that plan in some chapters when the subject matter requires it. In addition, a variety of questions and activities occur throughout chapters, though the text can be read independently of them.

Sociology in Practice is primarily aimed at meeting the requirements of the main GCSE Sociology syllabuses. However, we have set sociology in the broad context of social science and the humanities, and the book is also offered as a social science text. In addition, it covers the main requirements of the LEAG Community Studies syllabus and should also be useful in teaching integrated humanities.

Finally, there is more 'content' here than might be expected. This is partly because, in shaping this book for the 1980s and 1990s, we have had to make reference to issues and trends not yet widely dealt with elsewhere at this level. It also reflects our view that students best develop the skills of analysis, application and interpretation by employing them on interesting, topical and sometimes controversial issues and information.

We have taken the opportunity to update and make minor revisions in this reprint of *Sociology in Practice*.

Mike O'Donnell
Joan Garrod
April 1992

Acknowledgements

The authors would like to thank each other. Each of them feels that the book would not have been completed without the other. Mike O'Donnell would like to thank his colleagues, Jim Pey and Angela Bradding, for their helpful comments on parts of the manuscript. Thanks, too, to the GCSE classes of 1987–89 which cheerfully piloted much of his material. Valerie Hughes and Sandra den Hertog did the typing promptly and efficiently. Joan Garrod would like to thank her sociology students, and also Ray, for his support and encouragement.

The authors and publishers are grateful to the following for permission to use their work:

Mike Abrahams/Network p. 99; J. Allan Cash Ltd pp. 133, 227; All-Sport Photographic Ltd p. 213; Barnaby's Picture Library pp. 114 and Colin Cuthbert p. 46, Stuart Haden p. 84, David Alexander Simson p. 73; Camera Press Ltd p. 83; John Clark pp. 14, 65, 76, 106, 118, 136, 172, 197; Mark Edwards pp. 10, 72, 73; Mary Evans Picture Library pp. 255, 264; The Fotomas Index p. 110; The Francis Frith Collection p. 36; Glasgow Herald/IBM p. 227; Sally and Richard Greenhill pp. 78, 136, 180, 188, 200 (twice) 204, 247; Greenpeace p. 84; The *Guardian* pp. 10, 75, 79, 115, 120, 281; David Hoffman p. 175; The *Huddersfield Examiner* p. 113; Hulton-Deutsch Collection pp. 36, 110; The *Independent* pp. 105, 127; Hulton Picture Company/Keystone Press Agency Ltd p. 20, 142; Barry Lewis/Network p. 271, 279; Neil Libbort/Network p. 268; NSPCC p. 192; Humphrey Nemar p. 178; The *Observer*, p. 281 and Roger Hutchins p. 98; The Press Association p. 46; David W. Pratt p. 113; Rex Features Ltd pp. 46, 55, 63, 144, 151, 185; Chris Ridgers p. 118; Alex Ruhle p. 31; Topham Picture Library pp. 83, 91, 120, 174, 184, 255; Youth Training Scheme p. 170.

CHAPTER ## 1 Doing Sociology

What is sociology and social science?

You probably chose to study sociology because you are interested in people. If you aren't interested in people, you should close this book now and try to select another subject!

Sociology is the study of how individuals relate to each other within and between groups. A group consists of two or more people. A family is an example of a small group, and a school is an example of a larger group. The study of how fathers relate to their children is an example of the study of relations within the family. The study of how children's family background can affect how well they do at school is an example of the study of relations between groups.

Activity (class)

Working alone or in small groups, give as many examples as you can think of in a given time (say, ten minutes) of the following:

1 small groups other than families,
2 large groups other than schools,
3 relationships between family members other than fathers and children,
4 all the groups (large and small) of which *you* are a member.

As sociology covers the whole of social life, it is a good basis from which to study other social sciences, that is, economics, psychology and politics. These other social sciences specialise in particular aspects of society. Economics studies how people produce and consume (buy or use) goods and services; psychology specialises in the study of the individual mind and emotions, and politics studies power and decision making.

Doing sociological research

'Research' simply means 'finding out about a particular topic or thing'. In doing research, 'natural scientists' — physicists, chemists, biologists — have an advantage over social scientists. They can often use an experiment. It is usually quite straightforward to experiment with non-living substances and non-animal organic matter, e.g. rocks, light waves, plants, etc, but there are often both practical and moral problems in experimenting on people. For instance, a sociologist cannot make people live in poverty simply to find out about the effects of poverty on them. There would be general agreement that this would be morally wrong, and in practice, few people would volunteer for such an experiment! Instead, the researcher must investigate poverty as and where it actually exists in the real world. Of course, it is not only social scientists who face moral problems in the use of experiments. Many people feel that the use of animals in experiments on the possible effects of new drugs also raises moral issues.

Social scientists face some problems natural scientists don't.

1

There are different ways in which a researcher, whether a natural or a social scientist, might go about tackling a piece of research, but the steps shown in Figure 1.1 are useful as a model. The left-hand column gives the stages, and the right-hand column gives an example from sociology of how this might work.

Figure 1.1

The stages of research	**Example**
1 *Ask a question*	1 Do women spend more or less time on housework today than 40 or 50 years ago?
2 *Suggest a hypothesis* (in everyday speech, 'hypothesis' is often called a 'theory', i.e. *your* suggested answer or 'guess' to the question you have posed)	2 As there are now so many labour-saving devices, e.g. washing machines, microwave ovens, women are probably spending less time on housework than their grandmothers did
3 *Select your method(s)*	3 Checking earlier research into the topic; interviewing housewives
4 *Collect your data* (another word for information)	4 Find out what the average weekly time spent on housework was in the 1930s and 1940s. You may have to interview some elderly women to do this. Then, carefully choose a number of younger housewives and ask them questions which would show the average amount of time they spend doing different tasks
5 *Present your data*	5 Write a report on your question, your hypothesis, your methods and the information collected. This would probably include tables, an example of your questionnaire, and extracts from the interviews
6 *Draw conclusions*, particularly with regard to whether your data have tended to support your hypothesis — in other words, does it look as though your hypothesis might be correct?	6 How *does* the average time spent on housework by the women in your group compare with the earlier research? How can the findings be explained in relation to your hypothesis? Suppose women are spending as long or even longer on housework than they used to? What have you found which might explain this?

Activity (class)

Working alone or in small groups, take each of the following questions which a sociologist might ask about an aspect of society and try to suggest a hypothesis, and how you might collect the information to test that hypothesis. (We will be looking more closely at sociological methods in the next section, but you can start to develop your 'sociological imagination' and think of ideas.)

1 Why do some young people join gangs?

2 Why do many long-term unemployed people suffer from higher-than-average rates of depression and other illness?
3 Why do some people do better at school than others?
4 What is it like to live in a small, isolated, rural community, such as might be found in the Shetland Isles? (If you already live in such a community, develop a hypothesis about living in a large, urban area.)
5 What makes people satisfied with their work?
6 Do scenes of violence on television and in films lead some people to commit violent acts?

Sociological methods

Without perhaps realising it, you already use a whole range of methods to get information about your own society. For example, you watch, listen, ask questions, read, and perhaps send away for information. The main difference between all that and 'doing' sociological research is that sociologists are more *systematic* (organised) in choosing and using their methods, and in how they make sense of, and use, the information they collect.

Information you obtain for yourself, in other words, information which only exists because you have gone out and collected it, is known as *primary data*. Thus, information you obtain from people by questionnaires, or by watching groups of people going about their work, is *primary data*. Information which already exists, such as government reports or statistics, newspaper articles or textbooks, is *secondary data*.

Observation and participant observation

In the following description of sociological methods, each will be illustrated by an example based on a large supermarket, like the ones in which some of you may have part-time jobs. This will show you that the *social situation* can be investigated using a variety of methods, and that the different methods will give you different kinds of information — all useful, but different.

Observation

This simply means 'looking' — but you must first decide *what* you are going to look at, and *why*. Suppose you find that many people prefer shopping at supermarket X rather than at supermarket Y, even though the prices are largely the same. You might develop a hypothesis that the reason for this is that the check-out staff at supermarket X are particularly pleasant and friendly. You could then spend some time observing each group of check-out staff over a period of time, noting, for example, how many times they looked at customers, how many times they smiled, whether they said 'hello' and 'goodbye', how many customers they appeared to know by name, and so on. Your observations would need to be noted down accurately as soon as possible after you had made them, or even as you were making them. The good observer will find a way of blending with the background, otherwise the people under study will spend too much time looking at the observer looking at them! In the supermarket example, rather than hanging around the check-outs, you would probably volunteer to do the family shopping for a given period, and also accompany friends on their shopping trips too.

Activity (class)

Think of another situation where a hypothesis could be tested by observation — not necessarily in a supermarket.

Participant observation

This method is also about looking and listening, only this time, the sociologist is a part of the group, instead of a 'bystander'. In our supermarket example, suppose another hypothesis regarding the two stores were that employees in supermarket X were happy in their jobs because they had very good relationships with supervisors and managers. To do a participant observation study, you would need to be an employee. Again, you would need to think carefully about what you were going to observe — for example, what does 'good relationships' mean, and how can you tell if they are present? This time, you would be getting firsthand experience of how employees were treated by supervisors and managers, but you would need to observe and listen to the experience of all your fellow workmates as well; your own experiences alone would not be sufficient — you might be related to the boss! Participant observation can be carried out with the knowledge and consent of those being observed, in which case it is called 'overt' (open), or in secret, in which case it is called 'covert' (hidden). It is more polite and considerate to let people know if you are studying them, especially if the findings are going to be written up and read by other people. Unfortunately, when people know they are being studied, they may change their behaviour. However, as most participant observation takes place over a considerable period of time, it could be argued that behaviour may well go back to 'normal' as people get used to, or even forget, that they are being studied.

Activity (class)

Think of another situation, not necessarily in a supermarket, where participant observation would be a useful method of research. Say whether you think it should be overt or covert observation.

3

Stimulus question

The method of research used in the first extract is participant observation, and that used in the second extract is non-participant observation. Read the extracts carefully, and then answer the questions.

ITEM A (participant observation)

(Sallie Westwood was studying the largely female work force of a large knitwear factory.)

I was a participant observer in one department, where I watched and listened, talked and worked, and generally joined in the life of the shop floor. The problems associated with this method are well known, but though I am aware of the criticisms, I am unimpressed. This does not mean that there were no practical problems. I had to find a way of keeping lots of notes, but in ways which did not intrude on my relations with the women. I took notes during the day which formed the basis for field notes, which I wrote up at the end of every day, and it was not long before the writing-up period was longer than the hours I spent in the factory. It became more complicated once I started to move beyond the factory and into the women's houses, or when I started to go out with groups of women in the evenings or on day-trips.

(Adapted from Sallie Westwood, *All Day, Every Day*, Pluto Press, 1984.)

ITEM B (non-participant observation)

When I began my study of Churchmans, a tobacco factory in Bristol, I was met with astonishment from management; what could I possibly want to know about 'factory girls'? Was I, then, a 'troublemaker'?
On the shop floor I was met with a mixture of suspicion and curiosity. I was not an employee, and had to explain that I felt many people had no idea what factory life was like and I wanted to listen, learn and write about it. Slowly, I became a familiar figure, with notebook and cassette recorder in hand, and suspicion turned to amusement, even sympathy: 'Go on, my love; I think it's a good thing: people ought to know how people live — not just think about themselves.'

(Anna Pollert, 'Girls, Wives, Factory Lives', in *New Society*, 22 October 1981.)

Questions

1 Give one thing which Sallie Westwood did as part of her participant observation study. (Item A) (1 mark)
2 What practical problem did Sallie Westwood find in carrying out her study? (Item A) (1 mark)
3 How did she overcome this? (2 marks)
4 Would you say that the study in Item A was overt or covert participant observation? Give a reason for your answer. (2 marks)

5 Why were the management at Churchmans concerned about Anna Pollert? (Item B) (1 mark)
6 Why was Anna Pollert doing the research? (Item B) (1 mark)
7 Why did the employees begin to accept Anna Pollert? (2 marks)
8 Give *two* methods of collecting data referred to in the stimulus materials. Discuss *one* advantage and *one* disadvantage for each method. (10 marks)

Social surveys — interviews and questionnaires

A social survey involves the collection of information about a particular group of people, usually by interviewing or questioning members of the group. As it is not usually possible, for reasons of time or cost, to ask questions of everybody in the group you are interested in (for example, *all* housewives), researchers usually choose a *part* of the group, or a 'sample'. The aim of a sample is to make the people in it as similar as possible to the people in the whole group, so that if, for example, 53 per cent of the people in the sample answered 'yes' to a particular question, the researchers could know that, if they had been able to ask everybody, *about* 50 per cent would also have said 'yes' to that question. This is called making the sample *representative*. The people in samples have to be chosen very carefully. If, for some reason, the people in the sample are *not* representative of (not similar to) the whole group, we say that the sample is 'biased'. As a general rule, the sample should be as large as possible.

For example, if you were doing research in a school of 2000 pupils (1000 boys and 1000 girls), and if you interviewed only ten pupils, it would be very unlikely that you would have obtained a representative sample. Your sample would possibly have contained one girl and one boy from each of the third, fourth, fifth, lower sixth and upper sixth years. Try to think of *one* boy and *one* girl in your particular year group who is typical of *all* the pupils in your year. Even if you are able to think of such a person, he or she might not have been the one chosen in the sample! If you had been able to have 100 pupils in the sample, however, it would have been less likely to be biased.

There are two main types of samples — *random* and *quota*. Random samples are helpful in avoiding bias. A random sample is one in which every person in the whole group has an equal chance of being picked. A quick way of taking a random sample is to put everybody's name in the group on a separate slip of paper, fold them and put them in a hat, and draw out the required number for your sample, rather like a prize lottery. Sometimes, of course, the group involved is very large (such as all members of a political party), or the researcher may not even know people's names, such as when a whole town is being surveyed. In such a case, each person or household is given a number, and the sample will be chosen by selecting numbers, often from random number tables (yes, they really do exist!).

Sometimes, samples are *stratified*. This means that the whole group is divided into separate sub-groups which are then sampled separately. For instance, suppose that you wanted to take a sample of students in a college class in which there were 21 males and nine female students. If you wanted to be sure of representing both males and females, you would divide or stratify the class list into two parts — males and females — and sample each separately. This is called a stratified sample.

Note: once you have decided how to select your sample — you must not 'doctor' it.

Question

Using the example of the college class from the last paragraph, what would the number of (a) males and (b) females be in the sample if you sampled every third member from each group?

The second main type of sample is the *quota* sample. In this case, the researcher decides what groups he or she is interested in — rather as in the case of the stratified sample. He or she then takes a certain number (the quota) from each group. Many opinion polls are based on quota samples. For example, there must be a certain quota of middle-class and working-class people, males and females, young, middle-aged and elderly people, northerners and southerners, etc, if the opinion poll is going to be representative of the population as a whole.

Activity

Suppose that you are going to do a survey of your town or village, and you have to draw up a quota sample which will ensure that all groups are represented. Which categories (groups) would you put people in? The list above will help, but you should be able to think of others which take into account the nature of your particular area.

Interviews

Interviews take place when a researcher asks somebody (the respondent) some questions. There are different types of interview and different types of question, and the main ones are summarised below.

Structured interviews

Each respondent is asked the same questions in the same order.

Semi-structured interviews

The interviewer has a list of topics to be covered, but can choose the order and the wording of the questions asked.

Questionnaires can reach widely scattered possible respondents — but they are not always returned!

Unstructured interviews

The interviewer knows the general topic he or she is interested in, but is free to follow up things the respondent says and allow the interview to develop into what is more like a 'normal' conversation.

Interviews, particularly unstructured ones, are often tape-recorded, so that the questions and answers can flow naturally, and the respondent is not distracted by the interviewer trying to scribble everything down, and the interviewer is free to devote all his or her attention to the interview, also being able to notice gestures and facial expressions.

Closed questions

These limit the answers to either Yes/No/Don't Know, or give the respondent the choice of ticking one of a number of pre-selected answers. In other words, the researcher has decided on the range of answers allowed. An example of a closed question would be: 'Do you consider that there is a need for a new community centre in this area? Yes/No/Don't Know'.

Open-ended questions

These are like 'normal' questions, and the respondent is able to answer in any way he or she chooses. An example of an open-ended question would be: 'What are your views on the proposed new community centre?'

Questionnaires

The questionnaire is like an interview put into writing, and answers are usually written down. Some questionnaires are sent to people through the post, while others are directly asked by the researchers or their assistants. Questionnaires are like structured interviews: all the questions are identical and pre-set, though both closed and open-ended questions may be used. Usually, the questionnaire method is used to reach a large number of respondents. The postal questionnaire is probably the cheapest and quickest way of doing this.

The main problem with postal questionnaires is that not everybody sends them back, i.e., they have a low response rate. Most questions on postal questionnaires are simple and closed so that answers can easily be counted. The Census — a survey of all households in the country which takes place every ten years — is perhaps the best-known questionnaire. You or your parents may also have been stopped in the street by market researchers with questionnaires about shopping habits, or which television/radio programmes you have watched or listened to.

It is actually very difficult to write good questions for interviews or questionnaires. A 'good' question is one which is clearly worded, easily understood, obtains the information which is required, does not try to ask too many things in the one question, does not 'push' respondents towards one particular answer (i.e. is not 'loaded' or biased), and is not embarrassing or offensive. Social surveys are usually so expensive to run that a small-scale 'mini-survey', called the 'pilot study', is often carried out first, to try out the questionnaires in case something needs to be altered.

Activity (class)

The questions below are examples of poor questions — the sort to be avoided! Study them carefully, and try to decide what is wrong with each of them. Then, in a small group or as a class, discuss how each of them could be improved.

1 How old are you?
2 Do you watch television (a) occasionally (b) often (c) a lot?
3 Don't you agree that unemployed people get too much benefit?
4 Have you bought a new washing machine, microwave oven or vacuum cleaner within the last six months, and if so, are you satisfied?
5 Some people say that to have newspapers with models posing topless is a way of exploiting women and they should stop doing it. Do you agree?
6 Do you need a deodorant?

In the supermarket example below, it would be possible to find out why people preferred supermarket X to supermarket Y by the use of interviews or questionnaires. How staff felt about relationships with supervisors/managers could also have been investigated using these methods.

Questions

1 What would be the problems of using a postal questionnaire to find out why some people preferred supermarket X to supermarket Y? (3 marks)
2 If you wanted to find out how the staff felt about the way they were treated by supervisors/managers, would you choose a structured or an unstructured interview? Give reasons for your answer. (5 marks)

Quantitative and qualitative data

Information which is, or can be, expressed in terms of numbers, percentages, tables, bar charts, pie charts, etc, is known as *quantitative* data. Information obtained from questionnaires and structured interviews is often of this kind.

Information on people's feelings about issues or events, or descriptions of their life-styles, is known as *qualitative* data. Information from unstructured interviews and participant observation is often of this kind.

Stimulus question

Read the following extracts and answer the questions.

ITEM A

The fifth year in Jane's school had recently changed from single-sex (boys and girls separated for lessons) to mixed-sex classes. Jane had become interested in whether pupils really liked the change, and especially what the girls thought about it. She had a hunch that more boys liked the change than girls did. She decided to do a social survey on this topic as part of her Sociology GCSE project. Her teacher agreed, after having cleared the matter with the Head Teacher. Altogether there were 100 fifth formers, 25 in each of four sets. Jane decided that she would interview only twenty of the 100 in order to keep the survey down to a manageable size. There were 60 girls and 40 boys in the fifth year. Jane divided the fifth-year pupil list into boys and girls, and put them into two separate alphabetical lists. She then interviewed every fifth person on each list; twenty people in all. She was confident that this would produce a representative sample of fifth-year pupils.

Questions

1 How many pupils were in Jane's sample? (Item A) (1 mark)
2 How many girls were there in Jane's sample? (1 mark)
3 What is meant by 'respondents'? (1 mark)
4 Jane divided her sample into boys and girls. What is the name given to a sample divided in this way? (1 mark)

ITEM B
Extracts from Jane's Interview Schedule

Extract 1

Name of respondent .... Male/Female ....
Taught in: Class A   Class B   Class C   Class D

Extract 2

Do you prefer being taught in a mixed-sex or single-sex class?   Mixed/Single

Extract 3

Can you say a few words about why girls find boys a nuisance in class?

5 What is meant by a 'representative sample'? (2 marks)
6 Why was it important that Jane's sample was representative? (2 marks)
7 Give *two* reasons why Jane might have asked the pupils interviewed to state which class they were in. (2 marks)
8 Which question is open: Extract 2 or Extract 3? (Item B) (1 mark)
9 Which question is more likely to produce quantitative data: Extract 2 or Extract 3? (Item B) (1 mark)
10 What criticisms could be made of the way in which Jane has worded the question in Item B, Extract 3? Rephrase the question in your own words to deal with the criticism. (3 marks)

Activity: mini-project suggestions

As the point, you may find it useful to do a *very* small piece of primary research yourself (perhaps using secondary research to suggest a hypothesis or to compare against your own findings). You will need to discuss this as a class with your teacher. You should choose an area of social life which you know well already, such as the family, school, leisure or work. Your mini-project could take the form of a pilot survey, which could later form the basis of your GCSE project. You could also use this exercise as a piece of course work.

Suggestions

Family — Compare the leisure activities of two adults of the same sex, one of whom has two or more small children, and the other of whom has none. A hypothesis might be based on the guess that a person with small children will not be able to have many expensive or time-consuming hobbies and might have much less leisure time than a person with no dependent children. What would be the best method to use in this case?

School — Do teachers give equal amounts of attention to both boy and girl pupils, or does one sex get more attention than the other? If your school has links with a local primary school, you might be allowed to observe one or two classes for about half-an-hour each. If you were fortunate, you might even get permission to video the classes. What would your hypothesis be? Would it be a good idea to tell the teacher what the purpose of the observation was? How would you actually measure 'attention'?

Work — We have already used a work situation to look at sociological methods. In a mini-project, you would be attempting much less than in the examples used earlier. You could do an hour or so of observation, or half-a-dozen questionnaires, or an interview. You could even use more than one of these methods. Most good projects use more than one method to produce data, but it is not necessary for you to do so at this stage. You could investigate job satisfaction, or how people come to choose their present type of work, or how shop staff dealt with customers.

Advice for your mini-project

1 Don't try to do too much. At this stage you are mainly trying to gain the skill to design a piece of research and to gain research experience. Nobody expects world-shattering findings!
2 Do go through all the stages of research:
 Ask a question.
 (Perhaps) formulate a hypothesis.
 Choose your method(s).
 Collect your data.
 Describe and present your data.
 Explain your data.
3 Finally, assess how good your choice and use of method was.
 What went right?
 What (if anything) went wrong?
 What would you change if you did the same type of research on a larger scale?
 What would stay the same?

Activity (class)

1 Read somebody else's mini-project and try to give as much helpful comment on it as you can.
2 Give a summary report of your mini-project to the class who can then comment.

Structured questions

You are a sociologist who wishes to do research about why some teenagers become members of 'gangs'.

1 Suggest an appropriate method for carrying out your research, saying why you would choose that particular method. (4 marks)
2 Briefly describe all the different stages of the research, from start to finish. (8 marks)
3 What difficulties do you think that there might be in carrying out your research? How would you try to deal with them? (8 marks)

Key words

Data	Participant observation
Hypothesis	Questionnaire
Interview	Sample
Observation	Survey

CHAPTER 2 What is Society?

What is society? What is sociology?

Sociology is the study of society, but what is society? A simple definition is that society is made up of groups of people — which vary greatly in size, purpose, membership and in many other ways. In this brief chapter we will try to reach a clearer and more detailed idea of 'society' — the subject of sociological study.

All societies have certain things in common. The best way to understand what they have in common is first to try to work it out for yourself. The aim of the following activity is to help you to do this.

Figure 2.1. The individual in society. You, the individual, are part of many groups. Together, all the groups make up society.

Activity (class)

Imagine you are on a Jumbo jet flight. There are 380 people on board — a mixture of women, children and men of various races, nationalities and religions. Some children are travelling without their parents, and some adults without their husbands/wives. Most, however, speak English.

The jet gets into difficulties and is forced to land on a remote island. Extensive search operations fail to discover the plane; it is given up for lost and the search called off.

Meanwhile the passengers and crew on the plane have survived the first problems of being wrecked and begin to build a society for the long term. There is some food and water on the plane, but it obviously won't last very long.

Now decide how the marooned people will make their new society. (You can do this either individually or in groups.) Here are some of the main problems the islanders will have to face (don't write answers to these questions! They are just to help get you going):

1 How to survive — what is needed?
2 How the various survival tasks and everyday work will be organised — who will do what? Why?

3 How decisions are going to be made — will there be a leader — if so, who? Will everybody have an equal say? What if they cannot agree?
4 How children are going to be looked after — including any new babies who might be born.
5 How family life and sexual relationships will be organised.
6 How to share the things that people need and want — equal shares or will some people get more than others? If so, who and why?
7 How to organise leisure and religious activities (if any).
8 Do you think that people in your group will be able to get on with each other? Which groups might come into conflict? How would you deal with this?
9 How to deal with people who 'break the rules'.

Follow-up discussion

To get the best out of this activity, you should follow up the written part of the exercise with a report back to the rest of the class, before reading the rest of this section. Did you all end up with similar kinds of society? What differences are there between your societies?

What all societies have in common

Usually, three important general points about society become clear from the above activity. They are:

1 *In all societies, the family, the economy, politics and culture occur.*

In order for people to survive, society must provide for their basic needs. These needs are:

a producing and consuming (using) goods and services,
b bearing and rearing children,
c deciding how to deal with problems and making laws,
d the 'non-material' side of life concerned with leisure, pleasure and the meaning of life (e.g. religion, values).

Another way of putting this point is to say that every society must have a way or a 'system' for meeting these needs. So, if we think of society in total as *the* system, then the four smaller systems or *sub-systems* that make up society are:

i   the economy —   (production/consumption of goods) ⎫ Society
ii   the family —   (sex, bearing and rearing children) ⎪ (the
iii politics and law — (arguing, making and enforcing rules) ⎬ social
iv   culture —   (people's 'way of life')   ⎭ system)

Activity (class)

Check whether the 'blueprint' of society you drew up for the previous activity has the above four sub-systems in one form or another. List each of the organisations in 'your' society under one sub-system (e.g. culture — church).

---

2 *The exact way societies organise to meet people's needs and wants varies — sometimes greatly.*

Even today, economies vary, from those based on simple agriculture to modern, industrial, 'high-tech' economies. Similarly, family, political and legal, and cultural systems vary from society to society, and it is not the place of social scientists to judge which systems are best. The variety of societies will be illustrated throughout this book.

Societies vary greatly: i) Modern society, Birmingham   *ii) Agricultural society, Ethiopia.*

3 *Social conflict occurs in all societies.*
Some conflict exists in all societies. People inevitably disagree about things —
often because they are in different positions in society (e.g. the rich and the
poor). Usually, a society tries to organise or *regulate* conflict so that it does not
disrupt life too much. For instance, in Britain, the political parties often come
into conflict, but 'within the system'.

Karl Marx considered that deep conflict between rich and powerful property
owners and those who work for them is unavoidable. He thought that only a
classless society would end this conflict. Others stress that differences between
males and females (gender), races and age groups can also cause conflict.
However, it is only fair to say that there are countless examples of co-operation
between the two genders, members of different races, age groups and social
classes.

Figure 2.2. The individual and social group

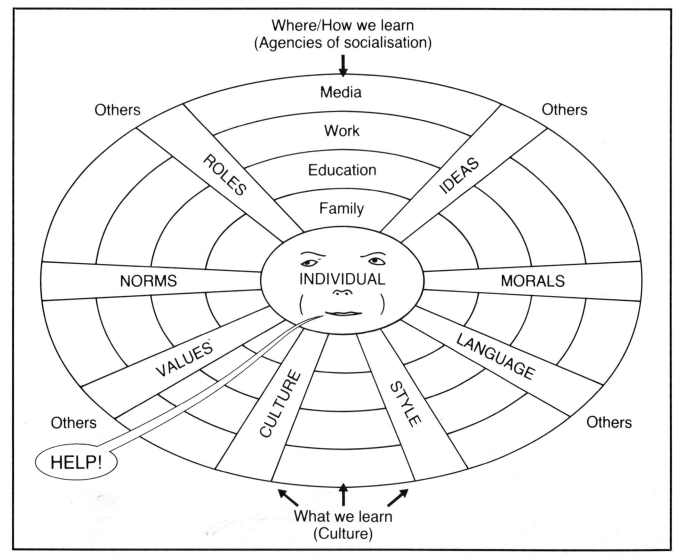

Definition of cultural terms (with examples)

Socialisation is learning to become a member of society. To do this, it is
necessary to learn a particular way of life or *culture*. Socialisation begins in the
family and continues throughout life. The following are the main areas or
agencies of socialisation — family, education, work, the media, religion and
other forms of belief (see Figure 2.2). Although members of the same culture
share a similar way of life, they remain unique individuals — perhaps because
they are partly able to decide not to conform (be like others) in every respect.

Values reflect what is felt to be important, e.g. patriotism — 'I love my country'.

Norms are the rules, written and unwritten, of a particular society, e.g. not laughing in church.

Roles are the (many) parts the individual plays in society, e.g. daughter, mother, wife, aunt.

Ideas are thoughts and notions about things — most of which are based on other people's thoughts', e.g. an idea about what your career might be.

Morals are beliefs about what is right and wrong, e.g. it is wrong to steal.

Language is the *meaningful* use of words, i.e. verbal communication, e.g. the English language. There are a number of non-verbal forms of communication, such as sign language, deaf and dumb language.

Style is the particular manner or way in which we present ourselves and do things. Usually our style 'says' something about us. It is a special form of language, e.g. dress, music — such as Punk 'style'.

Others are everybody else. Your experience of society is made up of your *interactions* (what you do) with others.

Significant others are people close to you and who affect you, such as your family, friends and, maybe, some teachers.

Activity (class)

The purpose of this activity is to look at the effect of socialisation on *you*. Select an agency of socialisation and give *one* example of how it has socialised you in terms of values, norms, roles, etc. Thus, in the family you might have learnt the value of truth, the norm of wearing pyjamas in bed, the role of child, etc...

Agency	*Example of*
Family	Value, norm, role, idea,
Education	morals, language, style
Work (you might have to ask your parents for help with this one)	
Mass media (e.g. television, films, newspapers)	
Religion	

From the point of view of having a good classroom discussion you may want to share out the agencies so that they are all covered by at least one person.

Sociology and the other social sciences

Sociology and history are closely related social sciences. Sociology is mainly the study of society in the present and history is mainly the study of society in the past. For that reason, it is useful to know some history before studying sociology. You cannot understand the present unless you know something about the past. The role of women in society, the long-running 'troubles' in Ireland, race relations in Britain (see Chapter Twelve) all illustrate how the present is influenced by the past. Sociology and history overlap with the other social sciences. Look again at the sub-systems model of society and see how much economics, politics and cultural studies are a part of sociology. Similarly, history is linked to other social sciences. For instance, there is economic history, political history and cultural history.

However, economics, politics and cultural studies are social sciences in their own right. To these we must add psychology, as well as geography, in so far as it deals with population and people in relation to the environment (material surroundings). Figure 2.3 summarises the social sciences and is followed by definitions of each:

Figure 2.3. The social sciences

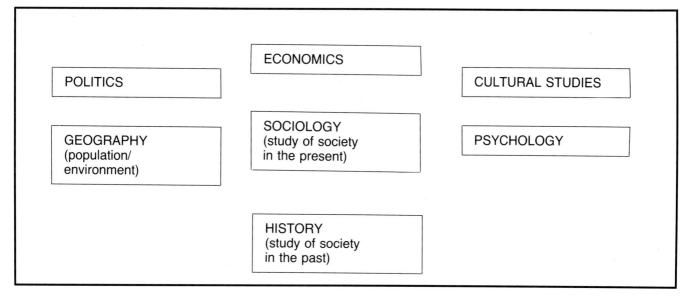

Definitions of the social sciences

Sociology is the study of the life of people in groups, e.g. why some schools get better examination results than others.

Economics is the study of production and consumption (buying) of goods and services, e.g. work — either paid or in the home — and what you buy and sell are economic activities.

Politics is the study of power, especially in relation to government, e.g. voting or not voting (either through choice or because the vote does not exist) are political activities.

Geography (human) is the study of the relationship between the physical world and people, e.g. the way you treat your neighbourhood is part of local geography.

Cultural Studies is the study of all forms of human expression and communication, including the media, literature, fashion and style (fashionable or not), and the way people live their everyday lives, e.g. what you choose to do with your leisure time this weekend is a cultural activity.

Psychology is the study of how individuals act, think and feel, and of relationships. It is a good balance to the more social emphasis of sociology, e.g. the study of intelligence and emotion are part of psychology.

Activity

1 Give another example to the one in the text of an area or activity studied by each of the social sciences mentioned above.
2 Choose two social sciences and in each case suggest a possible area that you might find worth studying.
3 Below is a list of possible chapter headings, from social science textbooks. Try to match each chapter heading with the appropriate social science:

'Making the News'
'The Coming of the Railways'
'Slum Settlements in the City'
'Individual Responses to Stress'
'Social Control and Deviance'
'The Causes of the Wall Street Crash'
'Party Conflict in the 1980s'

Key words

Culture	Society
Politics	Sub-system (of Society)
Role	System (Social)
Socialisation	Value

3 The Family

Family and marriage: types and patterns

Family types

How many people are there in your family? Whatever answer you have just given, the chances are that the people you counted were your parents, yourself, and any *siblings* (brothers or sisters) you may have. This type of family unit, consisting of an adult couple and their children, is called a *nuclear* family.

Another type of family occurs where the basic nuclear unit has been *extended*, either 'backwards' to include grandparents and even great-grandparents, or 'sideways', to include relatives, such as aunts, uncles and cousins. Of course, we are all part of an extended family in the sense that we all have grandparents, and most of us have some aunts, uncles and cousins as well. What distinguishes an extended family from a nuclear one, however, is that the members of the extended family either live together under the same roof, or live very close to each other and have a great deal of contact with one another. Do you think that *you* live in an extended family?

Today it is quite common for four generations of a family to be alive at the same time

The pattern of divorce and remarriage which has become quite common in Britain has led sociologists to identify another kind of family group, the '*reconstituted*' family. This contains a married couple, at least one of whom has been married before, and children from a previous marriage as well as the present one, i.e. step-brothers and step-sisters. Sociologists Michael Young and Peter Willmott introduced the idea of a *symmetrical* family, which they believed was a modern stage in the development of family relationships. A symmetrical family is a small, nuclear unit with both parents as breadwinners and sharing many household tasks and responsibilities. However, feminists in particular point out that evidence shows that relatively few modern families fit this pattern, and that although many families have two breadwinners, women still bear the major responsibility for domestic work and childcare.

About one in seven families in Britain are *single* or *lone*-parent families. This is because of the high divorce rate and the high rate of children born to non-married parents.

A nuclear family — The 'cereal packet norm' of the male breadwinner and female housewife with two children is often presented as typical — but the majority of families are not exactly like this. Is yours?

Activity (class)

One way of showing a particular family in diagrammatic form is to use the symbols shown below. A triangle represents a male, a circle a female, an equal sign shows marriage and downward lines indicate children. The letter 'b' shows the year of birth.

Study the diagram of the 'family tree' below and answer the following questions.

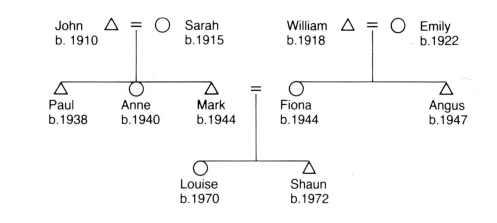

1 How many children did John and Sarah have?
(1 mark)

2 What are the names of Shaun's and Louise's grandparents? (4 marks)

3 How old was Emily when her granddaughter was born? (1 mark)

4 What is the relationship between Angus and Shaun? (1 mark)

5 What is the relationship between Paul and Fiona? (1 mark)

Now that you understand these diagrams, you can go on to the next activity

Activity (class/outside class)

Draw a diagram like the one above for your own family, going back at least to your grandparents, and showing as many other family members as you can. You might need to check some of the dates of birth with your parents, or you could leave out dates of birth altogether.

Although it is true that most families in Britain today live in nuclear units, the growth in the number of people with cars and telephones allows people to keep in close contact with their kin (relations). The increase in life expectancy (see Chapter Sixteen) has also resulted in a growing number of generations of a family being alive at the same time. On average, men today can expect to live fourteen years after the birth of their last grandchild, and women 23 years after the birth of their last grandchild. This has led to growing numbers of children in Britain with great-grandparents alive.

Marriage patterns

All societies contain 'families', that is, people linked together by ties of blood or marriage. The creation of a new family usually starts with a marriage, and different societies have different rules and customs about how many spouses a person may have. (A 'spouse' is either a husband or a wife.) Below are the different words used to describe the different kinds of marital arrangements:

Monogamy (only one spouse at a time):
Simple Monogamy   Only one marriage for each partner.
Serial Monogamy   Only one husband or wife at a time, but more than one spouse in a lifetime owing to divorce and remarriage.

Polygamy (more than one spouse at a time):
Polygyny   Men may have more than one wife.
Polyandry   Women may have more than one husband.

Polygyny (more than one wife) is more common than polyandry (more than one husband). Polygyny is found is some African tribes, and also forms part of Muslim culture. There are often economic reasons for polygynous marriages. Women form a very important part of the work force, and having several wives increases a man's wealth. Status is also often measured by the number of sons a man has, and in societies where many babies die in infancy, more than one wife increases the chance of a man having some children who grow to adulthood, and who can therefore take care of him in his old age.

Most people in Britain get married, although the number of couples 'co-habiting' (living together without being married) is increasing. Many people who cohabit later marry their partner. The increase in serial monogamy in Britain has resulted in the fact that over a third of all marriages taking place each year now involve the remarriage of at least one of the partners.

Activity (class)

Working in small groups, draw up a list of all the advantages and disadvantages you can think of for (1) marriage and (2) co-habitation without marriage. Discuss this as a class.

In other societies, they do some things differently — polyandry in Tibet

Divorce

An important feature of the family in Britain (and many other industrial societies) has been the increase in the divorce rate, which has risen in England and Wales by 600 per cent in the last twenty years alone.

Before 1857, a couple could divorce only if they could arrange for a private Act of Parliament, which was not only difficult, but also very, very expensive. Divorce was also considered to be a shameful and scandalous event, and very few divorces took place.

Since then, there have been many changes in the law and in people's attitudes towards divorce, both of which have contributed to the rising divorce rate, with one in three marriages now likely to end in divorce.

The last important change in the law was the 1970 Divorce Law Reform Act, which did away with the idea that one partner had to prove the other one 'guilty' of something which broke up the marriage. It is now recognised that relationships in marriage are very complex, and the ideas of 'innocence' and 'guilt' will often not be realistic. Divorces are now granted if the court is satisfied that there has been an 'irretrievable breakdown of marriage', which simply means that the people involved are very unlikely to get back together again and the marriage is really finished. An interesting feature of divorce patterns over the past 30 years or so is the growing number of *women* who go to the courts seeking a divorce ('filing a petition', in the legal jargon).

Activity (class)

Using the information from the table below, draw a graph showing:

1 the number of petitions filed by women 1961–87
2 the number of petitions filed by men 1961–87
3 the total number of petitions filed 1961–87

Table 3.1. Divorce

	1961	1971	1976	1981	1982	1983	1984	1985	1986	1987
Petitions filed (thousands)										
England and Wales										
By husband	14	44	43	47	47	45	49	52	50	50
By wife	18	67	101	123	128	124	131	139	131	135
Total	32	111	144	170	175	169	180	191	181	185

(Source: *Social Trends*, 1992)

Many people believe that the rise in the divorce rate is evidence of a breakdown in the belief in marriage and family life, but this is not necessarily the case. With every change in the law which has made divorce easier, the number of divorces has risen. This suggests that at any time there have always been many couples who wanted to divorce, but who were prevented from doing so by the law. It is also important to note that divorced people have a high remarriage rate. Seventy per cent of all divorced people remarry, half of them within five years of their divorce. This suggests that people divorce more because they no longer wish to live with a particular partner, rather than because they no longer believe in marriage and family life. Despite the fact that before they reach the age of sixteen one child in five is likely to have divorced parents, young people do not seem put off the idea of marriage, and most of them say that they expect to marry at some time in their life. The latest figures on divorce indicate that the trend has 'levelled out', and that the divorce rate, though higher than it was in the 1960s, may no longer continue to rise each year.

Reasons for the rise in divorce

There is no one single reason for the increase in divorce rates. As with other social institutions, the family and marriage are influenced by other changes taking place in society, some of which are shown in Figure 3.1.

Figure 3.1.

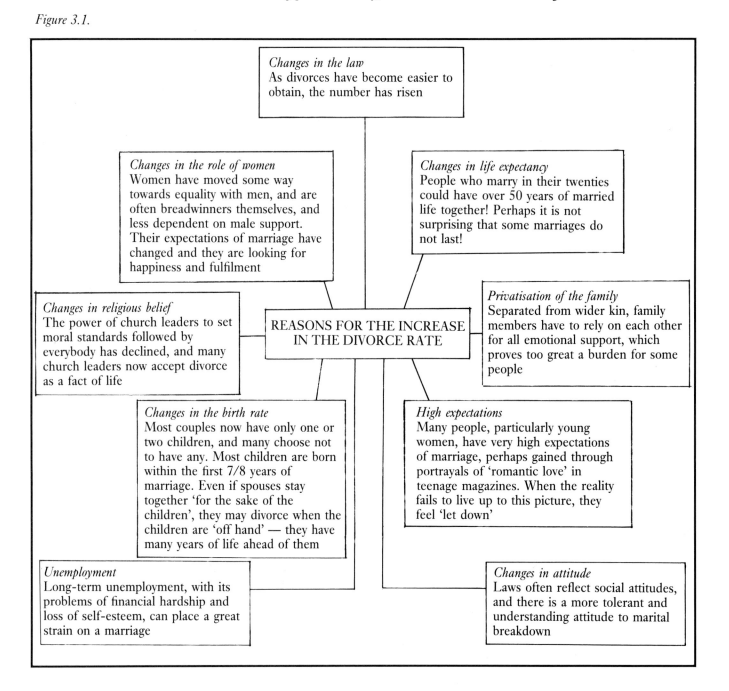

Changes in the law
As divorces have become easier to obtain, the number has risen

Changes in the role of women
Women have moved some way towards equality with men, and are often breadwinners themselves, and less dependent on male support. Their expectations of marriage have changed and they are looking for happiness and fulfilment

Changes in life expectancy
People who marry in their twenties could have over 50 years of married life together! Perhaps it is not surprising that some marriages do not last!

Changes in religious belief
The power of church leaders to set moral standards followed by everybody has declined, and many church leaders now accept divorce as a fact of life

REASONS FOR THE INCREASE IN THE DIVORCE RATE

Privatisation of the family
Separated from wider kin, family members have to rely on each other for all emotional support, which proves too great a burden for some people

Changes in the birth rate
Most couples now have only one or two children, and many choose not to have any. Most children are born within the first 7/8 years of marriage. Even if spouses stay together 'for the sake of the children', they may divorce when the children are 'off hand' — they have many years of life ahead of them

High expectations
Many people, particularly young women, have very high expectations of marriage, perhaps gained through portrayals of 'romantic love' in teenage magazines. When the reality fails to live up to this picture, they feel 'let down'

Unemployment
Long-term unemployment, with its problems of financial hardship and loss of self-esteem, can place a great strain on a marriage

Changes in attitude
Laws often reflect social attitudes, and there is a more tolerant and understanding attitude to marital breakdown

Activity

Which factors do you consider have most affected the divorce rate? List them in order of importance.

Stimulus questions

Read the following extracts and answer the questions.

ITEM A

Table 3.2. Percentage of women aged 18–49 cohabiting: by age

Great Britain	Percentage and numbers								Percentage and numbers						
	1979	1981	1983	1984	1985	1986	1987		1979	1981	1983	1984	1985	1986	1987
Age group (percentages)								Women in sample (=100%)(numbers)							
18–24	4.5	5.6	5.2	7.3	9.1	9.0	11.5	18–24	1353	1517	1191	1174	1182	1194	1277
25–49	2.2	2.6	3.2	3.3	3.9	4.6	4.9	25–49	4651	5007	4094	4094	4182	4320	4379
All aged 18–49	2.7	3.3	3.6	4.2	5.0	5.5	6.4	All aged 18–49	6004	6524	5285	5268	5364	5514	5656

(Source: *Social Trends, 1989*)

ITEM B

From the start of birth registration in 1837, children who were neither conceived nor born within marriage were classified as illegitimate. The percentage of births in England and Wales which were illegitimate fell steadily from a level of six to seven per cent of all births during the 1840s to around four per cent at the turn of the century. There were substantial increases in illegitimacy during both World Wars, but the ratio fell again after each period so that, in the early 1950s, the illegitimacy ratio in the United Kingdom was still only slightly higher than it had been 50 years earlier.

However, during the past 30 years, the illegitimacy ratio has risen steeply, stabilising only for a brief period in the 1960s, and by 1986 it had reached 21 per cent. At the same time, there has been an increase in the proportion of illegitimate births registered by both parents, from 38 per cent of illegitimate births in 1961 to 66 per cent in 1986. If a birth occurs outside marriage the name of the father may normally only be entered in the register if both the father and mother register the birth together in person. These figures suggest that at least half the children born outside marriage in 1986 had parents who were living together and were likely to be bringing up the child within a stable non-marital union. In about three-quarters of these cases in 1986, the parents gave the same address of usual residence.

ITEM C

Figure 3.2. People in households: by type of household and family in which they live

1 Data for 1961, 1971 and 1981 are taken from the Population Censuses for those years; the 1985 data are from the General Household Survey.
2 These family types may also include non-dependent children.

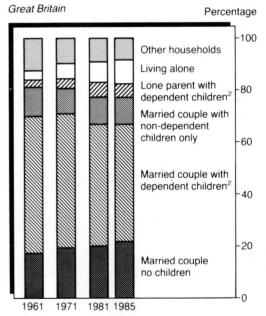

(Source: Office of Population Censuses and Surveys)

Questions

1 How many women aged 25–49 were in the sample in 1984? (Item A) (1 mark)
2 Which age group of women had the highest rate of co-habitation in 1987? (Item A) (1 mark)
3 What type of children are registered as 'illegitimate'? (Item B) (1 mark)
4 What percentage of illegitimate births were registered by both parents in 1986? (Item B) (1 mark)
5 Give *three* types of household which have shown an increase between 1961 and 1985. (Item C) (3 marks)
6 Give *five* reasons which have been put forward to explain the increase in the divorce rate. (5 marks)
7 Illustrating your answer with information from the items above and elsewhere, discuss the suggestion that the rise in the divorce rate in Britain indicates a rejection of family life. (8 marks)

Family structure and roles

Family structure

Family structure means how families are 'made up'. We have already seen that different *types* of families are made up or structured somewhat differently. Next, we are made up or structured somewhat differently. Next, we look at family structure in Britain during three different periods.

Pre-industrial

Sociologists *used* to think that as Britain became an industrial society in the nineteenth century this had led to a change in family structure, from a pre-industrial period of extended families to an industrial period of nuclear families. However, research by social historians has shown that things were not quite like that. Peter Laslett used church records of births, marriages and deaths to build up a detailed picture of family and household groupings in England in the sixteenth to eighteenth centuries. He found that the majority of people even then were living in nuclear family units. One of the reasons for this was that the average life expectancy (the number of years people were expected to live) was very low — just over 40 years. Together with the fact that most women did not get married until they were in their mid-20s or even later, this meant that relatively few people lived long enough to form three-generation families.

Even though the nuclear family was the commonest type in pre-industrial Britain, people did live more 'as part of the community' then than now. They had to! Not only did houses lack the many leisure facilities we take for granted, they lacked many basic amenities as well. Often, a source of fresh water or a toilet was shared between several families. Of course, living more in the community did not always mean people got on well together.

The working-class extended family remained a unit of protection and self-help even after the Second World War.

Industrial

It is quite possible that the extended family became *more*, not less common, as a result of industrialisation during the nineteenth century. Michael Anderson looked at families and households in some of the new industrial towns in the middle of that century, when industrialisation was at its height. If the earlier ideas had been correct, he would have found most people in nuclear family households. In fact, a surprisingly large proportion of people were living with relatives in some type of extended family grouping. One reason for this was that people needed somewhere to live when they first came to the towns, and often moved in with relatives already living there. Another reason was that jobs were often obtained by a person who already worked at the mill, in the mine or in the factory 'speaking for' a relative to get the manager to give him or her a job. People therefore relied a lot on their relatives, not only to help find jobs, but also to help out in times of sickness or unemployment, as there was no National Health Service or unemployment benefit then.

Late twentieth century

During the twentieth century, the small, nuclear family became increasingly common. This was partly the result of the development of mass education, which meant that employers could ask for qualifications and skills before they offered somebody a job, and the gradual introduction of sickness benefits and old age pensions. As a result, people need to rely less on the extended family.

However, in a study of Bethnal Green in East London in the late 1950s, sociologists Willmott and Young found a working-class community where extended family patterns were still quite common. There are fewer working-class extended familes now, but the extended family is still quite common among certain groups in Britain. Among Asians and Chinese in particular, the practice is to live in extended family groupings which provide a very important source of support for their members.

More recent research by Wilmott (1986) found that although kin are now less likely to live close to each other, contact remains quite frequent. He describes three kinds of kinship arrangements in Britain:

1   The local extended family — two or three related nuclear families living close to each other (such as in 1950s Bethnal Green). This now accounts for only about one-eighth of families.
2   The dispersed extended family — two or more related nuclear families live distant from each other but still have quite frequent contact. This now accounts for about half of families.
3   The attenuated extended family — this is like the dispersed extended family but contact is much less (attenuated). This now accounts for about three-eighths of families.

Changes in the family

The 'extended/nuclear' family issue discussed above is quite complicated. The following two changes in the family — in size and functions — are clearer and just as important in their consequences.

Family size

The average number of children born to a couple fell from about six in the early nineteenth century to just one or two by the 1980s. The reasons for this are discussed more fully in Chapter Sixteen. This was a *very* important change.

Family functions

The 'functions' of a family refer to the support and contribution it makes to its members and the society as a whole. Some people have argued that the rise of the welfare state and better standards of living and technology have 'stripped' the family of many of its functions. It is certainly true that some services, which used to be found within the family, are now provided by the state, but the family is far from unimportant — think of all the benefits your family has provided for you!

Activity (class)

Study carefully the list below, and then draw up a table as
shown. For each function, show by a tick in the appropriate
column whether you consider that it is provided only or
mainly by the family, only or mainly by the state ('society'),
or whether by both the family and society.

	Mainly or only by the family	Mainly or only by society	Mixture of both
Health care			
Gender role socialisation			
Ideas of right and wrong			
Education			
Entertainment/leisure			
Love and affection			
Care of young children			
Finding a job			
Sex education			
Religious beliefs			
Political views			
Discipline			
Care of the elderly			
Skills for employment			

Discuss your list with the rest of the class. Do the findings
lead you to believe that the family has been stripped of most
of its functions?

Family roles

A social 'role' refers to the way a person is expected to act in a particular social position. We all have an idea (though it may not be exactly the same as other people's ideas) of how a friend, or a policeman, or a teacher should behave. Roles and relationships within the family have changed over time. The typical Victorian father was very strict and stern, and expected that other members of the family would obey him. Parents had much more say over how their offspring behaved than many of today's parents. A young woman, for example, could not marry under the age of 21 without her father's written consent, and would be most unlikely to get engaged to anyone of whom her parents, especially her father, did not approve. Although working-class women were an important part of the labour force, middle-class women led very domesticated lives, running what were sometimes very large households with many servants to organise.

One very popular nineteenth century book compared the 'mistress of the house' with the 'commander of an army' when describing the qualities of leadership (over the domestic servants!) and organisation she should have.

In Victorian times, relationships between husbands and wives, and parents and children, while they might be loving and affectionate, tended to be very formal and correct. Children had very few rights, and would not be consulted about family decisions. Working-class children, until given some protection by the various Factory Acts, were a part of the work force, working in mills and factories, sometimes from as young as four or five years of age. Most families today have more open, democratic relationships, and there have been some changes in the 'conjugal roles' between husbands and wives, as discussed in Chapter Eleven.

Having a Nanny to look after the children gave middle-class women more time to manage their households. Today, many middle-class families employ a part-time 'helper' in their home.

(Source: *Illustrated London News*, reprinted in Jonathan Gathorne-Hardy, *The Rise and Fall of the British Nanny*, Arrow Books, 1972)

Lone-parent families

In 1990, nineteen per cent of all families with dependent children were headed by a lone parent, and in six out of seven cases, the lone parent was a woman. In all, nearly two million households are headed by a lone parent. In itself, this is not new. A century or so ago, there were also many families headed by a lone parent. The main difference is that, whereas in nineteenth century Britain the cause would most likely have been the death of a spouse (often a woman dying in childbirth), today more than two-thirds of lone parents are divorced or separated. It is important to remember that these figures represent a 'snapshot' of families at a single point in time — many lone parents will again form part of a two-parent family as a result of remarriage.

Family support

The welfare state is discussed in detail in Chapter Seventeen. As far as the family is concerned, it needs to be pointed out that the state now provides many services for families and individuals which once had to be found within the family or local community. The introduction of free professional health care, state education, retirement pensions, sickness and unemployment benefits, school meals and the support of social workers have all helped to add to, or replace, what families need to provide for their members. However, families, and women in particular, still provide primary care for their members, and many people argue that the extent to which the state has 'taken over' family functions has been greatly exaggerated. Indeed, many of the social policies pursued during the 1980s were intended to make people — including families — 'help themselves' more and rely less on the state. In turn, some argued that these policies went too far and that many poor families struggled as a result.

Stresses on the family

The section on divorce discussed a number of stresses on the family. Two signs of stress which were brought to the public's attention in the 1980s were wife battering and child abuse.

Teenagers are likely to be presented with the idealised 'cereal packet norm' version of the family. However, the situation described in the cartoon and Figure 3.3 are for many just as close to what actually happens.

Figure 3.3 Stress factors affecting families of abused children

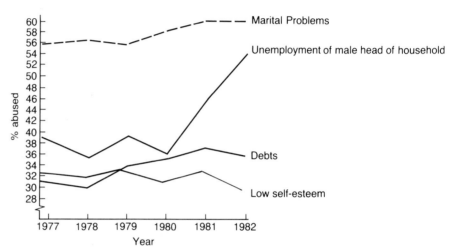

(Source: Creighton, S.J. *Trends in Child Abuse: 1977–82*, NSPCC, 1984, quoted in *Social Studies Review*, September 1986)

Privatisation

In their research on well-paid ('affluent') manual workers in the 1960s, Goldthorpe and Lockwood noted that the men they were studying, who had moved away from their 'families of origin' and were living in the growing town of Luton, spent a lot of their free time with their wives and children. In Goldthorpe and Lockwood's phrase, they had become more 'home-centred'. The stereotype of the working-class husband was an Andy Capp figure, who spent his leisure time with his 'mates' in the pub, at a football match, or at dog or horse races. The 'privatised' pattern of family life, observed by Goldthorpe and Lockwood, was one in which couples spent a lot of time together, watching TV, gardening, taking the children out, tackling DIY jobs around the house and so on.

Although the privatisation of the family can have important benefits to its members in terms of companionship, it can also be a source of stress. In a community where family members have several relatives living nearby, there is a wider circle of people to socialise with, and also to help and support each other. The old music-hall joke of the young wife packing her bags and 'going home to mother' after a row with her husband nevertheless described a situation where both partners could have a 'cooling-off' period before patching things up. Busy young mothers could have a welcome break by dropping the children off at 'Nan's house' for a few hours. When couples have no-one but each other to provide all the emotional support and companionship, it can pose a heavy burden on a relationship. The situation is often worse for young mothers at home all day with small children, in tower blocks or large estates with few facilities, and especially if their husband is one of the growing band of 'commuters', who leave early and come home very late because of the long journey to work. It is thought that situations like these can contribute to the break-up of a marriage.

Stimulus questions

Read the following extract and answer the questions.

ITEM A

We asked the wives to give us brief diaries of their days. Mum was rarely absent. 'After breakfast I bath the baby and sweep the kitchen, and wash up. Then I go up the road shopping with Mum, my sister Greta, and the three children. After dinner I clean up and then round about two o'clock I go out if it's fine for a walk with Mum and Greta and the children. This is an ordinary day. If anything goes wrong and I'm in any trouble I always go running round to Mum's.' The mother is the head and centre of the extended family, her home its meeting place. Sixty-eight per cent of married women last saw their mother at her home, and only 27 per cent at their own. When there, they quite often see their other sisters, and brothers too, particularly if they are still living at home, but even if they live elsewhere, the sisters may call there at the usual time in the afternoon for a cup of tea, or just happen to drop in for a chat on the way to the shops. Regular weekly meetings often supplement the day-to-day visiting. 'All my family,' said Mrs. Shipway, 'gather at Mum's every Saturday afternoon. We sit jawing, and get amused with the children when all of them get together, play cards, and listen to the wireless. No-one leaves till tennish at night. It always happens on a Saturday.'

(Source: Adapted from M. Young and P. Willmott, *Family and Kinship in East London*, Penguin, 1957.)

ITEM B

The largest housing estate in Europe rises in red-brick Lego-like blocks from the shoulder of the M4 and meanders through closes and cul-de-sacs to the very edge of Reading. At the heart of the estate, which will in two years hold 6,500 homes and nearly 20,000 people, is an enormous supermarket, which is used by families from all over the area, not just Lower Earley. The shoppers come by car, whizz their trolley round and depart the same way. The chances are they will never see a face they recognise.

Those who suffer most from isolation and loneliness are undoubtedly the many young mothers. Mrs. Valerie Godfrey, who runs one of the over-subscribed playgroups — with 90 children on her waiting list — thought many mothers must get depressed. The estate seems to have been built on the assumption that everybody has a car at their disposal all the time. For years there were no footpaths beside main roads, and the supermarket is a long walk from the furthest reaches of the estate. Life is not easy for those mothers at home without a car. Health Visitor Mrs. Margaret Macleod believes the absence of traditional extended families has caused special problems. Many young couples moved to Lower Earley from the north when development first began, and most others have moved well away from mothers, sisters and aunts. She said: 'In this huge estate there was a breakdown of communications. There were no little corner shops, no pubs and no churches.' Until last autumn, when the play areas were built, there was nowhere for children, she said. 'The nearest parks are quite a long way away. New mothers were cooped up in the house all day with just the television for company. All that would tend to lead to post-natal depression and a great deal of loneliness and distress,' said Mrs. Macleod. To make things worse, the average age of women having their first child in Lower Earley is much higher than average, at 28 years old. Many have given up careers to start a family, and cannot immediately cope with isolation and dramatic change.

(Source: Adapted from an article by Sarah Boseley, The *Guardian*, 24 February 1988.)

Questions

1 What percentage of women saw their mothers at her own home? (Item A) (1 mark)
2 How many people will be living on the Lower Earley estate in two years' time? (Item B) (1 mark)
3 What information in Item A suggests that the people described live in extended families? (3 marks)
4 What information in Item B is used to support the writer's claim that young mothers suffer most from isolation and loneliness? (3 marks)
5 Give three main differences in the lives of the families described in Items A and B. (3 marks)
6 What is meant by the term 'privatised family'? (3 marks)
7 How do you think that the life of the women described in Item B could be improved? (6 marks)

The 'consumer' family

Although we have by no means got rid of poverty in modern Britain, the average standard of living has risen considerably over the last century. Improvements in health, housing, diet, working hours and conditions and the quality and quantity of goods available have led to longer, healthier and more comfortable lives for most of us. Many households now contain goods which even ten or twenty years ago would have been considered luxuries.

The movement of family members away from work based on the home (e.g. farming, weaving) to work based in shops, offices and factories has resulted in people buying things they would once have grown or made for themselves. In other words, there has been a shift from *production* to *consumption*. Marxist writers believe that capitalist society increasingly depends on families as consumers being persuaded to buy more and more goods and services, whether they really 'need' them or not.

Activity (class)

Using the information in the extract below, complete Table 3.3 at the end. (You will not be able to fill in every box.) 'Consumer durables' are personal and household goods which have a relatively long life, such as cars, CD players, freezers and washing machines.

The General Household Survey has monitored the availability of certain consumer durables since 1972. Nine per cent of households had a home computer available to them for their own use in 1984. Twenty-four per cent of households had a video, an increase from 18 per cent in 1983. There was also an increase between 1983 and 1984 in the proportion of households with a colour television (81 per cent to 83 per cent), and with a deep freezer (57 per cent to 61 per cent). There was a sharp increase in the proportion of households with a telephone during the 1970s, but the increase between 1983–4 was relatively small, from 77 per cent to 78 per cent. In 1984, 66 per cent of households had central heating, a rise from 37 per cent in 1972. The proportion of households with a car increased relatively slowly, from 52 per cent in 1972 to 61 per cent in 1984. Over the same period, the proportion of households with more than one car or van almost doubled, rising from 9 per cent to 17 per cent.

(Source: *General Household Survey*, 1984.)

Table 3.3. *Proportion of households in Great Britain owning selected consumer durables 1972–1984*

% of households with:	1972	1983	1984
Colour television			
Deep freezer			
Central heating			
Telephone			
Video			
Home computer			
One car			
More than one car or van			

Table 3.4 summarises some of the changes that have taken place in the family over the last century or so. As it is not really possible to put actual dates, the table is headed 'Then' and 'Now'. Using the information in this chapter, plus your own knowledge of society, complete the table. Some of the boxes have already been filled in to help you. The box for 'conjugal roles' may have to wait until you have finished Chapter Eleven on 'Gender'

Table 3.4. *Changes in the family*

Feature	Then	Now
Average number of children		
Divorce		
Family type	Many extended families	
Conjugal roles		
Parent/child relationships		
Work group	Mainly members of family	
Entertainment	Provided by family/community	
Standard of living	Low for most people	
Family support		
Contact with wider family	Mainly face-to-face	
Health care		
Education of children		
Number of generations alive	Not many three-generation families	

Alternatives to the family

Although there are many different family types in Britain today, the majority of them are based on people linked by ties of blood or marriage. However, some people have replaced this type of arrangement to create what they see as alternatives to the family.

One example of this are the 'kibbutzim' of Israel. A kibbutz consists of a group of people who, although some of them may be married to each other, live as part of a much larger group, with communal decision making and with children being raised in 'children's houses' rather than by their parents. Kibbutzim women return to work soon after having their babies, who are cared for by trained staff in 'babies' houses'.

In the 1960s and 1970s, some groups of young people in Europe and America formed 'communes', where the accent again was on sharing life with a much bigger group of people than in the average nuclear family. There are still some communes in existence today, though the idea is less popular than twenty years ago.

It is important to remember, though, that our socialisation has conditioned most of us to think of 'families' as mum, dad and two children. Although that particular arrangement is one in which many people exist for a time, if we took a 'snapshot' picture of the households in Britain, we would find that only 45 per cent of the population were in households consisting of a married couple with dependent children.

Activity (class)

Read the article about the Merchavia Kibbutz and then do the activity which follows:

Today there are some 280 kibbutzim in Israel with a total population approaching 150,000. Although they make up only about four per cent of the population, kibbutzim members produce nearly 40 per cent of the country's agricultural output and nearly six per cent of the industrial output. One of the first kibbutzim, Merchavia, was founded in the 1920s.

There was to be no sex-based division of labour (i.e. no 'men's jobs' and 'women's jobs') and, in fact, women worked in heavy building and road construction, as well as irrigation works, quarries and agriculture. However, even in the early days, work in the communal kitchen tended to be reserved for women. Then, as now, there were no wages. Each kibbutz supplied all the needs of its members. At first, even clothing was considered communal property.

A member's first loyalty was to the kibbutz. Spouse and children came second. Couples tried to avoid working in the same job, and took their meals with everyone else in the communal dining room rather than in their private apartment. In Merchavia, as in many other kibbutzim, it was decided that children should be brought up not with their families, but in 'peer groups' of children of roughly the same age. After six weeks, babies would sleep in a separate 'children's house' and be looked after by kibbutz members during the day. This, of course, increased the number of workers available, though most child-care workers tended to be women.

Over the years many of these original ideas have been modified. The nuclear family has been slowly coming back, and now forms the basis of kibbutz social life, with family members choosing to work together and cooking their own family meal in the evening. Family apartments also serve as a place for entertaining friends or watching television. Last year for the first time, babies were allowed to sleep in their parents' apartment rather than in the 'babies' house'. In fact, many young children sleep in their parents' apartment, too, though older children remain in the 'children's house'. Apartments currently being built on the kibbutz have an extra bedroom, reflecting this new trend, though all babies and children are still under communal supervision during working hours.

(Source: Adapted from Nigel Pollard, 'To Each According to his Needs', *New Internationalist*, December 1982.)

Continued over page . . .

Questions

Working in small groups, discuss and prepare answers to the following questions, ready for a class discussion:

1 What are the differences between life in Merchavia in the 1920s and life in a 'typical' modern nuclear family?
2 What changes have taken place in the Merchavia kibbutz since the 1920s?
3 What do you think are the advantages and disadvantages of life on a kibbutz? Consider the question from the points of view of
   a married women,
   b young children who are brought up in a group of children the same age as themselves,
   c elderly people.

There are different points of view regarding the value of families, both to their members and to society as a whole. Opposite is a list of statements which could be made about families. Draw up a table like the one opposite with columns headed 'For' and 'Against', and write out each statement under what you think is the appropriate heading. You may also think of some statements of your own to add to the list!

The Family

Provides for the care of young children.
Puts a heavy burden on women in their role of housewives, mothers and 'carers'.
Provides the next generation of citizens and workers.
An important agency of socialisation.
Unequal power relationships between men and women, parents and children.
A source of violence for some women and children.
A refuge from the stresses of modern life.
An important unit of consumption
A source of comfort and companionship.

Stimulus questions

Read the following extracts then answer the questions.

ITEM A

Generally, Asian households (defined as those sharing food and shelter) are larger, with 4.6 members, than 'White' or 'West Indian' households with 2.3 and 3.4 members respectively. Households including more than one generation or where brothers and their wives live together, which sometimes means that adjoining houses are knocked together, are more common among Sikhs and East African Asians. Overall, however, the proportion of extended families living together is 21 per cent — higher than among other groups, but not the norm. The trend, in fact, is towards nuclear families but this does not mean that the importance of extended family ties has diminished. On the contrary, economic and material assistance as well as emotional support are found in these enduring links. To say, as many Asian people do, 'We are a family people', expresses a truth and a commitment to family life shown in the Sunday gatherings where food and news and the warmth and support of family members are shared across generations and households. People will travel miles to be together for family events, crammed into cars or into minibuses for the journey.

(Source: Adapted from 'Images and Realities', Sallie Westwood and Parminder Bhachu, *New Society*, 5 May 1988.)

ITEM B

As they get older, people who remain in private households are more likely to live with 'others' — and the vast majority of these 'others' are relatives. Living alone, or in a 'no family' household, however, does not necessarily mean that the elderly do not benefit from or contribute to family life. Living near relatives is often as important as living with them. A major survey of the elderly living at home found that of those elderly people with living relatives, over 50 per cent received a visit at least once a week, and almost a third 'several times a week'. The most frequent visitors to elderly people are their children and it is to the family that many elderly people turn to for help. At the same time many elderly people are themselves a source of help and support for their families; about a fifth say that 'they are able to do things to help' when they visit. And other forms of contact, telephone calls and letters, are also important. Overall, then, apart from a minority of the elderly, family networks are an important part of their daily lives.

(Source: Adapted from *Families in Focus*, Lesley Rimmer, published by Study Commission on the Family, October 1981.)

Questions

1 Why do some Asian families knock adjoining houses together? (Item A) (1 mark)
2 Who are the most frequent visitors to elderly people? (Item B) (1 mark)
3 What sort of activities take place at the Sunday gatherings mentioned in Item A? (2 marks)
4 Families can provide 'economic and material assistance as well as emotional support' (Item A) and many elderly people are 'a source of help and support for their families' (Item B). Give examples of the sorts of things which might be meant by these phrases. (6 marks)
5 Using material from Items A and B and elsewhere, discuss the view that people in Britain are 'a family people'. (10 marks)

Structured questions

1 Why are 'families' important for society? (4 marks)
2 What are the problems in talking about the 'typical British family'? (4 marks)
3 Discuss four important changes to the family which have taken place in Britain over the last 150 years. (12 marks)

Project and assignment suggestions

1 *A study of changing perceptions of 'childhood'* — This would be largely a historical study, showing how ideas of children and childhood had changed over time. Your material would come from a variety of sources — e.g. literature, paintings, historical documents, diaries. You might also be able to show how the popular image, for example of appealing Victorian children in the paintings of the time, compared with the reality, such as descriptions from Royal Commissions of children working as chimney sweeps, in the mills etc. Remember to make your study sociological, and not simply descriptive, by trying to analyse what helped to bring about the changes you will be describing.

2 *The family in the media* — A study of how 'families' are portrayed by the mass media, probably television. You could include the advertisers' ideas of 'families' by describing the situations in which the families are portrayed, e.g. at table, out shopping, on holiday, and also the various roles of the different members of the family. What age, ethnic group and social class are the families portrayed? A further development would be to look at 'families' in some of the popular 'soaps', such as 'East Enders', 'Dallas', and 'Neighbours', showing the type of situations shown, and the various 'problems' occurring in the scripts. You might take this project a stage further, by doing a survey into why people watch such family-based 'soaps', and the extent to which they consider that they are based on 'real life'.

3 *Family structure in the past* — For this, you would need to have access to some early census material for your area — ask at your nearest main library for details. You could then analyse the material to extract information on a variety of topics, such as average family size, size of households, the age of the children (which would tell you what space there was between births), and perhaps even the occupations described. If you are lucky, you might also be able to get access to parish register material

(again, ask at the main library; many parish records are now on microfiche). From this material, you would able to do research into topics such as the average age at marriage of grooms and brides, the average age at death, the number of infant deaths (you would note how sharply these went up if there were an epidemic of measles or cholera), and the number of infant baptisms.

4 *Family changes during this century* — For this, you could do an in-depth interview with an elderly person, perferably an old lady. You could have a list of 'agenda items' on which you would encourage her to speak — although people often need no encouragement once they get going! Topics covered could include childhood, courtship and marriage, childbirth, work, housework, domestic appliances (or the lack of them!), health, the effects of the World War (or even both wars if the person is old enough), holidays, leisure and entertainment, and special occasions such as Christmas or birthdays, and how these were celebrated. Such interviews are best tape-recorded, if your subject is agreeable.

5 *Attitudes to the family* — This would be a fairly large-scale survey into people's attitudes on a variety of issues relating to the family such as co-habitation, sexual 'permissiveness', divorce, abortion, 'working mums', sharing household chores, ways of bringing up children, the 'terrible teens' and so on. You will get some other ideas by referring to the British Social Attitudes Survey, a copy of which is sure to be in the nearest main library. Remember to give careful thought both to the design of your questionnaire and to the selection of your sample.

6 *Family problems* — This could be a study of what help is available for people with 'family problems' in your area. Possible examples would be Relate (which used to be the Marriage Guidance Council), a refuge for 'battered wives', charities dealing with issues such as homelessness or alcoholism, and, or course, the social services. Obviously, 'family problems' are sensitive areas, and your project would most probably consist of a survey of what help is available, and possibly some interviews with charity workers or counsellors to get some general information about the sort of issues they deal with — you naturally would not expect anyone to discuss any confidential information. You could also look around your neighbourhood to see how and where information about any such agencies is made available to people who might need it.

Key words

Cohabitation	Privatised family
Extended family	Reconstituted family
Family functions	Symmetrical family
Nuclear family	

4 Education

You have probably spent more time in school than in any other place apart from your own home. So, no doubt you have your own opinions about school and education. From the point of view of understanding the sociology of education this is both a good and a bad thing — good because you have real experience to draw on when trying to understand theories and research, bad because you might have rigid and fixed views (bias) which will prevent you from fairly considering theories and research. This chapter begins with two activities aimed at helping you to use your experience sociologically to understand education as a whole.

Your school as an organisation

Organisations can 'rule' your life. It makes sense, therefore, to learn to 'get by' or 'survive' in them. The school is probably the first big organisation you will have had to deal with.

All organisations have a *structure*. That means that individuals and groups carry out given roles which help to make the organisation function. Examples of individual roles in a school are: head teacher, head of department (or faculty) and pupil. Examples of groups that carry out given roles are heads of department committees, general staff meetings, department meetings, and, in some schools, a pupil (or pupil and staff) council. The given (required and expected) roles of all individuals and groups make up the formal structure of the school. The people occupying these roles have power to affect your life. They will influence the subjects you take and, probably, the job you get. And, remember, as a pupil or student, *you* are what the organisation is supposed to be about.

Activity (class/outside class)

The following activity is aimed at finding out who occupies what roles in your school or college. By finding out how your own school works, you should find out a lot about how schools work in general.

In this activity you will draw up and try to explain two charts. One chart will be of all the roles held by individuals in your school or college. The other will be of the most important committees, working parties, etc. On your list of committees etc, include the name of the chairperson. You might find it helpful in drawing up the second chart to divide the committees into Academic (to do with teaching and learning), Administrative (to do with organisation), and Pastoral (to do with the personal welfare of students).

1 *Getting the information*
Divide the class into two 'main' groups — one group for each chart. Then, sub-divide the two main groups into groups of two or three each — each sub-group to draw up its own chart. When all the sub-groups have drawn up their charts, they should pool their information with their main group, so that each main group produces one chart which is as complete as possible.

2 *Report back: discussion*
In reporting back, it is important that everybody gets the information — so provide photocopies of the two charts or draw them on a board. You might find it convenient to appoint a spokesperson for each main group.

Here are some questions you might ask in your discussion:

- What is the most powerful role?
- What is the least powerful role?
- Compare the number of women and men in positions of Head of Department/Head of Year or above.
- Compare the number of whites and blacks in positions of Head of Department or above.
- Do you think your school/college functions well or not? Give reasons.
- Would you describe your school as 'democratic'?
- What changes, if any, would you make in the way your school is run? Give reasons.

Table 4.1. Percentage of posts held by female and male teachers in England and Wales in January 1983

	Female	Male
	%	
Head teacher	16	84
Deputy head teacher	37	63
Senior teacher	19	81
Scale 4	22	78
Scale 3	37	63
Scale 2	50	50
Scale 1	63	37
N =	110,308	132,308

(Source: DES, *Statistics of Education*, HMSO, London, 1983)

How democratic can a school be?

Few, if any, schools are organised in a completely dictatorial way. All heads have to answer to pupils' parents and, in nearly all cases, to some overseeing or managing body, such as a board of governors. Nevertheless, day to day, some schools may be run very firmly by the head or by just a few senior members of staff. Probably most schools are run from the top downwards, even though there may be some representation of pupil and junior teaching staff opinion. There have always been some schools in both the state and private sector of education which have tried to organise in a highly democratic way. Examples of this approach are:

1   a school council which gives pupils a big say in making the rules, e.g. Summerhill School — private,
2   freer choice in choosing subjects and perhaps attending lessons, e.g. Dartington Hall School — private, now closed,
3   community access, so that the school is an educational and social resource for the community, e.g. Countersthorpe Comprehensive — state.

Summerhill School — More democratic than most

Why are schools seldom really *democratic?*
Do you think they should be democratic?

What are the purposes of education? (why go to school?)

Activity (class)

This activity is a 'warm-up' for this section which is about what schools are for. Not all the reasons might be as obvious as you think. Here is a chance for you to say:

1   The reasons you have for coming to school.
2   The reasons why 'society' requires you to come to school.

Divide a piece of paper into two and make a list of each of the two sets of reasons. See if you can match up the two sets of reasons by putting those most closely related opposite each other on the lists. Somebody should put their lists on the board. Discuss.

There are two ways of looking at why people go to school. First, there are the individual's own reasons and, second, there are the reasons why 'society' requires school attendance. Figure 4.1 compares these two types of reasons:

Figure 4.1

Individual's reasons	Society's needs
Ambition	*Preparation/selection for job*
1 To get good qualifications in order to get a better job	To prepare and sort out (select) pupils for the type of job to which they seem best suited
Self-development	*Socialisation*
2 To develop more fully as a person	To make sure the population is educated to the level of being able effectively to participate in social and political life
Compulsion	*Social control*
3 Because you *have* to be there	'Storage' of the young in school to 'keep them off the streets'

We will now discuss each of these pairings:

1   *Ambition — preparation/selection for jobs (economic purpose of education)*

Preparation:

The link between school-work and employment is a *general* one. Most people do not receive specific job training before the age of seventeen, but they do acquire the general skills and attitudes to get by in the world of work. Such matters as learning to relate to authority and concentrate on work, whether or not it is interesting, prepares pupils for similar situations they will meet as employees. Such learning is part of the *hidden curriculum* of schools (see next section).

Selection:

The public examination system grades pupils according to different levels of attainment. This greatly affects the jobs they get. To some extent, grading reflects intelligence and ability, but by no means completely. Thus:

- Working class and black children perform *on average* below their measured intelligence.
- Despite anti-sex discrimination laws, girls still tend to choose subjects which lead to less well paying jobs, e.g. home economics rather than craft, design and technology.

Two more comments can be made about qualifications and selection: Most employers say that their greatest need is for people with a sound *general* education (particularly in maths and English), rather than people with specific vocational training — they say most 'voc' skills can be picked up on the job. However, there *are* skills shortages — especially in engineering and computing. Second, 'qualification inflation' has taken place. The same qualifications now 'buy' you less in the job market than twenty years ago. For instance, the qualifications required for being a teacher or a librarian have 'gone up'.

So, there is no nice easy 'fit' between ability, qualifications, and the job you get!

2 Self-development/socialisation

Self-development:

> For many teachers, the main purpose of education is to help pupils become more fully developed people. They believe that in studying the range of subjects typically offered in schools, most pupils will learn to think more clearly and to develop their appreciation of the best of human achievement. Of course, this is very optimistic, and many teachers have grown weary and, indeed, ill trying to persuade pupils to pursue these ideals! Yet many pupils are aware that a good education might increase their appreciation of life, as well as improve their chances of getting a good job. Even so, what young people find interesting and enjoyable is probably influenced much more by their peers (own age group) than by teachers. George Michael is no doubt preferred to Mozart by many of today's teenagers, just as, twenty years ago, the Beatles were preferred to Beethoven.

Socialisation:

> Socialisation in schools should help self-development but it can hinder it. The school is the first *secondary* agency of socialisation. In contrast to the family, it is based on *formal rules and organisation.*
>
> There are two aspects to secondary socialisation at school:
>
> 1   The formal curriculum (subjects learned).
> 2   Learning how to behave in a formal organisation.
>
> Pupils learn to work hard — often in silence, to keep time, and to recognise authority — all skills required in the 'real' world of work that comes next. Because this non-classroom part of learning is not written down or often referred to, it is called the *hidden curriculum.*

3 Compulsory schooling/social control

Compulsory schooling (and training):

> 'I don't want to go to school,' cries the child.
>
> 'Well, you *have* to,' answers the parent.
>
> Few of us grow up without taking part in some version of that conversation. We do, indeed, 'have to go'. And the age at which we 'have to go' has gone on steadily rising. Since the First World War, the minimum school leaving age has been raised, first to fourteen, then to fifteen, and, more recently, to sixteen. Since the sharp rise in youth employment of the late 1970s, there has been an increase in the numbers of sixteen-plus year olds staying on in schools, going into further education, or joining job training schemes. At first, the Youth Training Scheme was voluntary, but in 1987 it was announced that those who refused a place would be liable to lose supplementary benefit entitlement.

Social control:

> Most people take it for granted that we stay on at school to obtain qualifications to get a better job. But some sociologists take the opposite view. They argue that in the post-war period, young people have not been needed in the job market, especially as increasing numbers of adult women have sought full or part-time work. School has solved the problem of where to put or 'store' young people. From this point of view, teachers are seen as enforcers of social control, 'soft cops' rather than educators.

Stimulus question

Read the following extracts and answer the questions.

ITEM A

'Right,' said the teacher, 'that's enough maths for today. Put away your books and walk quietly to the assembly hall. The Headmistress wants to talk to you.' Everybody had been in the assembly hall for several minutes before the Headmistress arrived. When she did, everybody stood up except one boy of about fifteen. The Headmistress noticed him and said:

'Do you mind standing up when I enter the room, young man?'

The youth got slowly and reluctantly to his feet.

The Headmistress glared but said no more to him. Instead, she started to address the whole school.

'I want to talk to you today about one of the most important reasons why you are at this school — to get qualifications. Last year our results were poor. I hear from your teachers that this year they are likely to be no better. I must warn you all that unless you get good qualifications you will have difficulty in getting a job. Qualifications are the first thing an employer looks for...'

ITEM B

Table 4.2. The factors employers consider important in candidates for jobs

| | Factors | | | | | |
	Specific vocational skills	General Skills	Personal appearance	Personal qualities	Personal potential	School achievement
School-leaver at 18+	3	21	7	22	17	30
School-leaver at 16+	6	12	12	37	15	18
YTS trainee	0	11	19	42	4	22

Figure in percentages — each percentage shows the relative importance of each factor for a given group.

(Source: Adapted from *Times Educational Supplement*, 8 May 1987)

Questions

1 What was the least important factor considered by employers when selecting sixteen-plus school-leavers? (Item B)   (1 mark)
2 Give examples from Item A:
   a where somebody refers to the *formal curriculum* (1 mark)
   b to the *hidden curriculum*   (2 marks)
3 a Define *social control*   (2 marks)
   b Give an example of social control from Item A (2 marks)
4 The Headmistress says that 'to get qualifications' is 'one of the most important reasons for going to school'.

a Give two other reasons why pupils might attend school.   (2 marks)
b Present and explain the evidence in Item B to suggest that the Headmistress might not be completely correct in her view 'that qualifications are the first thing an employer looks for'.   (4 marks)
5 Item B presents the factors considered important by employees for three different groups of candidates for jobs. Present and explain the main differences in what employers are looking for between the three groups of candidates.   (6 marks)

Activity

Write a paragraph in answer to the question 'what benefits do you think you are gaining from your education?' Bear in mind your own and 'society's' purposes for your coming to school.

The changing face of education: past and present

The Education Acts of 1870 and 1880

It was not until 1870 that a national system of education was set up in Britain. In 1880 the minimum school-leaving age was set at ten.

Various answers are given as to why education became national and compulsory at this time. They are much the same reasons that are given to explain why education is national and compulsory today — to prepare a more efficient work force, to enable people generally to operate better in 'modern' society, and to keep young people under control.

Worlds apart — girls in a working-class school 1913; boys at Eton College, 1908.

The Education Act of 1902

This Act set up a system of grants to grammar schools to provide free places for a limited number of clever children of families of limited means. This provision did, to a very limited extent, break down the class and education divisions so deep in British society, though the majority of working-class children remained much less well educated than their middle-class peers.

The Education Act of 1944: the tripartite system

This Act established compulsory *secondary* schooling for all for the first time. It set the school leaving age at fifteen, which has since been raised to sixteen.

The Act, also known as the Butler Act, is associated with the *tripartite system* of secondary education which developed in England and Wales between 1945 and 1965. Mainly depending on their result in an exam taken at eleven — known as the eleven-plus exam — children went to grammar, secondary modern or technical schools.

These three types of school were intended to provide an education for three types of children. The grammar schools were for the academically able, the technical schools for those thought suitable for qualifying as skilled, craft or technical employees, and the 'secondary moderns' were intended to provide a general education for non-academic children, most of whom were expected to find lower-level occupations. It was not originally intended to talk about children 'passing' or 'failing' the eleven-plus exam (it is the same situation today with GCSE). The exam was simply supposed to show which type of school a child was best suited for. According to the Act, all schools had 'parity of esteem' (i.e. were equally good). In practice, if you got to grammar school, you had 'passed' the eleven-plus, if you went anywhere else, you had 'failed'.

The total secondary school population divided up roughly as follows:

secondary modern	75%
grammar	18%
technical	2%
private (fee paying)	5%

The main criticisms of the tripartite system were:

1 *Eleven years old is too early to decide a person's educational (and possibly, occupational) future.*
2 *In practice, many intelligent children failed the eleven-plus and many less intelligent passed.*
   One of the main reasons for this was that many less intelligent middle-class children got more family support for their school work (e.g. a quiet room to do homework in) whereas many intelligent working class children, lacking such support, lost interest in school and left as soon as they could. Table 4.3 shows just how big this problem was.

Table 4.3. A comparison of pupils of different social class background but of similar high ability

	Upper-middle class	Lower-middle class	Upper-working class	Lower-working class
% Gaining good GCEs	77	60	53	37
% Leaving school in their 5th year	10	22	33	50

(Source: Adapted from J.W.B. Douglas, *All Our Future*, 1968.)

Questions

1 Give *two* explanations for the pattern shown in column 1 (across) of pupils gaining good GCEs.
2 Give *two* reasons for the pattern shown in column 2 (across) of pupils leaving school in their fifth year.
   (Note. We will discuss explanations about the links between class and educational performance later — this question is just to get you started.)

In any case, the belief that intelligence tests precisely measure intelligence — on which many eleven-plus exams were based — came increasingly to be doubted in the 1970s — and even before.

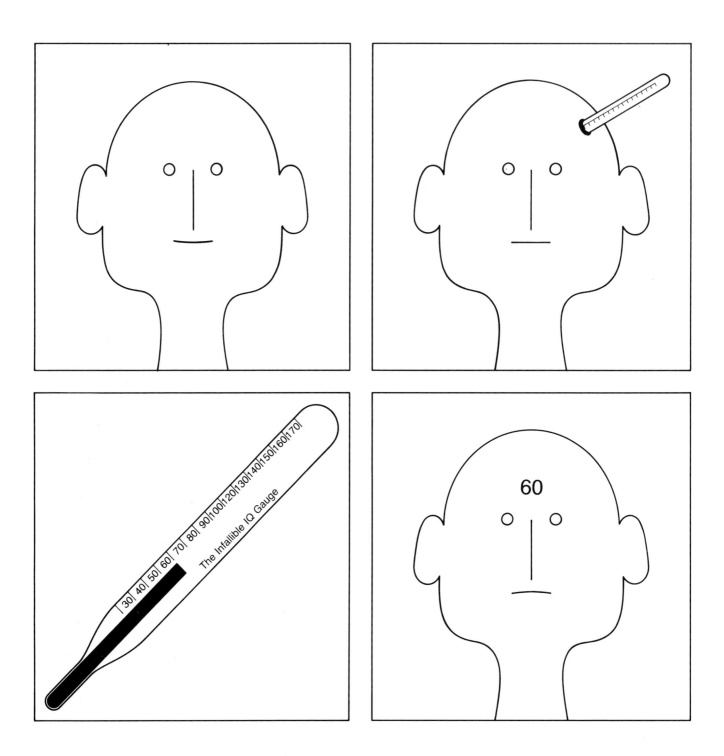

The widespread belief that intelligence could be precisely measured — on which the eleven-plus exam was partly based — was mistaken.

(Source: *Libertarian Education*, 12)

3 *Because of (2), the tripartite system came to be seen by many as socially divisive.* Most upper and middle-class children (even those of average intelligence) went to private or grammar schools whilst most working-class children (including many of high intelligence) went to secondary modern schools and left at fifteen with few, if any, qualifications. This reflected and helped to continue the class divisions in British society.

4 *The tripartite system created more 'losers' than 'winners' (i.e. more eleven-plus 'failures' than 'passes').*

5 *Because girls tended to do better at the eleven-plus than boys, in some areas it was made easier for boys to pass.*

6 *For all the above reasons, critics of the tripartite system argued that it did not provide equality of opportunity.*

The Labour Party accepted these arguments against the eleven-plus and the tripartite system. In 1964, it came to power, and set about promoting a different system of secondary education — the Comprehensive System. Supporters of this system hoped it would make equality of opportunity more of a reality.

The comprehensive system and equality of opportunity

A truly comprehensive school accepts children of all levels of ability except, in many cases, the educationally subnormal. Nearly all local authorities which 'went comprehensive' abolished the eleven-plus. In 1965, the Labour Government issued a circular directing local education authorities to prepare plans to 'go comprehensive'. At that time, only a small percentage of areas were already comprehensive. By 1971, 34.4 per cent of secondary schools were comprehensive, and by 1980, 85.9 per cent.

So far the comprehensive system has not achieved the highest hopes of its supporters:

1 *Academic results* — The academic results of comprehensive schools and grammar plus secondary modern schools of similar areas are roughly similar. All that change for nothing?

2 *Social mixing* — Fewer friendships between middle and working-class children develop in comprehensive schools than might be expected. This is partly because middle-class children are more likely to be put into higher streams and make friends there, and working-class children into lower streams where they make most of their friends.

The comprehensive system and the problem of class

Perhaps the hopes that the comprehensive system would soon provide a much broader avenue of opportunity for all children were unrealistic. All the sociological research into the matter in the 1950s and 1960s found that the social-class background of children greatly affected their academic attainment.

Here is a summary of the home-background factors that are known to be related to academic success. On all of them, working-class children are more likely to do less well than middle-class children:

- Parental attitudes to education.
- Educational level of parents.
- Family size (generally, it is an educational disadvantage to be a member of a large family).
- Quality of maternal care of young children.
- Material prosperity of the home.
- Neighbourhood disorganisation.
- Problems in family background (for example, a 'broken' home).

No school system — whether tripartite or comprehensive — can be expected to make up fully for disadvantages of home background. We shall see *how* class disadvantages tend to carry over into the classroom and school situation in the next section. First, however, we need to look at some more evidence of the effects of class background on educational success and failure.

National Child Development Study

This is a longitudinal (ongoing) study of all babies born in the week beginning 3 March 1958. At seven years old, the group was divided into three levels of achievement — high, medium and low. At eleven, about one third had dropped out of the top group and these were mainly working-class children. About one third had moved up from the low group and these were mainly middle-class children (Figure 4.2).

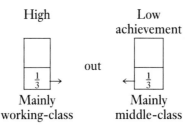

Figure 4.2. Movement between high and low achievement groups, according to class, between the ages of 7 and 11 for the group studied by the NCDS team

The failure of working-class children to achieve their potential is shown in Figure 4.3.

Figure 4.3

Numbers of children according to class (out of 10)

At Birth ○ ○ ○ ○ ○ ○ ○ × × ×
At University × × × × × × × ○ ○ ○

Key
× Middle-class
○ Working-class

Activity

Present the data in Figure 4.3 as a bar chart or in some other diagrammatical form.

The continuing importance of private education

Between 1981 and 1990, the percentage of pupils at private schools rose from about 5.5 per cent to about 7.0 per cent of the total school population. A small part of this increase was due to the *assisted places scheme* which provided grants to a limited number of less well-off children who, it was thought, would benefit from a private education.

The role of private schools in British education and, indeed, British society is far greater than the above percentages suggest. Within the private system, it is the so-called public schools which play such an important part in British society. Eton and Harrow are perhaps the best-known public schools. The function they fulfil is to enable most of the offspring of the elite (leading groups) in British society to become part of the elite of the next generation. They do this partly by providing a very good education and — just as important — by providing contacts. In this way, the public schools ensure that leadership in business, the professions and the armed services and social privilege will remain largely in the hands of the elite.

Of course, it is quite possible for a person of *any* background or schooling to join the elite if he or she becomes successful or rich, or both. However, the chances of a person going to a public school attaining elite status are far greater. For this reason, some people would like to abolish the public schools. At the moment, however, they are thriving.

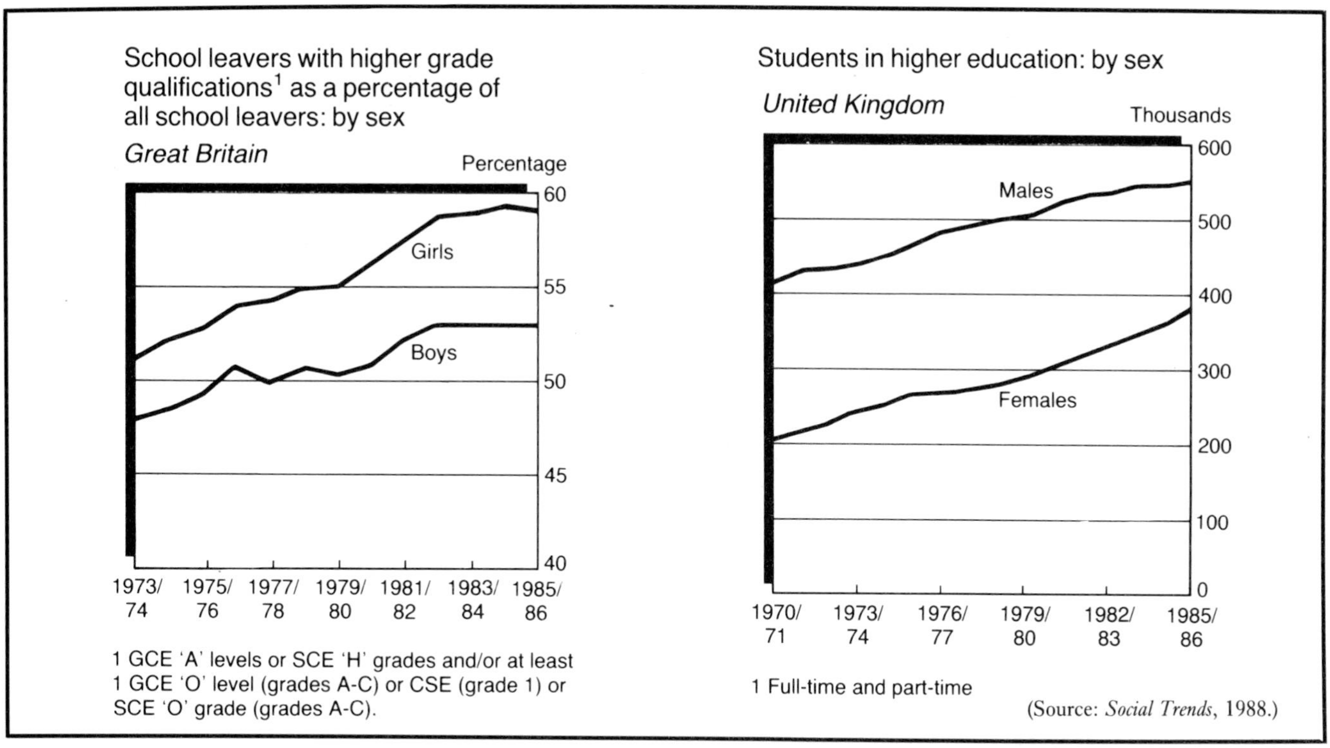
School leavers with higher grade qualifications[1] as a percentage of all school leavers: by sex
Great Britain
Percentage
60
55
50
45
40
Girls
Boys
1973/ 74
1975/ 76
1977/ 78
1979/ 80
1981/ 82
1983/ 84
1985/ 86
1 GCE 'A' levels or SCE 'H' grades and/or at least 1 GCE 'O' level (grades A-C) or CSE (grade 1) or SCE 'O' grade (grades A-C).
Students in higher education: by sex
United Kingdom
Thousands
600
500
400
300
200
100
0
Males
Females
1970/ 71
1973/ 74
1976/ 77
1979/ 80
1982/ 83
1985/ 86
1 Full-time and part-time
(Source: Social Trends, 1988.)

Figure 4.4. A larger percentage of females get higher grade qualifications than males yet a smaller percentage of females than males go on to higher education.

The classroom, the school and society

Society: class, gender and race

We have already looked at the relationship between class and educational achievement. Class is not the only important factor which explains educational attainment. Gender and race are also very important. For instance, females tend to under-achieve in maths and the sciences, and children of Afro-Caribbean origin under-achieve across a wide range of subjects, particularly English language and maths.

The problems females meet in education are much the same as they may meet in the family or in society generally. When studying the family, you will have noticed how females are *expected* and *socialised* to do certain things rather than others, and this can also occur in schools. Even though it has been illegal since 1975 for schools to insist that girls do certain subjects and not others, there is still a difference in how well the sexes do in given subjects (though differences are slowly reducing). For instance, *on average*, girls do better at English and boys at maths. However, overall, a larger percentage of girls get higher grade qualifications than boys (see Figure 4.4) *yet* fewer go on to higher education.

The problems faced by certain ethnic minority groups relate not just to education but to the whole of society. These include:

1 *Racism* — Blacks or others experiencing racism may lose trust and confidence in schools and teachers.
2 *Cultural differences* — It is not easy to be sure how differences in culture (the way groups live) affect educational attainment. Some Afro-Caribbeans use a language pattern called Creole which may negatively affect how they understand teachers and how teachers understand them. However, we cannot be sure that Creole dialect is any different in this respect from certain working-class dialects.
3 *Poverty and ethnicity* — In terms of income and wealth, members of certain ethnic groups, such as Bangladeshis, are typically lower working-class. Some of the problems their children experience in education may just be those faced by poorer children generally.

Although in comparison with, say, white, middle-class males, the groups we are discussing may lack certain social advantages, this is not in itself enough to explain the problems they meet in the educational system. Part of the problem is also that the *education system itself* has been geared to the middle-class, white, male. Things are changing in this respect, but not everywhere, and sometimes not very quickly.

We need to examine the argument that the educational system favours middle-class, white males because many of you may not readily agree with it.

Question (possible class discussion)

Explain the trends shown in the two diagrams of Figure 4.4.

Labelling in the classroom

Certain groups may get favoured in school and others disadvantaged as a result of what sociologists term *labelling*. Labelling is referring to a particular person or group in an over-simple and rigid way. 'All the kids from that part of town are thick' is an example of labelling. The labels people are given can affect the way they behave. They can become like their labels. This is called *self-fulfilling prophecy*. For instance, perhaps many males seem to be bad at needlework or cookery because in the past most people, including teachers, have labelled this 'women's work'. As a result, boys might feel that they would be considered 'sissies' if they did these things. So, they 'learn' to dislike doing them, to be 'bad' at doing them.

Don't confuse labelling with the *typing* of people and groups that we all do. There are, of course, certain types of behaviour that we *tend* to expect of given groups. Thus, we expect clowns to be funny and priests to be concerned about religion. It is only when we see people simply as types and not as individuals that labelling occurs. Labelling is not typing but *stereotyping* (which is another word for labelling). Labelling is like putting a person in a box, tying it up and sticking a label on.

Schools can make a difference

Although most people remain in the class that they were born in, about one in three working-class children move up the social scale, and about the same proportion of middle and lower-middle move down. Individual intelligence is one reason that partly explains upward movement, and going to a good school is another. But what *is* a good school?

Michael Rutter's study *Fifteen Hundred Hours* examined this problem. Rutter and his team looked at only twelve Inner London secondary schools so it is important not to over-generalise their findings. Rutter's research is summarised below:

Factors measured	*Factor linked with success in these four areas*
Attendance Academic achievement Behaviour in school Rate of delinquency outside school	Teachers who are: Punctual Well organised Patient Encouraging Inspiring Willing to share extra-curricular activities with pupils Consistent

(*Note*: Whether traditional or liberal, schools that were *consistent* (steady, reliable) did better.)

Question

How 'good' do you think your school is on the basis of the four factors measured by Rutter? Explain your answer.

Stimulus questions

Read the following extracts and answer the questions. Along with class, gender and race are among the most important factors linked with educational 'success':

ITEM A

Gender

The macho male is alive and well in the nursery school, according to new research on infant play patterns.

The research, by Seamus Dunn and Valerie Morgan, of Ulster University, confirms what we know already — that sexual stereotyping has a firm grip on children by the time they start school — but it is nonetheless disturbing.

In highlighting the early aggressiveness of boys and the compliance of infant girls, it illustrates the enormous difficulties that teachers, of all school levels, face in promoting true equality of opportunity, but is also shows the importance of starting young.

The researchers observed classes of four to seven year olds in Northern Ireland over a period of four months. As with other studies, they found that playgound games were clearly segregated according to sex and that boys tended to take over space, forcing girls to cluster on the edges.

Boys also took over the high-status toys, such as bicycles and sand pits, and used intimidating aggression to stop other children. Girls were only able to play with these favourite toys when boys were not using them or when the teacher made sure they could, and they often accepted the situation with resignation.

Boys were also more reckless with toys like climbing frames, whereas girls seemed to have accepted early socialisation so effectively that they lacked confidence and acted in a cautious way.

The method of using toys also differed. Although both sexes played with shop and house corners, girls acted out 'the usual female' roles such as cooking and shopping, and played nurse to the boys' doctor.

(Adapted from 'The Doll's House Blues', in *The Teacher*, 9 November 1987.)

ITEM B

Figure 4.5. School-leavers with higher grade results at 'O' level or CSE[1] in selected subjects: by sex, 1970/71 and 1985/86

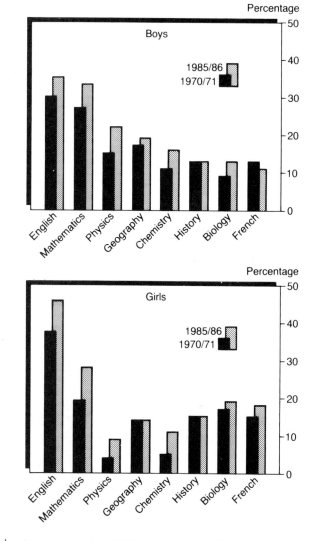

[1] 'O' level grades A-C, CSE grade 1. Excludes 'O' level passes on 'A' level papers.

(Sources: Department of Education and Science, quoted in *Social Trends*, 1988.)

ITEM C   Race

Ethnic minority groups are often clustered in inner-city poor housing areas and are sometimes referred to as the 'new poor'. Although there may be some important *cultural* differences which might affect educational achievement, it is most unlikely that there are any *genetic* differences which would account for poor performance.

Even so, the following generalisations appear to hold:

• Children of West Indian origins are more likely to be allocated to a school for educationally subnormal children than any other group.

• In general, pupils from India and Pakistan do better than other immigrants.

• West Indian and Turkish Cypriot children do worse than other immigrant groups.

• Pupils from most ethnic communities are likely to be over-represented in low streams of primary schools where streaming takes place.

(Source: Michael Williams (ed.), *Society Today*, Macmillan 1986.)

Continued over page . . .

ITEM D

Table 4.4. School-leavers: achievements, destinations and further education

CSE and 'O' level achievements	Asians %	West Indians %	All other leavers %	All maintained school-leavers in England %
No graded results (includes those attempting)	19	17	22	14
At least 1 graded result but less than 5 higher grades	63	81	62	66
5 or more higher grades	18	3	16	21

Note: All figures refer to leavers in six local education authorities.
(Source: Rampton Report, 1981.)

Questions

1 The second paragraph of Item A refers to 'stereotyping':
  a Give an example of the result of stereotyping in Item A. (1 mark)
  b Given an example of the result of stereotyping in Item B. (1 mark)
  c Define what is meant by stereotyping. (2 marks)
2 Did more boys or girls pass mathematics in 1970/71? (Item B) (1 mark)
3 Which sex had the greater increase in mathematics passes between 1970/71 and 1985/86? (2 marks)
4 Give any evidence you can find in Item A which might explain why boys achieve more passes in physics, chemistry and mathematics. (Item B) (3 marks)
5 What is the percentage difference between the number of 'West Indians' and the number of 'Asians' obtaining five or more higher grades? (Item D) (1 mark)
6 With reference to Item C, give some evidence that teachers and schools may be partly responsible for the low levels of academic achievement of 'West Indians'. (4 marks)

Activity (class)

Do you agree that social class background can have a big effect on educational attainment? Or do you think what matters most is the effort an individual makes? Discuss.

The educational issues of the 1980s and 1990s

In the 1980s, education has come to the fore again as an urgent national issue. It was one of the main issues, perhaps *the* main issue of the 1987 general election.

But why all the concern and argument about education in the 1980s? In fact, the 'great education debate' began in the mid-1970s.

1976: the great education debate — the Ruskin College speech

The Great Debate was launched by Labour Prime Minister, James Callaghan, in a speech at Ruskin College, Oxford. He made two points which were repeatedly taken up by others during the next decade:

1 Education was not satisfactorily meeting the needs of the economy — 'the world of work'.
2 The public were not convinced that teachers were doing a good job.

It was as though the teaching profession had just received a report saying:

As these criticisms were repeated through the 1970s and 1980s, many individual teachers and their unions got very concerned and even angry. They argued that what the nation and industry most needed was pupils who had a good general education and sound basic skills (especially the three 'R's' and, increasingly, technology). This they claimed, they were achieving. Figure 4.6 supports the view that pupil's educational performance improved steadily between 1953 and 1983, but that improvement slowed after 1983.

Figure 4.6. Achievements of school leavers

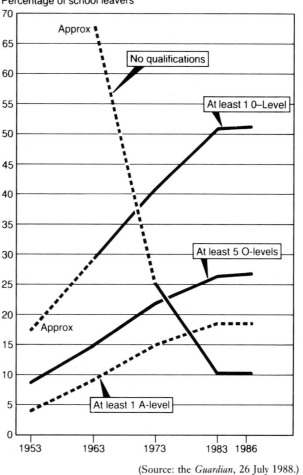

(Source: the *Guardian*, 26 July 1988.)

Questions

1 Reading across, write down the percentage differences between the number of school-leavers
   a achieving at least one A-level pass in 1953 and 1983,
   b achieving no qualifications between 1963 and 1983,
   c achieving at least five O-levels between 1983 and 1986.
2 Briefly try to explain why the rate of improvment in pupils' level of achievement slowed sharply after 1983.

The Government decided that educational change *was* needed, and pushed ahead. The pace of change increased with the election of the first Thatcher Government in 1979. Mrs Thatcher had herself been a Secretary of State for Education and had strong ideas on the subject. Both she and Sir Keith Joseph, who became Secretary of State for Education in 1981 believed the education system *could* do better — especially in relation to industry.

James Callaghan: *Labour Prime Minister 1976–9: He began The Great Debate*

Margaret Thatcher: *Conservative Prime Minister 1979–90: She was determined that education should improve its service to industry*

Kenneth Baker: *Secretary of State 1986–9: He introduced the Education Reform Act of 1988*

Education and industry: the new vocationalism

The Youth Training Scheme (YTS)

YTS was concerned with the seventeen-plus age group and with training rather than education. At first, YTS was a one-year course, but, by 1987, a two-year course was available. About three-quarters of the training is on the job and about one quarter is back-up. Some educationalists argue that this does not provide a balanced education. In 1987, young people refusing a YTS place lost welfare rights. The stimulus question at the end of the section deals with YTS and gives more information about it.

Other vocational programmes, such as the Certificate of Pre-Vocational Education (CPVE), have been introduced. The Conservative Government, also set up the Technical and Vocational Educational Initiative (TVEI). This is not a course, but is aimed at spreading vocational awareness and technological competence across the curriculum.

Question

Has education gone too far in trying to 'serve the needs of industry'? Discuss.

The General Certificate of Secondary Education (GCSE)

Given that you are reading this book, you probably know what GCSE is. It is an exam — open to virtually all sixteen year olds — which replaces the separate General Certificate of Education (GCE) and Certificate of Secondary Education (CSE). The first GCSE examination was in 1988.

The idea behind GCSE is to move away from off-by-heart learning of textbooks and to learn more *skills* by 'doing' (for instance, research projects). All GCSE grades, from A to G, are *positive*, which means they indicate the candidate has mastered certain skill levels. There are no 'fails' in GCSE.

It is early days in the life of GCSE, but two sociological points are worth considering. First, there are some signs that GCSE may favour middle rather than working-class students. This is because more examination-assessed work takes place at home than with 'O' level/CSE, where middle-class children generally enjoy better support and conditions. Second, it is hoped that GCSE will reduce the need for old-fashioned teacher control by increasing pupils' interest and participation.

Question

Are the ideals of GCSE being achieved? Compare your own experience of the public examination system with that of older relatives. Discuss.

The Education Reform Act (1988)

In 1988 an important new Education Act was passed. It was generally regarded as the most important piece of educational legislation (law) since the Butler Act of 1944.

The Act is summarised below. The idea of a core curriculum obtained wide support, but the other proposals were fiercely debated:

- The establishment of a national core curriculum (subjects that must be studied by all pupils).
- The introduction of national standardised tests in certain key subjects at ages seven, eleven, fourteen and sixteen.
- Local management of schools — head teachers and governors allowed greater control of budgets and to decide how much to spend on heating, books and teachers.
- Open enrolment: this means that schools will be able to expand their numbers if there is the demand without the local authority being able to stop them.
- Opting out: parents and governors will be given the right to receive money directly from the Government and so 'opt out' of local authority control. 'Opted out' schools will run their own affairs, including the hiring and firing of teachers.
- Inner London Education Authority to be abolished.

The core curriculum

What subjects ought every student to study and for how much of the timetable ought he or she study for each subject?

In 1987 Kenneth Baker, Secretary of State for Education, published discussion proposals for a national curriculum. His proposals are reprinted at the end of the chapter (Figure 4.9). Before looking at them, however, attempt the following Activity.

47

Activity (class)

Draw up your own core curriculum. Say what percentage of the timetable you would require for each compulsory subject or set of subject options (e.g. history or geography). How much time would you leave over for non-compulsory subjects? (For the suggested national curriculum, see p. 51.)

Testing, open enrolment and opting out

Arguments

For	*Against*
Testing: will help children and their parents to know how well they are doing — and to do something about it if needed	Will turn education into a ten-year rat race, making life miserable for many children — particularly if test results are published
Open enrolment: will enable better schools to attract more pupils and, over time, will force the less good to improve as well in order to survive. Thus, the whole educational system will improve.	Because less popular schools are likely to be in less well-off areas, some parents in these areas may not be able to afford to send their children to popular schools. The quality of those schools is likely to deteriorate.
Opting out: will enable the people on the spot — parents and governors including the Head — to run schools as *they* see the need. This could make schools more responsive to local conditions	Will, like open enrolment, hit schools in less favoured, possibly poorer localities. The local education authority will be less able to achieve balanced planning (of resources and curriculum provisions) for all schools in its area as opted out, 'free-enterprise' schools move out of its control

A testing time for children?
(Source: *Education Guardian*, 21 July 1987.)

Examples of the science knowledge that might be expected of the *average* sixteen year old, according to the National Science Working Party:

- How sex is determined in humans. The properties of gases, elements and compounds. That the periodic table groups together elements with similar properties.
- How to describe changes in the Earth's surface in terms of structural features.
- That energy sources may be renewable or non-renewable.

(Source: The *Independent*, 17 August 1988.)

Question

Examine the main features of the 1988 Education Act one by one. Try to agree on *two* lists: one of the groups you think will benefit from the Act and the other of those who will not.

Tertiary (16–19) and higher education

The national curriculum does not apply to education for sixteen–nineteen year olds and there has been slightly less change in this area than in others. However, the introduction of YTS, the extension of TVEI to tertiary (and higher) education and the appearance of 'AS' (half 'A') levels is still considerable change. Higher education has experienced sizeable cuts in government funding and faces the prospect of having to open up to private, commercial funding.

One of the main sociological questions about these sectors of education is how *open* they are to young — and sometimes old — people who want to use them. Recently, Britain has come into line with most other European Common Market countries by offering either education or training to all sixteen year olds. However, some consider that Britain divides up its sixteen year olds into winners and losers too sharply. The 'winners' are those who do 'A' levels, the 'losers' many YTS trainees; and there is another group that studies higher-level vocational courses (such as B-TEC).

With these groups in mind, Stewart Ransom had written of a 'new tertiary tripartism' (see p. 37 for 'the old' tripartism). He considers it unfair that only about a quarter of sixteen year olds do the high-status academic courses, when in many advanced countries *most* sixteen year olds continue with a general education. Inequality is accentuated by the much higher proportion of middle than working-class students studying 'A' levels.

Entry into higher education is also much more limited in Britain than in similar countries. For instance, in the United States, about 30 per cent enter higher education, compared with about 15 per cent in Britain. However, all the main political parties want to increase this percentage, and it remains to be seen whether, and how, this will be achieved.

Summary: education for one nation, or two?

There is general support for the idea of a national core curriculum. However, the proposals for testing, open enrolment and opting out are fiercely debated.

The strongest supporters of these proposals argue they will bring to education the spirit of competition and enterprise they believe it needs. This will be done by means of increasing choice and by letting the able flourish.

The strongest opponents of the proposals argue that they will create two nations: a better-off group able to take advantage of the proposed changes and a worse-off, in some cases, downright poor, group which will be disadvantaged by them. They believe that these proposals will divide the nation more sharply even than the grammar/secondary modern system did. What do *you* think?

49

Stimulus questions

Read the following extracts and answer the questions.

ITEM A

Figure 4.7. 16–18 year olds participating in education and training schemes

Percentage of population

16–18 YEAR OLD PARTICIPATING IN EDUCATION AND TRAINING SCHEMES

FEMALE
MALE

UK ITALY FRANCE JAPAN USA NETHER LANDS WEST GERMANY

ITEM B

Figure 4.8. Educational and economic activity of 16 year olds in England

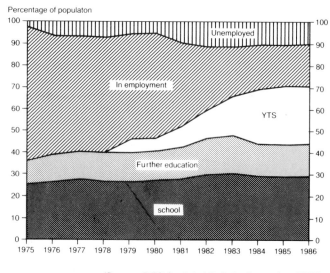

Percentage of populaton

Unemployed

In employment

YTS

Further education

school

1975 1976 1977 1978 1979 1980 1981 1982 1983 1984 1985 1986

(Source: *DES Statistical Bulletin*, September 1985.)

ITEM C

Arguments

| | *For* | *Youth Training Scheme* | *Against* |

1 YTS made a start in providing a national training scheme — which is sorely needed if Britain is to remain economically competitive (see Item B)

2 YTS is getting better — even though some of the early courses may not have been good. Courses such as those put on by IBM are concerned with social and community issues as well as work training

3 YTS provides something useful and constructive for young people to do

4 In the long run, both YTS trainees and 'the country' will benefit from YTS

5 Business control of YTS makes sure the scheme is about the 'real' world of work. For too long, British education has been anti-business. YTS and other schemes (Item A) are setting the balance right

YTS is a way of massaging the youth unemployment figures — which would be far worse without it (see Item B)

YTS is not real education. Most YTS trainers are not qualified teachers or educators. YTS is a deliberate attempt to create an under-educated, 'mindless' and conformist work force

YTS is a form of social control. It keeps 'bums on seats — and off the streets'. It is 'teen-minding'

YTS provides cheap labour for capitalism

YTS is helping to divide both education and society into losers and winners, exploiters and exploited. YTS 'kids' usually fail at school and go on to be exploited on YTS and at work. GCSE 'successes' get the better paid jobs

Questions

1 Which is the only country which had a higher number of females than males in education and training in 1985? (Item A) (1 mark)

2 Approximately what percentage of sixteen year olds were in employment in
a 1975   b 1986? (Item B) (2 marks)

3 Approximately what percentage of sixteen year olds were on a YTS course in
a 1978   b 1986? (Item B) (2 marks)

4 Do you see any link in the answers you gave to 2) and 3)? Give one reason to explain your answer. (2 marks)

5 Discuss the view that YTS was needed to help improve the British economy. (4 marks)

6 Using where possible actual examples, discuss the advantages and disadvantages of youth training schemes from the point of view of both employers and young trainees. (9 marks)

Activity

Look again at the details of the Education Reform Bill of 1987–8.

Divide the class into five groups. Each group should try to find out as much as possible about how any *one* of the Bill's measures is likely to affect (or is already affecting) your area. If you are an Inner London school, divide into six groups and include the abolition of the Inner London Education Authority measure.

You will probably have to interview teachers, maybe parents, and look at the local press to get data.

Decide how to report back.

Project and assignment suggestions

Probably more projects are done on schools than any other social institution. So beware of burying your school in questionnaires!

1 *Gender and education* — There are a number of projects on gender and education you could do, including: gender and pupil subject choice; gender stereotyping in the classroom; gender and posts of responsibility in the school.

2 *What makes a pupil leave or stay on at school at 16?* — You could do a project — perhaps questionnaires with some interviews — on why certain pupils plan to leave at sixteen-plus and why others plan to stay on. Are there any class, race or gender differences?

3 *Has GCSE been a success in your school or college?* — Find out by surveying either or both teachers and pupils. Is there too much course work? *Are* pupils doing more practical things?

4 *The 1988 Act* — There are several aspects of the 1988 Education Act you could do your project on. For instance, how has the core curriculum been organised in your school? What changes, if any, did its introduction require? Or you might do a project on opting out — particularly if your own, or another school in the area, has or is planning to opt out.

5 *Does your school or college take adult students*, and, if so, do they take classes with fourteen–sixteen, or seventeen year olds? This could be the basis of an interesting and unusual study. How well do the two age groups get on together, and how well do teachers deal with the situation?

Structured questions

1 What is meant by the 'tripartite system of education'?
(2 marks)

2 Discuss *two* important changes to secondary education in Britain which have taken place since the introduction of the tripartite system.
(6 marks)

3 Discuss the ways in which each of the following can influence a child's educational performance:
a) ethnic group, b) gender,
c) the organisation of the school.
(12 marks)

Figure 4.9. The national curriculum (from the 1987 discussion document) Note: in the 1988 Act exact time percentages for subjects were not *adopted. Pupils must now study history and geography.*

Secondary phase — years 4 and 5
Allocations of curriculum time

Foundation subjects	%	*Additional subjects e.g. for GCSE might include:*	
English	10	Science	
Maths	10	Second modern foreign language	
Combined sciences	10–20	Classics	
Technology	10	Home economics	
Modern foreign language	10	History	
History/ geography or history *or* geography	10	Geography	10%
		Business studies	
Art/music/ drama/design	10	Art	
Physical education	5	Music	
		Drama	
		Religious studies	

Key words

Afro-Caribbean	Racism
Comprehensive School	Social control
Ethnicity	Stereotyping
Labelling	Tripartite system
Longitudinal	

CHAPTER 5 Media and Communications

Introduction: the media and a media culture

The modern media are those means of communication which can reach large or 'mass' audiences. The media include television, radio and newspapers.

You probably give as much time and attention to TV as to any other single person or thing. Admittedly, you are unlikely to give it the same kind of attention as you give to, say, your girlfriend or boyfriend (though, you've heard of 'TV widows'!). Very likely, too, you will share the attention you give TV with some other activity — possibily one involving people.

Activity (outside class)

The survey shown in Figure 5.1 gives you some idea of the importance of television and other media-related activities in people's lives. This survey was of Americans in 1982, but the pattern is likely to be much the same in Britain in the late 1980s and early 1990s. You could do a small sample survey of patterns of leisure activities in your own area perhaps as the basis of your project.

Figure 5.1. We're a media culture!

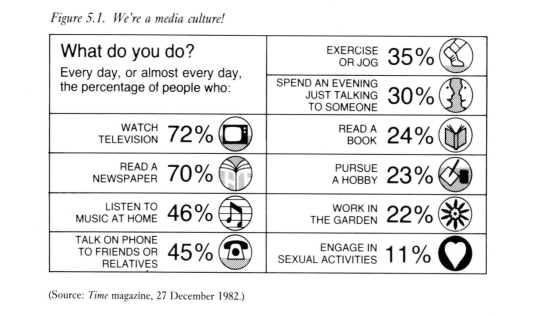

What do you do? Every day, or almost every day, the percentage of people who:		
	EXERCISE OR JOG	35%
	SPEND AN EVENING JUST TALKING TO SOMEONE	30%
WATCH TELEVISION	72%	
	READ A BOOK	24%
READ A NEWSPAPER	70%	
	PURSUE A HOBBY	23%
LISTEN TO MUSIC AT HOME	46%	
	WORK IN THE GARDEN	22%
TALK ON PHONE TO FRIENDS OR RELATIVES	45%	
	ENGAGE IN SEXUAL ACTIVITIES	11%

(Source: *Time* magazine, 27 December 1982.)

The age of information and communication

One of the main differences between modern and past societies is the amount of information that can be produced, stored, used and communicated. Computers linked to modern telecommunications help to do this. Information is now so important in running business and other organisations that some sociologists describe modern society as *'the information society'*. If the nineteenth century was the age of mechanisation, the late twentieth is the age of information.

The changing means of communication

The effects on society of changes in the means people use to communicate are immense. The following list illustrates some of the communications used at three different points in history.

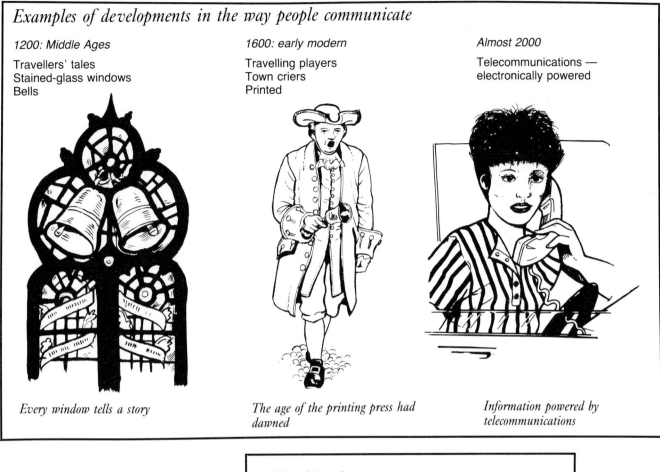

Examples of developments in the way people communicate

1200: Middle Ages

Travellers' tales
Stained-glass windows
Bells

Every window tells a story

1600: early modern

Travelling players
Town criers
Printed

The age of the printing press had dawned

Almost 2000

Telecommunications —
electronically powered

Information powered by telecommunications

Activity (class)

What do you think life was/is like in each period — as a result of the communications available to people? Before discussing this point, you could add to the three lists in each period.

Groups involved with the media

Apart from *you*, the consumer or user of the media, there are various other groups involved with them. Figure 5.2 shows these groups.

Figure 5.2

	Performers	
Owners		Producers
	Consumers	
Government		Managers
	Technicians	

Activity (class)

As a media consumer, you use the media for your own purposes, e.g. entertainment, information. However, for other groups involved with the media, you are part of 'the audience'. They pursue their own purposes which may or may not be the same as yours.

Draws up *two* lists: one of your own purposes in using the media, the other of what you think the purposes of the other groups in Figure 5.2 may be.

The media: control and freedom

Most sociologists agree that control of the media lies between the following four groups, but there is disagreement about which has the greatest control:

- Owners
- Management
- Government
- Consumers/audience ('the people').

Before it is possible to decide who controls the British media or how free the media are, it is necessary to *describe* them in more detail. At present, the media are divided between public and private operators.

The public sector media (broadcasting)

In 1926, the British Broadcasting Corporation (BBC) was set up as a public company. It was made responsible for *all* radio broadcasting and, when television broadcasting started in 1932, it was solely responsible for that as well. There are no major publicly run newspapers in Britain.

As a public company, currently financed by licence payments by the consumer, the BBC is supposed to be run in the public interest and not for profit. The BBC's charter requires it to be unbiased (fair) in its presentation of news and opinion.

To be independent in its programming, the BBC must generally be free of government interference. The corporation is run by an independent Board of Governors. It, not the Government, appoints the top BBC TV and radio managers.

The private sector media (broadcasting and the press)

1 The broadcasting media

To an increasing extent, the broadcasting media and all the main press in Britain are commercially operated.

Commercial television started in 1955 and commercial radio in 1973. Commercial radio is locally based and is known as Independent Local Radio (ILR). It is financed through advertisements. However, the owners of TV and radio stations often also own other businesses and can use the profit from these to support their broadcasting interests.

The commercial broadcasting media are not totally free, any more than the public broadcasting media are. Both are governed by the laws discussed below. The Independent Broadcasting Authority (IBA) oversaw the commercial broadcasting media, rather like the BBC Board of Governors oversees public broadcasting, but this was replaced in 1990 (see p. 57). The IBA grants franchises (rights to run a station) to fifteen Independent Television (ITV) companies, and this is now done by the Independent Television commission.

Table 5.1. Best sources of news

Most believable source	Any newspaper %	Telegraph, Guardian, Times or Financial Times %	Express or Mail %	Mirror, Sun or Daily Star %
TV	57	30	59	66
Newspaper	15	35	13	11
Radio	15	20	16	13
Don't know/ No reply	12	16	12	11

(Regular readers of)

(Source: British Social Attitudes — the 1985 Report, reprinted in *Sociology Update*, 1986.)

Questions

1 Which source of news is regarded as the most believable by most readers?
2 Which group of readers regards newspapers as the best source of news?

2 The press

The national press

In Britain, newspapers are privately owned. Three newspaper chains accounted for over 75 per cent of national circulation in 1986. They were:

	Newspapers	Percentage of adults reading each paper in 1986
Maxwell Communications Corporation (owned by Robert Maxwell)	*Daily Mirror*	20
	Sunday Mirror	21
	Sunday People	19
News International (owned by Rupert Murdoch)	*Sun*	26
	Times	3
	Today	2
	Sunday Times	8
	News of the World	29
United Newspapers	*Daily Star*	10
	Sunday Express	14

These chains account for: 74.8% of daily circulation, and
82.7% of Sunday circulation.

Robert Maxwell   *Rupert Murdoch*

Media conglomerates

For a person to own several national newspapers might seem to provide an opportunity to influence news and opinion greatly. When a person owns several different kinds of media, that opportunity is increased, and where ownership extends across nations and continents, opportunity for influence is even greater. Rupert Murdoch owns such an international multi-media 'empire' as did the late Robert Maxwell. These are referred to as 'conglomerates' (Figure 5.3).

However, the research shown in Table 5.1 suggests that people do not always believe what they see and hear, whether provided by Mr. Murdoch or others.

Figure 5.3. Rupert Murdoch's international conglomerate

	Britain	United States	Australia	Pacific Basin
Newspapers	*Times* *Sunday Times* *Today* *Sun* *News of the World*	*San Antonio* *Express-News* *Boston Herald*	*The Australian* Over 120 regional titles	*South China Morning Post* (Hong Kong) *Sunday Morning Post* *Fiji Times* *Sunday Times* *Post Courier* (Papua New Guinea)
Magazines & Books	*Elle* *Sky* *Times* supplements Geographia John Bartholemew Robert Nicholson Times Books Collins	*Automobile* *Elle* *New York* 19 other titles Harper & Row Publishers Salem House Zondervan	*TV Week* *Australasian Post* *Family Circle* *Better Homes & Gardens* Others include travel guides Bay Books Angus & Robertson Publishers Herald & Weekly Times books	*Pacific Islands Monthly*
TV and films	Sky Channel	Twentieth-Century Fox Fox Broadcasting TV stations in: Dallas Houston Los Angeles Chicago Boston New York Washington DC	None	None
Commercial printing	Eric Bemrose	World Printing	Over 20 companies	None

(Source: the *Guardian*, 9 August 1988.)

The local press

Nearly all regions have their own local press. This can be divided into newspapers that are bought and those that are free. The former are financed by the cost price and advertising, and the latter just by advertising.

The 'pay-for' local press has long been a part of regional life. *Your* school, *your* mate, even *you* might just appear in say, the '*Lancashire Evening Post*', the '*Southend Echo*', the '*Brighton Argus*' (and, if Ken Dodd is to be believed, the '*Knotty Ash Bugle and Tickling Times*'!). Recently, some of the traditional local press has come under the ownership of big media 'moguls', and it remains to be seen whether this will affect their regional character.

The new, advertising-based local press has *already* affected regional life. It carries the spirit of 1980s commercialism into many homes. On the plus side, it provides much information, including, of course, advertising information. Some papers have a special 'Community Links' service section and others provide reviews of local entertainments. On the minus side, the 'free' press arrives whether ordered or not, and some see it as just more useless clutter pushed through the letterbox — not so much free as another small invasion of freedom.

The law, the Government and the media

The media are not free to publish/broadcast just anything at all. Broadly, two types of laws limit their freedom: those that protect national security (1 and 2 in the list) and those that protect individual members of the public (3, 4 and 5). Many consider that the Official Secrets Act, which is intended to protect national security, gives the Government too much power to control what the media can say. In 1988, the Government proposed changes in the Act, but many journalists argued that these would limit their freedom even more. See if you can find out about how this debate is progressing.

The law and the media

1 *The Official Secrets Act*
   According to this Act, *every* official government activity is an official secret *unless* an official statement is made about it. As a former head of secret intelligence, MI5 said: 'It's an official secret if it's in an official file.' Over two million civil servants sign the Official Secrets Act.

2 *D (Defence) Notices*
   'D notices' are a set of voluntary rules by which the media agree not to report a variety of defence and security matters (such as the whereabouts of Russian defectors).

3 *The libel laws*
   A newspaper can be sued for libel if it prints wrong or damaging material about an individual. This partly protects personal privacy. *But* it costs money to sue.

4 *Contempt of court*
   Journalists are limited by the law about reporting cases before the courts or about to come before the courts. This is mainly so that jurors are not influenced by the media in reaching their verdict.

5 *Obscene Publications Act*
   This Act controls the publication of sexually explicit material. There is continuing debate about whether controls are too loose or too tight.

The future of British broadcasting: Government plans

The speed of change in the media has been and remains very rapid. The root cause of the change is technological invention. Currently, it is cable and satellite that underlie much media development. There will be more media as we move towards the year 2000. But more in quantity does not necessarily mean more variety (it could be more of the same) or better quality. These questions of variety and choice and of quality remain to be decided. Also to be decided is who will own the new media. Already among the leading 'players' in this potentially profitable game are Rupert Murdoch and Richard Branson (owner of Virgin Airways).

In 1988, the Government put forward a White Paper (proposals for discussion) which are likely to be the basis of a Broadcasting Act in 1990. The Government wants more commercial development of the broadcasting media, but is concerned about a possible loss of quality. Others argue that Britain already has the best broadcasting media in the world (especially the BBC) and that commercial development should not be allowed to endanger this.

Main Government proposals for broadcasting, summary: 1988
1 The BBC will continue to be funded by a licence fee, but other sources of income will also be permitted, including subscription and sponsorship.
2 The BBC to hand over some transmission time to other groups.
3 The IBA to be replaced by a commission with fewer powers of regulation.
4 ITV companies to be made more open to competition, *but* quality thresholds (controls) to be imposed.
5 The new (1988) Broadcasting Standards Authority to be given more powers to monitor sex and violence.
6 Channel 4 to keep existing programme instructions.
7 A fifth channel by 1993, and possibly a sixth, seventh and eighth later.

The media: control and freedom

By this stage, you are in a much better position to consider who controls the British media and how free it is and is likely to remain. Certainly, the British media are freer than the media in totalitarian countries, such as the Soviet Union and Chile, but perhaps less free than those in the United States.

Which, then, of the four key groups — owners, management, government and audience — has the most control over the British media? Not surprisingly, people differ in their views on this question. The following list summarises some of the views about media control and freedom (the next section will give you more information about the audience).

The British media: control and freedom — a summary of views

Free	*Not so free*
1 Editors are in charge of the content of newspapers (even though ownership may be concentrated in the hands of business people). An editor is part of the day-today management team of a newspaper	Owners can, and sometimes do, control editors. Harold Evans, editor of *The Times*, did not support owner Rupert Murdoch's views. He was sacked
2 Journalists are free to report and comment — within the limits of editorial policy and the law. This compares favourably with countries which have regular press censorship (i.e. where the media are constantly censored)	Despite many fine examples of independent journalism, the trend of some papers, especially the popular ones, is to reflect their *owner's* views. The result is a strongly Conservative press (biased towards business interests)
3 Legal limits on the press are necessary to protect the country's security and the individual's privacy	Legal limits go *too* far in this country — far further than many people realise
4 Politicians do not control or censor broadcasting or the press — apart from the Government's rights mentioned in 3, e.g. the book *Spycatcher,* written by an ex-MI5 employee, was both a breach of security and of his oath of secrecy (i.e. of the Official Secrets Act). The Government unsuccessfully sought the banning of its publication in Britain. When leading Conservatives accused the BBC of left-wing bias they were defending the principle of media fairness (see stimulus question below)	The Government has been heavy handed with its treatment of the media on security issues, e.g. although in breach of security, once *Spycatcher* was widely available in the United States, Australia and elsewhere, it was *public information* and pointless to ban it in England. The accusations of leading Conservatives against the BBC threatened its independence (see stimulus question below)
5 Anybody can set up a newspaper or, at least, a news-sheet	Only the rich can print *and* distribute many copies of a newspaper

Stimulus questions

Read the following extracts and answer the questions.

ITEM A

BBC faces new Tory broadside

The Conservatives are to press on with their attacks on the BBC, despite criticisms of party chairman Norman Tebbit's letter to the corporation protesting at its coverage of the American bombing of Libya.

'The Libyan coverage is not an isolated incident, but an example showing up more general BBC coverage which is subjective'[1] said a very senior Central Office official yesterday.

The largest number of complaints concern the very successful BBC1 Saturday night drama series 'Casualty.' The programme, which now has a 10 million audience, is based on the night shift of a casualty ward, and depicts in a very life-like way the problems of the unit. Central Office is concerned that the series emphasises health cuts, under-staffing and low pay of the workforce.

However, Michael Grade, the BBC's Director of Programmes, Television, responded yesterday that the series had 'taken hospital drama out of the cosy world of the 1960s.' He said: 'It is doing for hospitals what 'Z-cars' did for the police 20 years ago. What do the Tories want us to do? Make the blood blue rather than red?'

Richard Brooks, Media Editor

(Source: the *Observer*, 2 November 1986.)

ITEM B

Director-General of the BBC, Alastair Milne's response to Norman Tebbit:

The immediate reaction of Alasdair Milne, as Director-General, to this broadside, was to issue a statement accusing Tebbit of trying to intimidate[2] the BBC. 'We are determined to ensure that this idea' (that the Conservative Party was attempting to intimidate the BBC) 'gains no credence[3], not least because we are in the run-up to a general election and it comes at a time when the future of broadcasting is being discussed by a Cabinet committee.

On the other hand, Milne went on, it would not be in the public interest for the BBC to get into a confrontation with the Conservatives or any other political party. And he promised to come up with a rebuttal of Tebbit's charges as soon as possible.

(Source: From an account in the *Observer*, 13 December 1987.)

Glossary

[1] subjective — biased, an approach based on guesswork
[2] intimidate — frighten
[3] credence — belief, acceptance

Questions

1 What was the programme about which most complaints were received, according to Conservative Party Central Office? (Item A) (1 mark)
2 In your own words, describe Michael Grade's response to this complaint. (Item A) (2 marks)
3 Why do you think the (then) Director General of the BBC, Alasdair Milne, was *very* concerned that the BBC should not appear to be frightened by the Conservative Party '*in the run-up to a general election*' (1987)? (Item B) (3 marks)
4 What limits are there on media freedom in Britain? (6 marks)
5 How free do you consider the British media to be? (8 marks)

Activity (class/outside class)

Suppose you are about to set up your own newspaper. Write a sentence or two on how you would deal with each of the following problems:

1 Financing the newspaper.
2 Editorial policy — what would be the politics of the paper, what kind of causes would it take up?
3 What kind of readership would you aim to attract, and how would you do so?
4 Sources of news — would you use 'the usual sources', such as local authority departments, the police, prominent people, etc., or would you try to use 'alternative' sources? Explain your choice of sources.

Why people watch, listen and read — the effects the media have

TV — We watch it a lot — or do we?

Figure 5.4 seems to show that the British watch a lot of TV. As with most activities, however, there is a wide variation according to class and age, and some variation according to gender.

Figure 5.4. Television watching habits of the British

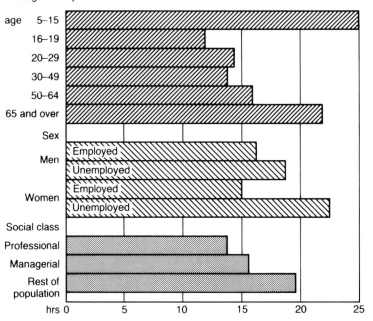

(Source: *Society Today*, Macmillan, 1986.)

Questions

1 a What is the pattern of viewing figures according to social class?
  b Which sex watches the most TV?
  c Who watch the most TV, the employed or the unemployed?
2 Give reasons to explain the watching patterns of age, gender and social groups.
Write a *brief* paragraph on *each* group.

Do people really watch TV for 20 or 30 hours plus a week? The answer seems to be 'yes', but often they are doing something else at the same time. Here is how one group of people describe the way they watch:

Vicky (27) — 'I couldn't sit and watch the telly doing nothing, I have to do something.'

Judy (23) — 'Yes, I watch television, and I can knit at the same time, you see. So I never think I'm wasting my time, if I sit and knit watching it.'

Des (34) — 'I'm married, got two daughters, one is four, the other fourteen months. Television is always on in the evening. That is not to say it's always watched. *We lapse off into conversation sometimes.*'

People listen to radio much less than they watch TV. According to *Social Trends*, the average listening time per week in 1986 was eight hours and 40 minutes. In addition, most adults at least glance at a newspaper each day, and there is a large readership of various weekly magazines which reflect the interest and activities of various age groups of both males and females.

Modern Britain clearly has a 'media culture' — whatever the precise effects of the media on people may be.

Activity (class)

Work out about how many hours a week you watch TV. For how much of the time are you doing something else as well? Do you watch more or less than the average for your age group (see Figure 5.4)? Compare your answers with those of other members of the class.

Why do people spend so much time on the media?

For pleasure — fun

The most popular TV programmes are the 'soaps', such as 'EastEnders' and 'Neighbours', and game programmes like 'Surprise Surprise' and 'That's Showbusiness'. Thus, most people appear to watch television for entertainment. Similarly, the most popular newspapers are the 'less serious' ones such as the *Sun* and the *Daily Mirror* which contain only short news items and lots of features about 'stars', 'sports', 'human interest' stories and photographs. These papers are sometimes referred to as tabloids (referring to their small size).

Sometimes, perhaps especially for the unemployed, watching TV is not so much for fun as to 'pass' or 'kill' time.

Activity (class/outside class)

1 Make lists of (a) tabloid newspapers, and (b) 'broadsheet' (those printed on larger pages) newspapers.
2 Now make a list of the differences between the two types. Follow up with a class discussion.

For information and education

Together the two main channel TV news programmes draw a bigger audience than 'EastEnders'. Far fewer people watch current affairs programmes, such as 'World in Action' and 'Panorama' — about a tenth of the audience of the most popular soaps. The 'high-brow', classical music-loving audience for Radio Three is tiny compared with that for BBC1 and most local BBC and commercial radio programmes. The more 'middle-brow' Radio Four audience, however, averages about two-fifths that of Radio One. The so-called 'quality' daily newspapers sell on average between a quarter (*Daily Telegraph*) and a tenth (*The Times*) of the total sales of the *Sun*.

To avoid loneliness: for 'company'

In their book *Uninvited Guests: The Intimate Secrets of Television and Radio*, Laurie Taylor and Bob Mullan found that, for many people, the TV is a kind of 'friend'.

Anne (45):	'It's a friend, really.'
Interviewer:	'A friend?'
Pat:	'Yeah.'
Judith:	'A companion.'
Janet (32):	'Yes.' [All:] 'Television is company.'

Many leave the TV on 'for company'. This probably explains why females watch TV on average rather more than men — it takes the edge off the loneliness of domestic work.

Television: a 'make-believe' community?

At a guess, probably more people know the names of the characters in 'Neighbours' and 'East Enders' than of other people living in their own street. Families have become smaller and more 'privatised', and there is less street and neighbourhood life in most areas. Instead, people often watch TV or do some other media-related activity. Media characters like 'Dirty Den' or (for an older age group), Dan Archer, can, for some, become more 'real' and important than real people. Judging by the letters these 'characters' get, some of their fans actually think they are 'real'. Even people less involved with media characters often make everyday conversation about their various 'doings'.

Is there anything wrong in the media playing such a big part in everyday life? The answer probably depends on what you think everyday life should be about. Taylor and Mullan discovered that a lot of people *do* feel guilty about the amount of TV they watch — partly because of the time it takes away from 'real' people and other activities (even though TV is often combined with doing other things). Sometimes parents think they should be doing other things with their children rather than watching television.

What would people do if they weren't watching 'the box'?

One way of finding out what people would do without television is to take it away from them. In *The Plug-in Drug*, Marie Winn reports on three experiments in which groups 'went without' TV for periods of up to a month. The following changes took place in these periods:

- More interaction between parents and children.
- A more peaceful atmosphere in the home.
- A greater feeling of closeness in the family.
- More help by children in the household.
- More outdoor play.

Nevertheless, when the experiments ended, *none* of the participants chose to continue without TV. Despite the above findings, it is also true that certain programmes can 'bring the family together' and provide the basis of much conversation. What examples of such programmes can you think of?

Was there life before the box? Or after?

What effects do the media have? — media socialisation

Nearly everybody has an opinion about how the media, particularly television, affect viewers. However, like many matters about which everybody has an opinion, it is not easy to *prove* anything. Experts agree that people are *socialised* by the media, i.e. they *learn* values, attitudes and behaviour through watching, listening or reading. What they disagree about is exactly *how* and *what* people learn. Here is a 'run-through' of some the main theories and issues.

Control theories

Control theories are based on the idea that 'the box in the corner' somehow controls what people think and do. There are two explanations of how control supposedly occurs. These can be called the 'brain-washing' theory and the 'cultural dope' theory.

The 'brain-washing' theory is that the media contain values and ideas (or *ideology*) which make people conform without much questioning about *why* they do so. Thus, Marxists argue that ideas like 'Britain is best' or 'it is natural to admire people who make and spend a lot of money' are mostly just taken for granted by the media. As a result frequent television watchers usually come to take these values for granted too. Similarly, it is sometimes argued that the emphasis on money and glamour in 'teenage' magazines helps to turn teenagers into capitalist consumers (buyers). For instance, *Just Seventeen* is a popular weekly for teenage girls. It contains lots of items like the two following ones:

Apart from being millionaire Hollywood superstars, they're just like you and me, really.

● The most recent Hollywood bash was held for **Bruce Willis** and **Demi Moore**. They were married for the second time at a £450,000 party held at Burbank Studios in L.A. The bride wore white and the minister, **Little Richard**, wore a sexy leather outfit.

The above are just two examples from a double-page spread under the heading 'The Price of Fame'.

CLOTHES COMFORT

Rick Astley, definitely not the Man at C & A

● Traditionally, famous persons have spent astronomical amounts on their clothes Rickolas Astley wears Anthony Price suits at £695 a time or Jean Paul Gaultier offerings which are equally expensive.

● ABC only wear designer clothes £300 Jean Paul Gaultier jackets, £135 Gucci loafers and a pair of trousers for £1,000!

(Source: *Just Seventeen*, 20 January 1988.)

Questions

1 What would you say is the main message of the items?
2 How do the items make their message?
3 Do such items make you want more money and possessions, i.e. do they make you more materialistic?
4 Do you think such items affect young people's values and ideas?
5 Do you think such items to any harm? Why or why not?
6 Why do you think that people might be interested to read things like this?

★★★★★★★★★★★★

★ **The selling of stars: stars as 'commodities'** ★

★ Today, some pop-music studios claim they can turn almost anyone into a 'star'. They have the technology to make a voice 'sound good' and the marketing to present and sell the 'singer' . . . This can be seen as making the 'pop star' into a commodity (saleable thing). ★

★ Hollywood is the most famous example of the star system where 'stars' were virtually owned by a given film company. The companies 'built up' their stars in order to sell pictures. The 'star system' did not occur in the European film industry to the same extent. ★

★★★★★★★★★★★★

Activity (outside class)

Make a list of stars that you see as 'commodities' and another of those you don't. What are the differences?

The 'cultural dope' theory argues that for many people TV is a kind of 'drug'. It keeps them harmlessly and pleasantly occupied and stops them thinking too much about their problems, particularly about how society could be made different and better. Karl Marx put forward the same idea about religion. He said it was 'the opium of the masses'. By this he meant that it blunts people's understanding of the earthly causes of poverty and suffering by promising hope of happiness hereafter in return for conforming in this life. The difference with TV is that the 'happiness' is *now*. But whether people would really try to understand and change society more if television (or religion!) did not exist has not been proved. What do you think?

Media stereotypes

A stereotype is an over-simple view or image of a person or group of people. For instance, the *Sun* tends to present women as 'sex objects'. Often, though not always, members of stereotype groups object to the way in which they are presented. Both Mary Whitehouse, the conservative leader of the National Viewers and Listeners Association, and Women's 'libbers' have objected to the stereotypical presentation of women as degrading and offensive.

Activity (class/outside class)

Read the following extract:

Pick out as many examples of gender stereotyping as you can.

Do you think reading material with a lot of such stereotypes would lead girls to behave stereotypically? Explain your answer.

The question of whether people actually believe media stereotypes is not easy to answer. It is most likely that if a stereotype occurs frequently in the media — such as that of the 'macho male' — it is already common in society as well. In such cases, the media probably only *reinforce* the images that already exist in society. For instance, a comparison of three women's magazines in 1949 and 1974 found an interesting change of emphasis in content which reflects a similar change in society. In 1949, *Woman, Woman's Own* and *Woman's Weekly* had two main themes: first, and most important, love, marriage and 'getting your man'; second, self-improvement and individual achievement. By 1974, the *second* of the two themes was strongest — the 'new' woman had become her *own* person, more 'liberated', and less dependent on 'getting a man' for her identity. This change reflected a change in society in the same direction.

There is some evidence that children can be more easily misled into believing in stereotypes than adults. One study was on the effect of the media on children's attitudes to race. Research showed that white children in areas with few blacks saw race more in terms of *conflict* than did those in areas of high black residency. Hartmann and Husband, the researchers, explained this partly in terms of 'news values', i.e. the preference for presenting the news in terms of 'drama', problems and conflict. In the case of race, such values can lead to a strong media emphasis on events such as 'muggings', 'riots' and 'illegal immigration'. As a result, children whose ideas of blacks came mainly from the media had built up a *negative* stereotype of black people.

Cannibal Island — one of the many examples of racial and sexual stereotyping at Blackpool's 'pleasure beach' (not strictly part of the media but experienced by millions). See how many stereotypes of this kind you can pick out next time you go to the seaside.

Media stereotypes can be unrealistically over- *positive* as well as *negative*. There are now many programmes, especially on American television, which present blacks and women in a very positive way. In fact, blacks are more 'successful' in careers in TV fiction than they are in real life! You might consider and discuss what you think of this trend.

Activity (class/outside class)

If you watch TV 'sitcoms' or 'soap operas', collect examples of *both* gender-role stereotyping (male and female) *and* occasions when stereotypes are reversed.

Discussion point in class: If characters are shown in the 'reverse' situation, e.g. a man running a home, or a woman running a company, but the situation is played for laughs by showing their incompetence at the job, is this overcoming or reinforcing gender stereotypes? Alternatively, carry out this activity in relation to racial stereotyping (though in this case reverse stereotyping is likely to occur less).

Violence and the media

Does watching violence on TV make some people more violent than they would otherwise be? Or, put a different way, does violent TV help to create a violent society?

It would be very useful for society if social science could give clear and definite answers to these important questions. If we knew for certain that violence on TV 'causes' real violence, action could be taken to reduce media violence and so reduce real violence. Unfortunately, the relationship between 'make-believe' TV violence and real violence is not so clear. The two examples of research into media violence show how difficult it can be to prove simple cause (violence on television) and effect (violent behaviour) as far as human beings are concerned.

Experimental studies

An experiment is an organised attempt (e.g. in a laboratory) to measure the effect of something on something else. Thus, there have been a number of experiments in which children have been exposed to a violent stimulus (e.g. a doll being beaten up, a violent film) in order to see what effect this has on them. The group of children who are the subject of the experiment is called the *experimental group*. In order to measure the effect of the experiment on the experimental group, a *control* group is also set up. The control group is as similar as possible to the experimental group *but is not exposed to the experimental stimulus*, i.e. does not see the doll being beaten up. If, following the experiment, the experimental group behaves differently from the control group, the difference is likely to be due to the effect of the experiment. In most cases, groups of children exposed to violent stimuli behave more aggressively *immediately following the experiment* than similar children who have not.

There are two problems with these experiments. First, we do not know whether children subjected to violent stimuli become more aggressive *in the long term*.

Second, the experimental situation is artificial — we cannot be sure that the experimental group would behave in the same way in real life.

How serious do you think these two criticisms are? Do you think they limit the usefulness of the experiment?

Correlation studies

A correlation study is an attempt to show a link between two things (factors), e.g. between watching violence on television and behaving violently. Some correlation studies do seem to show a link between watching violence on TV and behaving violently. However, it is not clear whether more violent people *choose* to watch more violence on television than others, or whether they are *made* more violent by watching more violence. Again, these studies do not allow the definite conclusion that watching violence on TV causes violent behaviour.

Trends in media violence

You may be surprised that since the 1960s the trend in Britain has been steadily towards a reduction of violence on television, measured on the basis of the number of violent acts per hour (Figure 5.5).

Figure 5.5. Violent acts per hour by year of production

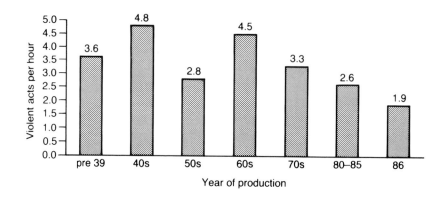

(Source: *Violence, and the Media*, BBC, 1988.)

Questions

1 In which decade did the number of violent acts per hour increase?
2 Can you think of any reason for this?
3 Working in pairs, try to think of at least *two* reasons to explain the trend towards fewer violent acts per hour.

Table 5.2. Programmes containing violence

	Prime time dramatic fiction %	Violent acts per hour
Japan	81	7.0
USA	80	5.5
Netherlands	80	5.8
New Zealand	66	5.7
Australia	66	7.4
W. Germany	Not known	8.6
UK	56	2.5

(Source: *Violence and The Media*, BBC, 1988.)

Questions

1 Which country has the highest number of violent acts per hour in prime-time dramatic fiction?
2 a What is the percentage of prime-time dramatic fiction programmes containing violence and the number of violent acts per hour for the US?
  b Try to work out *one* explanation of why the media in the US appear to be 'more violent' than in the UK.

Activity (class/outside class)

First, as a class, discuss how you would define a 'violent act' on television, if you were going to do research on this topic. The next part of the activity is individual. Next time you watch a film or an episode of a popular thriller series, try to count the number of 'violent acts' that occur. How closely did it match the UK figure in Table 5.2 (or the American figure if it was an American production)? Discuss your findings together as a class.

Advertising

According to the Advertising Standards Authority, an independent body, advertisements should be 'legal, decent, honest and truthful'. These objectives of the British Code of Advertising sound very grand, but they do not prevent advertisers from using sex, money, status, success, humour, or whatever to sell a product. The arguments about television advertising are as fierce as any about the effects of TV on its audience. Here is a summary of some of the main points.

Advertising

For	Against
1 Provides information about products	Uses sex, humour, etc, to persuade people to buy what they might not really want
2 Provides a way for 'brand' names to compete	Many products of the same type are very similar — advertising adds to the consumer's costs
3 Entertains people	Interrupts entertainment (TV programmes), destroys scenery (bill-boards)
4 Provides money which supports the commercial media	Because of their power to withdraw advertising if the media fail to 'deliver' buyers, advertisers have too much control over the commercial media and can lower broadcasting standards.
5 Helps to promote free choice in capitalist society	Can mislead people and make them greedy and materialistic

Whatever *you* think about advertising, there is certain to be more of it in the near future. A fifth TV channel, three new commercial radio channels by the early 1990s and more cable and satellite channels will make sure of that.

Stimulus question

Children 'not misled by TV adverts' study reveals

Children have a great interest in television advertising but their attention is attracted by commercials which are funny, feature animals, or cartoons, regardless of whether the product being advertised is aimed at them or adults, according to a preliminary Advertising Association study.

The study, covering 1000 children, was published yesterday and follows three years of investigation into the effectiveness, and effect, of advertising on children, aged seven to 14. It concentrates mainly on toys and sweets as well as alcoholic drinks and tobacco, goods which are aimed at adults, but whose advertising is increasingly criticised for encouraging children to start bad habits.

The association says that the research provides many reasons for rejecting the hypothesis that advertising to children unfairly manipulates the young, primarily because children often cannot remember brand names, and says that upbringing and parental attitudes are probably more important in areas such as sweet-eating.

The report found that beer and lager advertising, currently under attack, is very popular with children, primarily because of the entertainment value it provides. Where children do drink beer, they frequently do not know a brand, or recall one from the commercials. Trial tasting happens often at a very early age, usually through an introduction by parents or relatives. 'Reference is made to the effect of advertising in only a minority of cases.'

It says that cigarette advertising, banned from television, is virtually never mentioned by children, and there was a low level of recall of brands. Those who recognised all three cigarette advertisements shown to them were not significantly more likely to smoke than the general sample. As with alcohol, early smoking was more often linked to family influences and peer groups.

Children were found to to be widely aware of the names of toys and games being advertised, but often the product being promoted had little appeal to the child, though advertising was used to establish a new fashion or craze. Where children asked for toys in advance, as at Christmas, the reasons were given as: seeing a display in shops (50 per cent), friends and relatives (20 per cent), advertising (16 per cent).

The research found a high level of awareness of sweet advertising, though there was no link between frequent sweet-eating and watching ITV, or a clear link between the choice of sweet and awareness of brand advertising. 'Higher frequency of eating chocolate and sweets is associated with lower social class grading, the money available to the child, lower position in class, slower learning and being an only child.'

By Maggie Brown Media Editor

(Source: Adapted from the *Independent*, 26 February 1988.)

Continued over page . . .

Questions

1 How long did the study described in the above article take? (1 mark)
2 What was the hypothesis which the study found 'many reasons for rejecting'? (1 mark)
3 Give two examples from the study which suggest that advertising does not have a very great effect on children. How convincing do you find each of the examples and the evidence given to support them? (6 marks)

4 The study suggests that a child's social background has more effect than advertising on eating habits and on whether he or she drinks or smokes. Think of *two* examples of how this could occur. Explain your examples. (4 marks)
5 Describe what, in your view, are the main benefits or the main dangers to society of advertising. Discuss the extent to which you consider that *you* are affected by advertising. (8 marks)

Activity

The question of how much the media control the individual and how much the individual uses the media for his or her own purposes has been the main theme of this chapter. This activity is a final look at this problem:
1 List *all* the sources of information and entertainment that can be presented on a TV screen (e.g. video game, central computer bank information).

2 Divide the list into three
a cases in which information/entertainment is mainly user (i.e. the individual) controlled,
b cases in which information/entertainment is mainly supplier (e.g. Rupert Murdoch) controlled,
c cases in which you feel user and producer share control more or less equally.
3 On the basis of the activity so far, write *two* paragraphs on who controls what goes on *your* TV screen.

LIST WHAT CAN BE PUT ON THIS T.V. SCREEN

Structured questions

1 Briefly discuss the advantages to a society of a system of mass communication. (6 marks)
2 Using examples, discuss the possible disadvantages of mass communications in modern Britain. (6 marks)
3 Discuss *two* examples of a 'media stereotype', saying in each case what the stereotype is, and what the possible consequences of its use are. (8 marks)

Project and assignment suggestions

1 *Working in the media* — This may appeal particularly to those of you who hope to find employment in the media industry. Try to find a local person working for your nearest TV, radio station or local newspaper who will agree to answer your questions and allow you to spend a day (or possibly more, if you are lucky) 'shadowing' him or her in their daily job. Once you have found such a person, make sure you leave enough time before the interview and 'shadowing' to prepare your questions and do preliminary research into the particular medium — press, TV or local radio. Your project should not be simply descriptive, but should involve some analysis — what kinds of considerations appeared to affect whether an item was considered as 'news', or what made some 'news' more important than others. What kinds of pressures (e.g. the laws of libel, protecting the innocent) did the people working there appear to be operating under? Such things could also form part of your interview schedule.

2 *Ownership, control and freedom in the British media* — How free are the British media? There is plenty of material on this topic in this chapter, but try to use a couple of examples which have occurred more recently. Alternatively, you could do a detailed case study of an important dispute of the recent past such as the *Spycatcher* affair (ask your teacher about this case). What are the main issues of confidentiality (secrecy) and freedom which your case study raises?

   You could approach the same topic using quite different methods. For instance, if you wanted to find out whether people *think* we have free media, you could use questionnaires or interviews.

3 *'Images'/stereotypes in the media* — If you do a project on this topic, it is best to keep it within practical limits. For instance, you could study the way women, blacks, homosexuals, criminals or the unemployed are presented on, say, 'EastEnders' in a sample of six consecutive episodes. Don't just fill your project with opinion and criticism. Make sure you carefully *describe* and/or *present* (in the case of newspaper clippings) the images *before* analysing what they mean.

4 *Television viewing habits* — This topic is an obvious invitation to do a questionnaire and/or interviews. If you do interviews, you will need to describe whether they will be informal or formal. You might decide to concentrate on a particular age group, such as 'the elderly' or 'teenagers'. If you choose the latter, and an informal interview in, say, a coffee bar, you might get some relaxed and revealing answers. Or you may want to compare the viewing habits of two different age groups.

5 *Media effects* — Given that many professional studies of the effects of the media have run into great methodological difficulty and often produced very limited findings, you probably ought to avoid trying to find out the effects on behaviour of, say, violence or sex on TV, or of advertising. However, there is one *experiment* you might try, either on yourself and/or friends or family, *if* they will act as guinea pigs. Compare two weeks in the life of the participants in the experiment: one in which they watch their usual quota of TV and one in which they watch none at all. Participants must keep a record of what they do with the 'extra' time in the second week, and you may decide to set them a brief questionnaire on the effects of *not* watching TV!

   If your subjects won't deprive themselves of TV for a week, try two days!

Key words

Censorship	Experimental group
Conglomerate	(*see* control group)
Control group	Media
Correlational studies	Stereotype

CHAPTER 6 Religion, Beliefs and Values

Definition of terms

A belief is an acceptance of something as true, with or without proof. You may believe in miracles, but not be able to prove that they happen; on the other hand, you may believe that you had an egg for breakfast and be able to prove it to most people's satisfaction. Both are beliefs. A value is a principle or standard, such as honesty, self-interest, or caring for others. Values and beliefs are closely linked together, and people's strongest beliefs and values usually have a big effect on their actions. We can divide beliefs into religious and non-religious, or simply 'other'. The basis of religion is a belief in a god or gods, or some form of superior spiritual being, and usually a belief in life after death. Other beliefs can be about anything. People have beliefs about politics, about their country and nation, about violence and non-violence, about what are 'good' and 'bad' manners, and about how they and others should go about their work and, for that matter, their leisure. In fact, beliefs and values colour probably every area of life.

Religion seeks to give meaning to life and death.

Religion and society

Activity (outside class)

List, as briefly and clearly as possible, five of your most important beliefs/values.

Write a paragraph on how *one* of your beliefs has affected your life (or how it might affect your life in the future). Then write a paragraph about how one of your beliefs affects (or could affect) the life of others — how you act towards them, and how they respond. You might have religious beliefs, but equally you might believe in family loyalty, 'love', the importance of 'team spirit', or animal rights. The point of the exercise is to work out the effect of some of these beliefs.

Purpose and meaning in life

For many religious believers, their faith is most important and gives meaning to their lives. Such people sometimes say things like: 'Without my religion, I couldn't see the point of life.'

In traditional, non-industrial societies, religion plays a part in, and gives meaning to, all or nearly all aspects of life. The day, the year, the life cycle itself, all move to the rhythm of religious rituals (ceremonies) and festivals Usually, believers pray at important times of the day — such as before meals, or before going to bed. Wherever they are, strict Muslims pray daily facing Mecca, their holy city. Some Roman Catholics pray at odd moments during the day using rosary beads, and some Hindus use prayer wheels. Quakers take a few quiet moments to reflect and pray. All traditional religions mark birth, the coming of adulthood, marriage and death with religious rituals. For example, Jews recognise the coming to adulthood with the ritual of Bar Mitzvah, and Christians do so with the ritual of confirmation. Perhaps there are people in your class who can describe one or other of these ceremonies, or a different one from another religion and culture.

Religion and community

The French sociologist Emile Durkheim argued that the most important social function (purpose) of religion is that it helps to keep people together. In other words, it strengthens 'community'. In the days when everybody in a society believed in one religion, it helped to bind members of a society into one community.

Religion can help to create or destroy a community. i) A group of young Muslims reading a religious text.
ii) Anti-papist graffiti in Belfast — a city torn by religions strife.

Looking at present-day Britain, it is possible to agree with Durkheim that those who share a strong belief in one particular religion are more likely to form close-knit communities. Part of the strength of the mainly Hindu Indian communities and the mainly Muslim Pakistani communities lies in their religious beliefs and practices. Of course, when a member of a strong religious community tries to break from its practices, conflict can be very bitter — as some young Asians have found when they get very involved in a 'Western' life-style.

While a shared religion can strengthen a community, religious divisions can destroy the wider community. Religious disagreements play a large part in the conflicts in Northern Ireland and the Lebanon.

Activity (outside class)

Find out:
1   Who are the religious groups involved in the conflict in the Lebanon.
2   What causes, other than religion, there are for the disputes in Northern Ireland. Do you think that religion is the most important reason for the dispute? Why or why not?

Religion and conformity

In the past and in most present-day traditional societies, to conform to (obey) the rules of religion was also to conform to the main rules of society. The rules of religion *were* the rules of society, and in some cases today, still are. For example, under President Zia, Pakistan was run mainly according to the rules and punishments of the Koran, the 'holy book' of the Muslims. Among the rules are the total avoidance of alcohol and strict rules about how women should be dressed. Breaking the rules can result in punishment by public flogging, or even the cutting off of a limb.

In some Muslim countries today, such as Iran, there is a widespread belief that the decline of religion in the West has led to an increase in disorder, selfishness and corruption. This gives their leaders another reason for keeping the society running according to their strict Muslim principles.

Religion and oppression

Karl Marx wrote that: 'Religion is the sigh of the oppressed creature, the heart of the heartless world... It is the opium of the people.' By this, he meant that the majority of people are misled into accepting their 'oppression' by the promise of better things hereafter. Marx's view was that they should seek better things in this world, or, in his words, 'shake off the chain and cull the living flower'.

Religion and change

Religious beliefs can act as a force for change. This happens especially when members of one religion try to convert others — to persuade them to change their religious beliefs. For example, Christianity has affected most societies because, since the time of Christ, missionaries have 'spread the gospel' throughout the world.

Recently, the religions of the East — Buddhism, Hinduism and Islam (the Muslim religion) have probably had more influence in the West than Christianity has had in the East. Perhaps this is not surprising, as organised Christianity appears to have been declining in the West itself. The next section deals with this decline.

Science, secularisation and the decline of organised religion

Secularisation

Secularisation is a term which describes the decline in the power and influence of the church and of organised religion, together with a decline in religious belief and observance.

Activity (class)

Suppose that you had been asked to try to find out the extent to which secularisation was taking place in modern Britain. Working in small groups, make a list of all the things which you think would need to be considered to come to a conclusion about secularisation. When you have done that, write down against each item on your list, how you think you would go about finding the information, and how you would try to measure how much (or how little) secularisation was taking place.

Sociologists have looked at different things to show the extent of secularisation in Britain. Here are four of them:

1 The decline in church membership and religious practice.
2 The rise of non-religious ideas and ways of thinking, including science.
3 The decline in the influence of the church on the rest of society.
4 The extent to which people do non-religious things in their leisure time, including Sundays.

The decline in church membership and religious practice

Nearly all the statistics relating to formal (organised) religion show a steady decline. Between 1975–90, there was a reduction in the number of church members, ministers and buildings for all of the main religions practised in Britain. Formal religious observance ('going to church') also declined. Although there were some signs of a religious revival in the 1980s, it is not yet possible to say whether this trend will continue.

The rise of non-religious ideas and ways of thinking, including science

Science differs from religion in that it attempts to explain the world by reason and proof, rather than accepting things as 'God's will'. However, science and religion do not necessarily contradict each other. Sir Isaac Newton himself, one of the founders of modern science, believed in God, and many practising scientists today no doubt regularly practise a religion. However, in recent years there has often been a certain 'tension' between science and religion. Perhaps this is because science and religion are different ways of relating to the world: science is based mainly on reason, logic and proof, while religion is based mainly on faith and feeling. The conflict between science and religion was brought into the open by the work of the nineteenth-century biologist, Charles Darwin. In his book *The Origin of Species*, Darwin argued that human beings had developed ('evolved') through a process of natural selection, in which 'the fittest' survived and passed on to the next generation those characteristics which made them fitter than the rest. To many religious people, this theory of natural evolution (as opposed to the Biblical story of the creation) left God out of the picture, and also seemed to do away with the idea of a 'soul'. Darwin's ideas started a debate which still goes on to this day.

The decline in the influence of the church on the rest of society

One of the clearest signs of the decline in the importance of religion in many people's lives is perhaps the number of churches which are now used for non-religious purposes — flats, libraries, restaurants and shops.

'Churches' sometimes survive — for purposes other than religion: a church converted into flats.

Compared with earlier periods in British history, church leaders now have far less influence on political leaders and decisions. Monarchs used to have to be very careful about the possibility of losing the support of the clergy, and many bishops and archbishops had an influence on political decisions which would seem very surprising to us today.

The extent to which people do non-religious things in their leisure time

As church attendance has declined, so leisure activities, both inside and outside the home, have increased. People seem to have found other things to do rather than go to church, and for many people, Sundays in particular are days for relaxing, playing or watching sports, visiting friends, family outings, gardening or even washing the car!

However, what you have just read is only part of the picture. Even if there has been a decline in formal, organised religion, does this necessarily mean that Britain is now a secular, non-religious society?

The continued importance of religion

The continued importance of religion in Britain

Despite the fall in religious practice mentioned earlier, there is evidence that religion may be making a partial revival (see Figure 6.1).

Figure 6.1. Regional guide to religious revival (England and Wales)

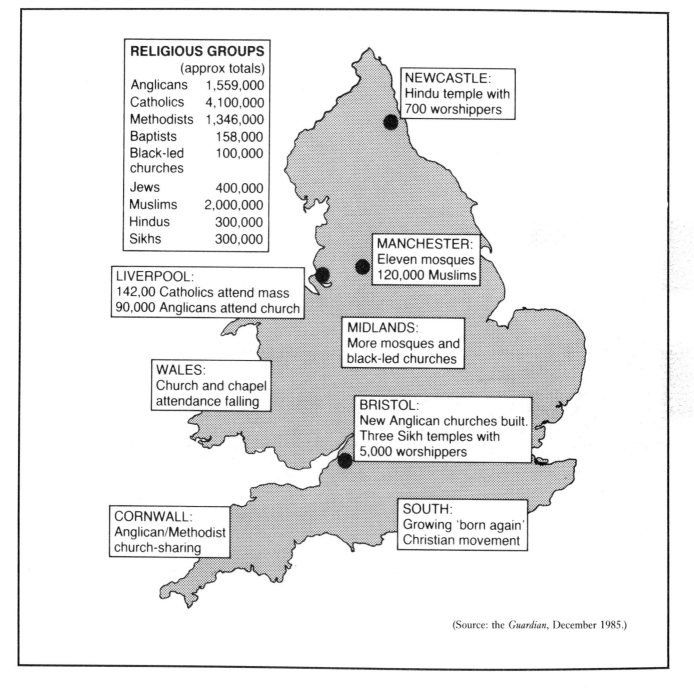

RELIGIOUS GROUPS
(approx totals)
Anglicans 1,559,000
Catholics 4,100,000
Methodists 1,346,000
Baptists 158,000
Black-led 100,000
churches
Jews 400,000
Muslims 2,000,000
Hindus 300,000
Sikhs 300,000

NEWCASTLE:
Hindu temple with 700 worshippers

MANCHESTER:
Eleven mosques 120,000 Muslims

LIVERPOOL:
142,00 Catholics attend mass
90,000 Anglicans attend church

MIDLANDS:
More mosques and black-led churches

WALES:
Church and chapel attendance falling

BRISTOL:
New Anglican churches built.
Three Sikh temples with 5,000 worshippers

CORNWALL:
Anglican/Methodist church-sharing

SOUTH:
Growing 'born again' Christian movement

(Source: the *Guardian*, December 1985.)

Questions

List four religions described in Figure 6.1 as part of a religious revival in Britain.

Many people are 'religious' in their own way, even if they do not regularly attend church. Many surveys have shown that far more people believe in God, or in some kind of spiritual force or being, than go to church. Some groups of people, rather than go to 'official' church buildings, hold religious services in people's homes — these are known as 'house churches'. Similarly, religious television programmes such as 'Songs of Praise' regularly attract large audiences. Such people would not, of course, appear in statistics on church attendance. Religious sects are groups which grow up outside the established churches. Sects often form religious communities, and many sects (such as the 'Moonies') have a particular appeal to the young. Many sects which have appeared in Britain have come from the United States, e.g. the Scientologists.

Religious enthusiasm continues in different ways — a Hare Krishna worshipper.

The Church of England also became more openly involved in social and political matters in the late 1980s. 'Faith in the City', a report calling for more government help to solve problems in the inner cities, was published by a commission set up by the Archbishop of Canterbury. In 1988, the Bishop of Durham said that it was 'wicked' that some poor people would become poorer as a result of the social security changes of that year. This led one Conservative MP to refer to the Bishop as 'anti-Christ'.

The Church of England and the politics of the inner city

'I'm not a very political animal — in fact, I find a great deal of politics extremely boring... So it is somewhat dutifully that I have entered into this question, the problems of the inner city.'

(Archbishop of Canterbury, quoted in the *Guardian*, 3 December 1985.)

'But if the policies of any government can be shown to be making the plight of some classes of citizens actually worse...it is the clear duty for the church to sound a warning that our society may be losing the 'compassionate' character which is still desired by the majority of its members.'

(From 'Faith in the City', quoted in the *Guardian*, 6 December 1985.)

(Source: the *Guardian*, December 1985.)

What responsibility does religion have for community — or lack of community?

Activity (class)

Discuss the second of these two statements as a class, making sure that you fully understand what is being said. Then write a few paragraphs saying whether or not you agree that it is 'the clear duty of the church to sound a warning' in such cases, giving reasons for your answer.

The continued importance of religion worldwide

Although the trend to secularisation, and particularly the decline in organised religion, is widespread, on a global scale the importance of religion and religious belief is apparent. The Muslim revival in Iran and Pakistan has already been mentioned, but even in Britain there is a Muslim community of approximately two million people. In the United States, the decline in religion has never been as apparent as in Britain, and the bible-based Christianity of the southern states has a powerful appeal to millions of Americans.

Figure 6.2. Membership changes in world religions and non-religions

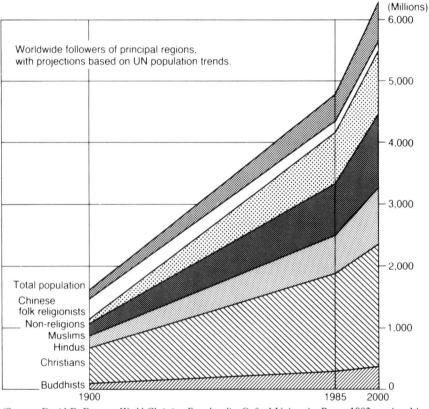

(Source: David B. Barrett, *World Christian Encyclopedia*, Oxford University Press, 1982 reprinted in *New Society*, 18 December 1987)

Activity (class)

In not more than two sentences, summarise the changes illustrated in Figure 6.2.

Latin America is another area where religion remains important. The experiences of Catholic priests in the poorer countries of Latin America helped to produce a new type of belief called 'liberation theology'. The message of 'liberation theology' is that the poor should not be content with their position on earth because their rewards will be in heaven, but rather that the worldly needs of the poor should be taken care of here and now. If doing this means that the power and wealth of governments, bureaucrats, landlords and businessmen should be challenged, then that is what must be done.

Stimulus questions

Read the following extracts and answer the questions.

ITEM A

Religion: 1950–1975

The statistics show that since 1952, secularisation continued and the story of religion was one of decline. In 1950, 67 per cent of children were baptised in the Church of England; in 1973, this was the case for only 47 per cent. In 1952, about 28 per cent of those aged 15 years in England were confirmed in the Anglican church: the proportion was below 20 per cent by the mid-1970s. Some 6.5 per cent of the population took Easter communion in the Church of England in 1953 — but 20 years later, fewer than four per cent did so.

(Source: adapted from Bryon Wilson, 'How Religious Are We?', *New Society*, 27 October 1977, reprinted in *M. O'Donnell, New Introductory Reader in Sociology*, Nelson, 1988.)

ITEM B

Evangelists lead revival of Britain

The decline of religion in Britain has been halted, with a strong revival emerging among evangelicals, house-church groups and ethnic groups according to a new survey.

The report by the Press Association, published as nearly 500 bishops of the worldwide Anglican Community assemble for next week's Lambeth Conference, shows that mainstream churches have largely stemmed losses suffered in the last 15 years and made modest advances in many places.

Outside the Anglican, Roman Catholic and non-conformist churches there is a thriving Christian movement, with black-led churches and house churches attracting many who seek a welcome and freedom of worship not always evident in established faiths.

Islam is also growing rapidly in Britain, with an estimated congregation of nearly two million. Hindu temples — one in a converted nightclub — and Sikh gudwaras attract large numbers from ethnic communities anxious to maintain their cultural and religious roots. Hindus and Sikhs each have an estimated 300,000 followers while Jews number 400,000.

(Source: the *Guardian*, 14 July 1988.)

ITEM C

In 1978, the EC set up a group to explore a wide range of values and beliefs, including religious beliefs. This European survey involved 12,500 people in over twenty countries. The following figures represent the reply of the British sample to the following question: 'Which, if any, of the following do you believe in?'

	%
God	76
Life after death	45
A soul	59
The devil	30
Sin	69
Hell	27
Heaven	57
Reincarnation	27

(Source: adapted from Ian Thompson, *Religion*, Longman, 1986, pp. 71–2.)

Questions

1 Give two pieces of statistical information from Item A which might be used to demonstrate the decline of religion. (2 marks)
2 Name two non-Christian religions mentioned in Item B. (2 marks)
3 How many people took part in the European survey described in Item C? (1 mark)
4 According to Item C, what percentage of British respondents expressed a belief in sin? (1 mark)
5 Define the term 'secularisation'. (2 marks)
6 Do you think that statistical evidence such as that given in Item A is sufficient on its own to show a decline in the importance of religion? Explain your answer. (5 marks)
7 Using material from Items A, B and C and elsewhere, discuss the suggestion that Britain has become a secular society. (7 marks)

Activity (class)

1 Working in small groups, take a map of your nearest town (or part of town, if you live in a large conurbation), and mark on it all the churches and chapels. Show how many of these buildings are still actually used for religious services. Now mark any other religious buildings, such as synagogues, mosques or temples.
2 Using a different method of marking (perhaps a different colour), show all the places of entertainment — cinemas and theatres, sports grounds, swimming pools, bingo halls, youth clubs, amusement arcades, etc.
3 Now outline the main shopping and business areas.
4 If you were an alien sent to study the people of your town, and you thought you would get an idea of their main activities by studying the different buildings and areas and their uses, what conclusions do you think that you would come to?

Non-religious beliefs and ideologies

Ideology is a term used to describe related ideas and beliefs about life or some aspect of life. Various religious ideologies were referred to in the previous section. Politics is another area in which there are many ideologies, for example, socialism, fascism and liberalism. Particularly since the nineteenth century, there have been many secular (non-religious) ideologies which, for some people, have replaced religious ideologies. Some of the most important of these secular ideologies are briefly described below.

Humanism

Humanism is the belief that the most important thing in life is the welfare and development of human beings. Such a belief is so broad that it can and does form part of many other ideologies. For example, many socialists would claim to be humanists.

It is not easy or practical to trace the influence on British life of so broad a movement as humanism. One example could be claimed to be the gradual move to more humane methods of treating criminals. Hanging, the stocks, birching, branding and amputation are now usually considered too inhumane.

Since the nineteenth century, humanism has influenced how the poor are treated, how the mentally-ill are treated, and how children are brought up and educated. Do you think that it would be possible to 'undo' the changes in these areas, and to go back to the previous way of doing things?

Nationalism and internationalism

Nationalism is a passionate loyalty to one's own nation or country, and a commitment to its independence. It has been a powerful and growing force during the nineteenth and twentieth centuries. In the twentieth century, the desire for nationhood arose in many areas of the world, including most of those which had been conquered by European powers. Dozens of nations have been formed following the break-up of the French, British, Belgian, Dutch and Portuguese empires. Nationalism can be constructive or destructive. National independence and pride in national history and culture are widely admired. For instance, the history and cultural variety of Britain has made it one of the leading tourist areas of the world — despite the weather!

However, there is often a less attractive side to nationalism. Firstly, in powerful nations, nationalism can grow into imperialism — which involves the control of other, less powerful, societies. Secondly, national rivalries between powerful nations can lead to conflict and war — such as those between Germany and other countries earlier this century. Thirdly, on a smaller scale, individuals and groups sometimes make national rivalry an excuse for aggressive and offensive behaviour to people from other countries. As a result of this kind of behaviour of so-called 'football fans' in 1985 English club teams were banned from European football club competitions.

Perhaps to try to overcome the problems of 'nationalism', there has been a strong movement in the twentieth century towards 'internationalism'. This can be defined as a belief that nations should solve problems co-operatively, rather than through conflict. The League of Nations, formed after the First World War, and the United Nations, formed after the Second World War, are both important attempts to achieve international co-operation. The European Common Market (EEC) is an attempt to remove trading barriers between member nations. From 1992, other barriers between EEC countries will be removed, making travelling, working and studying in other member-nations much easier. The tunnel under the Channel may also lead to Britain becoming more 'European'.

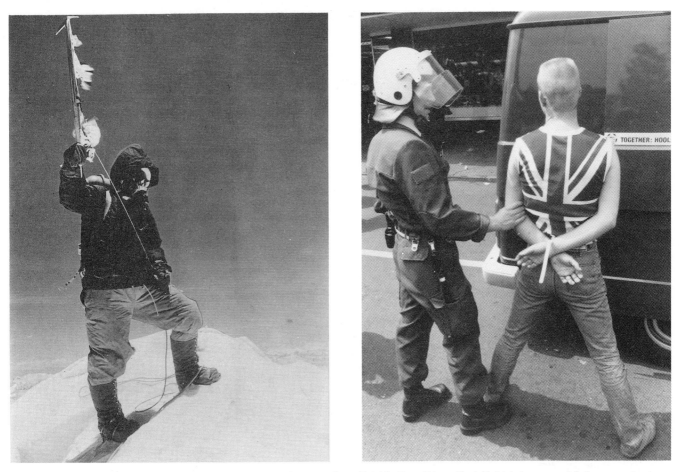

National pride and national disgrace. i) The conquest of Everest by a British Expedition. ii) A British 'supporter' being restrained at the 1988 European Football Championships in Germany.

Activity (class)

Discuss the advantages and disadvantages of Britain becoming more 'European'.

Political beliefs (intolerance and tolerance)

As there are many different religious beliefs, so there are many different political ones. Political beliefs are dealt with mainly in Chapter Fifteen, but it is relevant to make some points here.

Sometimes, political beliefs are held with as much strength of feeling and passion as religious beliefs. In the case of Communism, this can be partly explained by the fact that many early Communists believed that in Communism they had found a replacement for religion. They believed that Communism would provide the 'ideal' society here on earth. In their attempts to build such a society, some Communists have imprisoned, tortured and even killed those who did not, or would not, fit into this scheme, just as members of various religious groups have done throughout history.

The word to describe the attitude of not being prepared to accept people with different ideas and beliefs from your own is 'intolerance', and sometimes, people with strongly held religious or political beliefs are very intolerant.

Fascism is perhaps the least tolerant of all political 'creeds' or beliefs. Whatever the reality sometimes is, Communism at least preaches equality and 'togetherness' between people, whereas Fascism preaches the superiority of some races and people, and the inferiority of others. Racism is at the heart of Fascism, as in the attempt to kill off the Jews in the 1940s, surely one of the most inhuman crimes of modern history.

Not surprisingly, after the Second World War, many people decided that tolerance was one of the most important virtues. Tolerance is the opposite of intolerance — a willingness to 'live and let live', to co-exist with people and nations who hold different beliefs and practise different ways of life from your own.

Tolerance is a central principle of Western liberal political belief. In this sense, all of the major British political parties are 'liberal'. Given the increasing number of nations which possess nuclear weapons, tolerance may be an essential part of the survival of the human race.

There are many non-religions movements in present-day Britain. i) A Campaign for Nuclear Disarmament (CND) rally. ii) Greenpeace action against the dumping of waste off the North East coast of Britain.

Activity (class)

Here is a list of six non-religious movements found in present-day Britain. (You may choose different ones of your own if you wish.) Try to define the basic beliefs and aims of each movement in a sentence or two. Discuss one movement from your list with the rest of the class. How important is the movement? In your view, is it a good thing, crackpot, unnecessary, or what? Should it be banned? If so, why?

- Campaign for Nuclear Disarmament (CND)
- Friends of the Earth
- Animal Rights Movement
- Anti-Apartheid Movement
- Amnesty International
- Greenpeace

Do you think that a 'tolerant' society should accept any or all movements? What about Fascist movements within tolerant societies? Discuss.

Belief, socialisation and culture: conclusion

Where do our beliefs come from? We learn our first beliefs and values from those who bring us up — usually our parents. Children accept beliefs because they are told to, or because they seem 'normal', rather than because they fully understand them. People often remain very emotionally attached to the beliefs and values of their childhood. As people get older, other experiences and influences affect them, perhaps those gained through school, friends, work or the mass media. Sometimes, earlier beliefs are reconsidered in the light of new experience, though breaking away from them can cause feelings of guilt, such as those sometimes reported by 'lapsed' Catholics.

If children get their first beliefs and values from their parents, where do parents get theirs from? In general, family and parental beliefs reflect the culture or cultures around them. Britain is now very much a multicultural society, so Britain's children are brought up in various religious and cultural traditions, from almost all corners of the world. Sometimes, these newer traditions flow into the 'mainstream' culture and influence or change it. Yet we can talk of a 'mainstream' culture in Britain. The best aspects of this include a respect for individuality, a determination to survive, and tolerance — qualities likely to be tested in the future, as they have been in the past.

Stimulus question

Read the following extract and answer the questions.

J'Accuse

The murder of six million Jews by Nazi Germany was the greatest act of evil in the history of mankind.

It was nothing less than a deliberate, systematic campaign to remove a whole people from the face of the earth.

The victorious nations swore, when the last war ended, that it must never happen again.

But saying so is not enough.

How was it that a civilised, cultured nation could be turned by one madman into the nation of Auschwitz, Dachau and Belsen?

Unless we know, there will always be a danger that it could happen again. If not to the Jews, to another people. If not in Europe, in Asia or Africa. Pol Pot and Idi Amin were as wicked as Hitler, but not as powerful.

The Holocaust was not something horrible which happened to other people. Had Britain fallen to the Nazi armies in 1940, it would have happened here.

- It was in order to prevent it ever happening again that a unique conference took place last week in Oxford and in London.
- Several hundred scholars from 24 countries who have devoted the past 40 years to researching the State murder of the Jews and others presented the fruits of their work.
- Their purpose was not to dwell on the past. It was to prevent history repeating itself. That's why the conference was called, 'Remembering For The Future, The Impact of the Holocaust and Genocide on Jews and Christians'.

Let me declare my interest. My mother and father, my grandfather, three sisters and my brother were killed in the camps. My wife, Elisabeth, a French Protestant, organised the conference. We would both devote every hour we have left, every penny we possess, to prevent another Holocaust.

Yet how was this great conference, which culminated in a meeting at Central Hall, Westminster, London, on Friday, treated by the British Press?

With a few honourable exceptions, they ignored it.

Messages of support, moving and sincere, were sent to the conference by President Reagan, President Mitterrand, Mrs. Thatcher, Chancellor Kohl, President Herzog and M. Delors, President of the European Commission.

Yet the monopoly news agency in Britain, the Press Association, decided not to report it.

The *Star*, The *Daily Express*, The *Sun*, *Today* and *Glasgow Herald* wrote not a single word about the week-long conference. The *Daily Mail*, to its credit, gave a full page to the story of Elie Wiesel, a survivor of the camps and Nobel Prizewinner, who spoke on the last day.

Yesterday, only the *Financial Times*, *Daily Telegraph*, *Daily Mirror* and the *Independent* mentioned the conference at all.

As a publisher, as a journalist, but, above all, as a British citizen who lived through, and escaped from, the Nazi tyranny I am outraged at this indifference.

If evil comes when good men do nothing, then this silence contains the seeds of evil. When Hitler embarked upon his murderous course, the world's Press — again, with a few honourable exceptions — said nothing.

The British Press was guilty then. It is still guilty today.

Robert Maxwell
Publisher, Mirror Group Newspapers

(Source: Adapted from *Sunday Mirror*, 17 July 1988.)

Continued over page . . .

Note: 'The Holocaust' was Hitler's attempt to murder all the Jews.

Questions

1 What does Robert Maxwell believe was 'the greatest act of evil in the history of mankind'? (1 mark)
2 What was the purpose of the conference referred to in the extract? (1 mark)
3 What does Robert Maxwell mean when he says 'Let me declare my interest'? (2 marks)
4 In your own words, explain the phrase 'silence contains the seeds of evil'. Why is Robert Maxwell 'outraged' at most of the British Press? (4 marks)
5 Define ideology. What was Hitler's ideology? Why is it considered to be a particularly evil ideology? (7 marks)

Structured questions

1 What is meant by the following terms:
   a) humanism, b) ideology? (4 marks)
2 Outline and discuss *two* problems involved in the measurement of 'secularisation' in modern Britain. (8 marks)
3 Using examples, discuss how religious beliefs can a) strengthen 'community', and b) create conflict in a society. (8 marks)

Project and assignment suggestions

1 *Secularisation* — To what extent is your area 'secular'? You could approach this as a social survey — asking your sample questions about church attendance, belief in God, etc. Alternatively, or as well, you could interview several local people (including, perhaps, a local minister) who have been in a position to observe changes in religious practice over the years. However, make sure that you start off with a working definition of 'secularisation', in order to analyse your results.

2 *Religion and cultural variety* — You may want to examine one or two different religions in depth, and the way of life they wish their members to observe. If you are a member of religious family/community, you could make what is known as an ethnographic study — a carefully observed and recorded account of part of a way of life. However, you must ask sociological questions, such as whether the religion described is understood, or tolerated, by the rest of society, and what other functions, besides religious, it provides for its members and/or the wider community.

3 *A social history of a religion* — This would be a wider, more historical survey of the development and impact of a particular religion. You would need not just to describe the religion and its beliefs, but also how it has established itself in a particular society, what problems it faced and how it overcome them. You will need to use a lot of secondary sources, and it is particularly important that you seek the help of your teacher before you start on this one, to ensure a sociological dimension.

4 *Non-religious beliefs* — An examination of a particular group or movement, looking at its influence on public opinion and politicians.

5 *Religion and conformity* — There is not much recent sociological work on this topic, but you could do something quite simple. For example, you could do a small survey of five people who regularly practise a religion, and five who do not (the control group). You would need to ask questions to try to find out whether there are any differences in the degree of 'conformity' — which group conforms the most in such things as obeying parents, obeying school rules, obeying the law, etc.

Key words

Belief	Secularisation
Ethnic	Social control
Humanism	Value
Ideology	

CHAPTER 7 *The Economy and Work*

The economy and work

The economy

The economy is concerned with the production of goods (cars, washing machines, etc) and services (entertainment, education, etc). Work is economic activity — it is what people do in order to make a living.

There are three types of economies:

1 capitalist
2 socialist
3 mixed

Britain was the first capitalist economy but is now mixed. Capitalism is a system in which people produce goods and services for profit, in competition with others. These people are called producers. People who buy what is produced are called consumers. Buying and selling is referred to as 'market activity'. In order to function properly, capitalism requires a banking system which will lend money (also for profit) to capitalists who may then invest in business.

A socialist economy is one which is publicly owned — in practice this has meant that the state (government) plans and organises the production and distribution (who receives what) of goods and services. However, the original ideal of socialism was for the people to own the economy and to become increasingly involved in economic decision making. In reality the extent to which ordinary people are involved in economic decision making is limited but varies between socialist societies. For instance, there is more involvement in Yugoslavia than Russia. Many socialists argue that socialism does not exist unless there is meaningful democratic power and control over the economy.

A mixed economy is one which is *partly* (usually *mainly*) capitalist, and partly socialist. The two sectors of a mixed economy are referred to as the *private* (capitalist) and *public* (socialist).

Britain became a highly mixed economy after the Second World War, when several major industries, including steel, gas and electricity, were nationalised. Under the Thatcher Governments, these and other nationalised industries became part of a policy of privatisation (a policy of returning them to private enterprise).

Activity (class/outside class)

You cannot understand much about life in a society unless you understand the basis of its economic system — how its wealth is created and shared, and the variety of work people do. A starting point is knowing the difference between the main types of economies.

Carefully define *in your own words*:

1 a capitalist economy,
2 a socialist economy, and
3 a mixed economy.

Try to find examples of each, other than those given in the text.

Work

Work is economic activity — what people do to make a living. There are two main types of work in modern societies:

1 work for pay or profit, and
2 domestic work (housework).

Before the Industrial Revolution, more people were self-sufficient and far fewer worked for wages. People made a living mainly by farming or hunting — as they still do in many parts of the world.

The division of labour: who does what

The division of labour refers to how work is divided up — who does what. There are two main features of it:

- the *occupational division* of labour, and
- the *sexual division* of labour.

The occupational division of labour refers to the different jobs people have. There are tens of thousands of different jobs which are classified into certain main occupational groups (or classes), such as professional, skilled non-manual, and unskilled.

Table 7.1. Domestic division of labour.

	% Married adults		
	Mainly man	Mainly woman	Shared equally
Household shopping	6	54	39
Preparation of evening meal	5	77	16
Evening dishes	18	37	41
Main cleaning	3	72	23
Washing and ironing	1	88	9
Repair of household equipment	83	6	6

(Source: British Social Attitudes Survey.)

The sexual division of labour refers to how work is divided between women and men in a particular society. In Britain, women still tend to do most of the housework, though certain repair and maintenance tasks are usually done by men (see Table 7.1).

Most work for pay and profit is done by men, although matters are changing quickly in this area. This is shown in Table 7.2.

Table 7.2. Civilian labour force (paid, over 16)

	Percentage of males in work	Percentage of females in work
1971	80.5	43.9
1976	78.9	46.8
1981	76.5	47.6
1984	74.3	48.4
1987	73.7	50.0
Projection		
1995	73.3	53.0

(Source: *Social Trends*, 1989.)

According to the projection for 1995, the male paid labour force will outnumber the female by only 3:2 whereas only 24 years previously, in 1971, it had been almost 2:1. However, the increase in female employment has been mainly in part-time, low-paid employment. About a half of married female employees and about a quarter of unmarried ones are part-timers. Only a tiny percentage of male employees work part-time.

The changing economy: a service economy

During the past 200 years, the pattern of work in Britain has been through two great changes. First, there was the change brought about by the Industrial Revolution which eventually resulted in most people in Britain being employed in *manfacturing* rather than agriculture. This was the 'age of the machine' or *mechanised* production.

Second is the change from manufacturing to *service work* that has steadily taken place since the 1950s. Whereas manufacturing is concerned with the production of goods, service work meets people's non-material needs, such as education, leisure, health and welfare. About two thirds of the population now work in the service sector.

A service economy

Some examples of service work would be:

Occupation	Example
Higher-level salaried professional	Barrister
Managers	Marketing manager in ICI
Lower grade salaried professional	Teacher
Inspectors, supervisors	Bus inspector
Clerical workers	Invoice clerk

The figures in Table 7.3 show how rapid the change from a manufacturing to a service economy has been — measured by the number of employees in each sector. The figures also show the continued decline in agricultural employment:

Table 7.3

Sector	Employees, 1971	Employees, 1990
Agriculture, forestry, fishing	450,000	298,000
Manufacturing, mining	8,067,000	5,151,000
Services	11,627,000	15,368,000

(Figures based on data in *Social Trends*, 1990.)

The rise in self-employment has increased the trend to service work. The self-employed increased from 7.4 per cent of the labour force in 1979 to 12 per cent in 1988. Many of the self-employed work in distribution, catering, hotels, repairs and construction.

Summary of the change from a manufacturing to a service economy

1 From agricultural to industrial (nineteenth century).
2 From industrial to service (1950s onwards).

The continuing importance of manufacturing

Despite the huge drop in the number of people employed in the manufacturing sector, more manufactured goods are consumed (bought and used) in Britain than ever. This is made possible by:

1 the increase in automated production, and
2 the increase in imported manufactured goods.

Automated production is when computers rather than people operate machines. Microelectronics are used in over half of all production processes in Britain. The number of robots used in British industry doubled between 1984 and 1986. Eventually, automated production is likely to overtake mechanised production.

Britain — once known as 'the workshop of the world' — now imports more manufactured goods than it exports. The gap is partly made up by exporting services (including high-level services, such as insurance and financial services), tourism and oil (though oil exports are now in decline).

Where's it made?

Activity (class)

In small groups, look at the various items you have with you — bags, pencil cases, watches, calculators, pens, perhaps a personal stereo — and note, if you can, where each was made. Now do the same with your outer garments — sweaters, sweatshirts, shirts or blouses, skirts, jeans or trousers, shoes. You may need to peer at each others' labels! For each group, note the number of articles looked at, and work out (roughly) the proportion 'made in Britain' and the proportion imported. Discuss this in class.

The changing labour force and employers

The move from a manufacturing to a service economy has resulted in great changes in the labour force. In this section, we will examine the main recent developments.

The 'core' and 'reserve army' of labour

The core

The reserve army of labour theory argues that there are two main groups of employees in capitalist society. The 'core' labour force is skilled and, in return for secure work and 'good' pay, is expected to be flexible in its working practices and to co-operate with employers and management. Members of the 'core' labour force are typically male and white. Most full-time jobs in manufacturing industry and mining are 'core', though there are fewer of them than there used to be.

The reserve army (sometimes referred to as 'periphery' workers)

The reserve army of labour consists of workers who are usually semi-skilled or unskilled, and can be easily hired when business expands and fired when it contracts. They are generally low paid. Large numbers of part-time or temporary female employees and members of ethnic minorities (especially black) are members of the reserve army of labour.

Increasingly, less well-qualified young people are among this group, especially since the Wages Act of 1986 removed employees under 21 from the protection of the statutory minimum wage for industry. An example of the use of reserve labour is in parts of the textile industry where cheap female labour can be hired or laid off according to the employers' convenience.

The reserve army of labour theory applies to both manual and non-manual employees. It is as easy to have a reserve pool of teachers and nurses on part-time and/or temporary, less well-paid contracts as it is bricklayers or fruit pickers. Indeed, in the mid-1980s there was a rapid increase in the use of temporary teaching contracts in order to save money and to be able to hire and fire these teachers as the need arose.

The important thing which both the core and reserve army of labour have in common is that they sell their labour for money. From 'temp' typists to social workers, they are all answerable to employers, either private or public.

Managers

In the 1980s, great emphasis was given to the role of management both by government and private industry. Two points were often stressed:

1   The need successfully to manage change — especially the introduction of new technology and the reduction of the manufacturing labour force.
2   The management of the labour force and particularly the 'need' to make it more 'productive'.

Frequently, the Conservative Government appointed top managers from private industry to the chairmanship of public corporations, such as British Coal, British Steel and the British Broadcasting Corporation. These people and their middle managers typically sought greater productivity by labour force cuts, the introduction of new technology and the setting of 'targets' (aims to try to achieve) for employees.

Ian McGregor, the Chairman of British Coal during the bitter clash with the miners of 1984–5. He had previously been in private industry.

This style of management spread its influence far afield. Even doctors and teachers found themselves being subject to it, and not always liking it. Some argued that managers were interfering with their professional independence to do their jobs. However, others argued that the new emphasis on management led to greater efficiency.

The new 'technocrats'

The new 'technocrats' are the people who invent, develop and maintain new technology, especially the information and telecommunications technology on which so much of modern industry now depends. These employees do work which is essential to modern industry (see p. 102) and are often very highly paid. Some consider this group to be the *key* occupational group in modern society.

Employers: government and private

Whatever changes there have been in Britain's economy and occupational structure, Britain remains a mixed economy, most of which is run by the private sector. Most people work in capitalist enterprises and Britain is very much a capitalist society. This became even more so in the 1980s when the Government pursued a policy of *privatising* public industries such as British Gas and British Telecom. Table 7.4 shows a steady trend during the 1980s to more people in private sector employment and fewer working in the public sector.

Table 7.4. People in employment by sector (in millions)

Year	Public	Private
1961	5.9	18.6
1981	7.2	17.1
1985	6.6	17.9
1986	6.5	18.4
1990	6.0	20.9

(Source: *Social Trends*, 1992.)

Question

Try to find out why public sector employment was high in 1981, and lower later.

The Government and the economy

The Government has the power greatly to affect the economy. The economic aims of the Conservatives between 1979 and the early 1990s may be summarised as follows:

1 for British industry to become more competitive and more capitalist;
2 to reduce the power of the trade unions;
3 to promote an 'enterprise' culture in Britain;
4 to make the British work force more 'flexible', for example, more should be paid for the same type of work in higher than in lower cost of living areas, and promoting more short-term contract working so workers can be laid off when not needed.

These aims are an important part of the background to understanding many of the changes dealt with in the rest of this chapter.

Stimulus questions

Look at the following table and answer the questions.

Table 7.5. Trends in employment in Great Britain

	1973 %	1979 %	1983 %
Agriculture, forestry and fishing	2	2	2
Manufacturing	34	31	26
Coal, oil and gas extraction	2	2	2
Construction	6	5	5
Total industry	42	38	33
Wholesale, retail, hotel, catering	18	18	20
Transport, postal, telecommunications, electricity and gas	8	8	8
Banking and finance	5	7	9
Public administration	19	21	22
Other services	6	6	6
Total services	56	60	65

(Source: D.N. Ashton, *Unemployment under Capitalism*, Wheatsheaf Books, 1986.)

Questions

1 What was the overall percentage decrease in employment in 'total industry' between 1973 and 1983? (1 mark)
2 Give *two* reasons for the decrease in employment in 'total industry' between 1973 and 1983. (4 marks)
3 What was the overall percentage increase in employment in 'total services' between 1973 and 1983? (1 mark)
4 Taking any *two* occupational areas from the service industries, give *one* reason in each case for the increase in employment. (4 marks)
5 Discuss the consequences either for individuals or for society of changing patterns of employment shown in Table 7.5. (6 marks)

Activity (class)

This exercise is to help you check that you *can* tell the kinds of work which take place in each sector.

The following list of occupations is given in no particular order. Rearrange them under the headings of agricultural, manufacturing and service sectors:

kitchen hand	boilermaker
mechanical engineer	agricultural labourer
market gardener	assembly line worker
sales representative	architect
shepherd	

Work, prosperity and poverty

Prosperity

Income earned through work is the basis of the standard of living of most households, but other income, such as social security benefits, also contributes.

Apart from a drop between 1980 and 1981, average household income increased during the 1980s and particularly rapidly between 1983 and 1985. 'Real income' is the actual purchasing power of earnings — on average this was 14 per cent more per head in 1986 than in 1980 and 28 per cent more in 1986 than in 1977 (Table 7.6).

Table 7.6. Real household disposable income per head (1980 = 100)

1977	1978	1979	1980	1981	1982	1983	1984	1985	1990
86	93	98	100	98	99	100	104	108	128

(Source: *Social Trends*, 1988.)

Three important reasons for the increase in household prosperity were:

1 *The continued increase in national wealth* (North Sea oil was a big factor here) — This fed through to an increase in real wages in most job sectors.
2 *An increase in dual-income households* (by about one-and-a-half million) — A dual income household is one in which there are *two* earners. Even where the second income is low, the total of the 'dual income' could still be very comfortable. Two high incomes can mean real prosperity.
3 *An increase in people holding two jobs* — During the short period between 1983 and 1985, the number of people holding two jobs increased by 230,000 to 750,000. In 1985, the majority of second-job holders were not those who were poorly paid, but were managerial and professional workers (52 per cent of second-job holders).

Dual income household.

Holder of two jobs.

These were among the prosperous in the 1980s.

Causes of prosperity: luck or judgement?

An enterprise culture

Many Conservative Government supporters believe that Thatcherism has brought about a deep change in British society — that it has bred an 'enterprise' culture. The enterprise culture is based on the ideology (belief) that people should be willing to work hard for success and create wealth in the process. It arises from the belief that people should 'stand on their own two feet' and not simply rely on the state for 'handouts'. Conservative Minister Norman Tebbit's remark that unemployed people should 'get on their bikes' and look for work reflects the ideas of the enterprise culture. Another idea is that both employers and employees should be willing to retrain in order to compete in the modern world.

It may be possible to tell by the early 1990s whether the enterprise culture has created the basis of new work practices and stable prosperity. Meanwhile, critics point to the high rates of unemployment and low pay which they see as the price of Thatcherism.

The oil and the 'silverware'

Some argue that Britain's prosperity in the 1980s was due to the 'bonus' of North Sea oil and to little else. They suggest that as the oil runs down, so will prosperity. Critics also point out that privatisation — 'selling the family silver' — cannot go on for ever. Eventually, there will be no more nationalised industries to sell and no more 'windfalls' for the Government.

Unemployment and low pay: the other Britain

Whilst the majority prospered during the 1980s, about a quarter of the population did not. The main groups among among these were the unemployed and low paid.

Unemployment

Those who lost jobs in the 1980s — mainly in the 'old' manufacturing industries — were generally not the people who found the better jobs in the expanding service industries.

The better paid of the 'old' jobs were lost mainly in one area (roughly north of the Trent) and the better paid of the new jobs — such as those in finance and information processing — developed mainly in the south and, especially, the south-east. Nationally, the majority of new service-sector jobs — such as those in fast food or office work — were low paid and part-time. Unemployment increased by two million under the Conservatives — and then dropped by over 1.5 million in about 3 years. *Note:* The Labour Party argues that official figures understate the true extent of unemployment. Six major changes were made in how unemployment is counted between 1979 and 1989. The two main changes together took over one million out of the unemployment figures.

Figure 7.1. Unemployment in Britain

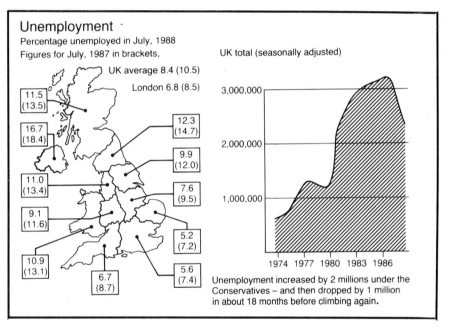

(Source: the *Guardian*, 17 March 1989.)

The levels of unemployment in the 1980s were high by historical standards. There is no doubt that unemployment, particularly long-term unemployment (one year and over), causes great material hardship and emotional suffering. These matters are discussed in Chapter Seventeen.

Government policy to deal with unemployment

Throughout the 1980s the Conservative Government pursued a three-pronged policy to bring unemployment down:

1 it encouraged private enterprise to expand and create jobs;
2 it introduced job training programmes to improve the skills of the unemployed and also a work 'Restart' programme, and
3 it 'tightened up' the benefit system to persuade those who were on benefit to try harder to find work.

Policies (2) and (3) came together in the introduction of a new programme in 1988 — (1) was discussed earlier in this section.

The New Employment Training Scheme for Adults, 1988

The scheme mixes work experience with training. Those joining the scheme receive £10 more than their normal unemployment benefit. The hope is to fulfil two guarantees — to provide opportunities for i) 18 to 25 year olds out of work for six months or more, and ii) those aged under 50, unemployed for two years or more.

Government ministers stress that the scheme is voluntary — though they expect over 600,000 a year will take it up. In the year before its introduction, stricter testing on availability for work was also introduced for those claiming unemployment pay. For instance, claimants are required to consider taking jobs other than their normal occupation and to be prepared to work at weekends.

Critics of the programme argue that the money incentive for retraining is inadequate (£10) and that training is often likely to be poor (depending, as it does, on what employers offer). You may recall that much the same arguments occur in relation to the Youth Training Scheme which is also part of the Government's training and employment policy (re-read p. 5 for this). It is too early yet to know how effective the New Employment Training Scheme for Adults will be.

The importance of training

Politicians may disagree about particular schemes, but all the main parties agree on the need to improve training for employment. There are several reasons for this.

First, it is estimated that one in three job vacancies occur because the workers with the skills to fill them are in short supply.

Second, because of a fall in the birth rate, there are going to be far fewer school-leavers to fill job vacancies — 23 per cent fewer in 1995 than 1987. This means that more adults will have to be trained and retrained.

Third, laws which come into force in 1992 will mean a much freer movement of workers within the countries of the European Community. If British workers are not adequately trained for jobs, there will be plenty of other European workers who will be.

Figure 7.2. Educating future professionals: the numbers gap

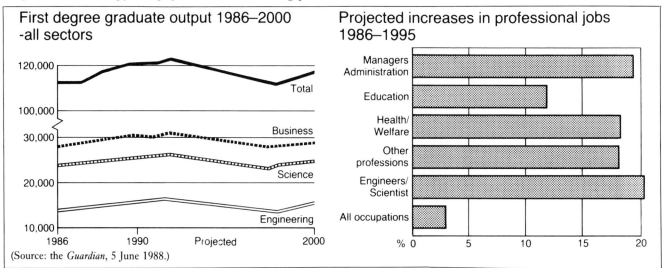

(Source: the *Guardian*, 5 June 1988.)

Questions

Write two paragraphs describing and explaining the estimated gap between the demand for professionals and the likely supply of graduates between 1986 and 1995.

Low pay

According to the estimates of the Low Pay Unit (1989), low pay increased in Britain between 1979 and 1988. The unit estimated low pay at £144.00 or less for a 38-hour week (two-thirds of the median male earnings). This may seem quite a high estimate but it is slightly less than that given by the Council of Europe.

Table 7.7. Estimated numbers and proportions of adult employees earning low wages* April 1988

	Including overtime pay %	Millions	Excluding overtime pay %	Millions
Male full-time workers on adult rates**				
Manual	22.3	1.25	35.8	2.01
Non-manual	10.0	0.48	11.6	0.56
All	16.4	1.71	24.1	2.51
Female full-time workers on adult rates**				
Manual	75.6	0.95	81.8	1.03
Non-manual	41.5	1.63	43.7	1.76
All	48.8	2.58	52.0	2.75
All full-time workers on adult rates**				
	27.2	4.27	33.5	5.26
Adult part-time workers				
Women			80.1	3.41
Men			77.5	0.68
All			79.8	4.09
All workers			44.9	9.35

*Under £144 a week, 3.80 an hour.
**Trainees excluded. Proportions derived from 'adult rates not affected by absence' and applied to total number on adult rates.
(Source: Low Pay Unit, 1989.)

Questions

1 According to the estimates in Table 7.7, what percentage of adult full-time workers were on low pay in April 1988 (including their overtime earnings)?
2 What percentage of part-time workers were on low pay in April 1988?
3 In your opinion, is two-thirds of the average wage too high, too low, or about right to set as the threshold of low pay? Explain your answer.

In cases where a low-paid employee is a member of a dual-income household, a reasonable standard of living is attainable. However, the steep rise in single people and lone-parent families in poverty between 1979 and 1988 is largely due to the increase in low pay (see p. 275).

A very low-paid group is school children in part-time work. According to a survey by the Low Pay Unit, about 2.5 million children were in part-time work in the mid 1980s, about two million illegally. Children legally and safely in part-time work can learn about the world of work whilst earning some pocket money. However, children whose parents are in manual occupations or unemployed are much more likely than middle-class children to be in part-time work. This suggests many children work because their families need them to.

'I used to work a 90-hour week to get the money I needed to live. My daughters used to come in from school, eat and start sewing...We were absolutely desperate for money...I challenge anybody to check, sew, and label a dozen sweaters at the rate they set and earn more than 66p an hour.'

Yvonne Smith

(Source: the *Observer*, 5 May 1988.)

There are over one million homeworkers in Britain. Many claim their wages are below legal rates, and some experience dangerous working conditions without legal protection.

Low-paid and, often, temporary workers make up much of what was referred to earlier as the reserve army of labour. Low-paid workers and trainee workers on grants can produce higher profits for employers. The following are among the main groups in the reserve army of labour:

* women in part-time work (especially service work);
* lower working-class males (including a relatively high proportion of members of black ethnic minorities);
* children in part-time work, and
* youths and adults on 'schemes'.

Stimulus questions

Read the following information and answer the questions.

ITEM A

The *Employment Gazette* describes trends in wages through the lifetime of Labour and Tory governments: in 1973–79, the gap between the top and bottom of the pay league narrowed, widening again in 1979–86.

But these shifts are swamped by the pay rises in the Thatcher phase for male non-manual workers as a whole: their real earnings rose by only 1 per cent in 1973–79, but 22.4 per cent in 1979–86, while manual workers scored roughly equally in both periods. For women the difference is less: non-manual earnings rose 14.9 per cent in real terms in 1973–79, 21.7 per cent in 1979–86; and manual earnings, helped by equal pay laws, rose faster in the first period.

Amongst men, professional and managerial groups (including those employed in education and health) suffered real income losses in 1973–79. By contrast, all occupations scored real increases in the second period, with the biggest rises mostly (but not entirely) going to professional and managerial groups.

(Adapted from the *Independent*, 4 February 1988.)

Figure 7.3. Wages

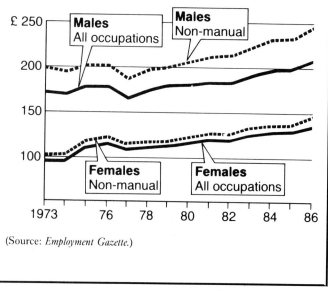

Real weekly earnings (1986 prices)

(Source: *Employment Gazette*.)

Continued over page...

ITEM B

Ten worst paid jobs

1 Hairdressers
2 Waitresses
3 Barmaids
4 Saleswomen
5 Check out operators
6 Sewing machinists
7 Kitchen hands
8 Counter hands
9 Receptionists
10 Cleaners

'Generally speaking, people undervalue what's involved in hairdressing. They say 'Oh it's only a trim isn't it — that can't take much.' They forget it takes up to five years to train. And we enable men and women to go out there and feel confident about their appearance. It helps them get on in the world.' Hairdresser (aged 44).

ITEM C

Education offers more hope to youngsters in run-down inner-city districts than schemes to create jobs in their neighbourhoods, according to a new study from the Economic and Social Research Council.

A council research team has discovered that employment does not depend on which part of a city youngsters come from, but on their educational and family backgrounds. Some city districts have higher-than-average levels of youth unemployment because young people living there are more disadvantaged — notably with low qualifications and unemployed parents. . .

- Some localities suffer high levels of unemployment simply because more young people leave education early.
- The lack of school qualifications was by far the most important disadvantage.
- There was some evidence of higher participation and attainment in some inner-city districts, probably reflecting difference in the quality of the schools.

And they argue that if the Youth Training Scheme is to help, it must enhance the qualifications and employability of young people living in disadvantaged districts, more than it does those of other youngsters.

Bleak outlook: Many Liverpool youngsters know nothing but economic decline.

(Source: *Times Educational Supplement*, 11 December 1987.)

Questions

1 During which period did the gap between the top and bottom of the pay league narrow? (Item A — text)
(1 mark)

2 For which group did wages rise most steeply between 1979 and 1986, males non-manual or females non-manual? (Item A — graph) (1 mark)

3 What does the list of the ten worst-paid jobs suggest they have in common? (Item B) (1 mark)

4 What two factors does the Economic and Social Research Council Report say are most strongly linked to success in getting employment? (Item C) (2 marks)

5 Look closely at the text and photograph in items B and C. Which two groups do they indicate are more likely than average to be either low paid or unemployed? (Items B and C) (2 marks)

6 Discuss *one* explanation why there is a large and recently (1979–1986) growing gap between high and low wage-earners. (2 marks)

7 Give reasons why women earn, on average, less than men. (4 marks)

8 In your view, are the current youth training schemes providing young people with what they need? (Give reasons for your answer.). Are there any ways in which such schemes could be improved? (7 marks)

The experience of work

Getting *satisfaction* out of work is the most important thing in life for many people after their family and personal relationships. In social surveys, over 75 per cent of Britons regularly *say* they are satisfied with their job. However, this may be because many have *low* expectations of it.

Activity (class)

List, in order of importance, five things you hope to get out of your job. Discuss this as a class.

The opposite to work satisfaction is, of course, *dissatisfaction* with work. *Alienation* at work is worse than just feeling dissatisfied; it means that the worker's abilities are hardly used or developed — perhaps resulting in severe boredom. Fulfilment or non-alienation is the opposite of alienation.

We will now look at the following four experiences of work in more detail:

- satisfaction
- dissatisfaction
- alienation
- fulfilment

Satisfaction: intrinsic and extrinsic

Work satisfaction can take the forms: *intrinsic* and *extrinsic*. Intrinsic satisfaction results from liking a job or some part of a job for itself. For instance, a teacher might 'love working with kids'. Extrinsic satisfaction results from liking something outside of, but related to, a job. For instance, a car assembly line worker may be 'happy' to do the job because of the 'good' wages.

'The money's awful, but I care about the patients.'

'The job's awful but the money's good.'

Dissatisfaction

Dissatisfaction with work occurs when the worker feels that neither the intrinsic nor extrinsic rewards of the job adequately compensate for the time and energy spent doing it. Levels of dissatisfaction, like satisfaction, vary with individuals. Some individuals would be very dissatisfied with being a traffic warden, whereas others would be quite satisfied.

Fulfilment (non-alienation)

Satisfaction is a matter of individual feeling. Thus, a highly intelligent person *might* feel satisfied stacking shelves in a supermarket. But such a person would *not* be fulfilled in the sense of being 'stretched' and challenged.

What makes for a non-alienating job? Robert Blauner suggests the following four features:

- power — control over the work;
- meaning — a sense of purpose and worth in the work;
- involvement — with the work and other workers, and
- fulfilment — through expressing ability and developing potential.

Many of you are probably saying to yourselves that few, if any, jobs are *that* good. Well, *some* are — and you can probably think of a few yourself. Nevertheless, it is fair to say that the above list is more a measure of what jobs *might* be like if they were fulfilling rather than what most are *actually* like.

Activity

List *two* jobs that you think are *fulfilling* according to Blauner's characteristics. Write down how *each* job meets the four characteristics.

Alienation

Alienation involves low levels of power, meaning involvement and/or fulfilment. Robert Blauner carried out a questionnaire survey of alienation in four different types of manufacturing industries. These are his findings:

Industry	Production Technology	Percentage of workers alienated
Printing	Craft	4
Textiles	Machine batch	18
Automobile	Assembly line	34
Chemical	Automated	11

As you can see, the more a worker is 'tied' to a machine, the more alienated he or she is.

Activity (class/outside class)

Make *either* a bar *or* a pie chart presenting the data in Blauner's list.

Service work and the 'deskilling' theory

Most work done in Britain is service work. How alienating is routine service work such as that done by typists or filing clerks? The question is open to debate. In the view of the American sociologist, Harry Braverman, capitalists sometimes deliberately deskill work (reduce the skill involved) in order to keep control over their workers. He gives an example of this approach from a handbook for office managers titled *A Guide to Office Clerical Time Standards:*

Open and close	Minutes
File drawer, open and close, no selection	.04
Folder, open or close flaps	.04
Desk drawer, open side drawer of standard desk	.014
Open centre drawer	.026
Close side	.015
Close centre	.027
Chair activity	
Get up from chair	.033
Sit down in chair	.033
Turn in swivel chair	.009
Move in chair to adjoining desk or file (4 ft. maximum)	.050

(Source: H. Braverman, *Labour and Monopoly Capital*, Monthly Review Press, 1974.)

Many would disagree with Braverman that capitalists *deliberately* cause alienation. They argue instead that it is certain kinds of technology (such as an assembly line or typewriter) or the way work is organised (just a few people giving all the orders) that makes things boring and alienating.

What can be done about alienating work?

Marxists argue that only when capitalism is abolished and when power and control at work, and what is produced, are more equally shared will people be more fulfilled. Others say this is a 'pipe dream' and the way to reduce alienation is to organise work so people are much more involved, and to make work technology more 'user friendly'. These points are discussed later (p. 106).

Stimulus questions

Read the following information and answer the questions.

ITEM A

The UK market alone in electronic machines and associated services is worth some £6 billion per annum, and growing at an annual rate of 20 per cent. IT employs more than 200,000 professional staff and needs an injection of at least 8–9,000 graduates, or equivalent trainees each year...

Many employers of graduates stress their 'all discipline' requirement, but the majority of entrants have a science background — computer scientists, electronic/electrical engineers, physicists, mathematicians and mechanical engineers...

Other trainees — and here the numerate arts graduate may appear — will be involved in applications programming, designing the software which meets clients' needs for payroll, stock control, staff records and forecasting.

(Source: the *Observer*, 17 January 1988.)

ITEM B

One in ten young people go from the classroom straight into hotel and catering. 'We must,' said Mrs Thatcher, 'expect that a lot more of our jobs will come from the service industries — from the McDonald's and Wimpys.' The hamburger economy has come to town.

McDonald's lights up three new outlets a month and has emerged as one of London's largest employers. Last year alone 4,000 people stepped into their uniform, bringing the total to 19,000. While **For Sale** signs appear outside locally run chippies and take-aways, the sales of the multinational fast food chains are growing by 25 per cent a year and profits even faster.

But the neon glare hides a reality that is more like the slum industries of yesteryear. McDonald's takes on those with few other opportunities open to them: women and ethnic minorities — who are twice as likely to work in hotel and catering as men or whites — and youths. Three-quarters of the work force are under 21 and individual store managers face a pressure to hire under 18 year olds who cost the company 50p an hour less. (The food and drink retail sector in Britain employs over one million people — a growing number of these are in 'fast-food'.)

Continued over page...

Many are still at school. In Slough, the senior education welfare officer took McDonald's to court in 1984 for breaking the child employment law on 14 counts. 'The whole industry gets away with it all over the country,' said the officer.

McDonald's secret recipe for success comes not from the Big Mac sauce but from a new production process, using a combination of the Fordist conveyor belt with a Japanese emphasis on flexibility. Each store is a factory where workers' skills have been kept down and labour costs kept to a bare minimum. No chefs, no apprentices wanted on this burgerline: everyone has been levelled down to the uniform "crew member" rushing between stations to perform tasks learnt in a day. Computerised machines do the cooking for you and regulate your movements to the second; the stated aim is to 'take the guesswork out of cooking.' From Oxford Street to Manila, McDonald's workers follow identical steps to produce identical burgers.

(Source: adapted from 'Big Mac is Watching You', *New Society*, 9 October 1987.)

Questions

1 Approximately how many professional staff are employed in Information Technology? (Item A)   (1 mark)
2 Approximately how many people are employed in the food and drink retail sector? (Item B)   (1 mark)
3 a What is the educational background of most of the entrants to careers in computing? (Item A)   (1 mark)
  b What *two* purposes do computerised machines achieve at McDonalds? (Item B)   (2 marks)
4 Some sociologists have argued that there is a link between 'alienation' and the 'level of technology'. Explain what is meant by (i) alienation and (ii) the level of technology.   (6 marks)
5 How would you describe the experience of working at McDonalds? Can you think of any way in which fast-food workers (such as those described in Item B) could make their work 'more fulfilling'?   (5 marks)
6 How do McDonalds manage to keep down their 'wage costs'? (Item B)   (4 marks)

Activity (class/outside class)

This activity is to give you a chance to measure alienation either in your part-time job (if you have one) or in your school work. Score your work according to the table:

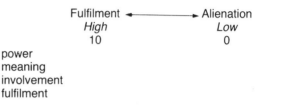

Fulfilment ←————————→ Alienation
High   *Low*
10   0

power
meaning
involvement
fulfilment

Give at least one reason for each score.
  Can you devise any other technique to measure alienation? If so, you might try out your measurement technique in a real situation (again, perhaps your own work). This activity might provide the basis for a project.

Industrial relations

There are three main groups involved in British industrial relations: employers, employees and government. They are mainly responsible for the degree of co-operation or conflict in industry.

Employers' organisations

There is an employers' organisation for most major industries. Altogether there are 335 employers' associations. They negotiate the national agreements with trade unions for their industry. Most employers' associations are members of the Confederation of British Industry (CBI). The CBI acts as a public relations body for British industry nationally and internationally. It also nominates representatives to important bodies such as the National Economic Development Council; the Advisory, Conciliation and Arbitration Service (ACAS), which deals with industrial disputes, and the Training Commission (which deals with job training).

Trade unions

Trade unions are associations of employees which negotiate pay and conditions of employment with employers. Trade unions have members in nearly all occupational areas, though some areas, such as restaurant work, are very weakly unionised. Union membership has been steadily falling from a peak of 51.1 per cent of the work force in 1979 to 38.4 per cent in 1985. The biggest manual workers' union is the Transport and General Workers Union (1.4 million members) and the biggest non-manual workers' union is the National and Local Government Officers' Association (750,000 members). Nearly 90 per cent of trade unions are members of the national body, the Trades Union Congress (TUC).

Stimulus questions

Use the information in the following tables to answer the questions.

ITEM A

Table 7.8. Trade unions: numbers[1] and membership[1] United Kingdom

	Number of unions	Total membership (millions)	As a percentage of working population	Percentage change in membership since previous year
1975	470	12.0	47.2	
1976	473	12.4	48.5	+3.0
1977	481	12.8	50.1	+3.7
1978	462	13.1	50.7	+2.1
1979	454	13.3	51.1	+1.3
1980	438	12.9	49.5	−2.6
1981	414	12.1	46.6	−6.5
1982	408	11.6	44.8	−4.2
1983	394	11.2	41.6	−3.1
1984	375	11.0	39.9	−2.2
1985	373	10.7	38.4	−2.5

1 As at December each year.

(Source: *Employment Gazette*, Department of Employment.)

ITEM B

Table 7.9. Trade union membership by selected industries

Industry	Total membership in thousands 1982	1985	Percentage change in membership 1982 to 1985
Metal goods, engineering and vehicles	1819	404	−78
Energy and water supply	413	213	−48
Education	745	794	+7
Medical/health	658	686	+6

Questions

1 What was the fall in the number of union members between 1979 and 1985? (Item A)
2 In what sector of industry (manufacturing or service) is the area which experienced the largest drop in union membership? (Item B)
3 In what sector of industry is the area which experienced the largest increase in union membership? (Item B)
4 Give *one* reason for the decline of union membership in certain industries and the rise in others. (Items A and B)

Government

A government can affect industrial relations by use of law. The Thatcher administrations have passed a series of laws, which have reduced the power (and so, probably, the membership) of trade unions but which the government claims have made the unions more democratic.

The following are the four main laws passed in the 1980s affecting trade unions:

1980 Employment Act — This Act limited lawful picketing to an employee's place of work. Picketing is trying to persuade fellow employees to join industrial action — usually a strike. The Act meant that *secondary* picketing — picketing at places of work other than one's own — was outlawed.

1982 Employment Act — From November 1984 this Act removed legal protection from all 'closed shops' which did not meet the requirements of the Act. A closed shop is a place of work at which all employees *must* be union members. The new Act meant a closed shop can only operate if it has been supported in a secret ballot (held in the previous five years) by 80 per cent of employees affected, or by 85 per cent of those voting.

1984 Trade Union Act — This Act requires unions to hold secret ballots 1) before strike action can be taken, 2) in electing their officers, 3) at regular intervals so membership can decide on whether or not to spend money on political purposes.

1988 Employment Act — This Act stops unions from disciplining members who break strikes (which now have to be supported by secret ballot — 1984 Act). Critics argue that the Government went too far in this measure in weakening the *collective* power of the unions over their members. The Conservatives believe it is right to allow the *individual* to choose whether or not to strike — whatever the majority decides. The Act also extended the secret ballot to overtime bans and 'working to rule' (working so carefully to the rules that things are slowed down).

Reasons for the low rate of strikes 1979–88: a summary

Judged by the usual measures, industrial conflict decreased fairly steadily between 1979 and 1988. Both the number of work stoppages and the number of days lost through stoppages tended to fall during this period. Even though the long miners' strike of 1984 pushed up the days lost in that year, the actual number of work stoppages was still less than in 1983.

Do the above trends suggest that the labour force was contented or frightened during this period? There is support for both of these and other views in the list of possible explanations for the reduction in industrial conflict between 1979 and 1986:

1 Government laws made it more difficult to call and carry out strikes.
2 The decline in union membership in the manufacturing sector — the traditional stronghold of unionism.
3 The 'white-collar' (service sector) unions that did experience a slight membership increase traditionally did not often use the strike 'weapon' — through to a limited extent the teachers (1985–7) and the nurses (1988) did.
4 The recession and high unemployment made employees wary of strike action — in case their jobs became threatened.
5 The large numbers of temporary and part-time female workers coming into paid work tended to be unorganised and ununionised.
6 Many better-paid employees became *more* prosperous during this period and may not have felt the need to strike.

Activity (class)

1 Rearrange the above list of 'Reasons for the low rate of strikes, 1979–88' in the order you consider to be most important.
2 Not all the reasons given apply equally to all types of employees. Try to give an example of *one* occupational group for *each* point in the list.
  Discuss with your teacher the current trend in strikes and try to explain it.

Just a striking coincidence, or, will strikes increase again? What goes down (the number of days lost through strikes) could go up. In early 1988 and again in 1989 there were signs of a revival in industrial militancy.

From conflict to co-operation?

Some sociologists argue that a high level of industrial conflict in capitalist societies is inevitable. Conflict is 'built into the system' because capitalists seek higher profits whilst workers seek higher wages and better working conditions. Such sociologists consider that the relative industrial calm of the 1980s may only be temporary. In time, the unions may successfully challenge at least some of the 'tough' laws of the Thatcher years, or a new government may change the laws altogether.

Use of the law is one way to reduce industrial conflict. Some alternative approaches are discussed below.

Examples of industrial co-operation

1 Company shares for employees

About 20 per cent of British adults now own shares. Many first-time shareholders bought shares at special cheap rates for employees in newly privatised companies. Thus, there are in total millions of employee shareholders in British Telecom, British Gas, British Airways, the Trustee Savings Bank and British Aerospace. Another way of bringing about employee shareholding used by many companies is to make an annual allocation of shares to employees as a kind of bonus.

It is too early to say whether employee shareholders will be less inclined to strike than other employees, or whether, individually, or in groups, they will exercise their full rights as shareholders to influence the company. In Sweden where employee shareholding has been operating for much longer than in Britain, employees identify more with what will become '*their*' company as they build up more and more shares. In Britain, large shareholders and management still dominate industry, but this could be open to some change *if* the employee-shareholder movement really 'takes off'.

2 Employee participation

Employee participation in the operation of a company can vary from a very little to a lot. An example of limited participation is the 'quality circle' developed by Japanese firms and now used by some British firms such as Jaguar. A 'quality circle' is a small group of workers which meets regularly to discuss problems, especially how to improve the quality and efficiency of work. In Japan, circles sometimes compete to achieve the best ideas, but this seems to have limited appeal to British employees.

Employee representation on company management boards is a much higher level of participation than 'quality circles'. In those countries in which employee representation is common, such as Sweden and West Germany, there tend to be fewer days lost through strikes than in Britain. Perhaps knowing more about a company and sharing in the running of it gives employees a greater sense of involvement and identity in the total work process. However, so far, in Britain, workers' participation has not proved popular. This may reflect the continued strength of the 'them' and 'us', 'two sides of industry', attitude.

3 Co-operatives

In the case of co-operatives, employees *control* the company, they do not simply take part in its running. Nevertheless, employees may choose to appoint managers answerable to them, or may rotate (take turns at) management roles among themselves. In the mid-1980s there were about 1000 co-ops in Britain with the trend moving rapidly upwards (400 were set up in 1984–5). The industrial sectors in which co-ops most commonly occur are building, entertainment, food retailing (the most prone to failure) and printing.

Most co-ops are small — four being the average number of workers. Many supporters of co-ops would say that for workers who want real control and involvement in their work, 'small is beautiful'.

The co-operative movement is again becoming more popular.

Stimulus questions

Use the following tables and extract and answer the questions.

ITEM A

Figure 7.4. Working days lost during year due to stoppages.

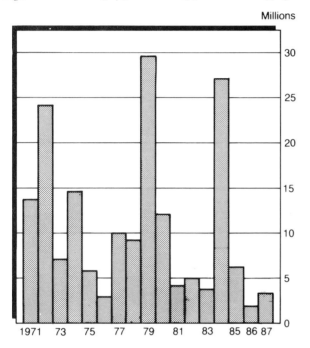

ITEM B

Figure 7.5. Unemployment rate: annual averages

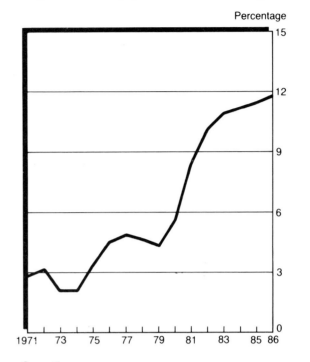

ITEM C

Fear of unemployment may be one reason why, in the 1980s, there was a trend for working days lost due to stoppages to decrease. As one unionist, Ron Todd, put it, 'We've got three million on the dole, and another 23 million (employees) scared to death.' But there were other reasons, too. Trade union membership fell by almost twenty per cent between 1979 and 1985 and the loss was especially great in unions in the manufacturing sector — traditionally the stronghold of the union movement. Looking back, the miners' strike of 1984–85 looks more like a struggle born out of desperation rather than strength. As the manufacturing working class declined in numbers and influence, millions of new, service sector jobs were created. The less well paid of these jobs were often temporary or part time, and held by women, young people or members of ethnic minorities. Often these employees were not unionised and could not risk taking strike action. Some sociologists have referred to them as 'a reserve pool of labour'.

(Source: Adapted from *Social Trends*, 1988 and 1989.)

Questions

1 a In what year between 1980 and 1988 were the most working days lost through stoppages? (Item A)
(1 mark)
   b What reason can you give for your answer to (a)? (Item C)
(1 mark)
2 What was the unemployment rate in 1980? (Item B)
(1 mark)
3 What connection is made in Item C between unemployment and working days lost due to stoppages? (Item C)
(2 marks)
4 Give *two* possible reasons for the decrease in working days lost due to stoppages *other* than the rise in unemployment. (Item C)
(2 marks)
5 a What is a 'reserve pool of labour'? (Item C) (2 marks)
   b In what ways might a reserve pool of labour be useful to employers?
(4 marks)
6 Discuss various ways in which the level of industrial conflict might be reduced. Which do you consider to be the most likely to succeed?
(7 marks)

Structured questions

1 Discuss the possible disadvantages of being a 'homeworker'.
(4 marks)
2 Identify and discuss *two* factors which may influence the level of satisfaction or dissatisfaction with paid employment.
(6 marks)
3 Discuss changes that have taken place in the nature of 'work' over the last 50 years or so and which, in your opinion, have benefited the workers involved.
(12 marks)

Project and assignment suggestions

Note: It is important, in this as in other topic areas, that you follow certain guidelines and procedures. You should always get your teacher to check over any questionnaire or interview schedule you intend to use. You must make sure that you have permission from someone in authority in the firm to carry out your study, and you must make it clear what method(s) of investigation you will be using, and roughly how long it will take. You must *never* just 'turn up' at a firm without having made a proper appointment. You will see that, in this as with all other projects, there is a lot of advance planning to be done!

1   *Job satisfaction* — There are several studies you could do based on your own part-time job or perhaps work experience placement. For example, you could look more closely at the question of 'job satisfaction', finding out what your fellow employees find satisfying or dissatisfying about their work, and perhaps comparing the responses of 'shop-floor', clerical, supervisory and management personnel. (Which categories are available to you will depend largely on the type of organisation it is.) You might also see whether differences emerge between male and female employees, younger and older workers, or full-time and part-time workers.

2   *An 'in-depth' study of a particular job* — Perhaps a teacher's. You might get permission to 'shadow' a teacher for a day, or you may be allowed to distribute a questionnaire to some members of staff. (How would you choose your sample?) It might be interesting to do a *comparative* study of, say, a primary or junior and a secondary teacher. You might be able to do something similar with a member or members of another occupation — perhaps family contacts could help you find something appropriate? (Note: many work places are very dangerous — do make sure you have received the proper permission if, for example, you will be going into a factory, and *do* observe all the safety rules!)

3   *Contrast the work and life-style of two people in very different occupations* — say, a professional or managerial worker and a manual worker. The first difficulty would be to find people willing to talk to you at length. Would you tell each of them that you were going to compare them with somebody else? Would it be fair *not* to tell them? Would your research go beyond just the work situation and cover things like training, standard of living and use of leisure time?

4   *A contrast between a paid job and housework* — perhaps focusing on the different aspects of satisfaction/alienation. (Remember to look again at what Blauner considered the 'four dimensions' of alienation.) One way might be to find someone who has worked for long periods, both as a full-time houseworker and as a full-time paid employee. Another way would be to compare two different people, one a houseworker, the other a paid worker. Of course, the nature of the paid employment is important — a teacher's answers might be very different from those of a factory worker.

5   *The effects of technological change on a place of work* — This might be difficult, at least to find a suitable example, but could be very interesting. You might be able to find a company which has recently changed its production methods (e.g. an engineering firm which has gone over to automated processes, the use of robots, or the introduction of computer-aided design and/or manufacturing). An alternative might be an office which has just switched from typewriters to word processors, or has just computerised its stock records or accounts system. Your own school or college might even be in this position.) Another place to look would be your local library or supermarket, as many of these are switching to computerised systems. You could talk to employees about their 'before' and 'after' experiences, to see what differences there are, and how they feel about them. You should also try to take a wider view, by looking at possible changes in the size and nature of the work force, changes in the organisational structure, and the systems of control — you would obviously need to talk to someone in a senior position for this part of the study.

Key words

Alienation	Private sector
Capitalist economy	Producers
Consumers	Public sector
Core labour force	Reserve army of labour
Division of labour	Satisfaction (work) — intrinsic
Mixed economy	— extrinsic
	Socialist economy

CHAPTER **8** *The Economy, Urbanisation and Community*

This chapter is about how changes in the 'world of work' (the economy) have helped to cause changes in where and how people live. We look at two periods of change. The first of these took place in the eighteenth and nineteenth centuries and the second began in the 1950s and is still taking place. The first change was the Industrial Revolution, which caused an increase in the number and size of cities which we refer to as *urbanisation*. The second change is the move from an industrial manufacturing economy to a service economy, which is resulting in *de-urbanisation*, people moving from towns to the suburbs or the countryside, although most Britons still live in urban areas and are likely to do so for some time. A service economy is one in which the majority of people are not involved in producing material goods (such as cars, televisions, etc) but work to meet non-material needs, such as education, financial and legal services.

The two great changes referred to above can be summarised as follows:

	Economy	Society (Way of life)
1	From agricultural to industrial (18th and 19th Century)	From mainly rural to urban
2	From industrial to service (1950s onwards)	Still urban but increasingly suburban/rural

Understanding these two periods provides a basis for understanding modern British society. We will examine them in turn.

Changing British society

The Industrial Revolution

The late eighteenth to the mid-nineteenth century is often referred to as the 'age of revolution' or the period of the 'dual' (two) revolutions. The two revolutions were political and economic. The political revolution resulted in a move towards democracy — led by the French Revolution. The economic revolution resulted in industrialisation — of which Britain was in the forefront. It is the economic, or industrial, revolution we are interested in here.

The following are the key factors which turned Britain into an industrial, urban society:

- *Technological invention* — The late eighteenth and nineteenth centuries were a great period of invention in Britain. Perhaps more than today, Britain's inventors of that time put their ideas to practical use. Arkwright's spinning-jenny and Hargreave's power-loom rapidly increased the production of cotton and woollen goods, and markets for these were found all over the world.
- *The factory system* — In the nineteenth century, the factory system of producing goods largely replaced the domestic or home-based system of production. The new machinery needed to be in larger buildings and to be driven by natural sources of energy such as coal and water. It was economically more efficient to have larger-scale units of production (factories).

- *The growth of towns and population* — Factory production required large numbers of factory workers, and miners to meet demand for coal. Factory and mining towns grew up in the North and the Midlands. Industrial areas such as Manchester and Birmingham soon outgrew in population ancient cities such as Oxford and Norwich. It was during the nineteenth century that Britain's greatest population explosion occurred.
- *A capitalist revolution: the private enterprise system* — The industrial revolution in Britain was carried out by capitalists. Through capitalism, Britain has become a much wealthier country. In addition, many private fortunes have been made. On the other hand, great inequality and considerable poverty occur under capitalism.

Adam Smith
Author of The Wealth of Nations,
Smith was an early writer on capitalism
and its benefits.

Friedrich Engels
Author of The Conditions of the
English Working Classes, *Engels was*
critical of the poverty he believed was
caused by capitalism.

What is a city? Urban characteristics

Before discussing the effects of industrialisation and urbanisation on the way people lived, we need to have a clearer idea of what a city is.

The following are important characteristics of the city. It is:

1 large in size,
2 large in population, and
3 contains a variety of inhabitants (e.g. various social classes or races).

110

Of course, cities do not suddenly appear for no reason. The reason so many cities developed at the time of the Industrial Revolution was because large numbers of workers were required in the factories. Towns and cities grew up around factories. However, before the Industrial Revolution, large towns and cities existed throughout Europe for different reasons. For instance in England, Norwich, once the country's second city, was a centre of the wool trade with the Netherlands, London was the centre of government, Chester was a military centre, and Canterbury a centre of religious devotion.

The industrial city: a model

Figure 8.1 shows a very approximate model of the industrial city of the late nineteenth and first half of the twentieth century. Of course, there are few cities in which the zones develop even roughly as concentric circles. However, the functions described in the zones take place somewhere in virtually all cities in the capitalist West.

Figure 8.1. The industrial city: a model

The central business district — a shopping and financial area — is still a feature of most cities. The zone of transition is where newcomers, often seeking work, arrive and settle. This area is often linked with social problems (see p. 124) The two housing zones are self-explanatory and in many cities a similar pattern still occurs, although a patchwork pattern of smaller, but separate middle and working-class housing areas is also common.

Did industrialisation and urbanisation cause a loss of community?

Defining community

Was there 'more community' before the Industrial Revolution? Whether there was or wasn't, many people *think* that there was. Many also believe that there is more 'community' in the countryside today than there is in towns. Both views are difficult to prove, but before examining them, it is necessary to define community. A community is a group of people sharing strong and lasting relationships and usually living in the same area, such as a neighbourhood, village or part of a town. However, the term community does not always refer to those living in a particular geographical area; we sometimes refer to any group that shares feelings and beliefs as a community, such as 'the world community' of Muslims or Jews.

We can now look at the arguments about whether industrialisation and urbanisation in the nineteenth century caused a loss of community.

The disruption of community due to industrialisation and urbanisation

There was certainly a disruption of community in the late eighteenth and early part of the nineteenth century. This was caused by the number of people moving from rural to urban areas to find work. Often, males would go first, leaving their families behind, whilst they organised work, and accommodation in a town. However, the term 'disruption of community' is a more accurate description than 'loss of community' as new communities did form in urban areas (see below).

To some extent, conflict must be part of community, too.

Arguments against 'loss of community' in the nineteenth century

1 'Cosy communities' did not always exist — There is plenty of evidence of division and conflict in pre-nineteenth century Britain, both nationally and locally. Like any group at the bottom of society, the peasants could be angry and rude about those above them — in their case, the gentry, the aristocracy and the clergy. Apart from rebellions, such as the famous Peasants' Revolt of 1382, popular ballads show a more everyday, simmering resentment. The very fact that Robin Hood, who 'robbed the rich to give to the poor', became a legendary folk hero suggests that all was not 'cosy' in medieval England.

2 During the nineteenth century new communities formed — The view that the community was only disrupted and not 'lost' during the nineteenth century is supported by the work of historians and sociologists. They have found that new communities were formed in the towns — some of them by the same people or descendants of families and groups who had lived together in rural areas. For instance, working-class communities formed around areas of work, such as the cotton mills of Preston and the docks of East London (see p. 115). These kinds of community are called 'occupational communities'.

3 Strong immigrant communities were formed in urban areas in the nineteenth and twentieth centuries — In the nineteenth century, there was a strong Jewish immigrant community in East London. Later, this became a prosperous, middle-class but still Jewish, community based in Golders Green, North London. Similarly, parts of London have become areas of Afro-Caribbean immigrant settlement, and East London and many Midland and northern towns areas of Asian immigrant settlement. Often the formation of these communities followed the same pattern as that of the nineteenth century working-class communities, with a male coming in first to establish a base, and others following later. This pattern of family and community self-help has often continued.

A working-class occupational community (late nineteenth century).

An immigrant community (late twentieth century).

De-urbanisation since the 1950s

De-urbanisation is another way of saying that since about the mid-1950s people have been moving out of cities and larger towns, particularly the inner-city areas.

Factors leading to de-urbanisation since the 1950s:

1 The decline of urban-based industry (and industrial communities) — Urban working class and ethnic communities were often based around manufacturing work. Between June 1971 and June 1985, the numbers employed in manufacturing industry fell by 32 per cent — over 2.5 million. Increasing numbers left the inner urban areas to find work.

2 The location of industry outside urban areas — Expanding service industries, such as banking and retailing, were increasingly situated outside city centres. Service industry towns, such as Oxford and Southend, attracted new populations. Even newly automated manufacturing industry was often located outside towns — close to the motorways.

3 Public housing and town and country planning — After the Second World War, it became government policy to attract people away from the inner cities. Public housing estates were often built on the edge of towns. The development of new towns took place rapidly following the Town and Country Planning Act of 1948. Model towns, such as Milton Keynes, provided better homes and environments for the mainly skilled workers and their families who tended to settle there. However, there were failures. Apart from the horrors of high-rise flats, concrete towns were not to every one's taste. The comment on Basildon by some locals — 'the town they forgot to finish' — gives an idea of their view of its architectural appeal.

Milton Keynes — arguably one of the more attractive new towns.

4 Private housing: the drift to suburbia — There has been a steep rise in the number of people owning their own houses (owner occupiers) since the War (see Figure 10.1). Millions of these people sought the peace and greenery of the suburbs.

5 The decline of the inner cities — As industry and younger and more skilled people 'fled' the inner urban areas, so a vicious cycle of decline set in. The old, less skilled and socially deprived tended to be left behind. Often Asian and Afro-Caribbean immigrants were caught in this spiral of decline. They seldom had the money to move to the suburbs, but the jobs they had come to do often disappeared before their eyes. The racism and hostility of some whites aggravated matters. Some inner city areas became squalid, tense and dangerous places. In 1981 and again in 1985 a series of major riots flared up in the inner cities.

An inner urban revival — for some

'Gentrification', 'yuppies' and the 'staying put'

It suits some middle-class people to live in the inner city — perhaps to be close to work in, say, government or the city of London.

The term 'gentrification' is used to describe how middle-class people may take over whole patches of previously working-class houses. There are several such areas in Islington, North London, one or two of which go back to the 1960s. Sometimes, better-off working-class and black householders do not sell up, and the interesting result is residential areas that are very mixed in terms of the class and race of the people living there. Some of the streets off Kingsland Road in Hackney are examples of this. Those who 'stay put' in this way can see their properties double or triple in value over just a few years. Of course, the problem for those on lower incomes comes when the rates do the same.

Yuppies (young, upwardly-mobile, professionals) sometimes find it convenient to live — at least part of the time — close to the city centre. Partly to meet their needs, London's former dockland area has been 'redeveloped'. Flats costing between £150,000 and £500,000 can prove attractive to yuppies, but are priced beyond the reach of most buyers.

The arrival of middle-class people to live in choicer inner urban areas does little, if anything, to improve matters for the majority. What is needed is economic revival — prosperity and jobs.

East London Docklands Development — It looks good, but does it help the majority . . . ?

The Neighbourliness Survey

In 1982, a survey was carried out by Market and Opinion Research International (MORI) into how neighbourly the British are. Interviews were conducted with 1801 adults (aged fifteen-plus) at 178 sampling points throughout Britain. These were the approximate results presented in terms of types of neighbours:

1 Superneighbours — about a *fifth*. They really know each other, e.g. always in and out of each others' houses.
2 Isolates — rather less than a *fifth*. They keep themselves to themselves.
3 Rubalongs — over *three-fifths*. Quite friendly with neighbours, but the home and the work place are the centres of life.

Note: There was more neighbourliness in rural than in urban areas — giving some support for the stereotype that 'country folk are more neighbourly'.

Question

What types of neighbours are yours? Perhaps this could be a topic for research.

115

Activity (class)

The aim of this activity is to get you to consider what, apart from the people, makes a 'community'. As we have discussed, the majority of communities have a particular geographical setting, as well as certain buildings and amenities (services) which serve the people of that community. Not everyone agrees about which particular buildings and services are the most important. This has led to many debates, such as whether many of the new towns have the right kinds of things to develop into 'communities'. Now it is your chance to decide what you think makes a 'community'. Read the description below, which tells you about the new town of Newburgh.

Newburgh

'Newburgh' is a new town in South-East England. At the moment, it has 40,000 inhabitants, though proposed new housing developments will mean that the population will eventually be much larger. Newburgh is well situated in relation to the main motorway network, yet is only 20 miles from the coast and is set in pleasant, open countryside. The area has excellent employment opportunities. There is a 'mix' of housing, ranging from large, executive-style homes to smaller terraced housing and bungalows. There are also some local authority houses and flats. The result of this housing mix is that the population consists of a wide range of people — young, single workers, young couples with small children, older couples with teenage or grown-up families, some lone-parent families and a fairly large number of retired people. Many people work some distance away from Newburgh, as there are few jobs available in the town itself, which leaves a large number of the mothers and elderly people being the main residents from Mondays to Fridays.

At present, Newburgh has a primary school and a doctor's surgery, but very few other services and facilities. The main shopping and recreational centre is Castletown, a busy market town fifteen miles away. However, public transport facilities are not good; there are only two buses a day between Newburgh and Castletown (four on Wednesday, which is market day), but the journey takes 45 minutes, as the route passes through all the neighbouring villages. It is also quite expensive.

Divide up into small groups of four or five people. Each group are members of the planning team trying to make Newburgh a pleasant town in which to live; in other words, to create a proper community which serves the needs of the population. There are many suggestions for suitable buildings and services but, as always, there is not enough money for everything, at least at present. Your team has 4,000 units to spend, and beside each building (or service) is the number of units it would take. Your task is to decide, as a group, how you would spend your 4,000 units in order to create a 'community' in Newburgh. You should note down your reasons for deciding which things to put in, and also your reasons for deciding to leave others out.

Below is the alphabetical list of proposed buildings and amenities, together with the number of points each would take. You may choose to have more than one of something, provided you multiply the number of points accordingly:

Anglican church (Church of England)   1,200
Antenatal and baby clinic   400
Baker   200
Bank   400
Butcher   200
Chemist   200
Children's playground (with swings, slides, etc)   600
Church hall   400
Community centre (all-purpose)   1,000
Crèche   200
Dentist   400
Fast-food takeaway   200
Fish and chip shop   200
General grocer   200
Golf club (greens and clubhouse)   1,600
Greengrocer   200
Launderette   200
Library (permanent)   600
Library (travelling, once per week)   200
Methodist chapel   1,000
Mothers and toddlers club   400
Newsagent and tobacconist   200
Night-club and discothèque   800
Old people's day centre   400
Park (landscaped with pond, flower beds, seats, etc)   1,000
Post Office   500
Pub   200
Recreation ground   800
Restaurant   400
Sports ground (marked pitches, tennis court, changing rooms)   1,000
Supermarket (large, edge of town, free parking)   1,200
Telephone box   50
Video-hire shop   200
Youth club   400
Wine bar   200

Now discuss your suggestions as a class. Was there general agreement on what should be included to make at least the beginnings of a community? Do you think that you have tried to meet everybody's needs — or did you think that some groups were more important than others? Can you think of anything which you would like to have been included but which wasn't on the list? Judging from the other things on the list, about how many 'purchasing units' do you think that your suggestion would have taken up?

Figure 8.2. De-urbanisation: population migration to rural areas and small towns

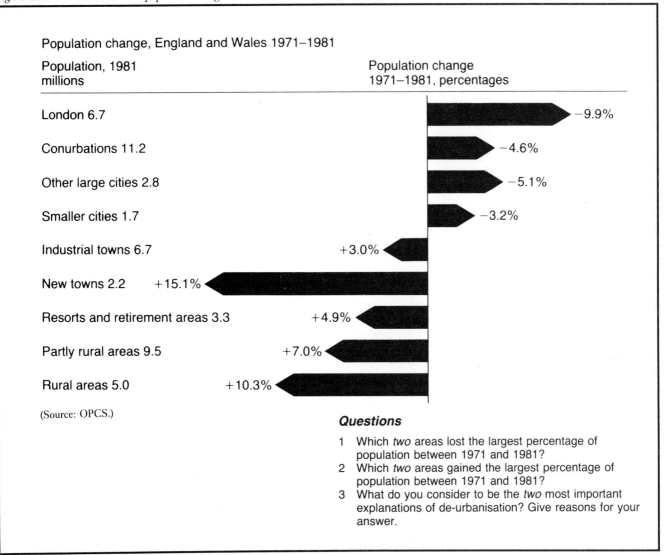

Population change, England and Wales 1971–1981

Population, 1981 millions	Population change 1971–1981, percentages
London 6.7	−9.9%
Conurbations 11.2	−4.6%
Other large cities 2.8	−5.1%
Smaller cities 1.7	−3.2%
Industrial towns 6.7	+3.0%
New towns 2.2	+15.1%
Resorts and retirement areas 3.3	+4.9%
Partly rural areas 9.5	+7.0%
Rural areas 5.0	+10.3%

(Source: OPCS.)

Questions

1 Which *two* areas lost the largest percentage of population between 1971 and 1981?
2 Which *two* areas gained the largest percentage of population between 1971 and 1981?
3 What do you consider to be the *two* most important explanations of de-urbanisation? Give reasons for your answer.

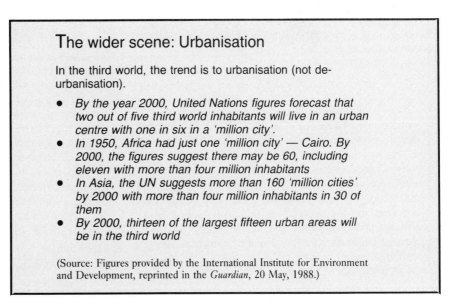

The wider scene: Urbanisation

In the third world, the trend is to urbanisation (not de-urbanisation).

- *By the year 2000, United Nations figures forecast that two out of five third world inhabitants will live in an urban centre with one in six in a 'million city'.*
- *In 1950, Africa had just one 'million city' — Cairo. By 2000, the figures suggest there may be 60, including eleven with more than four million inhabitants*
- *In Asia, the UN suggests more than 160 'million cities' by 2000 with more than four million inhabitants in 30 of them*
- *By 2000, thirteen of the largest fifteen urban areas will be in the third world*

(Source: Figures provided by the International Institute for Environment and Development, reprinted in the *Guardian*, 20 May, 1988.)

117

Stimulus questions
Read the following extracts and answer the questions.
ITEM A

A Survey of community life in the Hanover district of Brighton

As part of our project, we carried out an in-depth survey of local people in a district of pleasant terraced streets, which has the reputation of being a 'strong community.' It's an inner city area that's neither particularly deprived or affluent, though like a number of others it has had its fair share of gentrification.

Although most people liked living in the area, less than half thought it was a community. While the increased 'privatisation' of people's lives — more home orientated, with videos and washing machines — is one explanation offered for weakened local relations, being *outside* the home in paid work figured more prominently in people's comments. One woman who'd lived locally for 21 years, and was in her 60s, said that while she still knew a lot of people in the council flats where she lived, who had moved in when she did, and who were all friendly together, 'There are a lot of new people in now who are out at work all day and so I don't know them.'

'There's a lot of new people moving into this area but they never stay long — they do up the house and move on.'

A lifelong resident in Brighton's Hanover district.

One of the area's first-time buyers.

Our study indicated a clear class division over 'community.' Evidence of two broad groups emerged; middle-class people, who were likely to have lived and to stay in the area for a short time and who had a sense of local community; and working-class residents, who were older and had lived locally longer, who did not. More important, not only were their perceptions different, but the presence of one group seriously affected the 'community' of the other. This became clear in comment after comment of working-class residents:

'It's changed a lot since I was younger. There used to be a lot of older people. Now it's all young couples moving in and first-time buyers.'

'It was (a community), but gradually it's broken up. People come and go a lot — first-time buyers — and then they sell up and move.'

'There are some nice people around here, but though I've lived in this street almost 23 years, I only know a handful of people now.'

'There's a lot of new people and young people in flats. I nod to people, but they don't always take any notice.'

(Source: *New Society*, 17 July 1987.)

Continued over page . . .

ITEM B

Death of a Village

Picture an ideal village, listed in the Domesday Book, cottages with roses round the door, a river running by a water mill, a cluster of houses nestling in a sleepy hollow, a fine old church chiming the hour on the hillside.

Such a village is Netherbury in Dorset, the sort featured in Come to Britain posters and Hovis commercials, a village of the kind that city dwellers like to imagine is their ancient natural home. But like thousands of other villages up and down the country, Netherbury is dying, and dying fast.

The final blow came a few months ago when the last pub closed its doors. The District Council Planning Committee looks set to approve plans submitted by Palmers Brewery, the pub's owners, to demolish the old Brandon Hotel and build a row of seven new houses on the site.

Five years ago the village had two shops, a post office, a village school, a pub and a vicar of its own. Now all have gone. The village has turned into a dormitory, a rural suburb, whose population works, shops or goes to school somewhere else.

The villagers have protested vigorously, got up a large petition and begged the brewers to reconsider. But Palmers refused.

At first the protesters thought they could persuade the District Council Planning Committee not to grant a change of use to the brewers. It seemed to them self-evident that the last remaining village pub should stay, while there were still people wanting to run it as a business. But it appears that planning laws do not take such social considerations into account.

(Source: adapted from the *Guardian*, 16 December, 1985.)

Questions

1 In Item A, approximately how many people thought the area surveyed was a community? (1 mark)
2 In Item B, give one term used to describe an area 'whose population works, shops or goes to school somewhere else'. (1 mark)
3 Look at the photographs and part II of the text of Item A. Use the material to explain the break-up of community in the area. (4 marks)

4 Describe the changes which have led to the 'loss of community' in villages such as Netherbury. (Item B) (6 marks)
5 Describe what you think is meant by 'community'. What are the advantages and disadvantages to people of living in communities? (8 marks)

Activity (class)

Go back to the activity you did on 'Newburgh (p. 116). In the light of the extracts above, would you make any changes to the decisions you made?

Now each draw a rough map of your own area (about three miles across). Put in the main centres of community on the map.

Write a couple of paragraphs saying whether or not you think your area is a community. Some of you could present your work to the class.

Power and people in the city and countryside

A lot is said about 'the problems of the inner city' — high crime rates, high unemployment, urban riots and squalid environment. But what or who causes these problems? Are they avoidable?

People with power in or over the city are, at least partly, responsible for what the city is like. Of course, anybody living in, or even just visiting, the city has *some* power. The ability to drop or pick up a piece of litter involves power. Some individuals and groups have more power than others. By examining who has power in the city, we will get a better idea of the causes of urban problems and prosperity.

Business (capitalism)

Britain's industrial urban areas were, in the first place, the creation of capitalists. It was their money (sometimes borrowed) and their entrepreneurial (business) spirit that first created the 'modern' British city. The great industrial cities of the North and Midlands — Manchester, Leeds, Birmingham — were forged by capitalism. However, when capitalists *disinvest* in an area (i.e. take money/business out of it), unemployment and hardship can follow. This can be made worse when people are replaced by machines in production — *automation*. Parts of the North-East, North-West and Midlands have been hard hit both by disinvestment and automation.

Socialists argue that *where it is necessary in the public interest*, investment should be controlled by *government* so that people can be protected from loss of work and prosperity. Those who take a 'pure' capitalist view argue that capitalists must be left free to seek profit and efficiency in the best place and in the best way possible. They think too much government interference will damage business.

How far should government interfere to prevent the closure of factories and the sometimes disastrous consequences for local communities?

Government (and people)

Both central and local government play important roles in urban *and* rural life in both the economic and social welfare areas.

1   *Economic development*

All the political parties are agreed that what is needed for economic revival in the inner city is more business (whether public or private) and more jobs. We will briefly look at the policies of the Labour and Conservative parties in this area.

There are two main ways in which Labour governments have tried to foster regional economic development:

a   through the *nationalised industries*, for instance, by putting money into the coal industry, and

b   through providing *regional aid*, which was often channelled through local government or special regional authorities which required companies to fit into a regional development plan before providing grants.

Certain local governments, mainly Labour, have sponsored local enterprise, especially in the 1980s. This is an example of *municipal* (town) socialism (see p. 122) For instance, the Greater London Council (now abolished) set up an enterprise board which helped to finance scores of businesses varying from a 'rent a cleaner service' to an Afro-Caribbean restaurant. Often, Labour local authorities showed a fresher approach than Labour governments. Two examples typical of their approach are:

a   *Partnership:* local government often co-operated with private business in financing and managing enterprises. This sometimes resulted in socialist politicians and their advisers working with business people who were strongly Conservative, as, for instance, in Sheffield.

b   *Business co-operatives:* Socialist local authorities usually require some worker participation or even control in return for providing investment funds. In some cases, workers produce, manage and share the profits of the business. Partly because of the help received from municipal socialism, workers' co-operatives increased in number during the 1980s. The Greater London Enterprise Board was a very strong supporter of co-operatives. They particularly suited young people who wanted to pool labour, money and resources.

The Conservative Party has sought economic growth through the private sector. Recent Conservative governments have steadily privatised (returned to private ownership) several previously nationalised industries. Because of the severe plight of the inner cities, Conservative governments have felt the need to give private enterprise a 'helping hand'. Here are two examples:

a   *Urban Development Corporations (UDCs):* these corporations are one of the main means by which the Government hopes to revive the inner cities, as Mrs Thatcher promised to do in 1987. The UDCs hope to attract private capital, and, by 1988, the London Dockland Corporation claimed £2 billion from the private sector.

b   *Targeting money:* in 1988, the Conservative Government began a policy of *targeting* public money to selected *individual* companies which were prepared to locate in the inner city (rather than make grants to local government as Labour did).

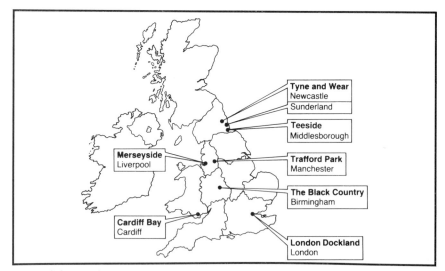

Figure 8.3. UDCs aiming to revive inner cities 'the Thatcher way'.

Employment News

THE DEPARTMENT OF EMPLOYMENT NEWSPAPER MARCH 1988 No. 163

| Twelve 'compacts' planned between schools and industry | More money for local enterprise agencies | Small Firms Service expanded in inner cities | Improved loans for small businesses in inner cities | Enhanced help for unemployed people |

ACTION TO REVIVE THE INNER CITIES

THE Government has announced new measures for the inner cities to help the unemployed, encourage enterprise and forge agreements between schools and local employers.

A key initiative is a plan to provide financial and organisational support from the Manpower Services Commission and the Derpartment of Employment to helop set up 12 inner city Compacts around the country.

Compacts are agreements between industry and schools and colleges by which employers aim to guarantee jobsd to local school-leavers in return for agreed standards of achievement and commitment.

This is how the official Department of Employment newspaper announced 'Action to Revive the Inner Cities'. Are its aims being achieved at the time you are reading this book?

(Source: *Employment News*, March 1988.)

2 The welfare state

One of the main purposes of the welfare state is to provide help for those people whose own income and resources are not enough for them to live at a level considered decent by society. The welfare state is so important that we have given a whole chapter to it (Chapter Seventeen). Here, we need only note that the welfare state is under great pressure and especially so in the inner city. Some of the reasons why the inner city has been especially hard hit are:

a   There are more problems to spend money on in urban areas — mainly due to economic decline.

b   Local governments which have wanted to spend more money than approved by central government have been financially penalised by central government, e.g. Liverpool, Lambeth and Haringey in London.

c   Points a and b have created a vicious circle — social problems have often got worse, which has created money problems, putting more pressure on the welfare state.

'Gatekeepers'

In 'city' terms 'gatekeepers' are not literally people that control gates; they are people who control access to what other citizens want — such as mortgages, bank loans, a local authority house, any kind of welfare benefit, or information about local social services.

More and more services have been provided by both the private and the public sector during the course of this century. Although this has brought great benefits, it has also meant the growth of a great 'army' of people who decide which individuals do or do not qualify for a given service. This is what is meant by the growth of bureaucracy — an ever-increasing number of people handing out and processing an ever-increasing number of forms, i.e. more and more gates to get through — or not. Many find the welfare state bureaucracy complicated and confusing — not least, many welfare recipients. There has been a reaction against bureaucracy, and, in some cases, measures have been taken to simplify and reduce bureaucracy and to help people deal with it, such as the setting up of citizens advice bureaux.

People: participation, protest and movements

People are not equal in the power they have. Every group mentioned so far in this section — business people, politicians, 'gatekeepers' — has enough power to help or harm others. This section concentrates on those with less power. Many citizens have little power, but virtually everybody has some. The following are the main ways in which citizens can and often do exercise their power in the urban context.

Participation

The right to vote in local elections is essential to local democracy. People may vote for positive or negative reasons. On the positive side, they may support certain policies — such as the privatisation of council houses, or the local bus or garbage collection service. On the negative side, they may be angry at something a group of politicians has done (or not done), such as build a road through part of a local park. The negative vote helps to control politicians — who know they can be 'got rid of'.

There are other forms of participation besides voting for local political representatives. People now have rights of representation in most areas of the welfare services. Thus, tenant rights of representation were extended in the 1980 Housing Act and an increase in the number of parent governors on school governing bodies was implemented by the Education Act of 1986. Both tenants and parents of school children have the right to vote for their representatives, but in both cases they can attend certain meetings in person as well.

Protest

People protest about a great variety of matters — either individually or in groups. For instance, an individual may protest about a long delay in dealing with damp in a baby's bedroom; groups may protest against, say, the dumping of nuclear waste in their area.

How people protest is almost as varied as what they protest about. It is important to distinguish between legal and illegal protest. Writing letters, giving speeches, canvassing politicians, holding meetings are rights within the law (subject to certain restrictions mainly relating to other people's convenience and public order). Sitting in front of traffic, drawing protest slogans on walls, withholding taxes are illegal forms of protest.

(Urban) movements

Sometimes a cause of protest attracts so much support that a movement develops. A movement occurs when a large number of people organise in support of a cause over a long period. The squatters' movement is one example. Its 'members' take the view that the rights of the homeless to shelter are more important than the rights of owners of *empty* properties to keep them empty. What do *you* think?

123

Of course, not all social movements are urban. The anti-nuclear weapons movement is one example. This movement is national and international. It included the women's peace camp at the small town of Greenham Common, close to the site of the Cruise missiles. Some of the women adopted tactics of non-violent protest against the siting of the missiles, such as trying to block their entry on to the site.

Questions (answer individually, then discuss in class)

1 Is illegal protest ever justified?
2 If so, give an example, or explain why you think it is never justified.

Citizenship and community

The above examples show that by acting together, 'ordinary' citizens can greatly affect the quality of their community, 'Democracy' should mean that citizens are the most powerful of the groups we have discussed — but only they can make sure that this is so.

Prosperity and problems in the city and countryside

Consumer city

The modern city developed as the main centre of industrial *production*. Of course, many goods and services are still produced in the city, but it has now increasingly become the centre of *consumption* (where things are bought). There are now many more things to be consumed, as a stroll along any main city shopping centre will remind you.

Some groups get more than others in the city. Those with high incomes or great wealth can enjoy the best, whereas, at the opposite extreme, the poor can only look and wish.

Goods and services are distributed (brought) to people for consumption through the private sector (shops, banks, etc), and through the public one, i.e. the welfare state. The welfare state grew up to guarantee basic services to everybody — including health and education. Today, many think it is not fully achieving this. Often, it is the inner urban poor that suffer most.

The urban poor often live within sight of the urban 'core' which is a centre for entertainment and pleasure as well as business. Watching yuppies 'at play' no doubt rubs home to the urban poor that they have missed out on the glamour and glitter of consumer city. Perhaps here lie the seeds of resentment and urban conflict.

Urban problems

The inner city is an area of rich and varied life. Nevertheless, it does have more than its 'share' of big and difficult problems. These include the following:

- unemployment
- poverty
- an underclass
- 'outsider' subcultures
- crime (of certain kinds)
- racism

Because these problems *do* occur in other places as well as the inner city, we examine them in their own right in other sections. Here, we will try to explain why they are often *worse* in the city than elsewhere.

Unemployment (and education/training)

In the mid-1980s, there were many inner city areas where unemployment was as high as 30 and even 50 per cent in places. Young people were particularly hard hit, some being unable to get a permanent job for years.

The decline of certain industries was a main cause of unemployment, but individuals with good qualifications stood a much better chance of getting the jobs that *were* available. A research report from the Economic and Social Research Council (1987) stated that employers preferred job applicants to have good educational qualifications rather than YTS qualifications. In the inner cities, there are often 'job training schemes' but far fewer young people than the national average with good educational qualifications (see p. 99).

Poverty

Not only is there more unemployment in the inner city than elsewhere, many of the jobs that *are* available are low paid and/or temporary. Jobs as cleaners, janitors, shop assistants or selling 'fast food' do not always provide enough income to support a family — and there are more one-wage-earner families in the inner city than elsewhere. Low pay and unemployment lead directly to poverty. In the late 1980s the number of homeless poor wandering in the central areas of big cities appeared to increase. Cuts in spending on housing and the closing down of several large mental hospitals contributed to this.

An underclass

The majority of people in Britain got better off during the 1980s. There were a number of groups which did not take part in this increased prosperity and some individuals and families experienced a real decline in their standard of living.

We can define the underclass as those cut off from prosperity either because they do not work (some retired and the long-term unemployed) or because of low pay. Among the retired, only those entirely dependent on the state pension would be likely to be part of an underclass.

A certain number of the unemployed or low-paid do 'drop out' of regular work more or less altogether. Some do so because they cannot find regular work; others perhaps drift into alternative life-styles through boredom or disappointment with the jobs they have done or had offered to them. For them, the alternatives of long-term dependency on social security or crime beckon.

'Outsider' subcultures

Those who are cut off from mainstream prosperity for years develop their own way of life — a life on the margin, an *'outsider' subculture*. In some areas, such as Toxteth in Liverpool and Handsworth in Birmingham, a second generation of the underclass has reached early adulthood. Like their parents, they are likely not to be in regular work and so work ceases to be at the centre of their lives. Some look for alternative ways to achieve a sense of *status* (importance) or *economic* 'success' (the money to get the things they want). Drug pushing and other forms of crime are one 'solution'. For some inner city kids, to be able to say 'I done my time' is a bit like a suburban kid saying 'I got five GCSEs'.

Once a subcultural way of life has lasted for two or more generations, only a deep change in circumstances is likely to alter it. Better education, better jobs, more money would be part of such a change.

Crime

Certain kinds of crime — such as large-scale financial fraud — are most likely to be committed by businessmen. Equally, other kinds of crime are more likely to occur in the inner city. Your car or your handbag are more 'at risk' in the inner city than in suburbia. So, for that matter, are you. Even self-destructive crimes, such as taking heroin, can lead to crimes against others — simply to get the money to maintain the habit.

Nevertheless, most victims of inner-city criminals are other inner-city residents. They are most in need of effective crime prevention measures.

Crime rise linked to bad design of estates

Badly designed housing estates have been a major factor in the large increase in crime, according to research carried out by London University.

The research shows that crime rates can be halved if features such as linking walkways between blocks of flats are removed. Other design features related to crime include shared corridors, stairs, lifts and entrances and open layouts.

Professor Alice Coleman, head of the research team from the Land Use Research Unit at King's College, says young people who live in the worst designed blocks are seven to eight times more likely to commit crimes than those who live in the best blocks. Yet the Department of the Environment is giving good design awards to new housing schemes that encourage crime, she says.

(Source: the *Independent*, 18 January 1988.)

Race and racism

A variety of ethnic groups are concentrated mainly in the inner cities, including those of Asian and Afro-Caribbean extraction. Typically, members of these groups have worked hard and many have been successful. However, as Chapter Twelve will show, they have often been victims of racism, including racism in the job market. Being 'blocked off' from the normal paths of progress through work has resulted in Afro-Caribbean youth sticking more closely together than they might otherwise have done. They have been more likely to form 'outsider' subcultures than any other groups. Perhaps, the best known are the Rastafarians (see p. 200)

Beyond the city: suburbia and the countryside

Some of the very rich have flats or houses in the urban core, and 'gentrified' areas of middle-class occupation also occur in the inner-city ring. However, most of the middle class live in the suburbs or in the more open country beyond. Since just after the War, better-off manual workers have also been part of the 'flight' from the city into suburbia.

Capitalists, politicians, 'gatekeepers' and ordinary citizens work and struggle in these areas as they do in the city. The difference is that, here, most people see themselves as fairly successful. There *are* areas of rural and suburban poverty, but most households are at least comfortable. A danger is that the problems of the less well-off in suburban and rural areas can easily be overlooked amid the general affluence.

The choice of living in suburbia or the countryside is partly made to gain a more spacious, pleasant and private home and environment. One of the most common issues to arouse middle-class protest is any threat to the local environment. Any proposal to extend building rights in the protected green belt of the Home Counties always provokes strong protests. The prospect of a new airport or a nuclear waste dump is usually enough to provoke those affected to protest.

It is almost 200 years since the peasantry moved from the countryside to the towns. It has often taken several generations of hard work for their descendants to become sufficiently well off to move back to the countryside. Having done so, many put much effort into protecting it. But what they are protecting is no longer the place where most of them *work* — except, perhaps, in the tourist season; it is the place of their *leisure* and *relaxation*.

Country estates plan for surplus land

A million acres of surplus agricultural land could be turned into small country estates for the well-off, if a proposal launched today by the Royal Institution of Chartered Surveyors wins government support...

It wants the Government to change its guidelines to make it easier for farmers to get planning permission for the building of new homes on unwanted land. Not any old houses, but the acceptable face of housebuilding — the small country estate...

Simon Pott, a RICS spokesman, said the typical estates would range from 50 to 100 acres and that one planning application would cover the main house, staff cottages, stables, barns, parkland, lakes and woods.

(Source: the *Independent*, 12 May 1988.)

Country manor: Simon Pott, of the RICS, which has launched plans to turn a million acres of surplus arable land into small country estates.

Questions

1 Who do you think might buy property on these proposed new estates?
2 What do you think of the idea of building these estates?

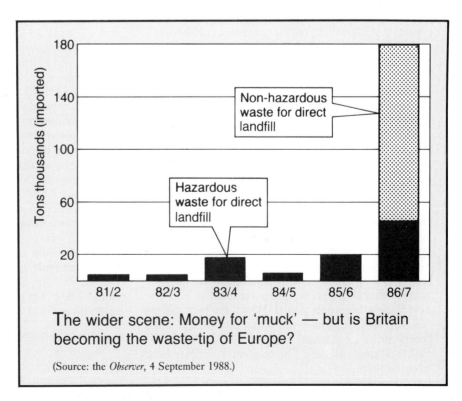

The wider scene: Money for 'muck' — but is Britain becoming the waste-tip of Europe?

(Source: the *Observer*, 4 September 1988.)

Stimulus questions

Read the following extracts and answer the questions.

ITEM A

'I used to pay £400 or £500, now it's £1,500. I can't afford it, and there's another increase on the way.'
Mohammed Zaib, Azim's Restaurant

'It's not just the insurance. Trade has dropped off since the riots. We need new blood, with new ideas and new types of business.'
Basil Clarke, electrical contractor

In the aftermath of the inner-city riots, there has been little general awareness of the problems which inner-city businesses face in getting insured.

What of those quite essential small businessmen who have suffered so much from inner-city disturbances?

Ahmed Ashraf owns three chemist shops in Birmingham. After the 1985 riots his previous insurance company refused to insure him despite the fact that his premises were well secured with alarms and security doors. After remaining uninsured for two months, he eventually managed to find a company that would insure his business at six times the original premium.*

* Note: A premium is the amount of money you pay each year to be insured.

Many of the businesses in riot-hit areas suffered twice over. During the Brixton disturbances in 1981, more than 70 businesses suffered damage. In 40 cases the damage was restricted to broken windows, but in 30 there were more serious losses through theft or damages to stock and property. In Toxteth in 1981 and Handsworth in 1985, there was also extensive fire damage during the disturbances. In Handsworth, 42 properties were completely gutted or badly damaged by fire. And in the aftermath — in Sparkhill, Sparkbrook, Moss Side, Tottenham and Toxteth — small businesses have faced serious problems in obtaining insurance cover.

These problems vary in degree. First, many insurance companies are demanding expensive security measures such as tougher doors, laminated security windows, metal shutters and alarm systems. Second, many companies have increased premiums to levels which are unaffordable for many small businesses. Finally, some businesses simply cannot get insurance at any price. This is particularly affecting ethnic businesses.

(Source: Adapted from *New Society*, 11 December 1987.)

ITEM B

Under the beautiful Isle of Purbeck lurk at least 200 million barrels of easily recoverable oil. British Petroleum this summer gained planning permission to expand a small oilfield on the peninsula, and by the end of 1989 Purbeck and Poole harbour will be producing 60,000 barrels a day — almost as much as a small North Sea oil field. After BP's announcement last week that fresh discoveries have been made in Bournemouth Bay, oil extraction at Purbeck may develop still further.

The oil works are mostly on the Rempstone estate, four and a half thousand acres of downs and poorish farmland where BP is digging a new pipeline and expanding two smaller oil well sites and a gathering station. . .

BP has also concentrated on a faultlessly smooth public relations exercise. It includes a local liaison group with parishioners, stalls at local fairs, a 24-hour information and complaints service, a local Wytch Farm development newspaper. Nearly everyone agrees that the PR (public relations) department act on complaints and are polite. Their success has nevertheless been only partial. While one lady told me 'There's an awfully nice one with a bow tie and a red sports car,' a local tenant farmer remarked, 'They've took it all over. (Pause.) The buggers. It'll never be the same no more.'

BP has had to try hard. Purbeck is an Area of Outstanding Natural Beauty and the pipeline runs through a series of Sites of Special Scientific Interest and out on to a Heritage Coast. According to local conservation groups, including the Nature Conservancy Council and Friends of the Earth, the company is doing quite a good job. BP sponsors preliminary archaeological digs. It monitors air and noise pollution. It is timing building programmes so as not to disturb the winter nesting grounds of waterfowl. Building contractors are issued environmental guidelines and workmen go through a training courses where they learn not to smoke cigarettes, play radios, dump waste or stray beyond demarcation lines.

For James Ryder, a local landowner, the real environmental problem isn't BP — who will be virtually gone in three years — but the 'grockles' (tourists or outsiders) who come in cars and caravans and block the public roads. He says: 'Ideally we would like to see them issue passports at Wareham to keep them out. But the problem is that we depend on them for our living. They help pay the rates and I have a share in a campsite and a couple of holiday homes.'

(Source: Adapted from *New Society*, 11 December 1987.)

Continued over page . . .

Questions

1 State in one sentence the main problem experienced by the traders in Handsworth. (Item A) (1 mark)
2 State in one sentence, the main problem experienced by the residents of the Rempstone estate. (Item B) (1 mark)
3 a Give *two* ways in which the traders of Handsworth lost money as a result of the urban 'riots'. (Item A) (2 marks)
  b Explain how *other* residents of Handsworth may have been inconvenienced by what happened to the traders following the 'riots'. (Item A) (2 marks)
4 a Give one way in which the environment of the Rempstone estate is officially protected. (Item B) (1 mark)
  b What does one resident of the Rempstone estate, James Ryder, see as a bigger problem than BP, and why is he prepared to put up with this problem? (Item B) (2 marks)
5 Why do you think the problems of the Handsworth traders seem less easy to solve than those of the residents of the Rempstone estate? (Items A and B) (3 marks)
6 With reference to Item A, what conclusions do you draw about the reasons for inner-city decline? (4 marks)
7 What suggestions can you give for making the inner cities more prosperous? (4 marks)

Activity (class/outside class)

Each of the following four groups of people contributes to urban life. Discuss the ways in which each group can play either a positive or a negative part in urban life. This list has some clues to help you:

Capitalists — creators of wealth or exploiters of people?
Government — helper of the poor or waster of tax payers' money?
Gatekeepers — providers of services or obstacles to people getting what they need?
The people — solvers of their own problems or failures in participation?

Structured questions

1 Describe what is meant by 'community'. (3 marks)
2 Discuss, with reasons, whether you think that *you* live in a 'community' or not. (5 marks)
3 Listed below are four aspects of modern life. For each one, discuss how that particular aspect might be different for people living in towns and people living in rural areas (if you think that there are no differences, say why): a) neighbours, b) housing, c) crime, d) amenities. (12 marks)

Project and assignment suggestions

1 *Exploring community* — Is your street or the immediate neighbourhood in which you live a community? It might be an interesting project to find out. Whatever your impressions are, you need to go about your investigation using proper sociological methods. First, however, you need to define what you mean by community — then, you can decide how to measure it in your neighbourhood. Make sure you keep your project within practical limits — for instance, you can't observe or interview everybody, even in *one* street.
2 *What are the main centres (or focal points) of your local community?* For instance a main centre might be a local church (or there may be some strong *joint* church activity). Who organises and who participates in church-run activity? Who does not participate? Again, you will need to use good methods of enquiry to find out. Vague impressions are no use. Other possible centres of community are pubs, launderettes and community centres. You might decide to study one in detail, or two or three in less detail. In either case, you will need to select appropriate methods.
3 *Who has power in your community?* — For this project, you might take a wider definition of community to include a whole town or region. Do certain *individuals* have a lot of power? If so, are they politicians, businessmen, or what? Or is it *groups* that seem to have most power, such as trade unions, political parties or the Rotary Club (a club for business people)? Your sources for a project along these lines are likely to include material from the local media.
4 *Investigating a community issue* — If the previous suggestion seems too broad, you might study one particular community issue that has occurred in your area. What have local people got concerned about and perhaps protested about? A nuclear waste dump? The building of a road through an attractive area? The closing of a school? Your project is likely to involve some library work researching press coverage of the issue, and perhaps one or two interviews with key participants.
5 *Make-believe communities* — A very different project would be to study community as it is portrayed in a piece of media fiction — such as 'Neighbours', 'Brookside' or 'EastEnders'. Part of the project would be descriptive — who are the leading characters and what are the main centres of community? How much like real life is the fictional community? Is the sense of community very important to the series or not? What do viewers get out of 'experiencing' the fictional community? Be careful not to spend to much space *merely describing* events and relationships.

Key words

Community
De-urbanisation
Participation (political)
Urbanisation
Urban movement

CHAPTER *9* Wealth and *Leisure*

Introduction: definitions

Leisure is the time when people do as they choose — their 'own time'. However, people's choices are influenced by many commercial interests. Many leisure pursuits are now big business.

Leisure: your time or theirs??

Often people think of life in terms of just work and leisure. However, as Figure 9.1 shows, in practice, people do not divide up their time quite so simply as that. Most people spend about half of any 24-hour period in activity that is neither strictly work nor leisure. This is *obligated* time — spent doing necessary things in relation to home, work or bodily functioning.

Figure 9.1. Two views of leisure time

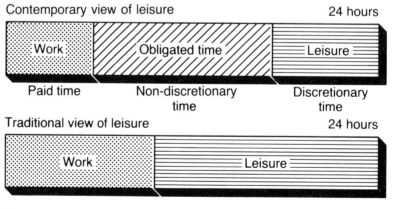

(Source: *Sociology Update*, 1987.)

Work

Work-related activities,
e.g. travelling to and from work

Catering for biological needs,
e.g. sleeping, eating

Family management (in addition to housework), e.g. planning a mortgage

Leisure

paid work or housework

} obligated (not free) time

discretionary (free) time

The amount of time spent on obligated (necessary) activities, can greatly affect the rest of life. Someone who has a one- or two-hour drive to work will probably have less leisure time than somebody who 'lives over the shop'. However, drivers may be able partly to 'convert' obligated time into leisure time by listening to a car radio or cassette tape, or even turn it into work time by using a car phone to make business calls. 'High-tech' can help to break down the barriers between work and leisure.

Activity (class)

Take three 'typical' days in your life, say, a Monday, a Saturday and a Sunday. For *each* day, work out roughly how much time in each 24-hour period (starting at midnight and ending 24 hours later) you spend on various activities. Try to make the estimates add up to 24 hours (even though they are approximate). The times you spend on various activities are likely to differ over the three days; for example, you might have a paid job on Saturdays, spend longer in bed on Sundays, do more school or college work on Mondays.

For each day, decide the amounts of time spent under the following headings (decide for yourself under which heading to put school or college work):

Work
Work-related activities
Obligated time
Discretionary time

Discuss this as a class. Where do you think time spent at school/college should go? What about homework? Were there any big differences between people in the group, for example, between those with part-time jobs and those without, or between males and females?

One person's leisure is another person's work

Leisure is a freely chosen activity, usually done for 'fun'. Once a person gets paid for an activity, it becomes a job. Doing ballet or playing football may be leisure activities to you or me, but for many people they are ways of making a living — work. Like leisure, work is not defined by the activity itself, but by the purpose for which it is done. The main purpose of work is to make a living or, in the case of domestic work, to maintain a home.

Activity (class)

1 List *two* of your own leisure activities that some people do not as leisure but as work.
2 List *two* of your leisure activities which, as far as you know, are not done as work by anybody.

An age of leisure

More people have more time and money for leisure than ever before in Britain. In addition, a greater variety of leisure pursuits are available. Britain is increasingly becoming a leisure society.

The most frequent home-based activity is watching TV, whereas listening to the radio is declining slightly. Gardening comes next, with DIY not far behind. Home is now the focus of most leisure activity.

Participation in sport is booming. Research by the Sports Council shows that between 1977 and 1983, sports participation increased by 25 per cent. This reflects both increased interest in keeping fit, as well as the pursuit of pleasure. However, much sporting activity is not competitive. The most popular sports are walking (perhaps better called 'recreation' than 'sport') and swimming.

131

Figure 9.2. *Viewing figures. Sport: Are more people participating rather than watching?*

	1985	1987
World Snooker Final	18.2m	10.6m
FA Cup Final	18m	15.4m
Wimbledon Men's Final	10m	8.2m
Wrestling	7m	4m
Big Match (recorded)	2.8m	1.8m

(Source: the *Observer*, 8 May 1988.)

Among non-sporting, out-of-home activities, going for a drink and/or meal tops the list. Going to the cinema comes next, but only just ahead of visiting the countryside. Total visits to the cinema are now only a fraction of what they were in the 1950s. Why do you think this is?

As Table 9.1 shows, the leisure industry persuades people to spend a great deal of money:

Table 9.1. *Selected categories of UK consumers' expenditure in 1985* £ million

Motor Vehicles	9916
Beer	8347
Cigarettes	6115
Electricity	4860
Furniture and floor coverings	4639
Sport including gambling	4366
Bread	4051
Gas	4046
Menswear	3981
Spirits	3861
Wines and ciders	3847
Sport, excluding gambling	3207
DIY goods	2616
Newspapers and magazines	2273
Pets	1278
Records	783
Bingo admissions	288
Cinema	125

(Source: The Economic Impact and Importance of Sport in the UK, Sports Council, 1987, quoted in the *Guardian*, 7 May 1988.)

Questions

How many of the above list of 18 items of expenditure are leisure items? Would you say the list provides justification for saying that Britain is becoming 'a leisure society'?

Causes of the increase in leisure activity

1   Science and technology

Improving technology based on scientific research and development is part of the foundation of modern changes in work and leisure. Science and technology have increased the amount of leisure time and the variety of leisure activities by:

1   releasing workers from manual labour — through automation;
2   enabling more people to work in the service (including leisure) industries;
3   creating more leisure time and wealth;
4   producing new leisure pursuits (e.g. computer games) and changing traditional ones (plastic football pitches), and
5   enabling people to travel more easily (better transport and communications)

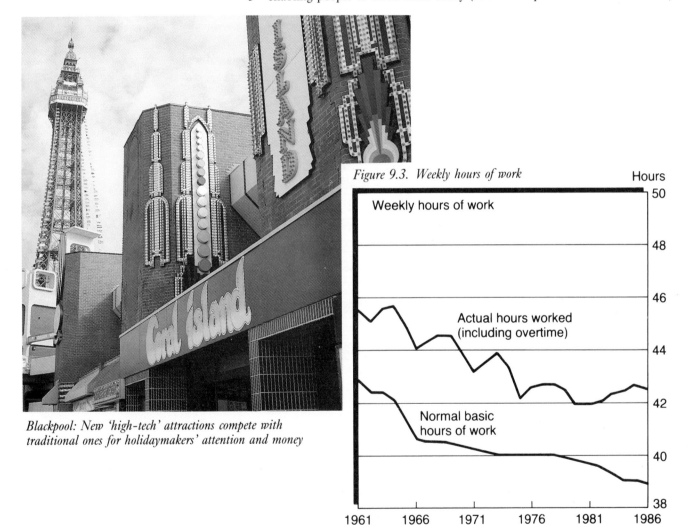

Blackpool: New 'high-tech' attractions compete with traditional ones for holidaymakers' attention and money

Figure 9.3. Weekly hours of work

(Source: *Social Trends*, 1988.)

2   Decline in weekly hours of work and increase in paid holiday entitlement

---

Activity (class)

What was the decline in weekly hours of work (including overtime) between 1961 and 1986 (Figure 9.3)? See if you can find out why the decline in actual hours worked temporarily stopped in about 1979.

133

The trend to fewer hours worked applies to all paid occupational groups. However, note that an increasing number of women work a 'double-shift' — of paid and domestic work.

Average paid holiday entitlement has increased in parallel with the decline in length of the working week:

- In **1961** 97 per cent of full-time employees were entitled to only two weeks paid holiday.
- In **1986**, 100 per cent were entitled to four weeks or more.

3 Increase in income and items to spend it on

The income of the 'average' Briton was twice as high in 1987 as in 1945. For most of those in work, income increased especially sharply during the 1980s. (In addition, people borrowed more money, particularly during the late 1980s.) The sizeable minority of low-paid and unemployed people largely missed out on this increase in prosperity (see the activity at the end of this section).

Figure 9.4 More wealth and consumption in 1980s Britain.

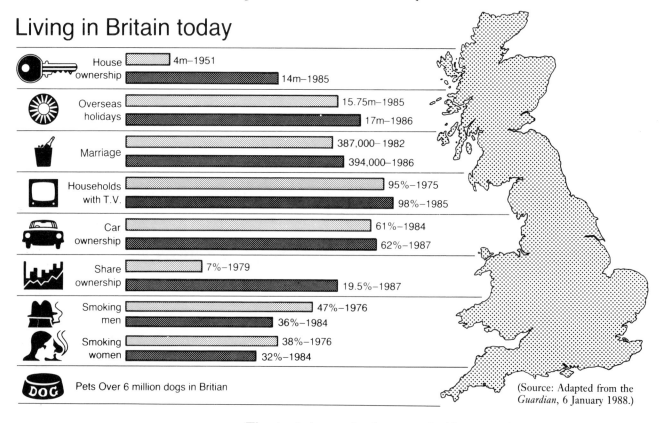

The rise in income has been matched by a massive rise in consumption. We now live in an age of *mass consumption* — even though there is great and growing inequality between what different groups can afford to consume. The term mass consumption means that a large number of items are bought by many households or individuals. In-home consumption is mainly on leisure items and new or improved household appliances. Television remains the most common leisure item: in 1987, 98 per cent of households had one television, over 50 per cent two, and 13.5 per cent three or more. In the same year, 13 per cent of households had a computer and nearly 44 per cent a video recorder. Many of the new or improved household appliances create more leisure (or work) time, such as microwaves (25 per cent) and tumble dryers (30 per cent).

Such is the boom in domestic consumption that the term 'the consumer home' is now sometimes used.

Stimulus questions

Read the following extracts and answer the questions.

ITEM A

Britain is a land of lager drinkers, take-away eaters and television addicts, according to the official view of the nation published yesterday. The book, *Britain 1988*, produced by the Government's information service for the Foreign Office, reveals many details about the way we spend our money and live our lives.

Those in work are clearly better off. They form the home-owning (more than 60 per cent), share-buying (19.5 per cent) democracy the Government has pledged to create.

The survey shows that most of their extra money goes on consumer goods. Nearly every household has at least one television (98 per cent) and half of them have two.

Ownership of telephones, freezers and cars has increased, and we spend more time watching television — 27 hours a week, on average — eating out, eating take-aways and doing DIY. Lager has overtaken traditional beer as the nation's most popular drink.

(Source: adapted from the *Independent*, 6 January 1988.)

ITEM B

Figure 9.5

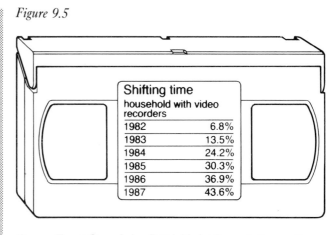

Shifting time household with video recorders	
1982	6.8%
1983	13.5%
1984	24.2%
1985	30.3%
1986	36.9%
1987	43.6%

(Source: Target Group Index, British Market Research Bureau, *New Society* Database, 13 May 1988.)

ITEM C

Levels of participation in sport have been rising due mainly to the increases in leisure time and facilities, greater mobility and rising living standards. A growing awareness of the importance to good health of regular exercise has been reflected in the upsurge of interest in jogging, keep fit and dance-related forms of exercise. It has been estimated that nearly half of the adult population regularly takes part in sport, men still outnumbering women. Walking is by far the most popular recreational activity, followed by swimming, snooker and billiards, darts, angling, athletics, football, squash, golf and cycling.

(Source: *Social Trends*, 1988.)

Questions

1 Name *two* items that are linked to 'the better off'. (Item A)   (2 marks)
2 What percentage of households possessed a video recorder in:
   a) 1982   (1 mark)
   b) 1987? (Item B)   (1 mark)
3 What is the most popular recreational activity? (Item C)   (1 mark)
   Give *one* reason why this might be so. (Item C)   (1 mark)
4 Define the term *mass consumption*.   (2 marks)
5 Using evidence from the stimulus material, discuss the view that Britain has become a consumer society.   (4 marks)

Activity (class/outside class)

People can be divided into the leisure rich and the leisure poor. As Figure 9.6 shows, there is only one way of being leisure rich — having the time and the money — but several ways of being leisure poor.

Make your own copy of Figure 9.6. Now put the people in the list below the figure into their appropriate boxes. Then add one more of your own to each box.

Low-paid worker
Unemployed father of a young family
Pop music superstar
Large company manager

Figure 9.6

The leisure rich	The time and the money
The leisure poor	The money but not the time
	The time but not the money
	Neither the time nor the money

Variety and differences in leisure and life-styles

Among the many factors that contribute to variety and differences in leisure are age, ethnicity (race/culture), gender and class. Others you might consider are local tradition (such as tossing the caber in the Highlands of Scotland) and local geography (boating in certain seaside areas).

Age

Certain leisure activities and life-styles are associated with particular age groups (see Chapter Thirteen and the Stimulus Question of this section). For instance, spectacular dress and make-up — partly to do with attracting possible mates — are especially associated with youth. Few elderly or middle-aged people could carry off the style of this young punk.

A young punk

A restaurant specialising in West-Indian food

Ethnicity

There is as much ethnic variety in leisure and culture as there are ethnic groups in Britain (see Chapter Thirteen). Jews, Italians, Afro-Caribbeans, Asians and many more contribute to the variety of cultural life in Britain. Many examples of ethnic cultural variety are given in Chapter Twelve.

Gender

Figure 9.7. Leisure time in a typical week, 1986, by sex

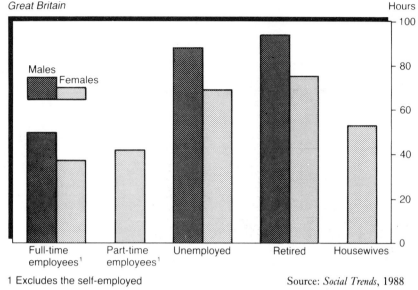

Great Britain

1 Excludes the self-employed

Source: *Social Trends*, 1988

Questions

1 What is the leisure pattern shown in Figure 9.7 according to sex?
2 How do you account for this pattern?

Class

Even though growth in national wealth has greatly increased the average amount of consumption per head, major differences in consumption between the social classes remain. These can be summarised as differences in:

- quality
- exclusivity
- taste

It is easiest to illustrate these differences in relation to the life-style of the rich, but they also apply to other social classes.

Differences in *quality* available to the rich can be easily illustrated:

Popular consumer item	Only the rich can afford a
Car	Rolls-Royce
Watch	Cartier
House	Mansion

No doubt you can continue this list for yourself.

There are certain items that cost so much that they are virtually *exclusive* to the rich. Only the very wealthy few can own race horses, furs, afford to dine regularly at top restaurants, and travel easily around the world.

Differences in leisure habits between the classes reflect differences of cultural *taste* as well as material (money) differences. Most upper and upper-middle-class people are socialised to like things different from the working class. Probably, most working-class males would say they preferred football to polo and most working-class women bingo to the opera. A less obvious difference — in the number of recreational trips taken to the countryside — is illustrated in Figure 9.8 and the questions are aimed at making you think why the difference exists.

137

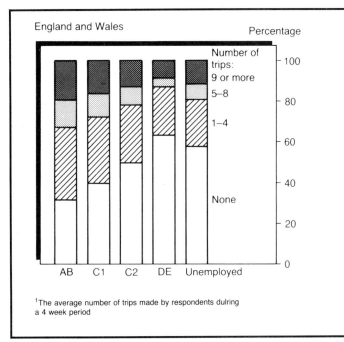

England and Wales

Percentage

Number of trips:

9 or more

5–8

1–4

None

AB   C1   C2   DE   Unemployed

[1]The average number of trips made by respondents dulring a 4 week period

Figure 9.8. Recreational trips[1] to the countryside: by social class of head of household, 1986

(Source: National Countryside Recreation Survey, Countryside Commission in *Social Tends*, 1988.)

Questions

1   Why do you think the unemployed take more recreational trips to the countryside than social class DE, but less than AB?

2   Write a paragraph explaining how recreational trips to the countryside might help children.

Do the above differences in leisure and life-style between the classes matter very much? Does the inequality that underlies them create gaps that are too big between people? There is much disagreement on the answers to these questions — not only among politicians but among the rest of the population.

There are several reasons for people being less concerned about these differences than might be expected. First, people usually compare themselves with others in a *similar* position — for most of us the rich are 'out of sight'. Second, the majority of households have been getting better off and improving their leisure facilities. Despite income differences, the majority have quite a wide choice of leisure activities. Third, the media rarely question unequal cultural and leisure opportunities. In fact, the popular media present the 'doings' of the rich as entertainment for the rest. Nevertheless, many people feel that more of the wealth of the rich should be used to improve the opportunities of the less well-off — including cultural and leisure opportunities.

Publicly and privately funded leisure facilities

Both publicly (through taxation) and privately (through business investment) funded leisure facilities have increased during the leisure boom. The idea behind publicly funded cultural and leisure facilities is to keep entry free or, at least, cheap, so that as many as possible can enjoy and benefit from them. In the past, local authorities have provided libraries, parks and museums — for all local citizens. More recently, some local authorities have provided sports and health-and-fitness facilities. The number of local authority sports centres grew from twenty in 1972 to 1500 in 1987.

Private enterprise provides leisure services for profit. In 1978, the top five areas of leisure activity in Britain were television, alcohol, sex related, tobacco and gambling — all multi-million pound industries. Newer markets, such as leisure centres, theme parks, and health and fitness clubs, are increasingly attracting commercial money. There are now over 1500 private health and fitness clubs operating up and down the country. Indoor swimming pools with such attractions as wave machines, water slides, sand and tropical vegetation have been built in several resorts, including Blackpool's 'Sandcastle'.

Entrance fees to privately operated leisure facilities can be quite high — too high for a poor family. At the same time, because of cuts in central government financial support, fees have also been introduced or increased for entry to many national and local public facilities. As the following report shows, this sometimes applied even to traditionally 'free' cultural facilities.

Museums plead for £22m lifeline

Britain's national museums and galleries need £22 million urgently to overcome the immediate problems caused by a shortfall in central government funding, the Museums and Galleries Commission said yesterday.

In the first report of its kind for almost 60 years, the commission said that, as a result of the shortfall, galleries had been closed, opening hours curtailed and security reduced. Museums had been unable to produce scholarly publications or to help schools, inefficient use had been made of staff time and the quality of service to the public had declined.

The commission's report, published yesterday, challenges the Government 'to live up to its responsibility for funding the national museums and their essential activities'.

The report suggests that trustees of the national museums should be free to decide to introduce admission charges as a means of producing extra revenue, but it warns that private funding, donations and business sponsorship cannot 'in the nature of things be relied upon as regular sources. They are liable to dry up in hard times or on change of policy.'

Nicholas de Jongh
Arts Correspondent

(Source: the *Guardian*, 5 May 1988.)

Two theories of leisure

The first of these theories is the work-leisure model. The theory is that the kind of work that people do is the main influence on their leisure. The second theory is that we have now entered a period in which leisure itself is becoming the most important part of people's lives. This is why earlier in this chapter the term 'an age of leisure' was used to refer to the present.

The work-leisure model

Stanley Parker argues that the type of work a person does greatly affects their leisure activities. A person's job and their class position are closely connected. In Figure 9.9, based on Parker, class, work and pattern of leisure are all related:

Figure 9.9

Class	Occupation (example)	Relationship of work to leisure
(Upper) middle	Lecturer	Extension
(Lower) middle	Clerk	Neutral
Working	Miner	Opposition

The *extension* pattern occurs when a person 'carries over' work into 'leisure' time — perhaps out of interest or ambition (members of high occupational groups are more likely to take work home). The *neutrality* pattern occurs when a person's leisure has little or no relationship to work — it is mainly for relaxation. The *opposition* pattern occurs when a person seeks an 'escape' from work in leisure — such as a miner or factory worker who 'washes away' the tensions and grime of work with a 'few pints'.

A big criticism of the work-leisure theory is that it does not apply to those whose main work is housework — still the majority of women. Domestic work does not easily fit into a nine to five routine, but has to be done as needed — at different times of the day and night.

The leisure society theory, is not opposed to the work-leisure model but it gives a different, perhaps more up-to-date view of leisure.

The leisure society theory

The 'leisure society' theory is that leisure is increasingly becoming a more central concern in people's lives. Increasing leisure time and facilities, and money to spend on them, has brought about the 'age of leisure'.

In this view, leisure is increasingly detached from work. People work to get money for leisure, rather than spend leisure recovering and preparing for work. As early as the 1950s, Goldthorpe and Lockwood found that a group of affluent (better-off) workers in Luton were not much bothered about work satisfaction, but worked mainly for money to spend on their homes and leisure. With more and more leisure items available, this is perhaps becoming the attitude of most people.

Both the variety of leisure opportunities and the variety of people's leisure choices is seen as separating off leisure from work. The majority of 'comfortably off' people — whether defined as middle or working class — increasingly overlap in their various leisure choices. The leisure society theory seems to suggest that what Parker referred to as the neutrality pattern of world-leisure is becoming more widespread.

Conclusion: is more leisure a good thing?

Most people would readily agree that having more money and time to spend on more things is a good thing. However, perhaps 'more' is not necessarily 'better'. How good is the *quality* of leisure life in modern Britain (pp. 64–5)? Is it possible that greed, perhaps fuelled by advertising, is on the increase? Should some of the money spent on luxury items be spent on the more basic requirements of the less well-off? In the end, does more leisure and more things make people happier — or does happiness depend on something else?

Stimulus questions

Read the following extracts and answer the questions.

ITEM A

Favourite leisure	Group 1	2	3	4
Sample No.	143	149	139	132
Watching TV	6	10	15	17
Home crafts	6	11	12	17
Reading	10	11	12	7
Creative arts	14	3	1	1
Listening to music	8	8	3	6
Theatre/film	10	3	4	2
Gardening	6	3	1	3
Sport/dancing	16	21	12	11
Walking/driving	5	6	5	3
Exploring/sightseeing	3	1	4	3
Being with family/friends	14	11	21	14
Other	14	10	11	15

Table 9.2. Favourite leisure activities by aggregated total and group (percentages)

From a survey in Birmingham in 1974, group 1 = social class I & II (professional/managerial); group 2 = social class II non-manual (clerical); group 3 = social class III manual (skilled); group 4 = social class IV & V (semi-and unskilled).

(Source: Adapted from 'Popular Culture and Everyday Life', Book 3, Unit 10, Open University Press, 1981.)

ITEM B

Table 9.3. Leisure activities of elderly people: England (Percentages)   (Source: *Social Trends*, 1979.)

Hobbies:	Men 65–74	75–84	85 and over	All 65 and over	Women 65–74	75–84	85 and over	All 65 and over
Knitting	1	1	—	1	54	37	29	47
Needlework	—	—	—	—	22	20	10	20
Gardening	45	25	20	39	22	12	6	18
Outdoor sport:								
Participant	14	5	6	12	3	—	—	2
Spectator	11	7	9	10	2	—	—	1
Sample size (= 100%)	565	375	54	994	789	688	151	1,628

Continued over page . . .

Questions

1 For which leisure activity is there the greatest difference in popularity between group 1 and group 4? (Item A)
(1 mark)

2 What was the *second* most popular leisure activity among group 3? (Item A) (1 mark)

3 Give *two* explanations why watching TV might be less popular with groups 1 and 2 than with groups 3 and 4. (Item A) (2 marks)

4 Which leisure activity of elderly people showed the *least* gender difference? (Item B) (1 mark)

5 What reasons can you suggest for the gender differences in the leisure activities of the elderly? (Item B) (4 marks)

6 Using material from items A, B and elsewhere, describe and explain *three* factors which influence people's leisure pursuits. (6 marks)

Activity (class)

Which age and/or social class groups are well catered for by leisure facilities in your area, and which are not? Get into groups of three or four people who live in the same area and have a 'brainstorming' session to produce the answers.

Structured questions

1 Explain what is meant by the term 'leisure rich', and give *two* examples of groups of people that you think are 'leisure rich'. (3 marks)

2 Explain what is meant by the term 'leisure poor', and give *two* examples of groups of people that you think are 'leisure poor'. (3 marks)

3 Discuss *three* reasons why, for many people, 'leisure time' has increased (6 marks)

4 Giving reasons for your answers, describe what you think might be 'typical' leisure pursuits of the following people: a) a highly paid business executive, b) a middle-class teenage boy, c) a housewife with two young children, d) a long-distance lorry driver. (8 marks)

Project and assignment suggestions

1 *A test of Parker's hypothesis that the type of work people do affects their leisure pursuits* — You would need to draw a sample of people from different occupational groupings (e.g. professional, clerical, manual) and design a questionnaire to obtain information on how they spend their leisure time. You would then need to analyse the results, to see whether your findings agreed with those of Parker. (It might prove helpful to look at a copy of Parker's book, *The Sociology of Leisure*, George Allen and Unwin, 1976.)

2 *A test of the 'leisure society' hypothesis* that leisure is an increasingly important part of people's lives, and that people of all classes work mainly to earn money to spend on leisure and recreation. You would need a sample drawn from different classes, and your questionnaire would need to be worded very carefully to be able to get information which would allow you to test the hypothesis.

3 *An examination of leisure outside the home* — You could make this a local study, by first doing a survey of all the leisure facilities available in your area, and then finding out (perhaps partly by observation and partly by interview) what sort of people use them. You might find examples of clear gender and age differences in the use of various leisure facilities.

4 *The leisure activities of a particular group* — This could be based on age, or you could look at a group of generally 'leisure-poor' people — mothers with young children. You might be able to persuade one or two of them to keep a diary for a week, so that you could analyse the use of time into work, work-related, obligated and discretionary time.

5 *The leisure activities of a particular ethnic group* — Your ability to carry out this research may vary according to whether or not you are a member of the ethnic group you choose to study. Keep the project manageable — focus on just one or two families, or a group of friends. You could then try to compare their leisure habits with those of 'average' native Britons to identify any similarities and differences.

Key words

Leisure

Obligated time

CHAPTER 10 Class

Class differentiation and stratification

The two systems of education: how much have things really changed?

(Source: Bert Hardy, *Picture Post*, reproduced in *New Society*, 26 October 1978.)

Into which social class would you put the boy on the left of the picture? In which class would you say the boys on the right belong?

Most of you have probably put the boy on the left in the 'upper' or 'upper-middle' class and the boys on the right into the 'working' class. How were you able to do this? The answer is that you were able to pick out certain visual clues about what class the boys belong to.

There are many 'clues' or *factors* relating to a person's class. The following activity is intended to help you think of some for yourself.

Activity (class)

There are two stages to this activity — individual and group, and its purpose is to help you to realise and use what you *already* know about class.

Individual stage — List *eight* factors which show to what class a person belongs. Examples are clothes or accent.

Group stage — In small groups (three or four), try to agree on the *five* most important factors and list them in order of importance.

Class discussion — Someone from each group should write its list on the board and the *group* should justify the order in which it puts the factors.

A useful follow-up activity is to divide the eight factors into two lists: material and cultural. Material factors are things you can see and touch, such as housing, clothes and money. Cultural factors relate to thinking and behaving, such as education and leisure pursuits.

It is on the basis of such *differentiation* (establishing differences) that *class stratification* (putting people into class groupings) is done.

Defining class

In the previous activity, you probably did not fully agree about the exact order in which to rank the factors which decide a person's social class. Neither do sociologists entirely agree on this matter. However, with the important exception of Karl Marx (see p.144), nearly all sociologists rank a person's class mainly according to occupation. Occupational differentiation is, then, a major basis of class stratification.

The most widely used occupational class scale has been the Registrar General's. However, this has become out of date especially because it does not provide enough occupational categories in which women are concentrated. In the early 1990s, it was replaced by the Standard Occupational Classification which, unlike the Registrar General's scale, is in line with the International Standard Classification of Occupations and better represents occupations in which women are concentrated.

The nine major groups of the SOC are given below. The nine major groups are divided into 76 minor groups which in turn are divided into 364 unit groups.

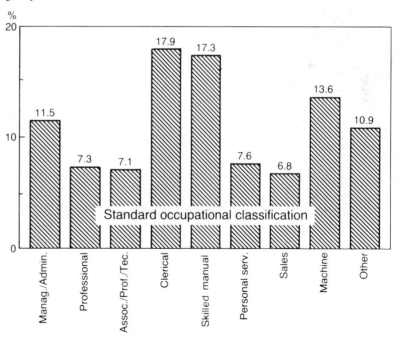

The Standard Occupational Classification (SOC)

Activity

Try to find out *one* occupation for each category ('other' includes cleaners and shop assistants).

In addition to the SOC, a group at Surrey University has also developed a new occupational class scale and this is given on page 146.

Comments on the Standard Occupational Classification

The SOC is both more up-to-date and less sexist than the Registrar General's Occupational Class Scale. However, it has still not solved the problem of classifying the main form of *unpaid* work — housework. This is part of a wider official tendency not to calculate and evaluate housework. For instance, it is not included in estimates of the country's gross domestic product (GDP) — the measure of what the country produces.

It is important to note that occupational *differentiation* (difference) is not the only basis on which a person's class can be calculated. Differences of property and unearned wealth (perhaps inherited) are also a basis for dividing people into different class groups. Thus, members of the *upper class* own much unearned property and wealth and the *poor* (or *underclass*) little or nothing. Therefore, in addition to occupational class, it is useful to use four broad class groupings:

Upper Class   Middle Class   Working Class   Poor (Underclass)

Activity

Try to agree among yourselves on *two* examples of members of *each* of the above four classes. (Remember, sociologists themselves do not fully agree on who goes into which class.)

Two views of class: Marx and Weber

Marx argued that in capitalist society, class conflict occurs between capitalists and workers. He believed that eventually the working class would win this conflict and that a socialist society would be formed.

Modern Marxists, appreciating that there are now fewer manual workers, often include service sector employees — many of whom are women — in their definition of 'working class'.

Karl Marx (1818–1883)
Ownership of the means of producing goods (or services) or lack of ownership is the basis of class, e.g. capitalist society in which the two main classes are divided into *capitalists* who own machinery and wealth, and *workers* who have to sell their labour for wages.

Weber argued that Marx had exaggerated class conflict and that a new 'white-collar' group was emerging which would act as a 'buffer' between the capitalist and working classes. Weber had far more influence than Marx on official occupational class scales. In any case, Weber did not think that class explained as much about people as did Marx. He argued that people chose their lifestyles (the way they live) in ways that often cut across class lines (e.g. religious groups).

Max Weber (1864–1920)
Qualifications, experience which give people a strong or weak position in the *job market* (i.e. when competing for jobs) is the basis of class. Weber argued that, in general, the better qualifications of non-manual (service sector) employees put them in a better position in the job market than manual employees.

Social mobility and life chances

Social mobility is movement up or down the social class scale. Social mobility may be *individual* or *group*. Individual mobility can be divided into *intra-generational* and *inter-generational*. Intra-generational mobility occurs when a person is socially mobile within his or her own lifetime. Inter-generational mobility occurs when an individual moves out of the occupational class of his or her parents.

Question

State which of the two situations below is an example of intra-generational mobility, and which is an example of inter-generational mobility:

1　A doctor whose father was a shop assistant.
2　A plumber who started work as an unskilled labourer.

Now think of two more examples of your own.

Group social mobility occurs when an occupational group improves its social class position. When the Registrar General considers that this has taken place, the group is *reclassified*. Thus, in 1961, engineers were moved up from social class III to II, whereas draughtsmen were moved down from II to III.

Life chances relate to social mobility. The term life chances means exactly what it says — the opportunities, good or bad, a person has in life to achieve his or her aims, including improving social position. Those born into higher social class positions nearly always have better life chances than those born into lower ones. What examples can you think of to illustrate this?

Factors affecting social mobility

This section covers the factors affecting *individual* social mobility.

1　A change in the occupational structure (types of jobs available)

When a society changes from being agricultural to industrial or from industrial to service, the types of jobs available also change. Changes in *the occupational structure* (jobs) of this kind were dealt with in Chapter Seven.

Questions

1　Think of an example of a) an occupation that declined due to the move to a service economy, and b) an occupation that increased.
2　Do changes in the occupational structure produce only better jobs?
3　Think of one high and one low service-sector occupation.
4　Which a) gender and which b) race do you think does proportionately more low-status service work?

2　Educational/vocational qualifications

Qualifications are the 'currency' of the job market — the more and better qualifications you have, the stronger your 'buying' power (provided your qualifications meet the needs and demands of employers).

3　Stratification

Life chances, including the chance of social mobility, are greatly affected by class, gender and race.

4 Intelligence and talent'

A certain level of intelligence or talent is required to do certain jobs. However, there are many highly intelligent people doing low-status, low-paid jobs and less intelligent people doing high-status, high-paid jobs. One of the main reasons for this is stratification — some people are born with advantages, such as money and 'contacts', which improve their life chances.

5 Chance

As in all areas of life, chance can make the difference. For instance, happening to see the 'right' job advertised or somebody on an interview panel 'really taking' to you can change the rest of your life.

6 Marriage

Most people marry more or less within their social class. It is mainly women who become upwardly mobile through marriage.

Trends in social mobility

Although the Oxford Mobility Survey, based on pre-1972 data, is now becoming rather dated, it still provides the broadest picture of trends in social mobility. This survey, plus some other data, provide the basis of the following points concerning trends in social mobility since 1945:

1 There has been almost *twice* as much upward (30 per cent) as downward (18 per cent) mobility.
2 There has been an increase in *long-range* upward mobility, partly because there is more 'room (jobs) at the top'.
3 Nevertheless, most mobility is still *short range* — most people end up close to where they started on the class scale.
4 The majority of the *top one per cent* of jobs are still filled by the sons (not the daughters) of fathers in similar jobs.
5 The top ten per cent of jobs are much more equally shared between the sons (and some daughters) of fathers of *various* social classes. Nevertheless, the sons of fathers in the top ten per cent of jobs have a much better chance of getting a job in the top ten per cent than the sons of working-class fathers.
6 According to the Oxford Mobility Survey, the middle class (mainly people in better service sector jobs) is growng in size, but is not very conscious (aware) of itself as a single class — partly because quite a lot of people move in or out of it. (Note: Marxists argue that most service-sector employees are *working class*.)
7 The industrial working class is reducing in size, but those remaining in it might well be conscious of themselves *as* working class.

Stimulus questions

Table 10.1. Surrey Occupational Class by employment status and sex

Surrey Occupational Class	Men full-time	Women full-time	Women part-time
1 Higher professionals	6.1	1.2	0.4
2 Employers and managers	13.4	5.3	1.7
3 Lower professionals	5.3	13.3	9.2
4 Secretarial and clerical	9.1	39.4	19.8
5 Foremen, self-employed manual	12.0	3.5	3.8
6 Sales and personal service	3.2	13.8	35.2
7 Skilled manual	32.2	5.1	3.0
8 Semi-skilled	15.2	16.2	9.7
9 Unskilled	3.4	2.1	17.2
Total	100%	100%	100%
N =	(7498)	(2967)	(2379)

(Source: *The Measurement of Social Class*, Social Research Association, 1986.)

Questions

1 In which occupational class is there the largest percentage of: a) women in full-time work? (1 mark)
   b) men in full-time work? (1 mark)

2 What is the total percentage of women in part-time work in occupational classes 6, 7, 8 and 9 together? (1 mark)

3 Do males or females tend to occupy the highest-status jobs? Give evidence from Table 10.1 to support your answer. (2 marks)

4 What is the term used to describe movement from a low occupational class to a high occupational class? (2 marks)

5 Briefly describe *three* reasons which may account for changes over time in the amount of movement up or down the class scale. (6 marks)

6 Give reasons for the gender pattern shown in occupational classes 4 and 6. (7 marks)

Activity (class)

Government statistics which refer to the class of a household or family use the man's occupation to do so.

What basis do you think should be used for classifying household or family class? Or, do you think that all adults should always be classified separately according to their own occupation? If so, how would you classify housework?

Income and wealth

Income: more income, less equally shared

Since the Second World War, Britain has steadily become a wealthier society, especially since the late 1970s. There are various ways of measuring national wealth. A useful one is *real income per capita* (per person). On this basis, according to A. H. Halsey, real income doubled between the Coronation of the Queen in 1953 and 1986. Put another way, *average* income per person increased by 100 per cent during this period, and there are few who have not benefited to some extent from this.

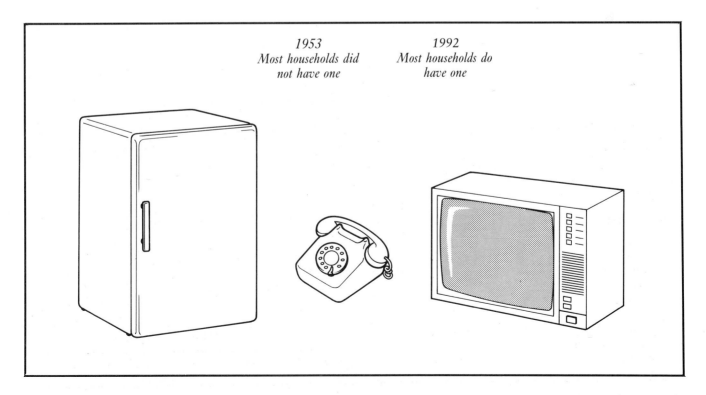

1953
Most households did not have one

1992
Most households do have one

Although average income increased quite rapidly between 1976 and 1985, relatively more of this increase went to the better off than the worse off. So, in terms of income, although the poor got richer in real or *absolute* terms, they got poorer *relative to the rich*. Table 10.2 clearly shows this growing gap.

Table 10.2. Income (after tax and benefits distribution) as a percentage of total household income

	Top fifth	Bottom fifth
1976	37.9	7.4
1985	40.2	6.7
1986	41.7	5.9

There are two different measures of wealth that need to be noted. First is *marketable wealth*, which refers to everything a person owns that can be sold. For nearly all the 62 per cent who are owner-occupiers, their house is their main marketable item. Second is marketable wealth *plus* occupational (job) wealth and state pension rights. Pension contributions require people to save and have proved a major way of equalising wealth. This second measure of wealth shows much greater equality than the first.

Table 10.3. Distribution of wealth: United Kingdom

		Percentages and £ billion			
		1971	1976	1981	1985
Marketable wealth					
Percentage of wealth owned by:	Most wealthy 1%	31	24	21	20
	Most wealthy 10%	65	60	54	54
	Most wealthy 50%	97	95	94	93
Marketable wealth plus occupational and state pension rights					
Percentage of wealth owned by:	Most wealthy 1%	21	14	12	11
	Most wealthy 10%	49	37	34	36
	Most wealthy 50%	85–89	80–85	78–82	81–85

(Source: Adapted from *Social Trends*, 1988.)

Questions

1 What was the percentage reduction in marketable wealth owned by the top one per cent between 1976 and 1985?
2 By what percentage did the ownership of marketable wealth plus pension rights of the top ten per cent fall between 1976 and 1985?
3 What percentage of marketable wealth was owned by the *least* wealthy 50 per cent in 1985?
4 Give an example from Table 10.3 which shows that there is less inequality between groups on the basis of marketable wealth *plus* occupational wealth and state pension rights than on the basis of marketable wealth alone.

The inequality question

Inequality and poverty are not the same thing. A 'mere' millionaire does not have as much money as a multi-millionaire but is obviously not in poverty! Inequality reflects *difference*, whereas poverty is a *lack of* what is needed to meet a decent living standard. All the main political parties say they want to reduce poverty, although they have very different methods of trying to do so (see Chapter Seventeen). However, they do not agree about how equal (or unequal) Britain should be.

Greater equality is one of the basic beliefs of the Labour Party. By contrast, many Conservatives see no harm in great inequality — as long as real poverty does not exist. Because the Conservatives were in power during the 1980s, it is their beliefs on inequality that have been put into practice. In 1988, three events occurred which *together* made Britain a less equal society.

1 *The 1988 Budget:* lowering income tax for the very rich

In the annual Budget, the Chancellor of the Exchequer decides how much money is going to be spent on various things (education, defence, etc) and how the money is going to be raised. The main source of government money is income tax. Table 10.4 shows what happened to income tax in 1988.

Table 10.4

Income tax	1987 %	1988 %
Basic rate	27	25
Top rate	60	40
Other rates	40, 45, 50, 55	40

Chancellor Nigel Lawson decided he could give money 'back' to all earners and gave most back to the very rich. Labour critics argued that if other government measures since 1979 were considered (such as raising Value Added Tax on certain items), basic rate tax payers had experienced no overall tax reduction during the Conservative period in government — however, the rich certainly had.

2 *The Social Security Act, 1988*

The Social Security Act introduced the biggest changes in social security since the 1940s (it is discussed more fully in Chapter Seventeen). The effect of the Act on inequality was mixed — some gained and others lost. The Government said this was inevitable when basic changes in the system were being introduced. Critics said it was wrong that many of the less well off should lose income at all, especially as the rich had gained so much in the 1988 Budget.

3 *The community charge (or poll tax)*

In 1988 legislation was passed to introduce a community charge or poll tax in the early 1990s. The poll tax is a tax on adults over eighteen and replaces local rates which are a tax on property (the tax is discussed more fully in Chapter Fifteen). Estimates are that the general effect of the poll tax will be that the less well-off will contribute more to local authority services, and the better-off less, than under the previous system. However, the poll tax proved so unpopular that the Conservative government decided to change it to a different system.

The basic government view is that everybody should pay the community tax because everybody benefits from community services. The poor receives extra in their social security payments or, in some cases, a rebate, to enable them to pay. The severely mentally handicapped is exempt from the charge. The severely physically handicapped, including those on low income, is not exempt but goes through the same system as everybody else. What do you think of this approach to the physically handicapped?

THATCHER'S OTHER BUDGET

Last week, Sir Ralph Halpern, boss of Burton's, got £5,134 tax rebate from the Budget. This week, he'll get another £5,134.

And next week. And the week after. And every week until the next Budget, when he'll get a bit more.

This week, millions of people who wouldn't get in a year what Sir Ralph gets extra EACH WEEK will be worse off.

What it means to YOU

Today marks the most drastic upheaval in state benefits since the war.

There will be millions of losers under sweeping new rules being brought in by the Tories. And the biggest sufferers will be young people, the disabled and couples with children.

Many will lose supplementary benefit. Others will lose housing benefit. Some will lose BOTH.

(Source: *Daily Mirror*, 11 April 1988.)

How the anti-Government Daily Mirror *saw the 1988 Social Security Act*

Note: The Social Security Advisory Committee which advises the Government on benefits said that 38 per cent of claimants would gain under the benefits and 43 per cent would lose.

The inequality question: conclusion

How equal people are materially is important in itself, but also because it affects other things such as education and ability to afford certain cultural pursuits. What is your view? Is Britain too unequal, not unequal enough, or about right?

The wider scene: Inequality

Inequality is, of course, an international as well as a national issue. In the last decade, the wealth gap between the richest and the poorest countries has got bigger.

Table 10.5. British overseas aid (as a percentage of gross national product)

1979	1987	Percentage Recommended by United Nations
0.52	0.28	0.7

From making the largest percentage contribution of its GNP of the seven richest nations, Britain has dropped to the second smallest.

The British Government has encouraged greater private contributions to overseas aid. The small increase in these nowhere near matches the decline in government aid.

What percentage, if any, of the gross national product of the rich countries do you think should go in overseas aid? Give reasons for your answer.

Class culture

It is only in a textbook that the economic or material side of social class — income, wealth and occupation — can be separated from the cultural side of class — the way people live. In real life, the money largely buys the way of life. You don't play polo, drive a Porsche or holiday in Monte Carlo unless you have the money, and if you don't do these things, you tend not to know the people who do, i.e. you don't share their culture.

It's true that knowing a person's income and wealth (the basis of the material side of class) does not tell you everything about his or her way of life (culture). But it can tell you a lot. The following activity illustrates the link between money and culture.

Activity (class)

Which *three* of the following leisure activities would you associate more with the upper and middle classes and which *three* with the working class and the poor?:
　　bingo, going to the theatre, playing darts, fox hunting,
　　betting on greyhound races, visiting an art gallery.
Try to add *two* more activities of your own to each list.

Comment: The above activities were selected because they are easy to associate with a particular class. This is not true of all activities. Thus, 'going out drinking' or 'going out to eat' could apply to any class. Even so, where and how people do these activities often indicates their class. Thus, the phrases 'going out for dinner' and 'popping down to the chippy' or 'going to a cocktail party' and 'going out for a few pints' strongly suggest the class of those speaking. Still, as we shall see, there are an increasing number of leisure activities not strongly associated with a given class.

With the top rate of tax reduced from 60 to 40 per cent in April 1988, perhaps the rich will not need tax ploys.

Upper-class culture

Who are the upper class? What makes them upper class? Even without the help of sociology, you probably already have a good idea of the answer to these questions. There are two main aspects to class, the economic and the cultural:

Economic — economically, the upper class is mainly made up of wealthy landed and business people. In the economic sense, the 'mega-stars' of showbusiness can be considered upper class.

Cultural — culturally, many of the upper class share a similar *life-style* (way of life), including similar education, leisure and social life. Going to the leading public schools of Eton or Harrow, regularly attending Ascot or Derby days, and belonging to an exclusive London club (mainly for males) might be part of such a pattern. Because members of the upper class share such a strong and exclusive culture, they tend to be very conscious (aware) of themselves as belonging to a particular class — a class of prestige, privilege, power and wealth.

The *nouveaux riches* (newly rich) may not fit easily into this pattern, and some of them, of course, may not want to.

Middle-class culture

Many members of the upper class are *born* into great wealth. The middle class has to *work* hard for its more limited wealth and comfort. Children born into the advantages of middle-class life know that they, too, will have to work hard to maintain them. *Achievement* through work is, therefore, an important middle-class cultural value.

Middle-class culture is also very *child centred* (concerned with children). Parents, especially mothers, typically spend a lot of time encouraging their children to develop their abilities and supporting their education. Even when middle-class parents, particularly mothers, 'play' with their children, they often intend to teach them skills or behaviour which will help them in later life. Helping children to learn language skills is most important of all.

The following extract gives a good description of the cultural links between educational and family socialisation, typical of the middle class.

> Research into the relationship between educational attainment and socialisation has tended to stress the importance of achievement motivation. The idea that society is a ladder which is there to be climbed is a familiar one to middle-class children; they are, moreover, likely to have learned that the rewards which life offers are consistently related to their own efforts. Research by the Newsons, for example, has shown that middle-class parents are more likely to use rewards as incentives and use physical punishment only rarely, in comparison with working-class parents, with the result that middle-class children grow up viewing the world as a place to be mastered through their own activities.

(Source: Adapted from R. King and J. Raynor, *The Middle Class*, Longman, 1982.)

Questions

1 Put in your own words the idea 'that society is a ladder which is there to be climbed'.
2 How does learning 'achievement motivation' help middle-class children when they go to school?

Working-class culture: 'traditional' and 'new'

The old working-class way of life, based on industrial communities, is now well in decline. This in turn, reflects the decline in the old industries and in the numbers of people working in them. Even so, traditional working-class culture continues to some extent in certain urban industrial areas. Yet this culture was already passing when Richard Hoggart wrote the following description of the working-class neighbourhood well over 30 years ago.

This is an extremely local life, in which everything is remarkably near. The houses, open on to the street; the street itself, compared with those of suburbia or the new housing estates, is narrow; the houses opposite are only just over the cobbles and the shops not much farther. For the things you want only periodically you may drop down two or three hundred yards to the shops on the main tram route or go into town; day-to-day services are just over the road or round the corner, and practically every street has its corner shop, usually a general grocer's or paper shop. The paper shop window is a litter of odds-and-bobs; if the light is kept on at nights the children make it a meeting-place...

The grocer, whose corner shop is the housewives' club as it is in most kinds of district, will hardly prosper unless he respects the customs of the neighbourhood. Newcomers may pin to the shelf at the back of the counter one of those notices which the local jobbing printers produce, 'Please Do Not Ask for Credit As A Refusal Might Offend', but whether the notice stays up or not most of them have to start giving 'tick' before long...

Life centres on the groups of known streets, on their complex and active group life. Think, for example, of the mass of financial arrangements which are transacted between house and house, the insurance collectors, the clothing clubs, the 'diddlems', the Christmas clubs, the 'Snowballs', the 'draws' of all kinds.

(Source: Adapted from Richard Hoggart, *The Uses of Literacy*, Pelican, 1966.)

Questions

1 What difference is mentioned in the passage between streets in working-class and suburban areas?
2 The two shops mentioned in the passage each serves a double purpose. What are these purposes?
3 Explain, with examples, what is meant by 'this is an extremely local life'.
4 How similar or different is the neighbourhood which *you* live in to the one described by Richard Hoggart?

In a phrase, the big change in working-class culture is that it has 'gone indoors'. In leaving the 'known streets', working-class culture has lost much of its shared, communal character. Now, the 'new' working class spend their time more like the middle class — though they watch television a bit more and read less. This change in cultural habits reflects three factors:

1 *Affluence* — working-class people can afford to buy more things for their houses.
2 *Consumerism* — the desire to consume items of leisure (e.g. videos) and convenience (e.g. microwave ovens) seems to increase as more and more become available.
3 *Privatisation* — many of the new leisure items can be consumed in private, whereas, in the past, most leisure pursuits required participation with other people. In the past, leisure was more communal, now it is more private. Today even watching football (on TV) can be done alone at home.

153

The culture of the poor (underclass)

The view that there is a 'culture of poverty' is now quite common in sociology. The culture of poverty refers to the way of life of the poor 'masses' below the 'solid' working class. Here are two descriptions of the 'culture of poverty'.

Taken as a whole, poverty is a culture...The poor are people who lack education and skill, who have bad health, poor housing, low levels of aspiration [ambition], and high levels of mental distress.

(Adapted from Michael Harrington, *The Other America*, Penguin, 1963.)

Certainly we observed the hopelessness and despair of slum life in Nottingham; we saw that the poor did not participate much in the important organisations of the larger society, even in trade unions where their own basic self-interest was involved.

(Adapted from K. Coates and R. Silburn, *Poverty, The Forgotten Englishman*, Spokesman, 1983.)

Today, the long-term unemployed, the lowest of the low-paid, single parents on supplementary benefit and many of the old and disabled are the groups most likely to be living a culture of poverty. Sometimes these groups are referred to as the *underclass*.

It is important to note that the culture of poverty is caused by difficult social conditions, such as unemployment and low pay, not by any inferiority on the part of the poor as a whole.

Is class becoming less important in Britain?

If you have read this chapter so far, you may already have developed your own point of view on this question. This section merely summarises the arguments for and against the view that the importance of class is declining in Britain. For the purposes of this section, class is defined as differences relating to occupation (e.g. income) and property and wealth.

Is class becoming less important in Britain?

For

1 The traditional manual working class is numerically declining
2 Since the 1979 general election, even the proportion of manual workers voting for Labour, 'the party of the working class', has declined (see pp. 232–233)
3 Most people are more affluent (better off) now — they depend less on the state for help and security
4 People are more 'into' consumption (enjoying their affluence)
5 Many *feel* class is less important. *Class-based culture is dying*. General prosperity has made people more individualistic — especially the growing middle-income band

Against

1 The extremes of British society are becoming *more* unequal, the rich relatively richer, the poor poorer
2 The Labour Party is bound to take time to adjust to the 'decline' of the traditional working class and to increase its appeal to other sections of the electorate, especially service workers
3 A large part of the population is either low paid, unemployed or elderly. In addition, other people may suddenly find they need state help
4 Most people still want good state health and education services. There is still a need for public welfare, as well as private profit and pleasure
5 People might feel less contented if prosperity decreased or levelled out. *Then* they might turn to the unions and the Labour Party

Some of the old class divisions are breaking down.

Is class 'a good thing'? Should class be abolished?

Most people in Britain appear more or less to take the existence of class for granted, even though they might think it is becoming less important. As long as some people earn and keep more than others, there will be social class. Only Marxists believe in the total abolition of class. They would replace the capitalist system, in which people compete for jobs, income and wealth, with communism. The principle behind communism is 'from each according to ability, to each according to need'. So far, this has not been achieved anywhere. Do you think it is possible to achieve it?

In Britain, people disagree about *how much* class inequality there should be rather than about whether class should be allowed to exist. The Conservative Party favours the most inequality. As Mrs Thatcher said, 'Let our children grow tall and some grow taller than others.' Under the Conservative governments (1979 onwards), the rate of tax for the rich has been greatly reduced. The Conservatives believe that those who cannot help themselves should receive help, but the other political parties argue that the Conservatives do not do enough about this. To a greater or lesser extent, the other political parties wish to do more to reduce class inequalities. They argue fiercely that more should be spent on public health and education.

Question

In what ways do you think that spending on public health and education might reduce class inequality?

Conclusion

This chapter does not try to tell you whether class is 'good or bad' or whether class inequalities should be reduced. Those matters are for you to decide for yourself in the light of the evidence. What it does tell you is that class changes. It does so mainly as the nature of work and jobs change. A class structure in which a large majority are service employees and in which an increasing number of women are in paid employment means a very different world from that of 50 years ago.

Stimulus question
ITEM A

It is becoming harder to classify Britons by social class. As more of them work in offices, rather than factories, the old labels which once defined and divided them become less distinct. Class is now less a matter of income and occupation, more of taste and culture.

The British working class was once typified by trade union members doing manual jobs in manufacturing industry. Today, less than a quarter of workers are in manufacturing, more people work with their minds than with their hands, and fewer than two workers in five belong to a trade union. So, the first point is that the manufacturing working class is getting smaller.

The second point is that people that remain in the working class are tending to follow the same general living patterns of higher social classes. More of them are owner-occupiers, more of them eat healthily, fewer of them smoke, and, generally, they have more money to spend on consumer items.

(Source: Adapted from *The Economist*, 16 January 1988.)

155

ITEM B

Growing inequality between the rich and poor

The official statistics show that, over the last decade, the trend has been towards greater inequality between the top and bottom income groups in society.

The bottom fifth had final household incomes amounting to 7.4 per cent of the whole in 1976 reduced to 7.1 per cent in 1984, while the top fifth raised their share from 37.9 to 39.0 per cent. The class problem thus...includes the fears and insecurities of the old, the sick, the insecurely employed, and indeed everyone who depends on welfare rather than earned income alone.

Within the bottom group are numbers of long-term unemployed who are not needed by industry. So the class structure of industrial societies, including Britain, is developing an underclass of those who cannot be placed in the regular workforce...

The underclass contains a large proportion from the young and the ethnic minorities and they tend to adopt a ghetto existence outside normal...citizenship and with little or no stake in official society.

They are the extreme social example of a class structure tending towards a richer rich and a poorer poor.

(Source: Adapted from A. H. Halsey, 'Britain's Class Society', the *Guardian*, 13 July 1987.)

ITEM C

Figure 10.1. Housing

Tenure by social class, 1985, %

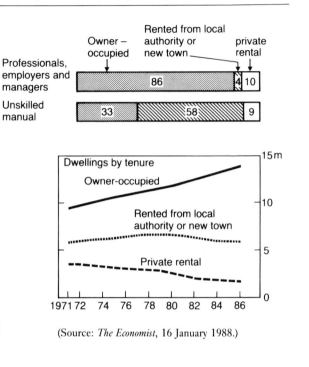

(Source: *The Economist*, 16 January 1988.)

Questions

1 Give one reason why 'it is becoming harder to classify Britons by social class'. (Item A) (1 mark)
2 What was the change in the final household income of the top fifth between 1976 and 1984? (Item B) (1 mark)
3 a) Which type of ownership of dewlings went up between 1971 and 1986? (Item C) (1 mark)
  b) What percentage of professionals, employers and managers lived in private rented accommodation in 1985? (Item C)
  c) What percentage of unskilled manual employees are in housing rented from local authorities or new towns? (Item C) (1 mark)

4 Give *one* piece of evidence from Item A to suggest that class differences are decreasing. (Item A) (1 mark)
5 Give *one* piece of evidence from Item B and *one* from Item C to show continuing inequality in Britain. (Items B and C) (2 marks)
6 What are the problems in modern Britain of measuring 'social class' simply on a person's occupation? (Items A and C) (6 marks)
7 Do you agree with the statement that 'class is becoming less important in Britain'? Give evidence for your answer. (Items B and C) (6 marks)

Activity (class)

Culture is the way of life of a given group. Does your neighbourhood reflect the culture of one class more than another, or would you say it has a class culture? Before deciding, make a list of *ten* items of culture (everyday life) in your neighbourhood (e.g. people's accent, dress, etc). Can you place the culture of your neighbourhood in terms of class?

Structured questions

1 What is the difference between 'income' and 'wealth'? (4 marks)
2 Explain why, although average income increased between 1976 and 1985, relative poverty increased also. (6 marks)
3 Discuss the ways in which people's 'life chances' can be influenced by their social class. (12 marks)

Project and assignment suggestions

1 *Social class and family background* — You could take two people from different social classes and give each of them an in-depth interview on their family background, the type of education they had, how they ended up doing their particular job and so on. You might find one of your teachers willing to be interviewed.

2 *Changes in class experience* — Interview an elderly person about what they recall of 'class structure' in their early days. Early this century, when many middle-class people still had servants, and many working-class girls and boys went into 'service' to earn a living, class differences were perhaps in some ways more noticeable than they are now. Many elderly people have very vivid memories of that period, and it could be a fascinating insight into class in your area many years ago. If your respondent is a man who served in one of the wars, he might have some interesting examples of differences between 'officers' and 'other ranks'.

3 *Class, occupation and status* — This would involve a survey, using a questionnaire, to see how people view the status (prestige) of certain jobs, and then to see whether there is a link between occupational class and status. For example, you could list about twelve to fifteen different occupations, covering all classes, in alphabetical order, and then ask your respondents to list them in order of status (you would have to make sure that they knew exactly what you meant by 'status' — how could you do that?). You would then need to analyse the results to see whether class 1 jobs were thought to have the highest status and so on. You would need to pay particular attention and give a lot of careful thought to the actual jobs which you chose. Make sure you discuss this with your teacher.

4 *Do people think social class has increased or decreased in importance?* — First, you will have to decide which group or population you intend to sample for information on this question.
Perhaps two quotas of five middle and five working-class respondents would produce interesting and contrasting findings. In your questionnaire or interview schedule, you will have to form your questions carefully to make sure that you get clear data about what respondents think about social class.

5 *Social class and leisure* — You could either study the leisure habits of a sample of one class or make your study a *comparative one* and study those of two classes. If part of your study involves participant observation, be careful not to be 'chatty' and disorganised in presenting your data. Participant observation seems to be the easiest but is, in fact, one of the hardest methods to use well.

Key words	
Class	Marketable wealth
Consciousness	Social mobility
Culture	Status
Lumpen proletariat	Underclass

CHAPTER 11 Gender

The study of gender is an important area in sociology. While 'sex' is used to refer to the physical differences between males and females, gender is used to describe the different patterns of behaviour associated with males and females — their gender roles. In all societies there are some differences in the ways in which males and females are treated, and are expected to behave. However, there are considerable variations between societies (and sometimes, within the same society) in what is considered 'masculine' and 'feminine' behaviour.

Gender socialisation and roles

Gender socialisation in childhood

Almost from birth, children are socialised into their male or female gender role. In Britain, this socialisation includes different types of clothes, toys and games, which in turn leads to different types of behaviour.

Activity (class)

Below is a list of words which can be used to describe people. Study the list carefully, then put each word into a column under the appropriate heading, depending on whether you think it is a word which is mainly used to describe males, females or equally used for both:

Word	Mainly males	Mainly females	Equally both
Clever			
Shy			
Aggressive			
Bold			
Dainty			
Attractive			
Sympathetic			
Ambitious			
Logical			
Strong			
Elegant			
Ruthless			
Witty			
Catty			
Powerful			
Gossipy			
Caring			
Emotional			
Athletic			
Creative			
Graceful			
Capable			
Domestic			
Sensitive			

Compare your list with the rest of the class. Was there broad agreement over some words? Did the results tell you that we do associate certain characteristics with different genders?

The lists below appeared in an advertisement in a local newspaper, advertising Christmas presents for children:

'Girls' Toys

Tinkerbell Jewellery & make-up e.g. lipstick
My Little Pony. Waterfall
Fashion Wheel
Tomy Dream Dancer
Wendy House — 42″ high
Peaches n' Cream Barbie
Crystal Barbie
Barbie's Dream Cottage
Shaping Up Sindy
Flower Fairies
Rainbow Brite & Starlite gift set
Sweet Secrets Transformers
Berjusa. A new baby just born

Boys' Toys

Masters of the Universe. Dragon Walker
Masters of the Universe figures
Masters of the Universe. Castle Greyskull
Zoids
Zoid Zilla
Big Foot 4 wheel drive truck
Transformers/Robo Machines
Hornby Thomas the Tank Engine
    Electric Train Set
Scalextric Escort XR31 Racing Set
Tonka Trencher
Wheelie Jeep Radio control car
Masters of the Universe. Battle Bones
Technic Lego. Car Chassis
Britains Farm Playbase & Animals
Britains Farm set. Tractor, trailer,
    farmer & animals

Questions

1 How would you describe the types of toy in each list?
(2 marks)
2 What differences are there in the kind of game or activity a child could engage in with 'girls' toys' and 'boys' toys'?
(4 marks)

Gender socialisation in school

Gender role socialisation also takes place at school. Feminists have criticised many of the books used to teach young children to read, as the stories and situations in them reinforced gender role stereotypes. The boys tended to be shown in active roles, often helping their fathers mend things, playing football, or climbing trees. The girls were much more likely to be shown helping their mothers with domestic tasks, or simply watching the boys admiringly. Perhaps more authors and publishers are now trying to avoid extreme gender role stereotyping. Can you find any examples of *good* practice?

Eileen Byrne carried out some research into gender role socialisation in English schools. She found that girls are praised for being quiet, clean, tidy and heplful, and criticised for being muddy, rough, noisy, lazy and untidy. She quotes these typical remarks from primary school teachers:

'There's a good girl, to help teacher.' 'Such a helpful child, she always offers to put the toys away.' 'A little boisterous for a girl, but she's quieting down as she settles into the class.' 'Jill is such a nice, polite little girl.' 'Alison, you won't grow up pretty if you scowl like that.' 'Emma, little girls don't fight like that, leave Jackie alone.'

On the other hand, boys are praised for toughness, strength, leadership, organisation, adult behaviour, initiative and originality. They are criticised for weakness, rudeness and 'sissy' behaviour. Here are more primary teachers' remarks quoted by Eileen Byrne, this time about boys:

'There's a brave boy, Bobby, real boys don't cry.' 'Big boys don't show when they're afraid.' 'Well done, Ian (he's a born leader, you know, always has his team ready first).' 'Kim, can you carry those boxes to the stockroom — there's a strong boy.' 'Alex, could you be very grown up and take this over to the junior school to Mr. Jones?' (Source: Eileen M. Byrne, *Women and Education*, Tavistock, 1983.)

Certain school subjects are still widely thought of as being more appropriate to one gender than the other. For example, maths, physics, chemistry and electronics are often seen as 'male' subjects; while biology, French, English, home economics and typewriting are often thought of as 'female' subjects. When boys and girls make their subject option choices at various stages of their school careers, they are likely to be influenced by these ideas, even if they are not consciously aware of them. Subject stereotyping is often reinforced by parents and teachers.

One of the reasons why we have so few women engineers in Britain, for example, is that relatively few girls take physics or electronics at GCSE or 'A' level. There are signs that this situation is changing slightly, with more girls opting for maths and science subjects at 'A' level. Also, many schools now structure their curriculum so that all pupils study a science up to the age of 16. However, differences do still remain in the subject choices of males and females, and these in turn are reflected later on in their occupations. It will be interesting to see whether the new national curriculum will alter this pattern.

One way in which children learn their gender roles is through 'role models' — adult males and females whose position and behaviour are unconsciously learned by the children as being 'typical' examples. Obviously, parents are powerful 'role models', and, in the school situation, so are teachers. One aspect of gender roles is the differences between males and females in terms of power and authority.

Gender socialisation and the media

The mass media (films, TV, radio, newspapers, magazines and comics) are very influential in the development of gender role stereotypes. The different portrayal of boys and girls in children's readers has already been considered, but these differences continue in many of the mass media.

Many children's comics, which cater for children from about seven years old to the early teens, are divided clearly into those for girls and those for boys, and there are quite marked differences between the two. For example, the action in the girls' comics tends to centre on the family or school (which limits the adventures somewhat!) while the action in boys' comics ranges everywhere in the world, and also in space. Many of the heroes in boys' comics are adult men — soldiers, spacemen, cowboys, footballers — who lead active, and sometimes dangerous lives, while in girls' comics, the heroines are usually teenage schoolgirls who spend much of their time sorting out family problems, coping with difficult teachers or classmates, and occasionally fighting through to the finals of the gymnastics competition or winning the school netball match.

Activity (class/outside class)

Try to get hold of a selection of comics for younger children. (You might work as a group, with each member contributing one comic.) Show the ways in which the content of the boys' and girls' comics differs, by looking at the following areas (you can probably think of other aspects to look at, as well):

- What do you notice about the titles of the boys' and the girls' comics?
- What is the setting of the stories?
- What activities are performed by the hero/heroine?
- What is shown in the illustrations?
- What words are used to describe the male/female characters?

The gender role stereotyping which is found in comics and teenage magazines is also shown in much advertising, especially TV commercials. Women are generally shown either as a wife/mother, in a panic because she can't get her floor washed and clean in time, or in raptures over the latest soap powder, or alternatively as a 'sex object' advertising products aimed largely at males, such as cigars or cars. Even when the product is aimed at women (e.g. detergent, perfume) the 'voice-over' who speaks the words which accompany the pictures is often male. This is because male voices are associated more than female voices with authority, and it is thought more likely that women will buy the product if a male is telling them that they should!

Men in commercials are more likely to be shown at work, playing sport, drinking in a pub, or doing something active, such as making/mending something or driving a car. When they are shown at home, they are often seen being waited on by a woman or trying unsuccessfully to cope with a piece of domestic equipment, such as a washing machine or microwave, even though they appear to have no trouble with saws and power drills! The world of television commercials seldom reflects the real world, where women have jobs, drive cars and take out mortgages, and where large numbers of men live alone and do their own washing, shopping and cleaning. However, perhaps you can think of some advertisements which avoid gender stereotypes and which reflect some of these realities.

Activity (class/outside class)

Make a list of *five* television commercials which, in your view, reinforce gender role stereotypes. Write a brief paragraph on each one, saying what the product is, what the setting is, what the characters are portrayed as doing, if there is a voice-over, whether it is male or female, and what it is about the commercial which made you select it for your list.

Sexism

To be sexist is to treat somebody as a sexual stereotype rather than as an individual. There have already been many references to sexist behaviour in this chapter. Thus, for a teacher generally to 'guide' girls towards English rather than physics at 'A' level, for a comic or magazine generally to portray 'girls' as 'after boys' are examples of sexism. Of course, the more people are socialised in a sexist way, the more they will act and think in a sexist way.

Sexism — an example from the language of journalism
News stories also tend to treat men and women differently. Women are often described by their physical characteristics even though these may have nothing whatever to do with the story, e.g. 'Mr. X's solicitor, slim, blonde 34-year-old Mrs. Blank, reported that her client...'

The National Union of Journalists believes that most newspapers, magazines and books discriminate against women so automatically that it is almost unconscious. They have published a list of commonly used phrases, together with a list of more appropriate substitutes. Here are some items from their list:

Instead of:	*Try:*
businessman	business manager; executive
newsman	journalist, reporter
foreman	supervisor
steward, stewardess	flight attendant
chairman	chairperson
mankind	humanity, the human race
man-made	synthetic, artificial, manufactured
housewife	consumer, shopper, cook
girls (of over eighteen)	women (especially in sport)
John Smith and his wife Elsie	Elsie and John Smith
authoress	author
spokesman	official, representative

The NUJ suggests that writers should use what they call 'the double-standard test' — *Would you use this description of a man?*

Activity (class/outside)

1 Find examples in newspapers or on television news where the words/phrases from the left-hand column rather than the right-hand column have been used. If in print, cut them out and stick them on a page, and underneath rewrite using the NUJ suggestions (or alternative words or phrases of your own if the 'sexist' language is not on the NUJ list). Which version do you prefer, and why? Do you think your changes would alter the way people would react to the story? Why or why not?

2 If you watch TV 'sitcoms' or 'soap operas', collect examples of *both* gender-role stereotyping (male and female) and occasions where stereotypes are reversed. (*Discussion point*: If characters are shown in the 'reverse' situation, e.g. a man running a home, or a woman running a company, but the situation is played for laughs by showing their incompetence at the job, is this overcoming or reinforcing gender stereotypes?)

The mass media can be very influential in shaping our ideas and knowledge about the world. If much of their content is sexist, this will reinforce the sexist attitudes which exist, and will also help to form them.

Conjugal roles

The social roles of husbands and wives within a marriage are known as *conjugal roles*. Conjugal roles refer to the parts played by husbands and wives in activities such as housework and other household tasks, child care, budgeting and family decision making. There are two main types of conjugal role, segregated and joint:

> *Segregated* conjugal roles occur where there is a very clear distinction between the husband's and the wife's household tasks and responsibilities. Typically, the husband does the traditional 'masculine' activities, such as household repairs and decorating, taking major decisions such as moving house and buying a new car, while the wife is responsible for the traditional 'feminine' activities of housework, cooking and child care.
>
> *Joint* conjugal roles are those in which household activities are seen as the joint responsibility of husbands and wives, and husbands play a significant part in child care and houswork, while wives are also involved in financial decisions. It is important to remember that probably very few couples fit exactly into one category or the other.

It has been argued that conjugal roles in modern Britain have shifted away from the traditional segregated pattern towards the joint. It is suggested that this is because of changing attitudes in society, influenced by things such as the increase in 'working wives' and the rise in male unemployment which has left many men at home during the day. It has also been thought that joint conjugal roles were more likely to be associated with middle-class than working-class couples.

However, research shows that both these views need to be treated with care. Many middle-class professional couples have segregated role patterns, and despite the increase in many men's participation in child care and housework, these areas still tend to be seen as the woman's *responsibility*, and the man's role as 'helping'. Men are also more likely to be involved with some household tasks than others. Sociologist Stephen Edgell studied 38 middle-class couples with young children. The men were scientists, engineers and dentists. Edgell divided the couples into those with segregated, joint and intermediate (not clearly one thing or the other) roles in domestic tasks and child care.

Table 11.1. Degree of conjugal role segregation and the household division of labour

	Segregated No.	Segregated %	Intermediate No.	Intermediate %	Joint No.	Joint %
Domestic tasks	18	47	20	53	0	0
Child-care tasks	6	16	15	39	17	45

(Source: S. R. Edgell, *Middle Class Couples*, Allen and Unwin, 1980.)

Questions

1. How many couples were involved in Edgell's research?
2. In which type of task did Edgell find the highest level of segregated conjugal roles?
3. What percentage of couples were judged to have intermediate conjugal roles in child-care tasks?
4. Give four examples of 'domestic tasks' and four examples of 'child-care tasks'.

Now study carefully Table 11.2. A sample of married couples were asked which tasks, in their households, were done mainly by the the man, mainly by the woman, and which were shared equally. The couples were then asked how they thought the same tasks *ought* to be shared out. Another group of people, who had never been married, were also asked how they thought that the tasks ought to be shared.

Table 11.2. Household division of labour: by marital status, 1984

	Great Britain								
	Married people						Never-married people		
	Actual allocation of tasks			Tasks should be allocated to			Tasks should be allocated to		
	Mainly man	Mainly woman	Shared equally	Mainly man	Mainly woman	Shared equally	Mainly man	Mainly woman	Shared equally
Household tasks (percentage allocation)									
Washing and ironing	1	88	9	–	77	21	–	68	30
Preparation of evening meal	5	77	16	1	61	35	1	49	49
Household cleaning	3	72	23	–	51	45	1	42	56
Household shopping	6	54	39	–	35	62	–	31	68
Evening dishes	18	37	41	12	21	64	13	15	71
Organisation of household money and bills	32	38	28	23	15	58	19	16	63
Repairs of household equipment	83	6	8	79	2	17	74	–	24
Child rearing (percentage allocation)									
Looks after the children when they are sick	1	63	35	–	49	47	–	48	50
Teaches the children discipline	10	12	77	12	5	80	16	4	80

(Source: Adapted from R. Jowell, and S. Witherspoon (Eds.), *British Social Attitudes*, Gower, 1985.)

Maybe he isn't as 'liberated' as the thinks.
Maybe she isn't so 'liberated' either — if she lets him get away with it.

Questions

1 What percentage of married women mainly did the household shopping?
2 What household task was likely to be performed by 83 per cent of married men?
3 What child-rearing task was most likely to be performed by married women?
4 Which household task was *least* likely to be performed by married men?
5 Which household task did most married people consider *ought* to be shared equally?
6 Which child-rearing task did half the never-married people think ought to be shared equally between men and women?

Stimulus questions

The following extract is taken from an interview between a woman who worked in a clothing factory and Sallie Westwood, a researcher who was interested in the ways in which the women in the factory spent a typical week. Read the extract, and answer the questions:

Kath was a woman who looked older than her 40 years; she was frail and had had pleurisy (a chest infection) the previous year. This had not stopped her working twenty hours a day for her husband and her children, who were all living at home; one son was working and another son and her daughter were still at school.

'We've got a dog so I hoover downstairs every day. I get up first...I get the tea on for the first lad and give him his breakfast because he has to go at 6.30 then it's me hubby. I make the lad's bed while the tea's brewing, then it's the other two and then I get meself ready while I make our bed, cut the sandwiches and I'm off out the door. I do the washing about three times a week because me hubby and the lad have overalls...I do all my ironing for the whole week on Sunday afternoon and pick up all the washing for Monday. The whole house gets a clean at the weekend.'

From her research, Sallie Westwood concluded that:

'Women spent all their waking hours working; they carried the responsibility for managing home life and the manual work it involved. The only assistance they received came, predictably, from their daughters...Mum made breakfast, cut sandwiches, washed clothes, shopped, cooked, cleaned and generally set the world in order for the other members of the household. It was this pattern that young men and women brought to their own marriages.'

(Source: Adapted from Sallie Westwood, *All day every day*, Pluto Press, 1984.)

Questions

1 Would you describe Kath's marriage as having joint or segregated conjugal roles? (1 mark)
2 Why should the author say that 'The only assistance came, predictably, from their daughters'? (2 marks)
3 What would be the likely effects on their own marriages of young men and women brought up in households such as that described above? (3 marks)
4 Describe what *you* consider to be a good pattern for sharing domestic tasks in a family of husband and wife (both with full-time jobs) and a teenage son and daughter (both at school). Give reasons for your answer. (9 marks)

Activity (class/outside class)

Look back at the survey on joint and segregated roles carried out by Stephen Edgell. Do you think you could carry out a similar but smaller-scale survey? List at least *two* difficulties you might experience doing such a survey.

Women and work

Domestic work

One type of work particularly associated with women is domestic work, that is, work concerned with preparing and serving food, washing clothes, cleaning homes and looking after children. Much of this work is 'invisible', in that other members of the household take it for granted, and often only notice it if it hasn't been done rather than when it has. Domestic work has another characteristic which distinguishes it from what is considered 'real' work — it is unpaid. However, domestic work takes up much of a woman's waking hours. In a survey of housework carried out in 1971, Ann Oakley found that the average amount of time spent performing domestic tasks by the women she interviewed was 77 hours per week. As well as the normal domestic tasks, women with small children can spend as much as an *extra* seven hours a day looking after them, as the following piece of research showed:

Table 11.3. Average time spent on looking after a young child	
	Minutes per day
Extra time for meals (cooking, washing up)	119
Washing and bathing	43
Clearing up and cleaning after child	48
Taking to toilet and changing nappies (day/night)	39
Getting children up and dressed	38
Putting to bed	38
Taking to nursery/childminder and collecting	35
Extra time for washing and ironing	34
Extra time for shopping	29
	423

Question

How do you think that Fawcett and Piachaud obtained the information shown in Table 11.3?

(Source: H. Fawcett and D. Piachaud, 'The Unequal Struggle', *New Society*, 20 December 1984.)

Despite the fact that in most industrial societies a growing number of women are in paid employment, the major responsibility for domestic work still rests with women. The picture in developing countries is similar; despite the fact that women make a major contribution to the growing and harvesting of crops and tending animals, they bear the major burden of domestic work.

Stimulus question

Read the extract below, and answer the questions.

There can be few generalisations that hold as true throughout the world: unpaid domestic work is everywhere seen as woman's work, woman's responsibility. It is important, vital work. Food must be cooked, infants fed, clothes washed and mended, water and firewood collected. And it all takes time. A woman in a Pakistani village, for example, spends around 63 hours a week on domestic work alone. Even in the rich world, where water comes from taps and cookers heat at the flick of a switch, a housewife works an average of 56 hours a week. And if she has children, that average jumps nearly 40 per cent.

Domestic work is not, however, the only work women do. There are relatively few women anywhere in the world who can claim to be 'just a housewife'. But a working woman in Europe can expect little or no help from her husband at home. In Italy 85 per cent of mothers with children and full-time jobs are married to men who do no domestic work at all. And in Europe as a whole, a working woman has, on average, only two-thirds the free time her husband has.

In the developing world the picture is the some. There is 'man's work' and there is 'woman's work'. And because many women do additional work outside the home, whereas few men would dream of doing any additional work inside it, 'woman's work' always ends up simply being 'more work'. In a village in Rwanda (Africa), for instance, men tend the banana trees and do most of the paid labour outside the home. Women, on the other hand, do virtually all the domestic work, three-quarters of the other agricultural work, and half of the work with animals. Taken together, women in this village work over three times as much as men.

Women do not choose to take on extra work in addition to their domestic responsibilities. They have no option. In most parts of the world, a woman's labour — in the fields growing food, packing transistors on a production line, typing a never-diminishing pile of letters — is absolutely vital to her family's survival.

(Source: *Women: A World Report*, Methuen, 1985.)

1 Give four examples of the 'important, vital work' that women do mentioned in the extract above. (2 marks)
2 According to the extract above, what percentage of Italian women with children and full-time jobs are married to men who do no domestic work at all? (1 mark)
3 What types of work do a) men and b) women in Rwanda do? (2 marks)
4 Why do women 'have no option' but to take on extra work? (1 mark)

Paid employment

Since the end of the Second World War, an increasing number of married women in Britain have been in paid employment. Whereas in 1921 fewer than one in ten married women were working or seeking work, by 1981 the proportion was one in two. By 1984, over 60 per cent of all women aged between sixteen and 60 had some form of paid employment. The 1980 'Women and Employment' study found that women are spending an increasing proportion of their lives in paid employment, although most of them take 'time out' to have children. It is increasingly the norm to return to work after having children, something made easier now that families are much smaller than they used to be.

The growing number of women in the labour market is often presented as a dramatic change in our society. However, although the figures have increased during this century, it is actually nothing new for women to have employment outside the home. Women in Britain have traditionally been engaged in farming, and in the seventeenth century, for example, women already formed a significant part of the work force, not only in agriculture but also in textiles, the retail and provision trades and a large variety of skilled occupations. Records show female bakers, brewers, millers, butchers and inn-keepers, and the medieval guilds of craft workers (which were rather like an early form of trades union) had female members who were printers, carpenters, shoemakers and blacksmiths. In the Industrial Revolution of the eighteenth and nineteenth centuries, women's labour played an important part in the factories, mills and coal-mines, not to mention the armies of female domestic servants who served the wealthier sections of society.

During the two world wars, women's labour was essential, and after the First World War in particular, the Government had to wage a propaganda campaign on the joys of housework and the duty of women to do it to get the women back into their homes again.

Activity (class)

The following 'Careers Quiz' was drawn up by the Equal Opportunities Commission. Say whether you think each statement is *true* or *false*.

1 You must be able to type if you want to be a journalist.
2 British girls cannot become coal-miners, but American girls can.
3 Boys can train as nursery nurses.
4 The law states that girls and boys must be paid the same amount of money if they are doing the same job.
5 The majority of girls employed in the engineering industry are working as secretaries.
6 Part-time workers, of which 84 per cent are women, do not always have the same rights and provisions as full-time workers.
7 Girls can join the Merchant Navy as deck officers.
8 Only boys can become pilots in the Royal Air Force, but girls can become pilots with commerical airlines.
9 You do not need to have studied maths to a high level to work with computers.

The women's movement and patriarchy

There are a lot of misunderstandings about so-called 'women's lib', many of them created by sections of the popular press. For a start, there is no single group or organisation; the phrase 'the women's movement' covers a number of different groups, in different countries, with different aims and methods. Again, the fact of women banding together to fight for certain rights, or to make people aware of a particular problem or injustice is not something new. Although many history books do not report the struggles of women to improve their condition throughout the centuries, such struggles have taken place, and have often been successful. In Britain this century, for example, women have successfully campaigned for the right to vote and the right to family planning.

However, what is now often referred to as the 'women's movement' developed from the 1960s, strengthened by what Sue Sharpe calls the 'double identity' of many women — that of wife/mother and paid employee. The general aim of the women's movement is to put an end to *patriarchy* (the power and control of men simply because they are men). It occurs in many families, organisations and societies. The women's movement wants to replace patriarchy with equality of the sexes. This is reflected in the following list of 'aims':

Equal pay — women usually get paid less than men.
Equal opportunities — women are less likely to be promoted than men.
Equal rights — in many countries, women do not have the same rights as men in voting, buying or owning property, getting jobs or getting married.
Sexual freedom — women should have the right to have as many or as few children as they wish, and should have access to reliable contraception.
Freedom from violence — women are frequently the victims of male violence, in the home or in the streets.
Men must change too — work, including domestic work, must be shared if women are to achieve real equality.

(Source: adapted from 'Figures for Feminists', *New Internationalist*, No. 150, August 1985.)

Activity (class)

Do you agree with the list of concerns above? Why or why not? Are they all equally important? Is there anything you would like to add? Discuss.

Obviously, some progress has been made in Britain on the issue of women's rights, though there is still a long way to go to worldwide sexual equality. What the 'women's movement' has done has been to alert many people, women and men, to the fact that there *are* changes to be made, changes which could improve the quality of life for both women and men.

Sex discrimination

The 'equality package'

To 'discriminate' in this context means to treat differently, in such a way as to cause unfairness or injustice. In the 1970s, two important Acts of Parliament were passed to try to prevent anyone from being unfairly treated because of her/his gender. Although the laws apply, of course, to everybody, in practice, the vast majority of people discriminated against, particularly at work, are females.

The Equal Pay Act of 1970, which came into force in 1975, stated that where men and women were doing 'like work' (i.e. the same job), they should be paid the same money. However, the 'sexual division of labour', which means that many jobs are done almost entirely by women and others almost entirely by men, meant that women's average wages continued to be much lower than those of men, as there were many cases where a direct comparison could not be made. The Act was changed in 1985 to refer to men and women doing jobs of 'equal value', but this is proving difficult to determine. Is a nurse's job of much less value than a sales manager or a bank manager? If not, why are nurses paid relatively little? Is it possible to decide on the 'value' of different jobs?

The Sex Discrimination Act of 1975 made it illegal to discriminate against anyone on the grounds of their sex. Examples would be not allowing girls equal access to the same subjects at school as boys, or by refusing a woman a job, promotion, or the chance of training, *because* she was a woman. Note that the Act does not apply to sport, to the armed forces, or where the employment of a woman would offend 'public taste or decency'.

Continuing inequality

Despite these laws, many women are still treated unfairly at work. Sometimes this is because they do not know about the laws, or they know that discrimination is taking place but don't do anything about it in case they lose their job. Some women do take their employers to the tribunals which deal with cases of alleged discrimination, but the number of women doing this has fallen. In 1982, there were 150 applications to the tribunals, of which 50 led to a tribunal hearing. Only seventeen cases were awarded compensation.

The Equal Opportunities Commission was set up to oversee the Acts, but there is no doubt that sex discrimination continues to exist, and remains a major barrier to equality between males and females.

What matters to women in paid work

Research has shown that men and women define 'success' at work differently, with women giving higher priority to things such as friendship and job interest, rather than promotion prospects, as Table 11.4 shows. One writer has suggested that this does not mean that women lack ambition, but that they face such difficulties at work from male colleagues when they do aim for, or reach, positions of importance, that many of them learn to value other things more.

Table 11.4. The proportion of working women rating seven different aspects of their jobs as 'essential' or 'very important'

	%
Work you like doing	91
Friendly people to work with	86
A secure job	76
Convenient hours of work	75
A good rate of pay	74
An easy journey to work	59
Good prospects	49

(Source: OPCS Survey, Department of Employment, 1980.)

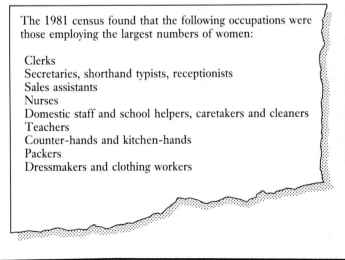

Stimulus question

Study the three items of information below carefully, and answer the questions.

ITEM A

The 1981 census found that the following occupations were those employing the largest numbers of women:

Clerks
Secretaries, shorthand typists, receptionists
Sales assistants
Nurses
Domestic staff and school helpers, caretakers and cleaners
Teachers
Counter-hands and kitchen-hands
Packers
Dressmakers and clothing workers

ITEM B

A newspaper report in December 1985 noted that in Britain, there were no female editors of national daily newspapers and no female heads of major television companies. Women formed eleven per cent of practising barristers, ten per cent of solicitors, and there was only one woman high court judge. Women made up only five per cent of top civil servants, one per cent of bank managers, eighteen per cent of practising GPs, seven per cent of architects and one per cent of engineers. Only two per cent of company directors are women.

(Source: Brenda Polan, 'Workface', the *Guardian*, 11 December 1985.)

Continued over page . . .

ITEM C

Employers still divide work into men's and women's jobs, unlawfully discriminating against women, according to an Equal Opportunities Commission study just published. Women had a particularly bad time in informal interviews, were often stereotyped as 'homemakers' without ambition and were steered into poorly paid, low-grade jobs. Men were classified as 'breadwinners' and were given higher paid, higher-status work.

The study of 45 private sector companies in the north-west of England found some interviewers priding themselves on giving women a harder time than men and reducing them to tears. A male personnel manager at a company selling office machinery said: 'We come down heavier, because we've got to see if they can take it. Most of them can't. They go out of here in tears. But it's part of the job and women have got to be able to take it.'

Other objectionable and unlawful practices included asking women candidates questions which would not be put to a man, such as whether they were career-minded and what their domestic arrangements were. The Commission found many personnel managers stereotyped women as lacking in ambition, but because women were conscientious and hardworking, they took them on as 'workhorses'. The study looked at more than 200 people over two years.

(Source: David Collinson, 'Barriers to Fair Selection', EOC Research Series, adapted from a report in the *Guardian*, 23 February 1988.)

Questions

1 How many of the jobs listed in Item A involve dealing with people in some way? (1 mark)
2 According to the information in Item B:
   a What percentage of solicitors are women? (1 mark)
   b What percentage of top civil servants are men? (1 mark)
3 Give two examples of 'unlawful practices' and two examples of the use of stereotypes reported in Item C. (4 marks)
4 Why do you think that the Sex Discrimination Act and the Equal Pay Act have not succeeded in overcoming sex discrimination? (6 marks)
5 Discuss the reasons for the 'sexual division of labour' in Britain today. (7 marks)

Activity (class)

Discuss the following questions in class.

1 Do you think the headline from *YTS News* is sexist or not?
2 Is there any difference between the number of boys and girls in your class who think the headline is sexist?
3 Substitute the words 'Tom' for 'Sharon', 'girls' for 'lads', and 'secretary' for 'mechanic' in the headline. If you thought the headline wasn't sexist before, what do you think now?

(Source: *YTS News*, Autumn 1987.)

YTS News

ACTION FOR JOBS

ESSEX MSC PUBLICATION   AUTUMN 1987

How the careers service can help

DO you want information on YTS programmes within daily travelling distance of where you live?

Would you like to know which programmes have vacancies? Do you want to know how to apply for a place on YTS?

These and many other more detailed questions about YTS can be answered by careers service staff.

Staff from the Essex Careers Service work closely with YTS programme providers and have full details of all the programmes available.

To help you find out more about YTS the careers service offers young people in Essex the following specialist assistance:

● Information on all YTS programmes in Essex including details of current vacancies
● Details of application procedures to all YTS programmes in Essex.
● Advice on which programme is most suitable for your intended career plan
● Assistance with finding full-time employment

Interested? Want to know more? Then contact your local careers office immediately — see the centre pages for addresses and telephone numbers or ask to see the careers officer who visits your school or college.

Also look out for the following FREE publications, which will give you further details 16 Plus Careers Service Magazine for 1988; Training Opportunities in Essex 1988.

SHARON'S JUST ONE OF THE LADS

SHARON Kenny's workmates think of her as one of the lads.

And that suits her just fine. For Sharon is training to become a motor mechanic.

All geared up to be a mechanic

TUNED UP: Sharon Kenny's glad she turned to YTS

Structured questions

1 Explain, with examples, what is meant by a 'gender stereotype'. (4 marks)
2 Give *three* areas of society which are important in the process of 'gender socialisation'. For each area, give an example of *how* it socialises people into gender roles. (6 marks)
3 Discuss the ways in which at least some males and females are beginning to break free of 'gender stereotypes'. (10 marks)

Project and assignment suggestions

1 *Design a questionnaire and conduct a survey into people's attitudes towards domestic tasks*, e.g. whether they think that some things are more 'men's work' or women's work'; whether they think that all/some household tasks should be shared; their ideas about responsibility for various aspects of child care, etc. You could also ask direct questions about who actually does what around the house, as well as their opinions on this matter.

   Try to ask different kinds of people, so that, in your conclusions, you can begin to examine whether there were differences between the opinions of, for example, men and women, older and younger people, employed women and 'housewives'.

Note: Drawing up a good questionnaire is not easy, and it is most important that you discuss this with your teacher, and get approval of the final result before you 'take to the streets'. You may also find it helpful to have a trial run, and ask the questions of your parents or other relatives before you run off a number of copies. This will help you to see whether all the questions are clearly understood and if there is something important you may have left out. This 'trial run' of a questionnaire is used by sociologists before they undertake a large-scale survey, and is known as a 'pilot study'.

2 *Ask an adult female (possibly, though not necessarily, your mother) if she will keep a diary for a week, showing how she spends her time* — It would help if you gave her a sheet for each day, with the times marked on it. At the end of the week, go through the diary and work out how best to classify the different tasks (e.g. paid employment, shopping, child care, leisure) and work out how many hours a week have been spent under the different headings. You could then try to compare this with something — either a similar diary kept by an adult male, or the sorts of activities a woman would have spent her time doing in another period of history. If you are going to do the historical comparison, you will have to do some research to find the information. On the other hand, you could run off several sets of diary sheets, and ask a number of women to fill them in for you, and make comparisons between them.

3 *Conduct an interview (taped if possible) with three or four women in paid employment* — Think of some questions to encourage them to talk about how they came to be doing that particular job, what they like/dislike about it, the hours, the training (if any), the nature of the work itself, and what they would like to do if they had the choice — it might, of course, be the same job! Try to get them to talk about their education, and how well or badly they think that it prepared them for employment. How do the answers relate to the work you have done in this part of the course?

4 *Collect information on an aspect of women's rights/ issues* — One area could be employment, but you might consider other areas, such as welfare benefits, health, the provision of child-care and nursery facilities, or women in politics. Remember, it isn't simply a matter of collecting the information; it has to be organised, and you have to decide what is important or significant about it.

5 *Undertake a study of 'Women in the Media'* — You could take a week's TV and radio programmes, and note how many news presenters, disc jockeys, sports reporters, etc, were male and how many female. You could also look at the types of radio and TV programmes presented by women — what kinds of programmes are they? When the 'credits' roll at the end of a programme, how many of the technical staff are female? You could also try to interview a female reporter on your local newspaper, or a female presenter on a local radio station, to talk to them about their work.

Key words

Conjugal roles	Sexist
Discrimination	Sexual division of labour
Gender roles	Stereotypes
Patriarchy	Women's movement
Role models	

Careers quiz

All statements are true.

CHAPTER 12 Race and Ethnicity

At a deeper human level: how much difference does colour really make?

Introduction: definition of terms

How racist is Britain? For that matter, how racist are *you*? Are race relations improving or getting worse in this country? Should race matter to you if you live in an 'all-white' neighbourhood? Further afield still, is it worth your while bothering about what is happening in racially divided South Africa?

Before tackling these questions, it is necessary to know what is meant by race and ethnicity. Strictly, members of the same race belong to the same broad biological type. The main races are Negro, Mongoloid and Caucasian (Indo-European) and there are many sub-groups. However, race is a very uncertain basis on which to generalise. First, billions of individuals are of mixed race — it is simply not possible exactly to classify them racially. Second, apart from certain obvious physical features, we do not know with any certainty what the main characteristics of the races are, or whether they matter very much. Most people agree that the basic humanity of all races is more important than minor differences, such as skin colour or size of nose.

An ethnic group is a group which shares a common origin (e.g. history) and culture. Culture is the way of life of a particular group. Language, religion, the sport and leisure activities of a group — indeed, almost any meaningful activity — are part of culture. You would probably have no difficulty in picking out a Chinese or Jewish ethnic area should you be passing through it. Most societies have an *ethnic majority* and *ethnic minorities*. The ethnic majority in England is white and has its 'roots' in English history. Its culture is referred to as the *host* or *indigenous* culture (though in reality there is great variety within the indigenous culture). The ethnic minorities vary greatly. Over time they adopt some of the habits of the host culture (see illustration) and vice versa. Minority cultures are often referred to as *subcultures*.

A fish and chip shop run by an Asian family — cultural 'mixes' are becoming increasingly common in Britain.

What is racism? Racism is believing or behaving as though another person or group is inferior on grounds of race or ethnicity, or both. Probably only one country — South Africa — is legally founded on the principle of racial superiority/inferiority; but racism exists, and on a large scale, in many Western, democratic societies, including Britain.

Racism in Britain is directed mainly, but not exclusively, against black people. Figure 12.1 shows the distribution of black people throughout Britain.

Figure 12.1. Percentage of economically active people in each metropolitan county or regional remainder who are from ethnic minority origins

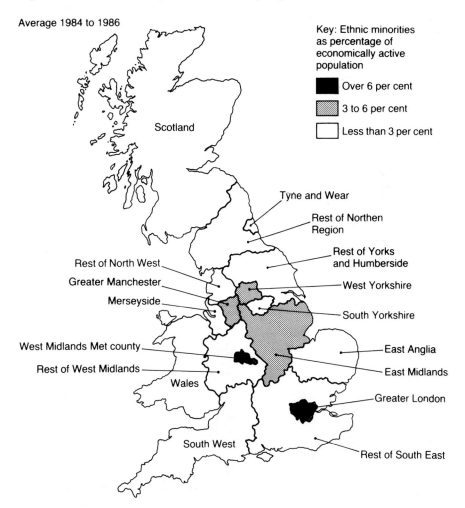

(Source: Adapted from *Employment Gazette*, March 1988.)

Activity (class)

Choose an ethnic group, other than your own, which you know something about.

1   Make a list of those things in the group's culture (e.g. clothes, religion, leisure activities) which are different from those of the ethnic majority.
2   Try to discover or work out the purpose behind each of the customs or other items of culture you listed in 1).

Note: Keep the list you made for this activity.

Why black people came to Britain
'We're here because you were there': forgetting history

How many times have you heard a white person say of blacks: 'Why did they come here in the first place?' This question shows an ignorance of history. As any black person knows, 'in the first place', whites went 'there'. 'There' is India, Pakistan, Africa, the West Indies and elsewhere. Britain had ruled some areas of the world for centuries before a number of their indigenous (original) inhabitants came to Britain.

The British Empire was held together mainly by military strength, which has been replaced by a voluntary association of independent countries known as the Commonwealth. The first members of the Commonwealth were countries with mainly white populations, such as Australia and Canada, but, later, India and many African and West Indian countries also joined.

Black and white Commonwealth troops fought together during the Second World War and there was much good feeling among member countries after victory. The 1948 British Nationality Act reflected this. By the terms of the Act, Commonwealth citizens were free to enter Britain, to find work, to settle and to bring their families. Seeking to improve their standard of living, hundreds of thousands of people from the 'new' or black Commonwealth countries settled in the 1950s and 1960s. Usually, adult males came first and brought their families over later. There was much encouragement from Britain for them to come, as there was a labour shortage in Britain at the time, especially in unattractive and low-paid work, such as cleaning, catering and transport.

Many black immigrants had affection and respect for Britain and had high hopes of life in the 'mother country'. The reality was often a disappointment, not to say a shock. The first photograph, Item A, illustrates the hope of early arrivals, and the second, Item B, the racist insults some experienced later.

Stimulus questions

Look carefully at the photographs and the extract, then answer the questions.

ITEM A

West Indian immigrants arriving at Newhaven in 1958. Most of the 'first wave' of immigrants were young.

ITEM B

Racist graffiti in a block of flats where an arson attack had taken place earlier the same day (London, 1985).

ITEM C

Given their relationship to the British, the West Indians tended to think of themselves as British and the British encouraged them to do so. Like the British, they were Christians; they spoke English; their history was closely tied up with that of Britain; they learnt English nursery rhymes; they saluted the Union Jack before starting their classes in schools: they studied and took pride in British history; the three major counties in Jamaica were called Cornwall, Middlesex and Surrey; Trafalgar Square and Nelson's Column in Bridgetown, Barbados were much older than the ones in London: the King or Queen's Birthday and Empire Day were the most celebrated days of the year; they looked upon Britain as their mother country, and so on. No doubt the West Indians knew that they were of African descent and black in colour, and therefore different from the British. However, they knew too that they were British in their political loyalties and that a large part of their culture was British...

The British in Britain saw them differently. To be sure, some of them did recognise the similarities in religion and language. For the bulk of British society, however, it was the colour of the West Indians that mattered more. They referred to them by negative labels such as 'niggers', resented their presence, and generally avoided them. The West Indians thought that they were black *but* British, and could not see why they could not be both. By contrast the British thought that they were black and *therefore not* British.

(Source: Adapted from The Open University, E354, Block 3, Unit 10.)

Continued over page...

Questions

1 Items A and B illustrate 'before immigration and a later situation. Contrast the feelings shown in the two photographs. (5 marks)
2 'Culture' means 'way of life'/'life-style'. Name *three* cultural similarities between West Indian immigrants and white Britains. (Items A and C) (3 marks)

3 Describe and explain:
  a how West Indian immigrants saw themselves, and
  b how the 'British in Britain' saw them. (4 marks)
4 What is racism? What evidence of racism is in the stimulus materials? (4 marks)

Activity (class)

The purpose of this activity is to pool knowledge about the cultures of various immigrant minority groups in Britain and to compare their cultures with that of the majority (i.e. the 'dominant' culture).

1 Divide up into small class groups (say, three or four). Each group should work with one of the lists of the cultural characteristics of an ethnic group drawn up in the previous activity (or draw up another list).

2 Draw up lists of the cultural characteristics of members of the ethnic group which have been imitated by, or have influenced, members of the majority culture.

At least one class group should deal with a black minority. Each class group should present its lists to the class for discussion.
  Which ethnic groups remain fairly separate from the majority culture and which have moved closer towards it? In each case, why is this so? Discuss.

Racism and racial disadvantage

Prejudice against blacks

In your discussion, someone might have suggested that black immigrants and their offspring often meet more prejudice than other groups. Why is this? It is understandable for people to prefer their own tribe or nation and to be cautious, if not suspicious, of others, especially when they first meet them. But this would apply to all 'outsiders', whether white or black. Another factor — colour prejudice — made it more difficult for white Britons and blacks to accept and respect each other enough to live peacefully together. Ever since the first visitors to African in the sixteenth century, many Britons have regarded blacks — especially those with negro characteristics — not only as physically and culturally very different from themselves, but as somehow inferior — a lesser people. Colour came to be a signal for prejudice against blacks.

Negative stereotypes and positive images

The idea that people 'fall into' certain 'types' can be useful. However, a danger lies in typing people in an insulting or too simple way, e.g. all members of a given ethnic group are 'greedy', 'sly', etc. This is called *negative stereotyping*.

In Britain, the Jews, the Irish and people of Asian and West Indian origin have probably been the victims of more racist stereotyping than any others. Here are two examples of negative stereotyping from the nineteenth century. (You may have to look up some of the words in a dictionary.)

Example of racial stereotyping from the Encyclopaedia Britannica

1810 — Negroes were described as having the following characteristics 'idleness, treachery, revenge, cruelty, impudence, stealing, lying, profanity, debauchery, nastiness, and intemperance'
1884 — 'No full-blooded Negro has ever been distinguished as a man of science, a poet, or an artist, and the fundamental equality claimed for him by ignorant philanthropists (lovers of the human race) is belied by the whole history of the race...'

Example of racial stereotyping in the nineteenth century from the American magazine Harper's Weekly

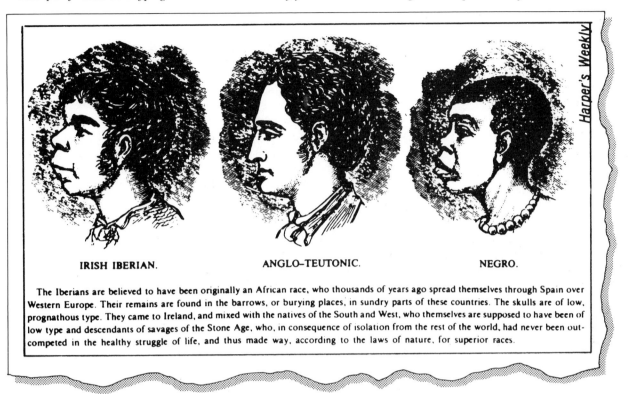

IRISH IBERIAN. ANGLO–TEUTONIC. NEGRO.

The Iberians are believed to have been originally an African race, who thousands of years ago spread themselves through Spain over Western Europe. Their remains are found in the barrows, or burying places, in sundry parts of these countries. The skulls are of low, prognathous type. They came to Ireland, and mixed with the natives of the South and West, who themselves are supposed to have been of low type and descendants of savages of the Stone Age, who, in consequence of isolation from the rest of the world, had never been out-competed in the healthy struggle of life, and thus made way, according to the laws of nature, for superior races.

In the 1980s, people of Asian origin have been subject to negative stereotyping at least as much as Afro-Caribbeans. Here are two extracts about 'Asians' from the *Sun* newspaper — both printed in 1986.

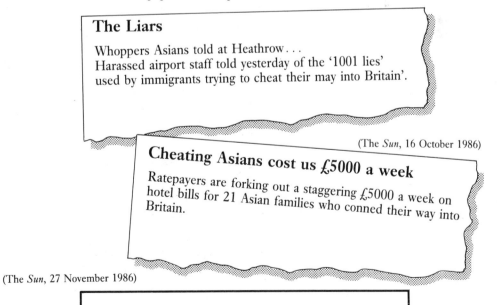

The Liars

Whoppers Asians told at Heathrow...
Harassed airport staff told yesterday of the '1001 lies'
used by immigrants trying to cheat their may into Britain'.

(The *Sun*, 16 October 1986)

Cheating Asians cost us £5000 a week

Ratepayers are forking out a staggering £5000 a week on hotel bills for 21 Asian families who conned their way into Britain.

(The *Sun*, 27 November 1986)

Activity (outside class)

1 In your own words, describe the stereotype of 'negroes' in the extract from the *Encyclopaedia Britannica*. Does this stereotype of Afro-Caribbeans exist widely today?
2 In your own words, describe the stereotype of 'Asians' in the extracts from the *Sun*.

The Odd Logic of the Stereotype!

Young British blacks, of both Asian and African origin, have rejected insulting and harmful stereotypes and tried to build up positive *self-images*. An image is a way of seeing and presenting oneself. Below is one example of how young blacks of today are trying to present a positive image for the young blacks of tomorrow.

Combating negative stereotypes with positive images

Star Apple Blossoms Company with their unique Zado doll.

(Source: *Caribbean Times*, October 1987.)

Teachers, parents and children alike are delighted with a new unique Afro-Caribbean doll named *Zadi*.

Zadi Wilkins (who named the doll after herself) and Sally Smith, raised their own money to fund the innovative *Star Apple Blossoms Company* which creates dolls to provide cultural role-models for children.

Sally whose degree in Child Psychology complements Zadi's training in fashion design, commented: 'Both Zadi and I feel strongly about the terrific lack of cultural resource available to children.'

The doll, which comes in a choice of African or Caribbean costume, is made entirely in England and its face is modelled on that of Zadi Wilkins' teenage daughter, Sharon.

African and Caribbean symbols decorate the silk-screened dolls dresses, which were designed by black artists especially for the toy.

Cultural awareness can be heightened by teaching children about the hummingbird or the parrot displayed on the Caribbean dress or about the meanings of the proverbs found on the African dress.

Sally and Zadi's ambitions include bringing out a Zadi doll in a second skin tone, producing Asian and European dolls whose costumes can be swapped with the Afro-Caribbean dolls. They would like to make male dolls, and looking further into the future, they hope to start up a multi-ethnic toy shop.

How racist is Britain?

In this section we will look at both social survey data and the personal experience of a victim of racism to answer the question 'how racist is Britain?' Table 12.1 presents the findings of two separate social surveys on the attitudes of whites to blacks.

Table 12.1. Percentage of sympathetic and unsympathetic feelings towards coloured immigrants (derived from Marsh, 1976, Table 1) compared with the results of the work by Bagley (1970, p. 21)

	Very hostile	Hostile	Unsym-pathetic	Neutral	Sympathetic	Positive	Very positive
Marsh	12%	13%	17%	25%	20%	10%	3%
	'Intense-outspoken'				'In the middle range'	'Tolerant'	
Bagley	14.2%			52%		33.7%	

(Source: The Open University, E354, Block 2, Unit 5.)

The two surveys seem to match quite closely. Bagley finds 33.7 per cent 'tolerant' and Marsh 33 per cent sympathetic, positive or very positive. This leaves almost exactly two-thirds of the population less than tolerant, most of them 'in the middle range'. A wedge of twelve per cent are 'very hostile' to blacks or, in Bagley's terms, 14.2 per cent are 'intense-outspoken' against them.

If more than one in ten whites are very hostile to blacks and most of the rest are more or less indifferent (neutral), then the chances of racists victimising blacks and getting away with it are probably quite high. The personal experience of a young Asian girl, recorded in her diary, suggests that this is so:

The diaries Nasreen has kept are surely material for future historians who wish to look beneath the surface of Britain in the 1980s.

The first entry was during the week they moved into their house. A gang of 40 attacked on the 25 January 1983. The gang threw stones, smashing the shop windows and gave Nazi salutes. They shouted: 'Fucking Pakis out!' They were able to do this, undisturbed, for six straight hours. Nasreen wrote in her diary: 'When the trouble started we phone the police, but they never came. Then again we phone the police, but they never came. Then my father went to the police station to get the police...we had a witness. The police said they didn't need a witness.'...

The entries in the diary for the weeks that followed, often written by candlelight in freezing darkness as the family huddled in an upstairs room, were repetitive and to the point: 'Trouble. Got no sleep. Had no telephone...three or four of them throw stones at our window.'

One night when she phoned me, Nasreen described her life as 'sort of like living under a table'.

(Source: the *Independent*, 2 February 1987.)

179

There are other forms of racism besides direct personal assault. Discrimination in housing, employment and education, although difficult to measure, still prevents many blacks from enjoying equal opportunity. (Racial discrimination means treating somebody as less than equal on grounds of race or culture.)

Some argue that as well as individual racism, institutional racism also occurs. *Institutional racism* happens when rules which are intended to be fair operate unfairly against a given racial group *in practice*. Those who believe that institutional racism occurs might argue that the lack of black policemen and women or of managers in big companies is an indication of institutional racism. They argue that if the rules operate to keep able blacks out, then the rules should be changed to enable their qualities to be rewarded and used. Thus, whether formally qualified or not, some blacks have a knowledge of their own community which could be useful in a variety of jobs, from social work to, say, marketing records.

A policy of *affirmative or positive action* adopted by some local authorities and private companies seeks to find out and use these qualities by appointing those who have them.

Despite high levels of racial discrimination in housing and unemployment, co-operation between the races is common.

Racial disadvantage

Racial disadvantage in accommodation and leisure facilities
Racial disadvantage refers to the problem experienced by members of a racial group as a result of racism. Many studies show that black Britons experience such disadvantage in employment, housing and in access to leisure facilities, education and other areas. The result is that, in general, they have worse jobs, houses, etc, than whites. One study of racial disadvantage was televised in 1988 as a series titled 'Black and White' which explored the extent of racism in Bristol.

Two journalists, Geoff Small, a black man, and Tim Marshall, a white man, researched racism in areas in which discrimination is illegal: housing, employment and places of entertainment (such as discos and night clubs). They used a method called covert (hidden) participant observation which they recorded on video. Their approach was for Geoff Small to apply for the job, or whatever, first, and for Tim Marshall to apply later. These were some of their main findings:

- five out of fifteen bed-and-breakfast proprietors discriminated;
- three out of sixteen landladies/landlords of rented accommodation discriminated;

- four out of ten employers discriminated, and
- two out of eight nightclubs discriminated.

Small argued that it was not just actual discrimination that damaged the prospects of blacks but the uncertainly and loss of confidence due to not always knowing when discrimination is taking place.

Racial disadvantage in education

Small and Marshall also looked at racial discrimination in education, although they produced no statistics. However, there is plenty of evidence to show that children of Afro-Caribbean origin do not achieve as high examination grades as those of Asian origin and indigenous British children. Racism — intended or not — in schools plays a part in this underachievement, but it cannot be the only factor because Asian children do more or less as well as white children and they are often victims of racism.

Sociologists have given the following reasons to explain the underachievement of Afro-Caribbean children, all of which play a part:

1 *Racism in schools (intended and unintended)*
   a   of teachers (stereotyping black pupils);
   b   of pupils (playground victimisation);
   c   of the curriculum (lessons), and
   d   of the way the school is organised (do blacks have more or less important jobs in schools?)
2 *Black pupils rejecting schools*
   Perhaps believing that schools might be racist, many black pupils seem to prefer to relate to each other than to teachers. Some black teenagers form strong peer groups that participate in subcultures, such as Rastafarianism (see Chapter Thirteen) which, if not anti-school, are fairly 'turned off' by it. Many black pupils can talk an alternative language of their own ('creole') which whites usually don't understand properly (see stimulus material).
3 *The majority of Afro-Caribbean pupils are working class.*
   The point about this fact is that working-class children generally perform less well than middle-class children in education. In fact, Afro-Caribbean children achieve about the same standards in education as other children of similar class background. So, class is probably a very important factor in explaining the achievement levels of Afro-Caribbean children.

The cycle of racial disadvantage

Disadvantage in education can lead to disadvantage in the job market (see stimulus question). Similarly, poor housing can lead to poor health and so to poor educational performance. Racism in any area can worsen problems in another — producing a cycle of racial disadvantage.

Race, class and gender

A black, working-class female is likely to experience disadvantage in three areas: race, class and gender. In practice, black working-class women have less power and wealth than any other section of the population.

In the case of Afro-Caribbean women, a large minority experience severe economic problems, because they are often both the main domestic as well as the paid worker in a family. For Asian women, the painful experience of being caught between two cultures is not uncommon — at home, they may still be expected to respect and obey the authority of males, yet, outside, they are increasingly taught to see themselves as the independent equals of men.

Race and class disadvantage often work together to reinforce each other. For instance, if there is an economic recession, working-class jobs are among the first to go. Blacks proportionately have more of those jobs than others, so more of them become unemployed.

Stimulus questions

Use the information below to answer the questions which follow.

ITEM A

Table 12.2. School-leavers: achievements

CSE and 'O' level achievements	Asians %	West Indians %	All other leavers %	All maintained school-leavers in England %
No graded results (includes those attempting)	19	17	22	14
At least 1 graded result but less than 5 higher grades	63	81	62	66
5 or more higher grades	18	3	16	21

(Source: Rampton Report, 1981.)

ITEM C

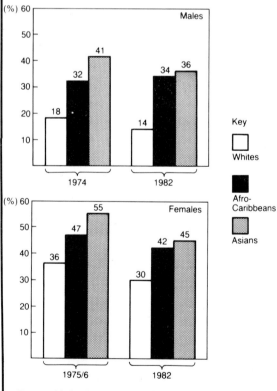

Figure 12.2. Low-status jobs: percentage of workers in semi- and unskilled work

ITEM B

West Indian pupils' language barrier

West Indian children do badly at school because they speak a different form of English from their teachers, according to a study published today.

This startling explanation of West Indian underachievement is one of the findings of a two-year research project carried out by Dr Ashton Gibson, director of the Centre for Caribbean Studies.

'The variety of English spoken by West Indian children needs to be treated virtually as a foreign language,' says the study.

More than half the 508 teenagers questioned did not place the same meaning on many everyday expressions as native Britons. Nearly 80 per cent sometimes had difficulty in understanding what the teachers were saying, and 56 per cent said they spoke differently at home from at school.

Dr Gibson says: 'Almost all English-speaking West Indians use a mixture of Creole and standard English that is neither one thing nor the other.'

The study quotes the example of the 20-year-old Jamaican woman who could read and write when she came to England at the age of eight. When she tried to explain that she had already completed the reading books she was offered, the teacher said: 'Please speak English.' She left school at 16 barely able to write her name.'

Judith Judd
Education Correspondent

(Source: Adapted from the *Observer*, 22 June 1986.)
(Source: Reprinted in *Social Studies Review*, March 1986.)

Questions

1   Give the percentage of Asian students who obtain five or more higher grades at CSE and O level. (Item A)
(1 mark)

2   What is the difference between the percentage of male Afro-Caribbeans obtaining low-status jobs in 1974 and in 1982? (Item C) (1 mark)

3   Give *two* ways in which the use of 'creole' might hinder the education of Afro-Caribbeans. (Item B)   (2 marks)

4   Give *two* explanations why more Asians and Afro-Caribbeans (of both sexes) than whites are in low-status jobs. (Item C)   (4 marks)

5   Look at the figures for 1982 for males and females in low-status jobs (Item C). Why are there proportionately fewer white men than white women in lower-status jobs? Why is there a higher percentage of women than men of all three groups in low-status jobs?   (7 marks)

Activity (class)

Read this poem.

Telephone Conversation
(or 'Almost Renting a Flat')

The price seemed reasonable, location
Indifferent. The landlady swore she lived
Off premises. Nothing remained
But self-confession. 'Madam', I warned,
'I hate a wasted journey — I am African.'
Silence. Silenced transmission of
Pressurized good-breeding. Voice, when it came,
Lipstick-coated, long gold-rolled
Cigarette-holder pipped. Caught I was, foully.

'HOW DARK?'... I had not misheard... 'ARE YOU
   LIGHT
'OR VERY DARK?' Button B.* Button A. Stench
Of rancid breath of public hide-and speak.
Red booth. Red pillar-box. Red double-tiered
Omnibus squelching tar. It was real! Shamed
By ill-mannered silence, surrender
Pushed dumbfoundment to beg simplification.
Considerate she was, varying the emphasis.

* Pay buttons were used to operate telephones in the 1960s.

'ARE YOU DARK? OR VERY LIGHT?'
Revelation came.
'You mean — like plain or milk chocolate?'
Her assent was clinical, crushing in its light
Impersonality. Rapidly, wavelength adjusted,
I chose, 'West African sepia' — and as an afterthought,
'Down in my passport'. Silence for spectroscopic
Flight of fancy, till truthfulness clanged her accent
Hard on the mouthpiece 'WHAT'S THAT?', conceding,
'DON'T KNOW WHAT THAT IS.' 'Like brunette.'

'THAT'S DARK, ISN'T IT?' Not altogether.
'Facially, I am brunette, but madam, you should see
'The rest of me. Palm of my hand, soles of my feet
'Are a peroxide blonde. Friction, caused —
'Foolishly, madam — by sitting down, has turned
'My bottom raven black — One moment madam!'
— Sensing
Her receiver rearing on the thunder clap
About my ears — 'Madam', I pleaded, 'wouldn't
You rather
'See for yourself?'

(Source: Wole Soyinka, 'Telephone Conversation', in G. Moore and U. Beior, *Modern Poetry from Africa*, Penguin, 1963.)

Question/discussion

1 How does the poem make fun of racism and racial stereotypes?
2 What aspect of racism does Nasreen's story (p. 179) bring out that this poem doesn't?

Racial conflict, control and tolerance

Immigration and race relations laws

Black immigrants first arrived in large numbers in the 1950s. They received little official help and surprisingly little thought was given to how they might affect British society. Probably the most common view was that they would gradually *assimilate* (take on) the British way of life. Today this view is seen as too simple as it has become obvious that ethnic groups prefer to keep some of their familiar way of life (e.g. religion, music). The view that recognises this is called *pluralist*.

It soon became clear that the settlement of about 1.5 million black immigrants of widely varying cultural backgrounds was not going to happen that easily. In 1958, there were race riots in the Notting Hill area of London, and racial incidents and tension began occurring elsewhere. In response, the Conservative Government of the day developed a 'carrot and stick' policy which has basically remained the approach of governments ever since. This was to reduce black immigration, but also to make racial discrimination in the main areas of life illegal. Figure 12.3 summarises the laws covering both sides of this approach. It can be argued that in passing the Immigration Acts of 1971 and 1988, and the British Nationality Act of 1981, the Government itself has been acting in a racially discriminatory way. What do you think?

Figure 12.3. British immigration/nationality and race relations laws

1948	*British Nationality Act* Commonwealth citizens allowed freely to enter and settle in Britain
1962	*Commonwealth Immigrants Act* removed the rights of the 1948 Act for most New (black) Commonwealth citizens. Instead, a limited number of *work vouchers* were issued
1965	*Race Relations Act* made discrimination in certain public places illegal — *but* the means of enforcing the Act were very weak
1968	*Commonwealth Immigrants Act* restricted the entry of East African Asians who held UK passports issued by the British Government
1968	*Race Relations Act* enlarged the scope of the 1965 Act (discrimination being made illegal in employment, housing and the provision of goods and services) *but* enforcement still weak — relying on the new *Community Relations Council* to take up *individual complaints*
1971	*Immigration Act* made a distinction between patrials (those born in Britain or with a parent/grandparent born in Britain) who kept full British citizens rights, and non-patrials (mainly black, New Commonwealth) who were required to obtain work permits prior to entry
1976	*Race Relations Act* extended the anti-discrimination laws to *unintended* as well as intended discrimination — a very important principle
1981	*British Nationality Act* restricted forms of British citizenship provided for those whose entry rights had been removed by previous laws — by now the entry of blacks for settlement is highly controlled and virtually limited to close relatives
1988	*Immigrant Act* An immigrant husband who wants his wife and children to join him must prove he can maintain them

Opinions on the immigration and race relations legislation vary. Some argue that although the immigration laws avoid racist language, they are racist in intention and effect, i.e. they discriminate against blacks. It is also true that whilst the immigration laws have been firmly, even harshly, enforced, the Race Relations Acts are weak and weakly enforced. This has contributed to confusion and mistrust between the races. What is certain is that, by the 1980s, Britain had retreated from the ideals of the 1948 British Nationality Act.

In 1958 West London erupted in race riots... which brought racial hatred bursting out into the open. This was one of the first occasions when Afro-Caribbeans in Britain acted together to defend themselves.

Racial violence and frustration

In the 1980s, racial violence in Britain increased. Racial attacks against blacks went up steadily, accusations of police racial harassment were common, and, in 1981 and 1985, urban disorders involving massive damage to property and serious injury to police and civilians took place. In 1985, the Tottenham disorders were triggered by the death of a black woman during a police raid on her home (in a search for her son). During the disorders, a policeman was brutally killed and there were even more police than civilian casualties.

What has caused racial conflict of this scale and bitterness to develop? There are various possible explanations — racism (especially in employment), the general rise in unemployment which has especially hit blacks, the failure of politicians to create a climate of racial tolerance (see the record of legislation above), and the disillusionment and anger of the second and third generation of black Britons, many of whom feel they face an unfair share of disadvantage, poverty and inequality. The stimulus material and questions enable you to examine this issue more closely.

The future of race and ethnic relations in Britain

Perhaps this chapter has given too negative a view of race relations in Britain. After all, millions of different ethnic groups relate well with each other every day. Such good relations make it possible to hope that full racial equality and tolerance will eventually be achieved in Britain. However, there is a long way to go before this is achieved.

To date we have been mainly concerned with the relations of blacks and whites in Britain. This also may give too simple a view of race and ethnic relations. For instance, there are many more people of Irish than of Afro-Caribbean origin in Britain. There are also hundreds of thousands of people of Jewish extraction, and as many as 200,000 people of Italian descent. Yet, little or nothing has been written here of these and other ethnic groups.

There are also great differences within both 'Asian' and 'Afro-Caribbean' ethnic groups. There are probably more differences among 'Asians' than among Europeans — and, of course, like Europeans 'Asians' sometimes disagree among themselves. Among 'Afro-Caribbeans', for instance, those of Jamaican and Trinidadian origin no more think of themselves as the same than do Lancastrians and the people of Norfolk.

Good race relations are not about destroying the differences between groups, but in accepting and even appreciating and enjoying them. Only by accepting the differences which exist between them can ethnic Britons become one people.

The wider scene: Apartheid

One of the main moral problems facing the world community today is the apartheid regime in South Africa. There, a quarter of the population — whites — control the majority who are of African or Asian origin. How to end apartheid has been the subject of great debate. Black South Africans who want to work inside the system to change it are faced with the difficulty that they are not allowed fully within it — but some try. Others — such as the once — banned African National Congress — are prepared to use violence. Their ageing, charismatic leader, Nelson Mandela, would probably have been released from prison many years earlier if he had been willing to renounce violence.
Internationally there was strong support for economic sanctions (stopping or reducing trade) against South Africa. However, Mrs Thatcher refused to support this policy, preferring to oppose apartheid by diplomacy. British companies remain by far the biggest foreign investor in South Africa, although as many as a fifth quit operating in there between 1985 and 1987. Often, however, they

Nelson Mandela, the leader of the banned African National Congress Party, before his imprisonment in 1964. He was released in 1990.

continue to supply their ex-subsidiaries with technological and management help.

Finally, there are those who ignore apartheid or say it is 'none of our business' — just as some have done with other inhumane regimes.

Activity (outside class)

Write a three or four-point plan to deal with apartheid.

Stimulus questions

ITEM A
Battle of Brixton*

A mob of 100 black youths battled with police in a London street last night.
The fierce clash broke out over a man who was stabbed in Brixton.
Angry black youths poured out of a cafe and surrounded officers who went to help him.
Three officers were injured as police used truncheons and called in dogs to fight off the youths.
Bricks and bottles were hurled through the windscreens of two squad cars as Scotland Yard reinforcements arrived.
They arrested eight youths and restored an uneasy peace.

By James Lewthwaite and Jim Hardy

(Source: The *Sun*, 11 April 1981.)

* Note: Brixton is an area in London in which a high proportion of the population is black.

ITEM B

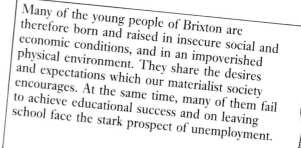

Many of the young people of Brixton are therefore born and raised in insecure social and economic conditions, and in an impoverished physical environment. They share the desires and expectations which our materialist society encourages. At the same time, many of them fail to achieve educational success and on leaving school face the stark prospect of unemployment.

(Source: *The Scarman Report*, Handsworth, Penguin, 1982.)

ITEM C

Figure 12.4. High-status jobs: percentage of workers in professional and managerial work

(Source: *Social Studies Review*, March 1986.)

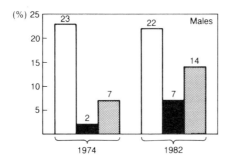

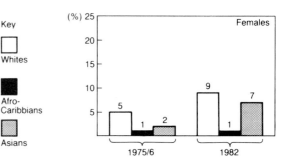

Questions

1 What is the percentage change
   a in white males in high-status jobs between 1974 and 1982 and
   b in Afro-Caribbean females in high-status jobs between 1975/6 and 1982? (Item C)   (2 marks)
2 Define what is meant by 'racial stereotyping'. Find a word or a phrase in Item A which might be considered an example of negative stereotyping.   (3 marks)
3 Do you consider the comments given in Item B help us to understand the civil violence described in Item A? Explain your answer.   (4 marks)
4 Look again at Item C. Comment on the percentage differences between Asians and Afro-Caribbeans in high-status jobs during the periods in question.   (6 marks)

Activity (outside class)

Select a newspaper or magazine which you or a member of your family read regularly. You may need two or three issues to acquire enough data:

1 How large is the publication's coverage of race issues?
2 Note any examples of racial stereotyping.
3 When an ethnic group is being written about, are members of the group consulted for their opinion?
4 What overall conclusion can you make about the coverage of race in that publication with regard to extent, accuracy and bias?

Structured questions

1 Explain the difference between a) individual racism and b) institutional racism, and give an example of each.

(4 marks)

2 Discuss the benefits to a society of having within it people from different ethnic groups. (4 marks)

3 Select *three* of the following, and discuss, using examples, how you think that each of them could try to improve race relations in modern Britain: a) employers, b) schools, c) the mass media, d) the Government, e) the police. (12 marks)

Project and assignment suggestions

1 *A study of an ethnic group* — Ideally, this would be a group you could interview, some of whose members live in or close to your area. Aspects of their culture which might be of particular interest include language/dialects, dress, food, music, folk stories, customs, proverbs, weddings, family life. If you want to narrow the study down, you could research a limited aspect of an ethnic group's culture, say, the role of a local church in the lives of those who attend it.

2 *Racial attitudes (in a mainly white area)* — If you live in an area in which nearly everybody is white, you might find it impossible to adopt project suggestion 1. However, people in your area, including students and teachers in your school, do have attitudes to other racial groups and these attitudes will affect how they behave towards them. Devising a questionnaire or interview schedule to discover attitudes in this very sensitive area is not easy and you will need your teacher's help.

3 *A study of the life-style of a specific age group within an ethnic subculture* (perhaps a particular group within the age group) — An interesting example would be the Rastafarians of the Afro-Caribbean subculture (although. Rastafarians are not exclusively young people). Although you might be able to interview one or more Rastafarians, this is a project that might depend quite heavily on secondary sources — see, for instance, E. E. Cashmore, *Rastaman: The Rastafarian Movement in England*, Allen and Unwin, 1979. If you do this project, you ought first to read the section on black youth in the Chapter Thirteen.

4 *The experience of being a member of an ethnic minority in Britain/what do members of a particular minority think of indigenous Britons?* — The responses you get to this enquiry are likely to vary greatly depending on which ethnic group you research. It might be interesting to pick a *small* sample from two contrasting ethnic groups (say, Italian and Bangladeshi) and compare responses.

5 *The experience and opinions of second, third or fourth-generation offspring of immigrants* — Are members of the generation you chose to study, treated as Britons? Do they feel they have equal opportunity with indigenous Britons of their own age? How do their attitudes and experience compare with those of their parents or grandparents?

6 *A detailed study of race and the media* — This could involve looking at how many ethnic minority groups feature in advertisements and in TV programmes, and how they are presented; a study of 'negative stereotypes' *and* positive images; research into whether members of ethnic groups tend to be associated with 'problems' in news stories.

Key words

Assimilate	Pluralism
Culture/subculture	Racism/institutional racism
Ethnic	Social control
Ideology	Stereotype
Life-style	Underclass

CHAPTER 13 Age and Generation

Introduction: the social construction of age

Biology is the basis of age. Everybody who lives a full life cycle is born, grows up, ages and dies. At each age, the body reaches a given stage of development, although variations between individuals are enormous. Sociologists are mainly interested in how different societies treat age groups, rather than in biological age as such. This varies greatly. For instance, in most traditional societies, old people have much more power and status (respect) than in modern societies. Another example of how the social treatment of age varies is the change in the treatment of children in Britain from, say, the thirteenth century to the modern period. Nowadays, most children go to school; then, few did; instead, they worked, more or less as 'mini-adults'. The different ways societies treat age groups is called *the social construction of age*. Literally, it means that society itself constructs or creates the way of life of people of a given age.

Aware that they are contributing to their families and society, Filipino elderly feel fulfilled.

The terms associated with this topic are straightforward. A full *life cycle* is made up of the *age stages* between life and death. The main age stages are:

- childhood
- youth
- adulthood
- old age

These main age stages can be sub-divided. For instance, there is young adulthood and middle age, early and late old age.

A *generation* refers to those born roughly at the same time — say, to within a year or so. The period between generations is about 30 years. Calculating from childhood, the generations are: childhood, young adulthood, early old age. Calculating from youth, the generations are youth, middle age and late old age.

Activity (class/outside class)

The purpose of this activity is for you to see for yourself how the different stages in the life cycle can change over time. Figure 13.1 deals only with the life cycle of women from the medieval to the modern period as the female life cycle has probably changed even more than that of men. Look at the figure and try to work out what years cover childhood, youth, adulthood and old age for women during the two different periods:

Figure 13.1. Historical perspective on the changing female life cycle in Britain

Years	Medieval (Middle Ages) female	Modern female	Causes of life cycle changes
0	Dependence		
5	....		
10		Dependence	Compulsory schooling to 16
15	Work, e.g. domestic and farm or textile production		
20	....	Paid work	Expansion of service (non-manual) work
25	Marriage/childbirth		
30	Rearing	Childbirth/rearing	State/family support for 'specialised' childrearing period
35	Domestic and other work	Childrearing, domestic and paid work (part-time?)	a Economy demands female labour
40	....		b Families seek higher standard of living
45	Death		
50		Domestic and paid work (part-time?)	c Effective contraception
55			
60			
65		Retirement	a State and occupational pensions
70		Domestic work	b Longer average life span/better health
75			
80		Death	

1 Draw up a diagram of the life cycle of a modern male (and of a medieval male if you think you can). Compare this with the female life cycle.
2 As far as is possible, compare the above description of the life cycle of the modern female against the actual life cycle of your mother and grandmother or some other suitable people. In what respects does the diagram agree and disagree with your real cases?

Childhood

The changing experience or childhood

History

In medieval Britain, childhood was very different from now for both females and males. There was a short few years of infant *dependency* on adults and then they were expected to help with work. In fact, this period of dependency was so short in medieval Europe, that the French historian, Philippe Aries, argues that 'childhood' 'did not exist then'. There was no long period of learning and total dependency as there is now.

Other cultures

In modern, Western societies, many think it 'normal' and 'natural' that the child's most important relationship should be with its mother. Some argue that only the mother-child relationship can provide the necessary love and security, and that without a relationship of this kind, the child will not grow into a healthy adult.

Yet, in some other cultures, the mother-child relationship seems to play a much less important role in children's lives, without their mental or physical health being affected. In these societies, the extended family or wider community gives the child love and support. The following extract gives an example:

> The close relationship between parent and child, which is so important in our civilization is not found in Samoa. Children reared in households where there are half a dozen adult women to care for them and dry their tears, and a half dozen adult males, all of whom represent authority, do not distinguish their parents as sharply as our children do. The image of the fostering, loving mother, or the admirable father is there composed of several aunts, cousins, older sisters, and grandmothers; of chief, father, uncles, brothers, and cousins. Instead of learning as its first lesson that here is a kind mother whose special and principal care is for its welfare, and a father whose authority is to be respected, the Samoan baby learns that its world is composed of a hierarchy of male and female adults, all of whom can be depended upon and must be respected.

(Source: Adapted from Margaret Mead, *The Coming of Age in Samoa*, Penguin, 1971.)

Question

State briefly in your own words what the passage says is the main difference between the relationship between parent and child in the two societies being compared (Samoan and 1920s USA).

Another example of a different method of child rearing occurs in the kibbutzim of Israel (see pp. 27–8). In the original kibbutzim, several children from different families would be brought up together by trained child-care specialists and see their parents only at weekends or holidays. According to Bruno Bettelheim who studied the kibbutzim in his book, *Children of the Dream*, this pattern of socialisation helped form people who worked well with, and had strong loyalty to, their peers (people of the same age and status), but who were less inclined to form deep relationships with individuals. Bettelheim concluded that the kibbutz children fared as well as many children raised in the nuclear family situation more familiar in Europe and the United States.

Children in modern Britain

The twentieth century is sometimes said to be 'the century of the child'. This is because both the state (government) and the nuclear family have become more concerned with the welfare of the individual child. Up to the second part of the nineteenth century, most children belonged to large families and went out to work. Their hard-working parents did not have time to teach them much, and children learnt as much from each other and the wider community as from their parents. Only the children of the rich received a long education, mainly from governesses and then in 'public' (fee-paying) schools, as they often do today. No wonder there was a so-called 'child' and 'youth' problem in Victorian England among the straying offspring of 'poorer folk'.

Free state education, the concern of the welfare state with children, and smaller families enabling parents to give more time to individual children, meant that the life of children in the twentieth century changed considerably. They certainly *seemed* to become the centre of attention. Figure 13.2 summarises the main ways in which the state and the family have become more involved with children:

Figure 13.2

The state
1 Child labour laws (protective/keeping children out of paid work)
2 Universal compulsory education
3 Laws dealing especially with children (e.g. 1980 Child Care Act)

NOT'S ALL THE FUSS ABOUT?

The family
1 Married couples have fewer children
2 As working time decreases, 'family time' increases
3 Families become 'child centred'
4 Family wealth increases
5 Producers and advertisers of toys 'target' the child/family market

Children's problems, child abuse

The material welfare of children has improved since the nineteenth century. Their emotional happiness has probably increased as well. Certainly, when asked which period they prefer, 'then' or 'now', children nearly always say 'now'.

But there is another 'side to the coin'. Children suffer in a variety of ways in late twentieth century Britain — some of them considerably. Probably the basic reason for most children's suffering is when their parents themselves are under pressure or behave in ways damaging to the child's well being. Divorce, separation and being the child of a lone parent are not in themselves *necessarily* harmful to the children involved, but the arguments and pain that usually go with them can be. At the *very* worst, the warm, supportive nuclear family can turn into something of a torture chamber for all its members, including its children, who may then be at risk of abuse.

Child abuse can be divided into four types:

● physical violence
● physical and emotional neglect
● emotional abuse
● sexual exploitation.

Much child abuse occurs within the family, although it does appear that children are more likely to be sexually abused by a stepfather than by their natural father. Outside the family, someone the child knows, as well as strangers, may turn out to be the abuser. A situation of particular risk is when young or mid-teenagers leave home and fall prey to adult — mainly male — exploitation. This seems to have increased since high youth unemployment has resulted in more young people travelling to the 'big city' to 'try their luck'. For

191

instance, once a week, the so-called 'Tebbit express' ('get on your bike') brings in scores of 'kids' to London from the North and Midlands. Although many travel back home for the weekend, they are clearly at risk. Who do you think can best solve this problem — the politicians, families, the kids themselves, or ought the exploiters somehow be persuaded to change?

Because child abuse often occurs in private, it is very difficult to know the extent of it, or whether the trends are up or down. People seem more willing to report child abuse now than in the past, which has led to an official increase in child abuse statistics. A 'moral panic' about child abuse might contribute to this.

Child sex abuse soars in new area

(Source: the *Observer*, 5 July 1987.)

Question

As a social science student, why might you be 'suspicious' of such a headline?

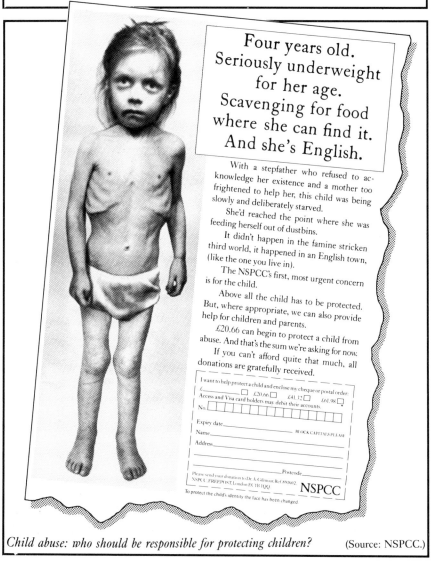

Four years old. Seriously underweight for her age. Scavenging for food where she can find it. And she's English.

With a stepfather who refused to acknowledge her existence and a mother too frightened to help her, this child was being slowly and deliberately starved.

She'd reached the point where she was feeding herself out of dustbins.

It didn't happen in the famine stricken third world, it happened in an English town, (like the one you live in).

The NSPCC's first, most urgent concern is for the child.

Above all the child has to be protected. But, where appropriate, we can also provide help for children and parents.

£20.66 can begin to protect a child from abuse. And that's the sum we're asking for now. If you can't afford quite that much, all donations are gratefully received.

I want to help protect a child and enclose my cheque or postal order:
£ ☐ £20.66 ☐ £41.32 ☐ £61.98 ☐
Access and Visa card holders may debit their accounts.
No. ☐☐☐☐☐☐☐☐☐☐☐☐☐☐☐☐

Expiry date_____
Name_____ BLOCK CAPITALS PLEASE
Address_____
_____
_____Postcode_____
Please send your donation to Dr A. Gilmour Ref 891602.
NSPCC FREEPOST London EC 1B 1QQ   **NSPCC**
To protect the child's identity the face has been changed

Child abuse: who should be responsible for protecting children?   (Source: NSPCC.)

Children's rights and protection

Who should speak for, and protect, children? First, children should be allowed to speak for themselves and should be carefully listened to (sometimes). Young children have not learnt to lie as well as adults and can usually say who or what they see as making them happy or not. In an everyday way, parents have the most 'say' over their children's lives, but, in cases where parents threaten or cannot protect the child's welfare, the state has the 'final word' — by taking the child into care.

To look at the matter more positively, what can be done to *improve* the welfare and happiness of Britain's children? Given that there is an increasing tendency for both parents to do paid work, there are frequent calls for better child-care and nursing facilities for pre-school children.

Stimulus questions

Read the following extracts and answer the questions.

ITEM A

The little boy was about 18 months old and sat in the front seat of the bus. The enormous pom-pom on his woolly hat was bouncing with the movement of the bus, and he clutched at it and sang, 'Jinger bow, jinger bow.' Everyone was smiling until his mother reached over and smacked him hard. 'Stop that and behave yourself.'

A child in a pusher was crying at a bleak, windy bus stop. A bystander offered her a coloured autumn leaf to divert her. The child took it with curiosity, but the parent threw it away. 'She's only interested in food.'

Neither of these young mothers would feature in a social worker's enquiries about child abuse. However, while most homes operate in private (fortunately for adults' civil liberties), parental behaviour in public can be observed at any time. It is research that costs nothing: you only need to take a clipboard on streets and buses, and watch how adults behave with children. Patterns of parental behaviour in public may well link up with grimmer statistics of destructive child abuse. The cruelty of the abusers may increase or decrease in line with the behaviour towards children by the 'normal' parents around them.

I carried out my own study in the streets, shops and buses of a provincial city. I watched a series of adult-child pairs for three minutes each, all of them matched with another pair of people for comparison. There were 85 of each set of pairs. I watched them on sunny afternoons, in places that were not crowded and not at peak hours, so that people were not busy hurrying, or dodging in the traffic.

The pairs that did not include a small child might be male/female, all female or all male. They ranged from teenage to elderly. But whoever they were, within my three-minute observation period, four-fifths had some speech together, or at least a glance or a smile.

By contrast, only a quarter of the adult-child pairs had any communication within two minutes of watching, and under half within three minutes. For two-fifths of my sample what took place was negative.

(Source: Adapted from Valerie Yule, 'Why are Parents so Tough on Children', *New Society*, 27 September, 1986.)

ITEM B

In the modern family women have usually borne the immediate burden of caring for children. That this is still the case is shown in *The Social Life of Britain's Five Year Olds*, a report by the Child Health and Education Survey (Osborn, Butler and Morris 1984). The report is based on responses by parents and health visitors to questionnaires about 13,135 children who were five in the second week of April 1975, the year the survey was carried out. Reviewing the report, Caroline St John-Brooks says:

'The report is, of course, focused on the lives of children. But the lives of their mothers actually emerge from it with extra clarity. Mothers are still by far the most important people in their five year olds' lives. The 'symmetrical family'. . . is hard to find.

'Quite rightly, it is noted that many women find mothering interesting and stimulating as well as hard work. But the mothers' answers to the questionnaire on maternal depression make disheartening reading. Over half 'often get worried about things', nearly half are 'easily irritated and upset', a third often have had headaches, a third often have backache, a third often feel miserable or depressed, a third feel tired most of the time.

'Assuming that the same third of the sample is not answering "Yes" all the time, it's a picture of pretty widespread exhaustion. And fathers do astonishingly little to help.'

(Source: Mike O'Donnell, *Age and Generation*, Tavistock, 1985.)

Continued over page . . .

Questions

1 The research described in Item A covered two sets of 85 pairs. Describe in your own words the main difference in the behaviour of the two sets of pairs. (Item A) (2 marks)
2 Why do you think that the researcher made the remark that 'none of these young mothers would feature in a social worker's enquiries about child abuse'? What point do you think is being made? (Item A) (2 marks)
3 What age were the children in the survey described in Item B? (1 mark)
4 With reference to Item B, describe, in your own words, why so many women find mothering 'hard work'. What connection might there be between overworked mothers and the kind of parent-child relationships described in Item A? (4 marks)
5 What is meant by the term 'symmetrical family'? (Item B) (2 marks)
6 Do you think the Government should provide more assistance for mothers, in paid work, who have young children? Explain your answer. (3 marks)
7 Describe *three* important changes in the lives of 'average children' in Britain over the last 200 years or so. What are the main reasons for these changes? (6 marks)

Youth

With the possible exception of the old, more generalisations and stereotypes exist about the young than any other age group. The young have been labelled 'rebellious', 'conformist', 'helpful', 'irresponsible', 'difficult', and much more. The fact that many of these labels contradict each other does not stop people using them. Such labels may serve the attention-grabbing needs of the popular media, but they are of no use to social scientists.

The experience of modern youth: being 'in between'

Modern youth is an 'in-between' or *transitional* stage between childhood and adulthood. Youth is a period of preparation for adulthood and of freedom from full adult responsibilities. The following are the main factors that 'construct' modern youth, i.e. the factors that make it the way it is.

Education and job preparation

Compulsory education separates young people from other age groups more than anything else. Young people *have* to spend a lot of time together, whether they like it or not. More and more young people are staying in education or training until the age of eighteen. This extends the period in which they are *dependent* on adults. However, a majority of sixteen to eighteen year olds now have some income other than from their parents, either from part-time work or in the form of a training grant. The longer a person stays in education, the longer is this period of dependency, and sometimes young people feel they lack real control over their own lives. For this reason, some leave school as soon as possible.

As well as educating young people, schools are increasingly trying to prepare them for the world of work. This is done by teaching general 'awareness' of the economy and the world of work, and by introducing more vocational courses (see p. 50).

Much of what pupils and students learn in educational institutions happens outside formal lessons in their own *informal* interactions and conversations. Where to pick up a part-time job, what the 'in things' are in music and fashion, the goings on in the neighbourhood are examples. Peer groups are very important in informal learning.

Romance, partner search and the peer group

The peer group is the key social grouping for youth other than the family, and for some it is more important than the latter. The peer group consists of people of about the same age who provide each other with support and identity. Young people build up their sense of identity by comparing themselves with each other and by experimenting with various roles (for instance, it is possible to try out the roles of 'ideas person', 'toughie' and 'joker', all within a week).

The peer group can be divided into the *clique* and the *crowd*. The 'clique' consists of from two to, at most, six peers who are close friends. In early adolescence, clique members tend to be of the same sex, but, in later adolescence, they are often of mixed sex. The 'crowd' consists of several cliques — the sort of grouping that might get together for a party. It is the clique that supplies close, immediate peer support. The crowd provides an opportunity to meet a wider section of people, including, possibly, a future marriage partner (Figure 13.3).

Figure 13.3. Cliques, the crowd and couples

The youth market

Like adults, young people have become much better off since the Second World War. Unlike most adults, a relatively small proportion of the income of young people has to be spent on things like mortgages, insurance payments, interest on credit, etc. This *uncommitted income* is an obvious target for the leisure and entertainments industry. After all, what else have most young people got to spend it on? Young people spend proportionately much more than other age groups on records and cassettes, discos, the cinema, clothes and cosmetics.

Not all new 'fashions' are started by the leisure industry. Young people sometimes start them for themselves. Music and dress are part of the 'language' of youth (i.e. part of the way young people communicate with each other) and are always changing. For instance, punk music and style began with the 'kids' before it became 'commercial'.

Different generations . . . different worlds . . .

The 'ordinary' majority of youth

Most young people, like most of the rest of the population, more or less conform and are more or less satisfied with life. Again and again, surveys report that young people tend to get on quite well with their parents, recognise that school is necessary if not always fun, and are no more politically rebellious than the rest of the population.

Of course, the kind of life a young person conforms to depends on his or her social background, including class, race and gender. For instance, Figure 13.4 shows that most working-class children think and behave in a way that will lead them to similar jobs and lives as their parents.

Figure 13.4

	'Adolescent boys in East London', P. Wilmott, 1966	%		'Schooling ordinary (working-class) kids', P. Brown, 1985	
Attitudes to work/class	Those with middle class ambitions	20	Attitudes to school	(Males and females) 'Swots'	Pro-school minority
	Satisfied 'solid' working-class	70		'Ordinary kids'	'Making an effort' majority (mainly 2–4 grades, CSE)
	Delinquents	10		'Rems'	Anti-school minority

Figure 13.5. British young 1974: parents O.K.; school/teachers — not so good

Activity (class/outside class)

The data below are from a survey of teenagers of over fifteen years ago (not quite old enough to be most readers' parents).

Either:
1 Do a survey of your own class covering the same points as Figure 13.5,
or:
2 Devise a larger survey — perhaps as the basis of a project.

1974 growth survey

Parents: four out of five teenagers get on well with mother and father
Dress and hair: Main source of friction with parents, but frequently so only in 11 per cent of homes
Smoking: two-thirds don't — and only one in 20 smoke 10 a day or more
Marriage: considered a good idea, with two children about right.
Television: the top spare-time activity with two out of three watching it 'often'
Drinking: Many admit going to pubs although it's illegal
School: nearly a third don't like it and over half admit to occasional truancy

(Source: National Children's Bureau.)

The problems of youth, and youth as a 'problem'

The fact that most young people get on with life in a pretty ordinary way does not mean that they don't have particular problems. Long schooling, the pressure of exams and just growing up in a competitive society contribute to tension and high rates of some mental illnesses among the young. Teenage girls, for instance, are the group most likely to suffer from anorexia nervosa (self-starvation due to the desire to be very slim). In Western society, slimness is thought to be attractive and desirable, and for some teenage girls, the ideal of slimness turns into a dangerous obsession.

In Western society, to be very slim is thought to be attractive. But to be very slim isn't necessarily healthy for everyone. Do you see any problems with this kind of advertisement.

In the process of growing up, a minority of young people become 'a problem' for their parents and other 'authorities'. Learning itself involves mistakes. Having plenty of time and (sometimes) money to 'play around with' can increase the chances of 'disaster'. Learning to drink alcohol, learning one's own strengths and weaknesses, learning to drive, learning to 'chat someone up', can all lead to mistakes and conflicts with others, including authorities. About a quarter of all crime is committed by those in the sixteen to nineteen age group. However, as most young people do not get convicted for crime and as most who do never 'do it again', it does seem that the young 'learn from their mistakes' (or don't get caught making them).

The 'extraordinary' minority of youth

The free time and freedom from responsibility of youth gives the opportunity to experiment in various ways. A minority of young people take this opportunity with both hands and, for a time, develop *subcultures* (ways of life) different in many ways from the majority of the population. Examples of youth subcultures are teddy boys, mods and rockers, hippies, hell's angels, punks, goths and casuals.

Youth subcultures don't just suddenly appear. They usually 'stand for something' and relate to society — even if only to oppose it. For instance in the 1960s, the hippies opposed the Vietnam war and wanted 'peace and love'; in the 1970s, the punks tried to sing for (and sing like) unemployed youth; in the 1980s, the casuals reflected the emphasis on success and looking good.

Semiotics and subcultures

Semiotics is the science of the meaning of signs. Working out what dress styles mean is an example of semiotics (i.e. treating dress as a 'sign system'). Dress style is one of the main ways in which members of subcultures convey their meanings and messages. For instance, the 'rag-tag' dress of the punks could be interpreted (taken to mean) that they did not mind being poor or that they wanted to shock 'glam' people.

One of the best known subcultures are the skinheads who first appeared in the early 1960s. At first, most 'skins' were East End working class and in many ways resembled a 'souped-up' or dramatised version of their dads (see Figure 13.6).

Activity (class/outside class)

1   List the style characteristics of a youth subculture, e.g. hippies, punks.
2   Interpret the meaning of their style.

Figure 13.6. Semiological interpretation of the skinheads

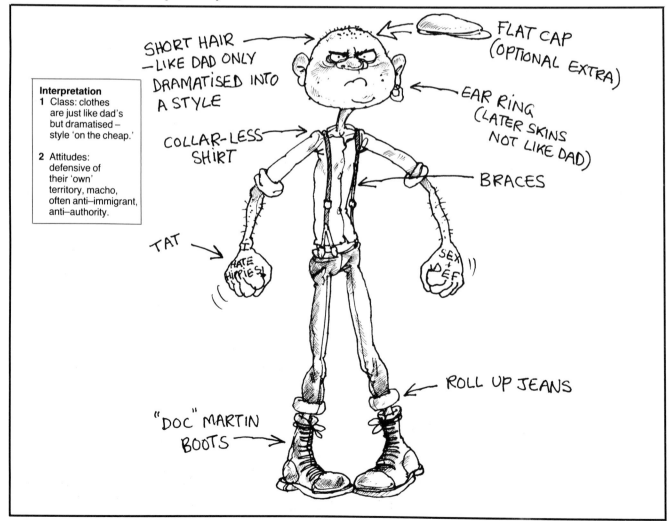

Gender and youth

Again and again in this book you will meet evidence that girls are brought up to think, behave and feel (yes, *feel*) differently from boys. The way girls are socialised varies considerably, depending on class and ethnic group, but few girls experience completely equal opportunities to males, whatever their social situation.

Christine Griffin's *Typical Girls? Young Women from School to the Job Market* is a study of mainly working-class school girls. She examines their experience and expectations in what she calls three 'markets':

1 the labour (job) market
2 the marriage market
3 the sexual market.

Points (2) and (3) are not, of course, the same thing.

The girls surveyed by Griffin were mainly hoping for office rather than factory work, and reflect the kind of work that is now mainly available for females. In the areas of the sexual and marriage markets, the girls by no means all conform to the 'pant and swoon' stereotypes of the more romantic teen magazines. Perhaps the increased opportunity of earning their own living — for most of their lives — is providing a basis for more female independence. The following activity gives you a chance to assess what is happening in the three 'markets' among young females (and males) you know.

Activity (class/outside class)

1 Discuss the differences between males and females in the three 'markets' and try to explain why they exist. Are things changing as the study by Griffin suggests they might be?
2 You could carry out a small social survey into male and female differences in relation to the three markets (see project suggestions).

Race and youth

You can't generalise about young people of Asian and Afro-Caribbean origin any more easily than about the rest of youth. The one generalisation that stands up is that they are all *at risk* of racism in this country, although the extent to which they are *actually* victims of racism varies between individuals.

Despite racism, a small but growing minority of Asian and Afro-Caribbean young people are achieving high status and well-paid jobs. The official figures show it is mainly males, especially of Asian origin, who are achieving better jobs. However, there are signs that Afro-Caribbean females, a group very under-represented in better jobs, are beginning to make some progress in promotion in lower white-collar work, such as assistant management in office or retail work. This is limited, but it may be a start.

A far higher proportion of Afro-Caribbean youth are either unemployed or are in low than high-paid jobs. Some get involved in a 'street and club' way of life. Like other youth subcultures, black youth subcultures are about having fun, looking for romance and trying to find some meaning in life. The music and dress styles of black youth subcultures usually come from the West Indies. In the 1960s, the tough, street-wise style of the West Indian 'rude boy' was used by Afro-Caribbean youth before it was partly taken up by the skinheads.

The Rastafarians are perhaps the best known Afro-Caribbean subculture. Part of Rasta style is dreadlocks (see photograph) and their music is reggae. Generally, Rasta is a mellow, peaceful way of life, bringing hope of better times to racially exploited blacks. There are different interpretations of what dreadlocks stand for. Maybe you know, or can find somebody who does...

199

More young blacks drift in and out of subcultures than do young whites. This is mainly because of the lack of opportunities offered by the mainstream system, and because of the popularity of the subcultures themselves. For the same reasons, black adults are more likely than whites to live 'on the margins' of society and, more than mainly white youth subcultures, black youth subcultures are often training grounds for a long-term 'outsider' life-style.

The 'success'

The 'outsider'

Stimulus questions

ITEM A

In the 1930s, as now, these worries settled around a cluster of directly familiar themes. Newspapers sensationalised motor-bandits, razor gangs and bag-snatches in the city streets. There were major disturbances at football matches — such as pitch invasions and attacks on referees and players — and the Hollywood cinema and Chicago gangster movies were regularly blamed for lowering public morals and inciting 'copy-cat' crimes among the young.

Youthful crime was often a linked with these problems.

(Source: Adapted from Geoffrey Pearson, 'Hooligans and Youthful Crime: 'Permissiveness' and Tradition', *Social Studies Review*, March 1988.)

ITEM B

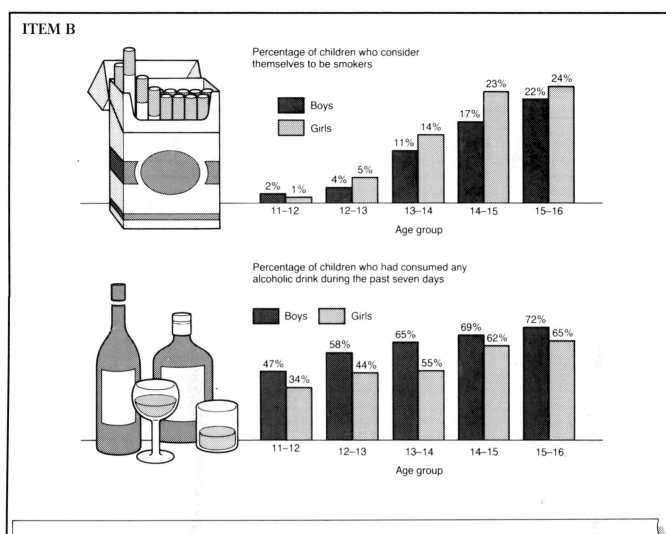

Percentage of children who consider themselves to be smokers

Boys / Girls

Age group	Boys	Girls
11–12	2%	1%
12–13	4%	5%
13–14	11%	14%
14–15	17%	23%
15–16	22%	24%

Percentage of children who had consumed any alcoholic drink during the past seven days

Boys / Girls

Age group	Boys	Girls
11–12	47%	34%
12–13	58%	44%
13–14	65%	55%
14–15	69%	62%
15–16	72%	65%

Pupils take pub and homework in moderation

The parents of Britain's pre-teens and early adolescents can forget what they read in newspapers about 14 year olds taking part in drunken orgies at unsupervised parties or watching hours of porno movies on a friend's video when they should be doing homework.

If the replies of 18,002 pupils aged between 11 and 16 in a survey published yesterday are sincere and honest, not even somebody else's children are doing it.

The times may be changing, with less homework, more paid work, more under-age drinking, less reading of books for pleasure, more 'steadies' at 11 or 12, more dieting, more high-fibre meals. But significant numbers still do not smoke, drink alcohol, or go to discos. And many more take a lot of showers and baths, wash their hair at least twice a week, save money — and don't eat chips...

Just under a third of the 11 and 12 year olds said they had been given no homework on the previous day, while this proportion had risen to almost three out of five by age 15 and 16.

On the topic of TV, 18.5 per cent of 11 and 12-year-old boys and 11.2 per cent of girls of the same age said they watched more than five hours the previous day. As they get older they watch less.

By the age of 15–16, 68 per cent of boys and 54 per cent of girls confessed to reading not a single book for pleasure at home on the previous day.

Quite a few children, even at the earliest ages surveyed, do paid work, with just under a half at 15–16 getting their own income, not just pocket money. Of the later group, a fifth work in the evenings, during term-time; one in 10 does more than 10 hours a week; and 16.8 per cent of boys and 19.2 per cent of girls get more than £10 a week.

(Source: the *Guardian*, 16 December 1987.)

Continued over page...

ITEM C

Listed are some of Britain's institutions. From what you know or have heard about each one, can you say whether, on the whole, you think it is well run?

Table 13.1. Faith in institutions	Adolescents (per cent)	Adults (per cent)
Banks	91	85
The police	74	72
Independent TV and radio	76	69
The BBC	69	67
The press	50	49
The National Health Service	42	49
Prisons	42	46
Manufacturing industry	54	40
The civil service	57	40
Local government	41	33
The trade unions	36	27
Nationalised industries	51	20

(Source: Adrian Furnham, 'The Ways of the Young', *New Society*, 8 January 1988)

Questions

1 Name one problem often linked with youth in different periods of recent history. (Item A) (1 mark)
2 Why do you think the general public sometimes gets a bad impression of youth in general when the 'hooligans' are only a limited number? (Item A) (1 mark)
3 a) Which sex of eleven–sixteen year olds consumes alcohol most frequently? (Item B) (1 mark)
 b) Give one possible sociological reason for this. (2 marks)
4 How many people took part in the survey (Item B)? (1 mark)
5 Which is the only institution in which, according to the details of the survey given in Item C, adults have more faith than adolescents (teenagers)? (Item C) (1 mark)
6 Examining the evidence given in Items B and C, would you say most young people seem fairly conformist (like the rest of society) or not? Give reasons for your answer. (Items B and C) (5 marks)
7 Despite exaggerations and sensationalism, there are some young people who *do* behave in ways that seriously worry most adults. Give *two* examples of such behaviour and try to explain why they are particularly associated with young people. (8 marks)

Activity (class/outside class)

Figure 13.8 gives you information on youth sub-cultures from 1953–54 to the early 1980s. As you can see, the information is given under the following headings: date, subculture, class and race, style, music and meaning. For each subculture up to 1978, one piece of information is missing. After 1978 less and less information is given in each slot and from 1982 no information is given at all. The activity is to fill in the missing information up to your own time — if you want to go that far.

To get information, you will probably have to ask older brothers, sisters, cousins, etc, and perhaps younger teachers. You will find the answers up to 1978 at the end of this chapter; after that date, you are on your own! You might find that from the early 1980s, youth styles and music are less easy to link with class (if not race). On the other hand, you might well be able to find differences amongst youth reflecting regions — given the relative affluence and poverty of different areas.

Figure 13.8

Date	Sub-culture	Class and Race	Style	Music	Meaning (Semiotics)
1953–4	Teds	Unskilled working class	Drapes	————	Newly better off working-class kids 'putting on the style', having fun
1955–6	Teds				
1958–61	Beats/CND		Duffle coat, beards	Jazz/Folk	Artistic/intellectual, pleasure-seeking
1963	Mods	Semi-skilled		R 'n' B/Tamla	Sharp and stylish
1964	Rockers		Motor-bike	Rock 'n' roll	Rough and ready
1967–72	Hippies	Middle class/student		Progressive rock	Protest, the 'alternative' society
1967	Rude boys	Black underclass	Hustling		City survivors
1968–9	Skinheads		Boots 'n' braces	Ska	
1970	Glams	Working class?		Glamrock	'Mixed up' world
1970	Rastas		Dreadlocks	Reggae	Rastafarian religion
1976–8	Punks	Working class?	Absurdity		Anarchy?
1978–81	Mod/ted/skinhead revivals	Less clear? (Styles spread and change quickly among youth...)			
1981	New Romantics				
1982	?				

Adulthood

It may seem unfair to adults to give them so short a section here. If so, this at least reflects the way in which many hard-working adults feel they are taken for granted by other generations (particularly, their offspring)! However, the authors' intention is not to 'short change' their own generation. In fact, most of the rest of this book is about adults. They dominate economic and family life, and in dealing with these matters, we deal with their concerns and problems.

Adults are the 'power-house' which generates and regenerates society. They do this in two ways:

- work (paid) — production of goods and services, and
- family life — reproduction and socialisation of children, maintenance of the home.

The central position of adulthood in economic and social life results in the following relationship with other generations:

Adults		*Others*
Power	$\longrightarrow$	Responsibilities for
Independence	$\longrightarrow$	Dependence on

Activity (class/outside class)

This activity is to let you explore further the relations between the generations. You could choose any two generations but those selected here are youth and adulthood.

Draw up two lists: one of the areas of power which your parents have over you that you find acceptable, the other of those areas which you find difficult to accept. You could do this individually or in small groups and then discuss as a class.

Does any pattern emerge from your lists? Are there any areas of 'parent power' in which you are able to *negotiate* and perhaps gain some power for yourself? How do you think you will deal with your own teenage children — will you 'give' them more or less freedom than you have? If so, in what areas of their lives?

You could carry out the same exercise in relation to teenagers and teachers as well as/instead of the above.

Old age

Perhaps the most common stereotypes of the old are that they are 'useless' and that they 'have problems'. The phrase 'when I'm old and useless' illustrates the negative thinking about old age still widespread in British society.

Low status and negative images of the old are *not* inevitable. The position of the old in society is created by members of society itself, i.e. it is *socially constructed*. For instance, in most traditional, agricultural societies, elderly people have more power and status and do more work than in modern Britain. It is not *necessary* to retire people compulsorily at 60 or 65 years, and in Britain to pay them one of the lowest state pensions in Western Europe. Indeed, in the United States, compulsory retirement was abolished in 1988.

Of course, there *is* a biological basis to old age. The body does 'run down' and eventually dies. However, humans have managed to affect the ageing process itself. Medicine has both lengthened old age and made at least the earlier part of it healthier for most. These changes have made it necessary to divide old age into *early* (65–75) and *later* (75+) old age. In addition, the greater wealth of modern societies has increased the possible comfort and opportunities of old age.

Early old age should be, and often is, a period when people do some of the things they have always wanted to do, but perhaps never had enough time for. Travelling, seeing more of friends, spending more time on leisure pursuits, or perhaps on a charitable activity are all options — though some do require money. Older adults often go to classes of a leisure or educational kind. With the number of sixteen to nineteen olds falling, many schools and colleges have opened some day courses to adults. This provides an opportunity for mixing across the age groups and for breaking down age 'segregation'.

Later old age is more likely to bring physical and mental health problems. In turn, this puts pressure on either relatives or the welfare state to 'care for' the ailing aged. In Britain, it is accepted that the old should receive the help and care they need. In theory, if relatives cannot or will not provide the necessary support, the state will. But how well are the needy elderly being cared for? The answer is that the situation varies greatly. For instance, some *sheltered accommodation* is very effective. Sheltered accommodation provides residents with considerable freedom and independence, whilst enabling them to receive support and services and to call for help when they need it. On the other hand, in some homes for the elderly, there have been cases of cruelty and neglect. The only solution to this is to provide more resources for training and facilities and proper, regular inspection.

Sheltered accommodation is growing in popularity among the elderly.

Recently, the Conservative Government introduced a policy of *community care* for the old. But what is meant by 'community' and who pays for the caring? Some are suspicious that 'the community' will turn out to be the old person's daughter who perhaps has a growing family and would like to have a part-time job. Again, community care can only work if it is properly organised and paid for.

Many 75 and 85 year olds might object to the previous paragraphs on the grounds that they stereotype post-75 year olds as either sick or dying. Far from it. Many of them do not feel old at all and prove it by continuing to remain highly active in a wide range of activities. It is as dangerous to generalise about the old as any other age group. Differences of class, gender and race help to produce great differences in life-style. For instance, what do a recently retired miner and the Queen Mother have in common, other than their right to draw the old age pension? The answer is 'not much'. (For more information on old age, see Chapter Sixteen.)

Stimulus question

ITEM A

'Gerontologists (researchers into old age) have coined the term ageism to refer to the negative image of someone who is old simply because of his or her age. Like racism or sexism, it is wholesale discrimination against all members of a group, though usually it appears in a more hidden form. Threatened cutbacks in social security and failure to provide meaningful outlets or activities are examples of ageism.

ITEM B

A stereotype is an oversimplified belief which tends to persist despite contradictory factual evidence. Table 13.2 shows a high level of negative stereotypes about old age among the American public:

Table 13.2. Differences between personal experiences of Americans aged 65 and over, and expectations held by other adults about those experiences

	Very serious problems experienced by the elderly themselves %	Very serious problems the public expects the elderly to experience %	Net difference
Fear of crime	23	50	+27
Poor health	21	51	+30
Not having enough money to live on	15	62	+47
Loneliness	12	60	+48
Not having enough medical care	10	44	+34
Not having enough education	8	20	+12
Not feeling needed	7	54	+47
Not having enough to do to keep busy	6	37	+31
Not having enough friends	5	28	+23
Not having enough job opportunities	5	45	+40
Poor housing	4	35	+31
Not having enough clothes	3	16	+13

(Source: adapted from Mike O'Donnell, *Age and Generation*, Tavistock, 1985.)

Questions

1 a Define 'ageism' (2 marks)
  b Give two examples of ageism. (Item A) (2 marks)
2 In what area of concern is there the biggest gap between the *actual* experiences of the elderly and expectations of the public? (Item B) (1 mark)
3 a Define the term stereotype. (Item A) (1 mark)
  b Look at the responses of the public given in Item B. How would you sum up the stereotype of old age held by much of the American public? Illustrate your answer with examples. (Item B) (3 marks)
4 b Briefly discuss what problems can result from members of the public viewing certain groups as *stereotypes* (as in the case of some members of the public and the old). (6 marks)

Structured questions

1 Explain, with examples, the difference between 'biological' and 'social' definitions of age groups. (4 marks)
2 In some societies, the passage from 'youth' to 'adulthood' is marked by a ceremony. In Britain today, young people take on various adult rights and responsibilities over a long period. Drawing on your own experience, briefly discuss the possible problems arising from the long drawn-out passage to full adult status. (6 marks)
3 Age is one form of stratification, others are based on class, gender or ethnic group. Using examples, discuss whether age is more, or less, important than these other forms of stratification. (10 marks)

Project and assignment suggestions

1 *Compare adult-adult and adult-child interactions (the way they act together)* — This might take the form of repeating on a smaller scale the observational survey of Valerie Yule described in detail in the first piece of stimulus material on p. 193.
2 *Child poverty* — You could cover both the extent (statistics) and experience (case studies) of child poverty. *Social Trends* provides some information on the former and you could probably get information from the Child Poverty Action Group and/or Dr Barnado's to cover the whole topic.
3 *Youth: An attitude survey* — What do young people think about school? Their parents? The Prime Minister? Capital punishment? A problem with this kind of survey is that it has been done so often before — and nearly always with much the same results. Most young people seem more or less to conform to their class, family and racial background. You could vary your approach, either by comparing the attitudes of the young to those of another generation, or, if you can find a survey of a previous generation of youth, with their attitudes (see p. 196).
4 *Youth subcultures* — If you want to find out about the fun and excitement, then research one of the minority youth subcultures. 'The History and Views of the Punks' or 'The Hippie Movement' are titles that will take you in very different directions. Among your sources might be newspaper and magazine articles of ten or twenty years ago, if your local library can provide them. Try to avoid making your project too simple and descriptive. Perhaps, look into the views of members of the subculture or do a semiological analysis of their dress.
5 *Old age* — What are the differences between what the old think and do and what other generations *believe* they think and do? The second piece of stimulus material on p. 205 should give you some ideas of how to organise your research into this question.

Key words

Age stage	Life cycle
Elique	Peer group
Crowd	Subculture
Generation	Uncommitted income

Answers to Activity (p. 202)

1/2 Rock 'n' roll, 3 Middle class, 4 Scooter, 5 Unskilled, 6 Long hair, psychedelic drugs, 7 Ska, 8 Unskilled, 9 Unisex, 10 Black underclass, 11 Punk rock.

14 Social Control and Deviance

Rules, norms and social order

We are all familiar with the idea of 'rules'. There are rules in school, rules in sport, and rules about driving on the road. Some rules only apply to certain people, or only at a certain time or place. For example, most school rules apply to pupils but not to teachers, and driving on the left-hand side of the road applies when driving in England, but not when driving in France or Spain. The laws of a country are intended to apply to everybody living in that country.

Many important rules, such as laws, are written down. Other rules of society are not necessarily written down, but we are socialised into usually taking notice of them. For example, not going out in pyjamas, not playing in church, not pushing to the front of a queue are all examples of unwritten rules in our society which most people obey.

The need for rules is obvious!

One reason for rules is to make people behave in a certain way — a way which is considered to be 'right' in certain circumstances. (We will look later at the question of who decides what the 'right' way should be.) Those rules and ways of behaving which are generally approved of in a society are known as '*norms*'. By more or less conforming to society's norms people create *social order*.

Activity (class)

Norms may be written down (e.g. laws), or simply 'understood' (e.g., how to behave in the classroom). Write down *three* examples of *each* type of norm.

Social control: sanctions and rewards

The process by which members of a group of a society are encouraged or made to conform to the norms of that society or group is known as *social control*. Social control operates by means of *sanctions*, a term which refers to what can happen to people if they break rules or norms, e.g. punishments. Social control can be *formal* or *informal*. Formal social control operates through rules and laws which are usually written down. There are particular sanctions for each type of offence, and the sanctions too are usually written down. Examples of formal social control are the *fines* imposed for offences such as speeding, *detentions* given for misbehaving at school, or *imprisonment* for more serious crimes such as robbery.

Informal social control operates when other people (often our families, friends or peers) show us in various ways that they don't approve of our behaviour. The type of sanction in such cases can range from a disapproving look, a smack (much used as a sanction against small children!), scorn and ridicule ('Don't be such a silly twit!') right through to being shut out of the circle (e.g. 'sent to Coventry').

Of course, social control doesn't only operate by 'punishing' us in some way when we break a rule. It can operate just as effectively by 'rewarding' us when we do something which is considered right, such as getting a medal for bravery, or applause for winning a race for the school, or the smiles and admiration of our friends.

Activity (class)

Below is a list of examples of cases where rules have been broken. Draw up a table like the one shown below, and copy out the 'broken rules'. For each one, say what you think the likely sanction will be, and whether this is an example of formal or informal social control.

Rule broken	*Sanction*	*Formal/informal control*
Smoking in school		
Laughing at a funeral		
Getting drunk and being sick at a party		
Not paying a TV licence fee		
A player swearing at a referee in a football match		
Drinking under age in a pub		
Killing somebody		
Spreading lies about a classmate		
Cheeking a teacher		
Cheeking a police officer		

Did you find some of those difficult to answer — did you find yourself saying 'Well, it all depends…'? If so, you have discovered for yourself one of the 'problem' areas of this topic, something which will be discussed later in the chapter.

Norms and socialisation

Most of our knowledge about the rules and norms of our society is learned as part of our socialisation. There are a number of different 'agencies of socialisation' involved in this process. The most important ones are the family, the school, peer groups, the mass media, the work place, the police and the legal system, which includes judges, magistrates and law courts. From each of these, and in different ways, we learn what is considered 'acceptable' behaviour in different situations. Religious beliefs and institutions form another agency of socialisation, though for many people, these are not as important a guide to behaviour as they have been in the past. For other people, they remain very important indeed.

Activity (class)

Alongside is a list of norms which could be found among groups of Britons today. For each one, state from which 'agency of socialisation' you think the norm would have been learned. For example, if you think that 'good manners' are learned within the family, write 'family'. For some norms, you might decide that there is more than one agency of socialisation involved.

Norm	*Agency of socialisation*
Good manners	
Not cheating	
Beliefs about birth control	
The importance of good qualifications	
What kind of clothes to wear	
Respect for royalty	
Political beliefs	
Views about crime	
Ideas of 'femininity' and 'masculinity'	

Deviance

A 'deviant' is someone who does not behave according to the norm, either written or unwritten. Committing a crime or insulting somebody are both deviant acts. Crime is just one form of deviance in which the rule that is broken is a law.

However, it is not at all easy to define any particular act as deviant. It will depend on *what* is happening, *where* it is happening, *who* is doing it and *who* is making the decision about what it means. For example, if someone shoots another person, this may not only be deviant, but criminal, unless it is happening in wartime, in which case the 'deviant' may be awarded a medal for bravery. Laughing during a funeral is deviant; during a comedy show it is quite normal. Nowadays, we are quite used to seeing girls and women in trousers or jeans, but 100 years ago in Britain, it would have been regarded as highly deviant. Some people think that brightly coloured dyed hair or shaved heads are highly deviant forms of fashion, but for punks or skinheads, these are 'normal'. What all this means is that deviance is *relative* — it depends on the situation, and on who is making the judgement, as to whether an act will be labelled deviant or not.

Labelling

To label someone deviant means to treat them publicly as deviant. Some people and groups in society have much more power than others to label a person or an act as deviant. Police officers, judges and magistrates, teachers, doctors, the mass media — all of these, under certain circumstances, have more power than other groups to label another person or group as deviant and to make that label stick. 'Troublemaker', 'criminal', 'failure', 'terrorist', 'mentally disturbed', 'welfare scrounger', 'loony lefty', 'poofter', 'vandal' are all examples of deviant labels which some groups are able to apply to others.

To treat somebody as a *stereotype* means to label them as 'a type' without considering them as individuals. For instance, a police constable may stop a male 'skinhead' merely because he 'looks suspicious', whereas a smartly dressed but rather drunk young woman may just get a concerned look. The stereotype here of a skinhead is 'young criminal'. What would you say the stereotype of the young woman might be?

Sociologists, particularly Marxists, are very interested in the ways in which the very powerful people in society are able to get *their* kind of behaviour accepted as 'right' and 'lawful', and *other* people's behaviour defined as 'deviant'.

Marxists point out that some have more power to make the rules than others.

Who commits crime and why?

This section will set up a picture of the 'typical' criminal and then ask whether it is quite as true as it seems. An examination of crime statistics would show that a large proportion of *recorded* crimes are committed in urban areas by young, working-class males. There have been a number of suggested explanations of *why* this particular group of people appears to commit more criminal acts than other groups. The following are some of the suggested explanations.

Boredom
Young males have quite a lot of free time, and often not enough money to pay for entertainment. They spend much of their time 'hanging around' in groups, and this often leads to their 'getting into trouble' — fighting, vandalism, joyriding, petty theft, etc.

Status frustration and the desire to 'get rich quick' (the economic motive)
Young working-class males know, from their socialisation and their exposure to the mass media, which occupations and possessions are valued and sought after in our society, in other words, which have 'high status'. Lacking the money and the qualifications to get these things by legitimate means, they turn to crime as an alternative way of gaining status. There have been several TV series about criminal gangs in which the gang leaders wear Armani suits, Gucci shoes, own a luxury yacht, a villa in Spain, and drive a Porsche or Mercedes.

Macho image
Young men are often under a lot of pressure to conform to a 'macho' stereotype. Lacking the ability to present an image through possessions such as fast sports cars, they 'prove' their masculinity by activities such as fighting or engaging in criminal or delinquent acts.

Criminal subculture
Many young working-class males are brought up in areas with very high crime rates, where, it is suggested, crime is seen as a 'normal' way of life. Through the process of socialisation, they accept such behaviour as normal.

Poverty and unemployment
For most people, unemployment brings not only poverty but boredom. These, in turn, can lead to crime and delinquency.

Opportunity
More crimes are recorded in cities because there are not only more people, but more *opportunities* for crime — more cars to steal, more houses, to rob, more shops to break into, etc, whereas legal opportunities to obtain wealth — jobs — are *more* limited.

Figure 14.1

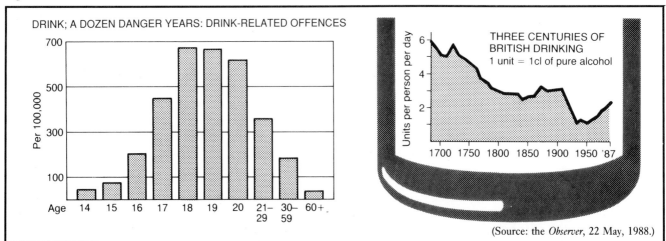

(Source: the *Observer*, 22 May, 1988.)

Question

Do you think it is drink which causes some young males to be violent (mainly against each other) or some other factor? Discuss.

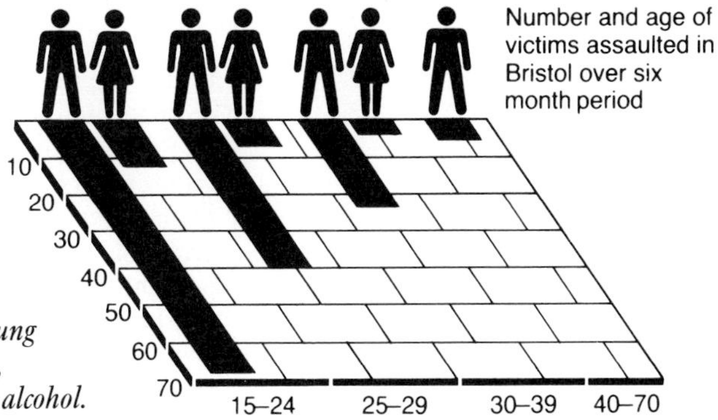

Number and age of victims assaulted in Bristol over six month period

Figure 14.2
Most assaults are on young men, not elderly women, and most are fuelled by alcohol.

(Source: the *Observer*, 26 June, 1988.)

Age

Young males often go through a 'wild' stage in which official figures indicate they commit much more crime than other sections of the population. As they get older, they 'settle down' and also acquire adult responsibilities — a wife, children, a mortgage — and these responsibilities lead them to try to keep out of trouble.

Activity (class)

Below is a list of statements which a young man might have made to one of his friends after having been 'nicked' by a police officer. Try to fit each statement with the appropriate 'reason' as given in the headings above, from 'Boredom' down to 'Age'. Some of them may overlap.

'What was he picking on me for — everybody does it round our way!'
'Well, I ask you, leaving all these fancy cars lined up outside the nightclub — what do they expect?'

'I've always wanted a stereo like that one, and I'm not going to afford one on my poxy wages, am I?!'
'Of course I joined in the fight in the pub — I couldn't just walk away, could I?'
'Well, it seemed a bit of a laugh at the time — there was nothing much going on.'
'If he spent all his time down the Job Centre or hanging around street corners, he might start sniffing glue, as well.'
'The old fogies are all the same, picking on us just 'cos we're still able to have a bit of fun. They're only jealous!'

Criticisms

Each one of the explanations of crime suggested above has its critics — people who do not agree with it. One of the main objections put forward is that none of these explanations really helps us to understand why only *some* people from each of the groups mentioned commit crimes.

Another important criticism concerns the fact that the explanations above all treat the crime statistics as though they were a complete and accurate account of the crimes committed in our society. With this in mind, some sociologists have studied the way in which the crime statistics themselves are arrived at, and instead of asking 'Why do certain types of people commit crimes?', they ask 'Why are certain types of people more likely to be accused and found guilty of crimes than others?' They have, of course, suggested some answers to this question, which are discussed below.

Police discretion

On the whole, those people who appear in court accused of a crime are there because of some action taken by the police — a summons to appear in court, or an arrest. Some sociologists have recognised the importance of the fact that both police forces and police officers often have a *choice* to make, either about which type of crime to concentrate on, or whether to charge someone, let him or her off with a 'caution' (a warning), or simply to ignore the law-breaking.

This point of view is expressed in the extract below, and you should keep it in mind when reading the following parts of this chapter:

Full enforcement of the law is not possible. Law-breaking is so common that to investigate every law broken, to prosecute every known offender, would require such large police forces and cost so much money that it would not be practical or acceptable. So small police forces with small budgets have to enforce laws selectively. Both as an organisation and as individuals, the police have considerable choice about how to organise, which crimes and criminals to prosecute, how to allocate what number of officers to different law-enforcement tasks, and so on.

The point is that the policeman is not, and never has been, simply a 'law-enforcement officer'. He had discretion (choice) — in almost all circumstances except catching a murderer actually on the job — about whom he will arrest, investigate or harass, and whom he won't. In this exercise of discretion — which is central to all his work — the policeman's own private view of the world comes into play: his opinion, as a citizen, of other citizens; his reaction, as a member of one class or race, towards other classes or races.

(Source: Adapted from John Lambert, 'The Police can Choose', *Society Today*, Vol. 5.)

Juvenile delinquency: two issues

(1) Football hooliganism

In 1985, over 30 Italian soccer supporters were crushed to death by a wall which collapsed during an attack on them by Liverpool supporters before the European Cup Final at the Heysel Stadium in Belgium. This terrible tragedy has not stopped soccer hooliganism.

The root of football hooliganism lies in the aggressive defence of 'territory' and 'community' — with 'the Kop', 'the Shed', 'the Stretford End', etc, standing for real territory. Usually, the ritual chants and waving and, of course, the contest on the pitch, are enough. However, sometimes real violence breaks out. This happens all over the world — from Holland to China — not only in Britain. 'Soccer warfare' is often at its worst when two foreign teams, particularly national teams, are involved.

However, as one sociologist put it, 'English troublemakers remain top of the league.' Why is this? In the past, the tough, macho nature of working-class culture may have accounted for the particularly rough behaviour of fans. However, an increasing number of hooligans seem to be quite well off and well dressed, and many have middle-class jobs. English soccer hooliganism may be worse because of the crude and extreme nationalism of certain young males (i.e. the view that England and the English are best, and that foreigners and everything 'foreign' is inferior). Perhaps these narrow attitudes are encouraged by the fact that Britain is an island. Hooligans may also be aware that, in the past, Britain was an imperial power, and be frustrated at its second-best status now (especially if the team is also second best!).

Crude nationalism sometimes takes the form of racism against black footballers. Many black British footballers experience racial abuse, including John Barnes, the 1987–88 footballer of the year.

Barnes was the first black player to make a lasting impact at Liverpool or Everton and everybody knew it. When, on that autumn night, he turned out against Everton for the first time in a Liverpool shirt, the inter-communal soccer sparring, a Merseyside tradition, took on a disturbing new aspect, expressed in a chant from a substantial section of Everton's fans: 'Everton are white! Everton are white!'

John Barnes' skill has not protected him from racial abuse.

Barnes was booed brutally every time he touched the ball. When the play took him to the edges of the field, he was spat upon, badmouthed and showered with bananas. Among the perpetrators were grown men with young sons at their sides. It was, perhaps, the most conspicuous display of football bigotry for years. It put racism briefly back on the agenda of a city for whom the issue has been a long-standing blind spot. It took a football derby to show it up, last time, it had required a full-scale revolt.

(Source: Adapted from The *Independent*, 4 March 1989.)

Question

The author refers to a 'full-scale revolt' that had shown up racism in Liverpool. When was this? (See Chapter Twelve.)

Crude and violent nationalism was also very much on display by English fans during the European soccer championship of 1988. (See page 83.)

Both sociologists and football administrators believe that soccer hooliganism is a social rather than a football problem. It is just one example of the broader issue of 'mainly' juvenile delinquency. Why delinquency *appears* to be increasing and how it can be reduced are questions that football management cannot be expected to answer.

"SOME TALK OF ALEXANDER, AND SOME OF HERCULES; OF HECTOR AND LYSANDER, AND SUCH GREAT NAMES AS THESE..."

The joke (for the reality, see p. 83).

(2) Rural crime — crimes of the prosperous young?

For those who believe that hooliganism is only a working-class and urban phenomenon or those who have gone to live in rural areas partly to escape crime, Figure 14.3 may come as a nasty shock. Police statistics for 1987 seemed to show an upward trend in serious public order offences in rural areas. More than 250 'riots' occurred in these areas.

These outbreaks of group violence typically involve white, employed, quite well-off males. Half of them took place on a Friday or Saturday night and alcohol was probably a factor in about 90 per cent of incidents.

Figure 14.3

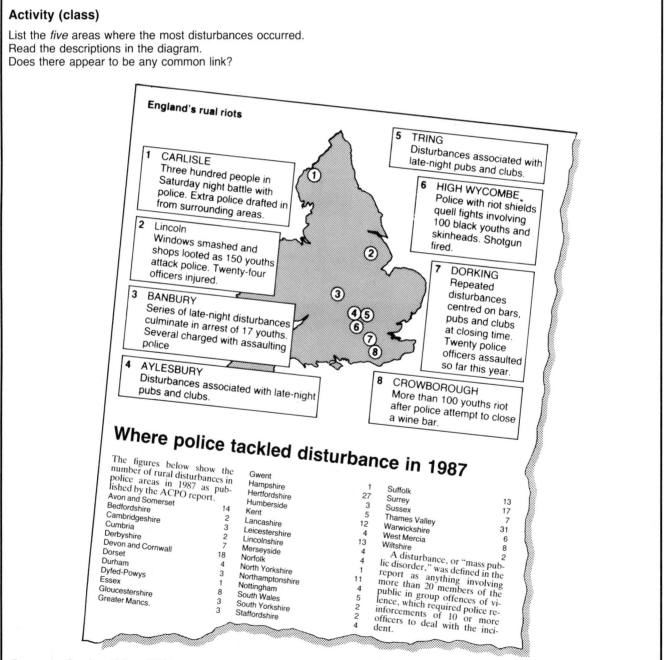

Activity (class)

List the *five* areas where the most disturbances occurred.
Read the descriptions in the diagram.
Does there appear to be any common link?

England's rural riots

1 CARLISLE
Three hundred people in Saturday night battle with police. Extra police drafted in from surrounding areas.

2 Lincoln
Windows smashed and shops looted as 150 youths attack police. Twenty-four officers injured.

3 BANBURY
Series of late-night disturbances culminate in arrest of 17 youths. Several charged with assaulting police

4 AYLESBURY
Disturbances associated with late-night pubs and clubs.

5 TRING
Disturbances associated with late-night pubs and clubs.

6 HIGH WYCOMBE
Police with riot shields quell fights involving 100 black youths and skinheads. Shotgun fired.

7 DORKING
Repeated disturbances centred on bars, pubs and clubs at closing time. Twenty police officers assaulted so far this year.

8 CROWBOROUGH
More than 100 youths riot after police attempt to close a wine bar.

Where police tackled disturbance in 1987

The figures below show the number of rural disturbances in police areas in 1987 as published by the ACPO report.

Avon and Somerset	14	Gwent	1
Bedfordshire	2	Hampshire	27
Cambridgeshire	3	Hertfordshire	3
Cumbria	2	Humberside	5
Derbyshire	7	Kent	12
Devon and Cornwall	18	Lancashire	4
Dorset	4	Leicestershire	13
Durham	3	Lincolnshire	4
Dyfed-Powys	1	Merseyside	4
Essex	8	Norfolk	1
Gloucestershire	3	North Yorkshire	11
Greater Mancs.	3	Northamptonshire	4
		Nottingham	5
		South Wales	2
		South Yorkshire	2
		Staffordshire	4

Suffolk	13
Surrey	17
Sussex	7
Thames Valley	31
Warwickshire	6
West Mercia	8
Wiltshire	2

A disturbance, or "mass public disorder," was defined in the report as anything involving more than 20 members of the public in group offences of violence, which required police reinforcements of 10 or more officers to deal with the incident.

Source: the *Guardian*, 10 June 1988.)

'Loadsamoney' and 'loadsatrouble'?

(Source: the *Observer*, 9 October 1988.)

Factors underlying rural disturbances

The rural disturbances have not been fully researched yet, but the following are some of the explanations put forward:

De-urbanisation — the population movement from city to countryside/suburbs. People, especially young people who were tough and inclined to violence in the town, may behave in the same way in the countryside.

Prosperity and leisure — A long working week can 'keep people out of trouble'. A well-paid, short working week can leave plenty of time to cause havoc. A cheque card and a sharp suit do not mean that newly well-off youths have suddenly become 'middle class' and conformist in the way they behave.

Drink — Increased alcohol consumption seems to be directly related to increased violence, and advertisers often make a special target of 'the young consumer'. Of course, so-called 'lager louts' appear not only in rural towns but in cities too, including the business area of the City of London.

Some people also see a *moral crisis* underlying the seeming wider spread of violence in society. Family, education, religion and community are all sometimes seen as having failed to give young people a moral basis to guide their behaviour. Others blame 'Thatcherism' for 'preaching' selfishness, greed and materialism.

However, it is important for sociologists to be cautious — especially when explanations get emotional. Crime in rural areas may not be worsening *so* much. Perhaps one reason for the police presenting the statistics of rural crime so dramatically was to get more public money to recruit more officers. Stirring up a bit of a moral panic about crime could help them to do this. It may also be that this 'outbreak' of group crime is just another form of one of the oldest crime threats of all: 'youth gangs and violence'.

Activity (class)

The following questions are all about juvenile delinquency. Read them carefully, and try to guess the date when each was written. (Answers are at the end of the chapter.)

1 'Our young people have no idea of discipline or subordination.'
2 'Relaxation of parental control...a growing contempt by the young person for the procedure of juvenile courts... The problem is a serious challenge, which is intensified by the extension of freedom which, for better or worse, has been given to the youth in the last generation.'
3 'Fifty or 60 years ago...under infinitely more subjection than they are now, they were content to submit to family government.'
4 'Children who have been brought up within these 30 years, have nothing like the same reverence or submission to their parents...This is the chief cause of the increase of crime.'
5 'Over the past 25 years, we in this country, through misguided sentiment, have cast aside the word 'discipline', and now we are suffering from it.'
6 'The morals of children are tenfold worse than formerly.'

'Moral panics' and the amplification of deviance

A 'moral panic' is said to occur when police, politicians, the mass media and members of the public all become extremely publicly concerned about a particular type of crime or type of behaviour. Stan Cohen, in his book *Folk Devils and Moral Panics*, looked at the so-called 'mods and rockers' disturbances of the 1960s. A few minor incidents which took place one spring bank holiday at a seaside resort were reported in such a way that a stereotype was created about the sorts of people 'mods' and 'rockers' were, and the kinds of things they got up to — mainly fighting pitched street battles with each other. Not only the police and the public, but the mods and rockers themselves responded to this stereotype, with the result that everybody expected scenes of violence between the two groups on bank holiday weekends.

What kinds of issue are likely to be the subject of a 'moral panic'?

The attention of the media, and public concern, resulted in extra police activity in the resorts, with the result that more and more arrests were made, thus apparently confirming that the public was right to be concerned about these groups of youngsters. The saga went on each year until other issues took up people's attention. A build-up of action and concern around supposed deviant behaviour is called a *deviancy spiral*. The result of such a spiral can be an increase in, or *amplification* of, a deviant behaviour.

Since the mods and rockers, there have been a number of 'moral panics', including those about hippies, 'pot' smoking, gays, muggers, granny bashers, glue sniffers, football hooligans, drug addicts, punks and Hell's Angels. The point is that when a 'moral panic' is on, anyone who comes into the category associated with the offence is more likely than others to be arrested, accused and found guilty. It is difficult to say, therefore, that a rise in the statistics for this type of offence really does indicate a rise in the actual number of such offences. This had led some sociologists to talk of 'phantom crime waves'.

'Moral' panics and 'real' problems

Just because a particular form of deviant behaviour is amplified by public concern it does not, of course, mean that it does not exist. Clearly, the mods and rockers did cause considerable disturbances and they were against the law. However, media sensationalism and sometimes public (including police) over-reaction can make it almost impossible to get an accurate idea of the size and nature of 'the problem'.

A recent example of a moral panic was over child abuse (see pp. 191–192). In some cases, it became difficult to know what was real, and what was panic, though the problem is certainly a big one. Another example is the huge concern over the trafficking and consumption of the drugs, cocaine and heroin, in the United States. This became the number one issue of the 1988 Presidential election. Whether the billions of dollars 'thrown' at the problem are being spent 'in panic' or effectively, remains to be seen.

Stimulus question

Study Figure 14.4 and answer the questions. (The break in the graphs is because, from 1977, different methods were used for counting court procedures. This shows one of the difficulties of trying to compare statistics over time.)

Figure 14.4. Offenders found guilty of, or cautioned for, indictable offences: by sex and age

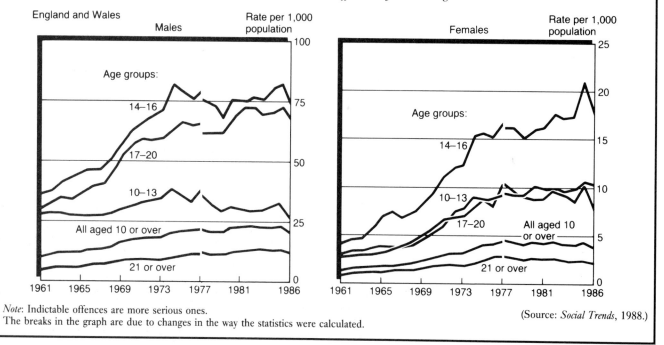

Note: Indictable offences are more serious ones.
The breaks in the graph are due to changes in the way the statistics were calculated.

(Source: *Social Trends*, 1988.)

Questions

1 What is very important about the *scale* of the two graphs? (1 mark)
2 In which age group were the highest number of offenders, both male and female? (1 mark)
3 Which age group of males had an offence rate of just above 25 per 1000 in 1986? (1 mark)
4 What was the approximate offence rate in 1986 for all females aged ten or over? (1 mark)
5 Give explanations for the high official rate of juvenile crime. (8 marks)
6 Give explanations for the much higher official rate of crime among males than females. (8 marks)

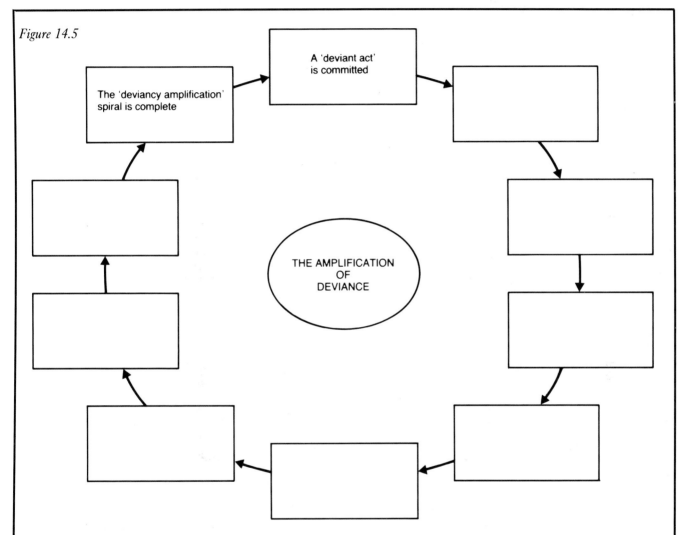

Figure 14.5

Activity

Look carefully at Figure 14.5 which represents the 'amplification of deviance'. Underneath the diagram is a list of statements, each one of which should be placed into its correct box so that the various steps of the process are shown. The first and last stages have been filled in. Try to work out the whole sequence *before* you start filling in any of your boxes, or you may have a lot of rubbing out to do!

- Partly due to the increased police activity, more arrests are made, which are reported in the press.
- The behaviour catches the public attention, which makes it even more 'newsworthy'.
- The 'deviant group' finds it more difficult to engage in the behaviour without being arrested. People who 'look like' the deviants are increasingly under suspicion.
- This leads to even more reports in the mass media, and demands for 'action' to be taken.
- Press reports of increasing arrests lead people to talk of 'a major crime wave' sweeping across Britain.
- Reports of the deviant behaviour, often sensationalised, begin to appear in the mass media.
- Public interest begins to die, as other news items compete for people's attention. The deviant behaviour is no longer 'big news'.
- Responding to the calls for action, greater police attention is focused on the act, with officers being taken off other types of investigation.

217

The problem of measuring crime

Table 14.1. Notifiable offences recorded by the police: by type of offence

England & Wales, Scotland, and Northern Ireland   Thousands

	England & Wales			Scotland			Northern Ireland		
	1971	1986	1990	1971	1986	1987	1971	1986	1990
Notifiable offences recorded									
Violence against the person	47.0	125.5	184.7	5.0	11.6	13.8	1.4	4.2	3.4
Sexual offences	23.6	22.7	29.0	2.6	2.7	2.9	0.2	0.8	0.8
of which, rape and attempted rape	..	2.3	3.4	0.2	0.4	0.4	..	..	0.1
Burglary	451.5	931.6	1,006.8	59.2	96.9	98.6	10.6	20.0	14.8
Robbery	7.5	30.0	36.2	2.3	4.1	4.6	0.6	2.2	1.6
Drugs offences	..	7.3	10.0	0.9	5.3	4.7	..	0.3	—
Theft and handling stolen goods	1,003.7	2,003.0	2,374.4	104.6	212.8	223.5	8.6	30.8	29.3
of which, theft of vehicles	167.6	411.1	494.2	17.1	28.0	26.2	..	..	7.0
Fraud and forgery	99.8	133.4	147.9	9.4	30.6	31.7	1.5	4.2	4.2
Criminal damage	27.0	583.6	553.5	22.0	78.9	76.4	7.4	4.1	2.2
Other notifiable offences	5.6	9.4	21.2	5.0	21.0	29.6	0.5	1.7	1.0
Total notifiable offences	1,665.7	3,847.4	4,363.6	211.0	463.8	481.2	30.8	68.3	57.2

(Source: *Social Trends*, 1992)

Notes
1. The basis on which official statistics are compiled can vary from year to year — this affects comparison of crime rates over the years.
2. The basis on which statistics are compiled is not exactly the same in England and Wales, and Scotland and Northern Ireland.

Official crime statistics are based on 'crimes known to the police', which leads to a further problem: many types of crime are seriously under-reported. Sex-related crimes, especially child abuse and rape, fall into this category, along with blackmail, fraud and wife beating. Following considerable criticism of their treatment of rape victims, many police forces introduced new procedures to deal with the reporting of this crime. Recorded figures for rape in England and Wales increased by 24 per cent, to 2288 between 1985 and 1986 (*Social Trends*, 1988). However, as *Social Trends* pointed out: 'A large part of this increase may be attributable to changes in police practice, since an increasing proportion of cases reported are now recorded as offences due to a more sensitive approach to victims. The new approach may also have encouraged more women to report offences.' This indicates that what some people might regard as a 'major new crime wave' of rape is simply highlighting the fact that earlier figures for rape were considerably lower than the actual number of offences, and this is still probably the case (Figure 14.6).

Figure 14.6. The 'dark number' of unrecorded crimes

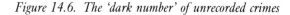
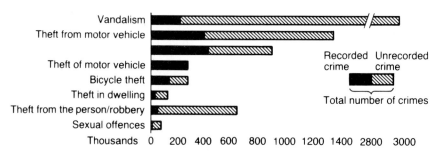

(Source: *Social Trends*, 1986.)

Alternative measures of crime: self-report studies and victim surveys

Two alternative ways of estimating the extent of crime typically produce much higher figures than official statistics. These are *self-report* studies and *victim surveys*.

A measure based on a self-report study of crime counts the crimes a respondent *says* he or she has committed, not just the ones which have been reported to the police. Clearly, people are only likely to self-report crimes either anonymously or to people they trust.

Victim surveys measure the amount of crime on the basis of those claiming to be victims. Criminologist Jock Young carried out a victim survey in Islington, London, the results of which suggested that the scale of crime was perhaps two or three times higher than that based on 'notifiable offences recorded by the police'.

Activity (class)

How many of your class have been victims of crime, and how often? Carry out a victim survey of your class. Do the results seem to support the view that the actual number of crimes committed is much higher than the official figure?

White-collar crime — an example of the measurement problem

White-collar crime refers to those crimes typically carried out by people in 'white-collar' jobs: crimes such as tax evasion, fraud and embezzlement ('cooking the books' to gain money from one's firm). Again, evidence points to the fact that these types of crime are seriously under-reported. Where crimes against companies are concerned, many employers prefer to deal with the matter themselves, rather than have shareholders lose confidence in the firm. Many white-collar crimes are simply not discovered. The Inland Revenue, for example, estimates that hundreds of millions of pounds a year are lost through tax evasion, but relatively few people are caught.

White-collar crime. Is there one law for the rich and another for the poor?

Scandal of the real scroungers

Cost of dole fraud .... £500 million	Cost of tax fraud ... £5,000 million
Number of prosecutions 14,000	Number of prosecutions 20

(Source: the *Observer*, 23 October 1988.)

Prisons and prisoners

The growth in the prison population

During the last ten to fifteen years, there has been a steady growth in the number of people in prison. The figures and estimates shown in Table 14.2 are from the National Association for the Care and Resettlement of Offenders (the estimates of the Home Office are over 7500 lower).

Table 14.2

Year	Prison Population
1977	41,570
1987	48,425
1988	50,000 (estimate)
1995	61,900 to 67,400 (estimate)

Despite the building of more prisons, the rapid growth in the prison population has resulted in great overcrowding, which itself has been a factor in many of the disturbances in prisons.

Are there better alternatives to imprisonment?

Most agree that those who have committed serious crimes, particularly involving violence to people, should go to prison. However, a large proportion of the prison population are there for *relatively* minor acts of theft or burglary (though *not* so minor to the victims, of course).

The following are the four main arguments *for* imprisonment of offenders:

- punishment,
- to protect the public,
- to deter them from further crime,
- to resocialise the offender not to commit crime.

The arguments *against* putting less serious offenders in prison are less well known and are therefore explained more fully:

- Prisons seem to operate as 'universities' of crime — ex-convicts are the most likely group in the population to commit (further) crime.
- Imprisonment leaves a stigma or stain on a person's character making people less willing to give them opportunities to fit into ordinary life, e.g. offer a job — this may lead them to turn again to criminal activities.
- Loss of work and family situation — again, making rehabilitation (settling back to non-criminal life) difficult.
- The cost to the public is more than it costs to keep the average student in higher education (in 1987, the total cost of prisoners and prison officers was £756 million).
- It can be argued that criminals ought to pay back their victim and the community rather than cost society so much. Ways in which this has already been done are by sentencing the offender to:
    - community service, or
    - repaying the victim (either financially or through service).

Who goes to prison?

Males are more likely to go to prison than females, the working class more likely than the middle class, and blacks more likely than whites (proportionate to their numbers in the population).

Although Figure 14.7 is based on American data, the same trends are true of Britain:

Figure 14.7

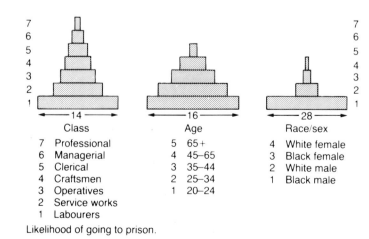

Class	Age	Race/sex
7 Professional	5 65+	4 White female
6 Managerial	4 45–65	3 Black female
5 Clerical	3 35–44	2 White male
4 Craftsmen	2 25–34	1 Black male
3 Operatives	1 20–24	
2 Service works		
1 Labourers		

Likelihood of going to prison.

(Source: John Lea and Jock Young, *What is to be Done about Law and Order?* Penguin, 1984.)

Poorer whites and blacks commit most of the recorded crimes against property which is the type of crime accounting for most imprisonment. Is it possible that if there were less poverty and more equality, they would feel less need to commit crime? What do *you* think?

Explanations of crime and criminals: a summary
The following is a summary of the various explanations of crime and crime statistics given in this section:

Social causes	e.g. poverty, unemployment, lack of opportunity.
Psychological causes	e.g. boredom, status frustration, 'adolescence'.
Cultural causes	e.g. criminal subculture.
Labelling	e.g. of social security but not tax fraud.
Reporting and recording of crime	e.g. victims not reporting, police not always recording.

Other forms of deviance (besides crime)

Every area of life can be roughly divided into 'normal' and deviant behaviour, not only non-criminal and criminal behaviour. This is because every area of social activity is governed by norms and it is always possible to break these norms, i.e. commit a deviant act. Think of any situation you can, in the family, school, sport, whatever, and it is almost certain to be governed by norms.

Of course, norms change and what people regarded as deviant can become widely accepted (divorce is an example of this). The whole area of moral behaviour — what is seen as good and bad conduct — has become more open to disagreement and doubt in recent history. So, in fact, the 'line' between moral/immoral or normal/deviant can become very blurred. For instance, is sex before marriage always immoral? The answer for some people is 'yes', for others 'no', and others 'don't know'.

Aids and deviance
Aids illustrates many of the problems in modern society about how to respond to certain forms of deviance.

If health is normal, then, in a sense, illness is deviant. However, few people attach much blame or *stigma* to a person who has fallen ill. Generally, both the public and the medical profession take a caring rather than a blaming attitude towards the sick. This includes Aids patients as well as others.

However, a quite different attitude to Aids exists among some sections of the public. In their view certain Aids sufferers — usually homosexuals or those who have had many sexual partners — 'deserve what they get' *and* should also be 'punished' by society for their immoral behaviour. This attitude is usually not fully thought out, but those who hold it might want to see 'guilty' Aids patients isolated as much as possible and perhaps receive less public funding for their treatment.

A possibility also exists of a 'moral panic' being directed at Aids sufferers. This might involve a media campaign and perhaps some kind of witch-hunt against Aids sufferers, or those in 'high-risk' groups, such as homosexuals.

Conclusion: conformity, deviance and freedom

All societies (and organisations) have some rules, written or unwritten, to which members are expected to conform. Conformity to these rules usually helps the society to function and benefits the majority. However, too much conformity could result in a society of 'clones' or 'lookalikes' or 'thinkalikes'. It is often 'deviant' individuals who bring interest and variety to society. Further, it is only individuals, willing to act in a free and independent way, who can point out when society may be moving in the wrong direction (e.g. Hitler's Germany). So deviants can contribute to society — although in a different way from conformists. One test of a free society is the way it responds to its deviants. A society which readily persecutes those who are deviant and different will not be very free.

221

Stimulus questions

Read the information in the tables and extract, then answer the questions.

ITEM A

Table 14.3. Police forces and police auxiliaries: manpower England and Wales, Scotland, and Northern Ireland

Thousands

	1961	1971	1981	1987
Police forces — strength				
England & Wales				
Men	73.5	93.5	108.8	111.5
Women	2.3	3.8	10.7	12.6
Scotland				
Men	8.8	10.4	12.4	12.5
Women	0.3	0.4	0.7	0.9
Northern Ireland				
Royal Ulster Constabulary				
Men	2.9	4.0	6.6	7.6
Women	0.1	0.1	0.7	0.6
United Kingdom total	87.9	112.2	140.0	145.7

(Source: Adapted from *Social Trends*, 1989.)

ITEM B

Table 14.4. Clear-up rates for notifiable offences: by type of offence England and Wales, Scotland, and Northern Ireland

Percentages

Notifiable offences recorded	England & Wales		Scotland		Northern Ireland	
	1971	1986	1971	1986	1971	1986
Violence against the person	82	71	87	82	28	57
Sexual offences	76	71	77	76	87	79
Burglary	37	26	26	19	27	26
Robbery	42	20	29	29	7	19
Theft and handling stolen goods	43	31	37	29	46	38
Fraud and forgery	83	67	80	75	84	71
Criminal damage	34	21	32	22	10	31
Total notifiable offences	45	32	38	34	32	37

(Source: Adapted from *Social Trends*, 1988.)

ITEM C

An offence is said to be cleared up if a person is either charged, summoned, or cautioned for the offence, or if the offence is admitted, or if there is sufficient evidence to charge a person but the case is not proceeded with for good reasons. The number of offences cleared up by the police in England and Wales in 1986, at under 1.2 million, was five per cent lower than 1985. Some offences tend to have much higher clear-up rates than others. For example, only 20 per cent of robberies and 21 per cent of criminal damage offences recorded by the police were cleared up in 1986, compared with 92 per cent of homicides. Thus the differences in the clear-up rates between years can be as a result of changes in the pattern of offences; for instance, in 1986 there were larger-than-average increases in recorded numbers of thefts of and from vehicles, which have low clear-up rates, and a drop in the recorded numbers of theft from shops, handling stolen goods, forgery and drug trafficking, which have high clear-up rates.

(Source: Adapted from *Social Trends*, 1988.)

Questions

1 How many police officers were there in the UK in 1987? (Item A) (1 mark)
2 By how much did the number of women police officers increase beween 1981 and 1987? (Item A) (1 mark)
3 What was the offence with the highest clear-up rate in England and Wales in
    (i) 1971
    (ii) 1986? (Item B) (2 marks)
4 Which part of the UK showed the highest clear-up rate for criminal damage in 1986? (Item B) (1 mark)
5 When is an offence recorded as 'cleared up'? (Item C) (3 marks)
6 Using information from Item C, state three offences which have high clear-up rates. (3 marks)
7 Why do you think that the clear-up rates for thefts from cars and for criminal damage are lower than the clear-up rate for homicide? (Item C) (4 marks)
8 Explain, in your own words, why a fall in the clear-up rate does not necessarily mean that the police are getting worse at doing their job. (Item C) (5 marks)

Structured questions

1 Give *two* reasons why crime statistics may not show an accurate picture of criminal activity in a society. (4 marks)
2 a What is meant by 'white-collar crime'? (1 mark)
   b Discuss, with examples, the reasons why 'white-collar crime' is more 'invisible' than many other types of criminal activity. (5 marks)
3 Using 'football hooliganism' as an example, describe what is meant by a 'moral panic' and 'the amplification of deviance'. (10 marks)

Project and assignment suggestions

1 *A 'discovery' of 'hidden' norms* — Every group conforms to certain rules, some of which may be hidden in the sense of not formally written down. You could study the hidden norms of any convenient group, but an interesting choice would be your own peer group (friends/people you know). You might *observe* such areas as:
dress
going out with the opposite sex
attitudes to school work
behaviour in the pub, disco, or club

2 *A study of football supporters* — There has been a lot written on this topic, some of which you can find in past copies of the *Social Studies Review* and *New Society*. Otherwise, the section on 'Youth' in your local library should provide you with relevant material. Don't concentrate *only* on 'hooliganism'. There is a lot of 'folk culture' in football supporting, including performing songs, chants and rituals and collecting pictures and mementoes of local football heroes. Apart from secondary sources, your project would benefit from some participant observation of crowd behaviour at your local football ground.

3 *Gender and crime* — Do males *really* commit much more crime than females as the official statistics suggest? Again, there is now plenty of material published on this matter which your teacher may be able to advise you about. Your own survey could include self-report questionnaires by a sample including both sexes and perhaps a couple of in-depth interviews. You could also analyse reports of crimes in your local newspaper to get an idea of the relative male/female ratio.

4 *Policing society* — Some of you may well be considering the police force as a career and might find a sociological analysis of the police would be useful. You could examine such issues as the compilation of police statistics, police stereotyping, alleged police racism, the position of women in the police force, and how the police 'see' their job. Be careful to make your analysis *sociological* and not just a general description of the police force.

5 *Crime and the media* — Over a period of about a month, collect newspaper reports about various types of crime. You should also watch out for reports on TV and radio news. Divide the reports into different types of offence, e.g. hooliganism, burglary, fraud, and analyse each in a sociological manner. For example, is there any evidence of labelling? Is any emotive language used, such as 'thug' or 'scum'? Is the offence currently part of a 'moral panic'? You must make sure that you actually analyse and discus the reports — a thick wodge of newspaper cuttings with no sociological comments is not much use!

Key words

Amplification   Social control
Label   Social order
Norm   Stereotype
Sanctions

Answers to questions on p. 215.

1) **1904** Evidence to the Inter-departmental Committee on Physical Deterioration; 2) **1939** A. E. Morgan, *The Needs of Youth*; 3) **1738** Daniel Defoe, *The Complete English Tradesman*; 4) **1828** Edward Irving, *The Last Days: A Discourse on the Evil Character of these Our Times*; 5) **1958** Conservative and Unionist Party Annual Conference; 6) **1843** Lord Ashley, later Earl of Shaftesbury, House of Commons.

15 Politics and Government

Politics, power and decision making

Politics is about power and the decisions which are taken by those who have it. A narrow definition of politics is that it is about how government works. A broader definiton is that it is about the contest for, and use of, power in *any* situation. For instance, is power in your family held by one or two individuals, or is it shared fairly equally among several members? How power 'operates' in the family is called 'the politics of the family'. Power between the sexes is referred to as 'the politics of gender', and power in education as 'the politics of education'.

Personal politics, like national politics, involves 'debate' and solutions.

In general, this chapter will use the narrower definition of politics. However, the wider issues of power cannot be entirely separated from an examination of government.

Activity (class)

Power is having the means to do what you want to do, and also being able to make other people do what you want them to. With this in mind, consider each of the following and discuss who has, or might have, power — and why.

Family	'Dating' couple
School	Football match
Work	Parliament
Courtroom	

The Government and the state

Britain is regarded as a 'democratic' society. 'Democracy' literally means 'government by the people', and the word 'democratic' is used to describe any situation or organisation in which the members have a say in how things are run.

It is important to distinguish between the Government and the state. A Government official handbook describes the British Government as 'the body of Ministers responsible for the administration (running) of national affairs'. A broader definition would include Parliament as well. Ministers are answerable to Parliament, and through Parliament to the people.

The state includes the Government, but is wider. It also includes the civil service, which advises Ministers and puts government decisions into practice. Judges (the judiciary) also form part of the state. Judges decide the meaning of both parliamentary law (laws passed by Parliament) and common law (laws which have come about during the history of the country). Many people would also include the armed forces as part of the state, as the defence of the country is usually considered one of the state's most important jobs.

The national state is a huge set of organisations, employing millions of people. It affects nearly all areas of our lives. Despite its size, in a democracy, the state should serve the people, and not the other way round. It is worth remembering this as we examine democracy.

Types of government: democratic and non-democratic

In Chapter Two you were asked to imagine how you would organise 'society' if you and others were wrecked on a desert island. Part of that exercise involved setting up a government. You probably realised that in a society of only a few people it was possible to have a very democratic government — if that is what you wanted. This is because it is easier for everybody to 'have a say' and even to do a government job when there are not many people. For instance, many pre-industrial societies were both small and, in certain respects, democratic. Tribal societies, as well as having chiefs, often have councils of elders and hold general tribal meetings.

Today, most societies are large nation-states. It is, of course, not possible for all people in a country to gather to discuss and decide on important matters. Instead, other, less direct, forms of democracy have been developed.

Types of democracy

Representative democracy

Representative democracy is a system in which people appoint somebody (their representative) to stand in their place. British Members of Parliament represent the people from a certain area, their constituency. Once elected, representatives can represent their constituents as they think best, that is, they make up their own mind about which policies or programmes to support. However, if they fail to represent the interests and opinions of a majority of their constituents, they can expect to lose popularity and may not be re-elected.

In a representative democracy, the people 'in power', e.g. ministers and MPs, are referred to as a 'democratic elite'. They do the day-to-day running, but, in the end, are responsible to the people.

Activity (class/outside class)

Working in class, see how much of the following information you know. (If the members of your class come from a wide area, some of the answers may be different.) Your teacher will help you decide which particular questions apply to you — it depends on which area of the country you live in. Complete the exercise in your own time — your local library will be a useful source of information.

I live in the constituency of . . . .

My Member of Parliament is . . . .

He/she is a member of the . . . . Party

My local metropolitan or county council is . . . .

My local district council is . . . .

My local elected representative(s) on this council is/are . . . .

My local parish council is . . . .

Delegatory democracy

Unlike a representative, a delegate is given certain instructions which must be carried out. Usually, the instructions are about which w. ' to vote on a given matter. For instance, a local constituency branch of the Labour Party might delegate one of its members to vote a particular way on the issue of an independent nuclear deterrent at the Labour Party Conference.

Direct democracy

Direct democracy is the representation of a person by him- or herself. When most people live in small tribes or villages, direct democracy is possible, though it doesn't always happen! Today, in large industrial societies such as Britain, even areas of local government are so big, and cover as many people, that direct democracy is not seen as practical. However, a limited form of direct democracy does continue in the form of the public meeting. Public meetings can be called to discuss important local issues, such as a plan to close a village school, or to site a nuclear waste dump in the area, and anybody can go along and speak at them.

Types of non-democratic governments

Dictatorship

A dictatorship is a government in which power is controlled by a single person. In recent European history, Adolf Hitler is the best-known dictator. Hitler provides an example of the main danger of dictatorship — when dictators pursue bad or evil policies, there may be no simple and quick way of getting rid of them. Democracies may sometimes be less efficient than dictatorships (in certain respects, Hitler's Germany was very efficient), but they are safer because power is spread more widely.

Oligarchy

An oligarchy is a government in which power is controlled by a few people. It seems that since the death of Stalin (another example of a dictator), the Soviet Union was ruled by an oligarchy composed of the most powerful leaders of the Communist Party, though the General Secretary of the Party was usually the leading figure in the oligarchy. In the mid- and late 1980s, certain changes were attempted in the Soviet system of government to make it less oligarchical and more democratic (see p. 238), but this did not prevent the collapse of the Soviet Union.

Political rights

There are two basic political rights in a large-scale democracy:
1   the right to vote,
2   the right to freedom of expression (under the law).
In a democracy, the people have the right to elect a government into or out of office. The electorate are those people registered to vote. In Britain, adults over eighteen are entitled to register to vote.

If democracy is to work properly, politicians and the people they represent must be able to express and listen to different views. The law supports the right to freedom of expression, but also limits it in certain circumstances. For instance, in Britain the libel laws make printing lies about people illegal, and the Race Relations Act of 1965 makes it illegal to make any statements that might stir up racial hatred. Citzenship carries responsibilities as well as rights. In the late 1980s, the need for citizens to create decent communities was obvious as violent crime and environmental problems increased.

Parties, pressure groups and public opinion in a democracy

Democracies must be organised in a way which lets people express their views and influence what the government does.

Parties

The right to vote is meaningless unless there are candidates to vote for. Nowadays, nearly all political candidates are members of political parties. The biggest political parties in Britain are the Conservative ('Tory') and Labour parties. In the United States, the biggest parties are the Democratic and Republican parties. There are also some smaller parties in Britain: the Democrats, the Liberal Democrats, the Scottish and Welsh Nationalist parties, and the Ulster Unionist Party. The majority of seats in Parliament are, however, held by Conservative or Labour members.

Political ideologies

A political ideology is a broad framework of political ideas, values and beliefs. The ideology of the Labour Party can be summed up by the phrase 'democratic socialism'. This means that the Labour Party wants to achieve a more equal society (socialism) by means of the British democratic system. The main way the Labour Party has tried to bring about greater equality is by policies of *collectivisation* which means public ownership. Parts of the economy and key public services, such as health, were collectivised by Labour. From the late 1980s, many in the Labour Party considered that collectivisation is not the only or best way to achieve greater equality and were considering other ways of doing so.

If a party is to achieve power, its ideology must appeal to those whose votes it wants. In the past, the Labour Party strongly supported the interests of the manual working class. For instance, the setting up of the National Health Service and the expansion of comprehensive schools were seen as means of providing greater equality in society.

The ideology of the Conservative Party is based on support for tradition and capitalism, and, especially in the 1980s, the value of individual enterprise and responsibility. Generally, support for tradition includes not only a strongly pro-national view of Britain's history and institutions, but also an acceptance of class and many other inequalities as an inevitable part of life. Sometimes, the pro-tradition and pro-capitalist strands in Conservatism can conflict with each other. For instance, in the late 1980s property developers who wanted to build in rural England, including on some protected 'green belt' land around towns, clashed with local residents who wanted to preserve the traditional, rural character of England. Members of both these groups typically vote Conservative.

Sometimes, 'traditional' and 'new' Tories come into conflict over the 'development' of rural areas.

The main supporters of the Conservative Party are the upper and middle classes. However, in the elections of 1979, 1983 and 1987, a clear trend emerged of better-off working-class people voting Conservative, though, overall, the Labour Party still obtains more working-class votes than the Conservative Party.

The 'centre' party, the Liberal Democrats, and the SDP, are pro-capitalist but also believe in greater equality. They try to appeal to all social classes. Centre parties have tended to increase their total percentage share of the vote in elections since the Second World War, although their small number of seats partly reflects the 'first past the post' system of British voting, rather than that only a very few votes are cast for them.

Party policies and issues

When political parties are trying to win support, they publish a 'manifesto', which is a broad statement of their ideology, and also what their policies are on important *issues* (i.e. matters like defence, taxation and unemployment). Here are some extracts from party manifestos from the 1987 general election:

Conservative Party

1   Reduction in basic income tax from 27p to 25p in the pound.
2   Privatisation of British Airports Authority, water authorities and electricity industry.
3   Education Bill giving governors and heads of secondary schools more control, and allowing schools to 'opt out' of local authority control.
4   Tighter controls on immigration.
5   New broadcasting Bill to encourage independent production, and to protect against sex and violence on TV.

Labour Party

1   Reduction in unemployment of one million in two years.
2   Increase in pensions and benefits, to be paid for by higher taxes on highest five per cent of earners.
3   Gradual reduction of Britain's dependence on nuclear energy.
4   New law to strengthen legal rights of trades unions and their members.
5   Non-nuclear defence policy by international consultation.

Liberal/SDP Alliance (now dissolved)

1   Unemployment to be cut by one million in three years.
2   Constitutional reforms, including introduction of proportional representation.
3   Restructuring of tax and social security to help the poorest.
4   Opposition to the sale of water authorities and electricity industry.
5   Maintenance of minimum nuclear deterrent until it can be negotiated away.

Activity (class)

List the points in each manifesto you strongly agree with.
Which manifesto do you agree with most?
Discuss the manifestos and your views of them as a class.
How does each party's 1992 Manifesto compare with that of 1987?

Pressure groups

Pressure groups are organisations of citizens who try to get politicians to act in support of the pressure group's interest. In fact, pressure groups are also known as 'interest groups'.

There are literally thousands of interest groups in Britain. Broadly, the groups fall into two main types, *protective* and *promotional*. Protective groups are concerned with looking after the needs of their members. Examples are trades unions, employers' associations and the Automobile Association. Promotional groups, on the other hand, are mainly concerned with putting forward the needs of others. Examples are the Child Poverty Action Group (CPAG), the National Society for the Prevention of Cruelty to Children (NSPCC), and groups such as Band Aid, Sports Aid and Comic Relief. Although interest groups do not seek power for themselves, they are as much a part of the life of a modern democracy as are political parties. The term 'pluralism' (meaning 'many') is often used to refer to the variety of ideologies and groups typically found in a modern democracy.

Activity (class/outside class)

The purpose of this activity is to increase awareness of the aims and activities of pressure groups:

1   Get hold of some copies of recent newspapers, local or national. Look for a mention of a pressure group, and, if possible, an account of its activities. What methods do you think that pressure groups *could* use to achieve their aims?
2   Working in small groups, list as many pressure groups as you can think of. How is it that you know about them? What methods have they used to bring themselves to your attention?

Public opinion and the media

The right to express an opinion on political and other matters is part of democracy. Mostly, individuals do not personally express their opinion on important issues in public. However, if democracy is working well, most shades of opinion should be expressed through the media. People who often do express opinions in public include spokespersons from pressure groups, media commentators and 'experts' on the subject in question. Sometimes an individual may feel strongly enough about an issue to write a letter to the press about it, or try to get time to comment on an appropriate radio or TV programme. However, there is no guarantee that the letter will be published or the air time granted.

How democratic are the media themselves? Do they reflect all shades of opinion without bias? Are they controlled by the rich and powerful? These are questions discussed in Chapter Five.

Activity (class/outside class)

Working alone or in small groups, obtain two national newspapers for the same day, a 'quality' and a 'tabloid':

1   Look at the letters section and compare both the subjects covered and the type of opinion expressed. What similarities and differences did you find?
2   Now look at the news pages. Is the main front-page story about the same event in both papers? If so, are there are differences in the way the story is presented? What kind of differences (if any)? If the main stories are different, does each paper at least mention the other's main story somewhere? If not, why do you think this is the case?

Democracy (or not) in everyday life

Democracy is both a form of government and, more broadly, of organisation, in which power is shared widely rather than concentrated in one or a few people. The first activity in this chapter was to look at who has power in particular areas of life, such as family, school and work. There are various ways of referring to power controlled by one person, such as authoritarian father, tyrannical headmaster, autocratic managing director, dictatorial ruler.

In most organisations in modern societies, power is not held by just one person. Most modern organisations are hierarchical, which means that they have several levels, or tiers, of power, although a few people (oligarchy) at the very top may have by far the most. Most schools and colleges are good examples of hierarchies. The following is a typical school hierarchy, but you will find much the same form of organisation in most commercial companies as well:

Head Teacher

Deputy Head (Academic)	Deputy Head (Pastoral)
Heads of department	Year heads
Teachers	Form tutors

Activity (class/outside class)

Make a list of five ways in which your school/college could be made more democratic. Do you think that such changes would be for the better, or not? Read out and discuss some of your answers with the rest of the class.

British democracy: a summary

Arguments in favour

It allows more people more 'say' than any other system could in a large society.
It gives the ultimate check on government — it can be voted out of office
It allows peaceful change and helps create a fairly peaceful society
Despite its faults, it is the best form of government there is for modern societies

Criticisms

The rich and powerful have more 'say' than others. They largely own and control the media, and can more easily afford to get involved in politics, including becoming politicians
People conform in capitalist society because they are misled by the capitalist-controlled media
'Capitalist' democracy is not 'real' democracy — most people have little control over their everyday lives

---

Stimulus question

Note: This stimulus question is different from others in that you will find some of the answers in different chapters of the book.

Consensus means general agreement. Compared to the 1940s, the general consensus in the late 1980s favoured Conservative *individualism* rather than Socialist *collectivism* In Figure 15.1 the arrows show Britain's consensus moving towards individualism on several important issues but on three, i.e. the welfare state, taxation more collectivist view. Two matters do not easily fit into the diagram — nuclear defence and law and order. Labour's problem is convincing a majority of the electorate that it has an effective defence policy, and the Conservatives are embarrassed by a rise in violent crime despite higher expenditure on law and order.

Figure 15.1

Collectivism		Individualism
Trade unions	$\longrightarrow$	Reduction of their power
The welfare state	⇄	Reduction in size
Housing	$\longrightarrow$	Selling off council housing
Education	$\longrightarrow$	Opting out
Taxation	⇄	Reducing taxes — especially of the better-off
Public ownership	⇄	Privatisation

(Source: adapted from an idea in *Politics Pal*, 1988.)

Questions

1 Define the meaning of the following and give *one* example of each: political consensus, socialist collectivism, and conservative individualism.   (9 marks)
2 Describe the policies of the Conservatives in *two* of the areas listed above (trade unions, etc). In what way would you say these policies are individualistic?

(11 marks)

Local government

The different levels of government in England and Wales, with their particular functions, are as follows:

Level	Function
Central	Overall and final power
County councils	County-wide planning
(There are 47 of these, but they do	Transport planning
not include London or the six	Highways
metropolitan [biggest city] areas)*	Traffic regulation
	Consumer protection
	Refuse disposal
	Police service
	Fire service
	Education
	Personal social services
	Libraries
District councils	Environmental health
	Housing
	Local planning decisions
	Refuse collection
Parish councils (in rural districts)	Serve mainly as a means to express opinion and recommend action

* London and the six metropolitan areas had their own county councils until they were abolished in 1986. Now the districts within these areas have taken over their functions, combining together to fulfil some functions.

As with Parliament, county, district and parish councils are elected — that, of course, is what makes them democratic.

The struggle between central and some local governments in the 1980s

During the 1980s, certain local authorities — nearly all Labour controlled — wanted to spend more on things such as housing and education than the Conservative Government agreed with. The Government felt that there was a lot of waste and overspending in local government, which it was determined to control. For their part, local authorities, such as Liverpool, believed that they ought to meet the needs of their constituents, many of whom they saw as 'victims' of high unemployment and welfare cuts. At this time, local authority spending was made up of the rates (a tax on housing and other property), and a rate support grant, which comes from central government. The latter decided to get full control of both these sources of income. This was achieved by the following measures:

1 The introduction of a Block Grant System (1980) which meant that central government would now decide how much the rate support grant would be, and on what it would be spent.
2 'Rate-capping' (1985) which set an upper limit on rates.

The effect was to put control of local authority taxation and spending in the hands of central government. In addition, the Government abolished the Greater London Council and the six metropolitan councils which had provided the main local authority opposition to its policies.

The community charge (or 'poll tax')

In 1988, an Act was passed requiring the rates to be replaced by a community charge. Whereas the rates were a tax on property, the 'poll tax' is a tax on each individual over the age of eighteen. Broadly speaking, this means that people who own expensive, or a lot of, property pay less under the new system, and households with several people in them pay more. The exception to this is the very poor, for whom special allowance is made. The poll tax was abolished partly in response to popular protest against it.

231

Figure 15.2

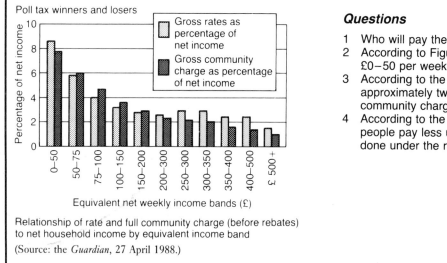

Poll tax winners and losers

Gross rates as percentage of net income

Gross community charge as percentage of net income

Equivalent net weekly income bands (£)

Relationship of rate and full community charge (before rebates) to net household income by equivalent income band

(Source: the *Guardian*, 27 April 1988.)

Questions

1 Who will pay the community charge?
2 According to Figure 15.2, will people earning between £0–50 per week pay more or less under the 'poll tax'?
3 According to the figure, which group of earners will pay approximately two per cent of their net income as a community charge?
4 According to the figure, from what level of income do people pay less under the poll tax than they would have done under the rates?

Conclusion: local democracy

This section has concentrated on the framework of local government. Day-to-day participation and struggle in local areas is described in Chapter Eight (p. 123) and some of the project suggestions at the end of this chapter are about local politics.

Although local politics affect people's everyday lives, they often have less knowledge about local than national politics. The following activity is designed to improve your own knowledge of local politics.

Activity (class/outside class)

1 Find out which party (or parties, if there is a coalition) holds power in your county council (or district council if you are in a metropolitan area).
2 Where does your local district council meet? How often?
3 Obtain reports of a recent district or parish council meeting from a local newspaper, and stick it in your folder.
4 Is there any local issue on which you have strong feelings? Discuss this as a group with your teacher.

Study the letters page in your local newspaper to get an idea of the style and length of published letters, then write a suitable letter to the editor expressing your point of view (you may like to do this as a small group of two or three). If you are lucky enough to get your letter published, cut it out and stick it in your folder.
5 After discussing it with your teacher, invite a local councillor to talk to the class about his or her work with the council.

Voting behaviour

Factors affecting voting behaviour

Democracy means that people can make a choice when voting — or even when not voting. However, many things can influence that choice, and this section discusses some of the main influences. However, other changes in society have meant that many of these are not as important as they used to be, and it is becoming more difficult to predict how people will vote.

Class

From 1945 until the General Election of 1979, the Conservative Party was largely the party of the middle classes, and the Labour Party that of the working class.

In the 1987 election, it was still true that the majority of both professional/managerial and office/clerical workers voted Conservative. However, in 1979, about the same percentage of skilled manual workers voted Conservative as Labour, and in 1987, nine per cent more voted Conservative than voted Labour. By 1987, therefore, Labour's grip on the working-class vote had been broken — even though just over 50 per cent of semi-skilled/unskilled manual workers and the unemployed voted Labour. Whereas in 1945 62 per cent of the whole working class voted Labour, in 1983 the figure was only 38 per cent.

The Labour Party has the added problem that its working-class and (limited) middle-class supporters have very different attitudes. This was clearly brought out by the British Social Attitudes report of 1987. For instance, a majority of the former favour capital punishment, whereas a majority of the latter oppose it; most of the working-class supporters favour the nuclear deterrent, whereas most of the middle-class supporters oppose it, and on homosexuality, middle-class Labourities tend to be much more permissive. It is not easy to lead a party of such different supporters. By contrast, the attitudes on social, economic and moral issues held by Conservatives of all classes are more similar.

Region

The tendency of 'the South' to vote Conservative and 'the North' to vote Labour was especially strong in the 1987 election. This reflects the fact that the south of Britain is relatively more middle class and prosperous than the north. However, members of the working class in the south are more likely to vote Conservative than those in the north. This is partly because they are more likely to belong to the 'new working class', which is discussed later in the chapter.

Age

There is not much relationship between age and voting behaviour. The 1987 election results showed a slightly greater than average tendency for the young to vote Labour and a similar tendency for the old to vote Conservative. This tendency has been noted in other elections, but is only very slight. It has been suggested that this pattern is a reflection of gender patterns, in that women (at least in the past) have tended to be more likely than men to vote Conservative, and women outnumber men in the upper age groups.

Gender

As stated above, historically, a greater percentage of women than men have voted Conservative, and a greater percentage of men than women have voted Labour. The explanation sometimes given for this is that more men than women were in paid work, and were more likely to get involved in union and possibly Labour Party activity. However, in the elections of 1983 and 1987, there was very little difference in the way the sexes cast their votes, perhaps reflecting the large proportion of women who are now in paid employment (Figure 15.3)

Figure 15.3. Gender and voting behaviour

(Figures in percentages; changes since 1983 in brackets. Source: ITN/Harris exit poll)	Con	Lab	Lib/SDP	Others
ALL	43.3 (−0.2)	31.6 (+3.3)	23.1 (−2.9)	2.0 (−0.2)
Sex: MEN	41 (0)	33 (+3)	23 (−3)	3 (−1)
WOMEN	43 (−1)	31 (+3)	23 (−3)	3 (+1)

(Source: The *Independent*, Saturday 13 June, 1987.)

Ethnicity

There is a strong tendency for voters of Asian and Afro-Caribbean origin to vote Labour. However, this is probably due more to the fact that the majority of them are working class than because they consider Labour to be the party most concerned with the problems of ethnic minorities. A Harris Survey of

1983 found that the most important issues of concern among those of Asian and Afro-Caribbean origin were:

Asian Origin	*Afro-Caribbean Origin*
Unemployment (71%)	Unemployment (67%)
Immigration (36%)	Cost of living (27%)
Cost of living (19%)	Education (23%)
Education (17%)	Immigration (17%)

Unemployment, the cost of living and the quality of education are the sort of problems that concern many working-class people — black or white. Labour is seen by many as the party most likely to help lower wage earners and the unemployed. On the specifically racial issue of immigration, Labour's policies are also seen as more sympathetic to black ethnic minorities.

Why do people vote the way they do? Two models

1 The class model

The class model of voting behaviour is that it is 'normal' for the majority of working-class voters to support Labour, and for the majority of middle-class voters to vote Conservative. The reason given for this is that the Labour Party represents the interests of the working class and the Conservative Party those of the middle class. To a large extent, this model explains the way that most people voted between 1945 and about 1970, although there have always, of course, been 'cross-class' voters — voters who did not vote according to the working-class Labour/middle-class Conservative pattern.

The concept of *political socialisation* plays a key role in the class model of voting. Political socialisation refers to the influences that shape and affect political thought and behaviour, including voting. Loyalty to Labour was learned by working-class children from their parents, and loyalty to the Conservatives by middle-class children from their parents. However, the elections of 1979, 1983 and 1987 showed that this simple class model is no longer an adequate explanation of many people's voting behaviour. Instead, many sociologists now talk about the 'new working class' — manual workers who are likely to be buying their own home ('owner-occupiers'), working for private companies rather than in the public sector, and who are less likely than the 'traditional working class' to belong to a trade union. In the 1987 election, the Conservatives had a larger share of the vote than Labour among these members of the 'new working class', who typically lived in the south rather than the north. Labour, on the other hand, had a larger share of the working-class vote than the Conservatives among council tenants and union members, who typically lived in the north.

	THE NEW WORKING CLASS				THE TRADITIONAL WORKING CLASS			
Party	Lives in South	Owner Occupier	Non-union member	Works in private sector	Lives in Scotland or North	Council tenant	Union member	Works in public sector
Conservative	46	44	40	38	29	25	30	32
Labour	28	32	38	39	57	57	48	49
Lib/SDP Alliance	26	24	22	23	15	18	22	19
Conservative or Labour majority in 1987	Con +18	Con +12	Con +2	Lab +1	Lab +28	Lab +32	Lab +18	Lab +17
Conservative or Labour majority in 1983	Con +16	Con +22	Con +6	Lab +1	Lab +10	Lab +38	Lab +21	Lab +17
Category as percentage of all manual workers	40	57	66	68	37	31	34	3
Change since 1983	+4	+3	+7	+2	−1	−4	−7	—

Note: Figures have been rounded to the nearest whole number, so totals do not always add up to 100%.

Table 15.1. The divided working class: the parties' shares of the vote among different groups of manual workers (%)

(Source: *Social Studies Review*, Vol. 3 No 1, September 1987.)

Questions

Study Table 15.1 carefully, and answer the following questions:

1 What percentage of working-class owner-occupiers voted Conservative in 1987?
2 What percentage of all manual workers works in the private sector?
3 Which category of all manual workers has decreased the most since 1983?

---

2 The consumer model

The consumer model of voting behaviour suggests that voters are increasingly 'picking and choosing' among the parties and their policies. Instead of voting out of loyalty or tradition, more and more people are voting for the party which they think is the most likely to help *them*. This is called 'instrumental voting'.

According to the consumer model, in the 1980s, Conservative policies and personalities (especially Mrs Thatcher) appealed to the electorate more than those of Labour. In fact, Ivor Crewe suggests that certain key, traditional Labour policies were unpopular with many voters, including some traditional Labour supporters. These policies included nationalisation (a policy under which certain industries are taken over and run by the state — the opposite of 'privatisation'), wanting to change some of the 'Thatcher' laws controlling trade unions, and Labour's non-nuclear defence policy. Perhaps realising this, in 1988, the Labour Party began a re-examination of all its main policies.

The consumer model of voting fits in with the idea of the consumer society. In the late 1980s, a large proportion of voters associated the Conservative Party with higher consumption (the buying of goods and services) and greater personal prosperity.

The two models: a summary

The class and consumer models of voting can be seen to complement rather than contradict each other. Many votes still reflect the class position of the voter, but, on the other hand, there is a growing tendency for some voters to 'shop around', as the consumer model suggests.

As far as class and voting is concerned:

1 The Conservative Party remains by far the most popular party among the middle and upper-middle classes.
2 The majority of semi-skilled and unskilled voters still support Labour.

As far as the consumer model is concerned:

1 The Labour Party did not win the biggest vote from skilled workers in the three elections to 1987.
2 There has been an increase in people switching votes (known as 'volatility') from election to election.
3 There has been a steady increase in the percentage of the vote cast for the centre parties (former Liberals and others) — but voters often move away again, too.

The parties: past and future trends

Voting trends

Figure 15.4 clearly shows the pattern of voting since 1945. These trends are the key to understanding the past performance and future electoral prospects of the Conservative, Labour and centre parties

Figure 15.4. Voting trends, 1945–87

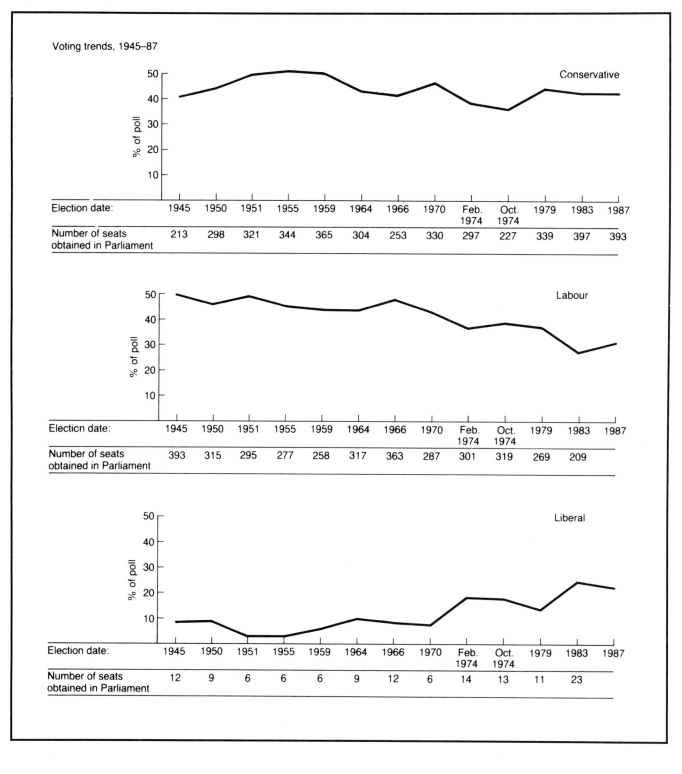

Voting trends, 1945–87

Conservative

Election date:	1945	1950	1951	1955	1959	1964	1966	1970	Feb. 1974	Oct. 1974	1979	1983	1987
Number of seats obtained in Parliament	213	298	321	344	365	304	253	330	297	227	339	397	393

Labour

Election date:	1945	1950	1951	1955	1959	1964	1966	1970	Feb. 1974	Oct. 1974	1979	1983	1987
Number of seats obtained in Parliament	393	315	295	277	258	317	363	287	301	319	269	209	

Liberal

Election date:	1945	1950	1951	1955	1959	1964	1966	1970	Feb. 1974	Oct. 1974	1979	1983	1987
Number of seats obtained in Parliament	12	9	6	6	6	9	12	6	14	13	11	23	

Note: *The Liberal figure for 1983 includes votes for their partners in the Alliance, the Social Democratic Party.

(Source: Butler and Sloman, 1980, adapted. Reprinted in original form in N. Abercrombie *et al.*, *Contemporary British Society*, Polity Press, 1988.)

Stimulus questions

Use the information in the table and extract to answer the questions which follow.

ITEM A

Table 15.2. 1987 election — vote by social class (%)

	Cons.	Lab.	Lib/SDP
Skilled manual			
Vote in 1987	43	34	24
Change from 1983	+4	−1	−3
Change 1979–1987	−2	−11	+14
Semi-skilled/unskilled manual			
Vote in 1987	31	50	19
Change from 1983	+2	+6	−8
Change 1979–1987	−1	−5	+5
Unemployed			
Vote in 1987	32	51	17
Change from 1983	+2	+6	−9
Change 1979–1987	−8	+2	+6

ITEM B

The shifts in a divided working class

The Conservatives' vote only held steady because they made further inroads into the working class. At 36 per cent its share of the manual workers' vote was the largest for any post-war election, including the victory years of the 1950s when the national Conservative vote was much higher.

Its success among the newly affluent working class of the South was crucial. Among working-class home owners it led Labour by 44 per cent to 32 per cent; among those who had bought their council houses it led by 42 per cent to 31 per cent. In the South — not just the Home Counties, but London, East Anglia and the South West — the Conservatives won a larger majority among manual workers alone (46 per cent to 28 per cent) than in the electorate as a whole. Among first-time buyers of shares in the newly privatised industries, of whom half were manual workers, the Conservative vote was 54 per cent.

It is in the contrasting shifts of a divided working class that Conservative success and Labour failure is most apparent. Labour's 1987 campaign was geared to recovering those working-class supporters whose large-scale desertion had produced the defeat of 1983. It concentrated unswervingly on what has always appealed most to its traditional class base: full employment, the welfare state and the genuine working-class roots of its leader.

The strategy only half worked. Labour remobilised the 'rank and file' working class of semi-skilled and unskilled manual workers (and the unemployed), among whom its vote rose by a full six percentage points — twice the national average. But Labour failed spectacularly in the other half of the working class — the foremen, supervisors, craft and high-tech workers — who make up the skilled, secure and affluent 'new working class'. Amongst this group there was a *further* swing to the Conservatives of 2.5 per cent since 1983.

(Source: Adapted from Ivor Crewe, 'Why Mrs Thatcher was returned with a landslide', *Social Studies Review*, September 1987.)

Questions

1 What percentage of semi-skilled and unskilled manual workers voted Conservative in 1987? (Item A)   (1 mark)
2 Which party showed the greatest percentage fall in votes from skilled manual workers between 1979 and 1987? (Item A)   (1 mark)
3 Which party showed the greatest percentage fall in votes from unemployed voters between 1979 and 1987? (Item A)   (1 mark)
4 What percentage of manual workers voted Conservative in 1987? (Item B)   (1 mark)
5 Item B talks about the 'newly affluent (well-off) working class of the South'. Give three characteristics of this group mentioned in the article.   (3 marks)
6 Give three things which the Labour Party campaign concentrated on, and say what the reason for this was. (Item B)   (2 marks)
7 Give three groups of voters whose support for Labour went up, and three groups of voters whose support went down. (Item B)   (3 marks)
8 Using material from Items A and B and elsewhere, discuss the problems of talking about 'the' working-class voter.   (8 marks)

Activity (class)

1 Discuss the trend for each of the parties in the general elections since 1945.
2 Look carefully at the number of seats won by the parties, together with their share of the vote in Figure 15.4. Why do you think that the Liberal and SDP parties believe that the number of seats should be based on the share of the votes gained (a system known as 'proportional representation')? Do you think that this would be a fairer system?
Can you think of any arguments against it?

The Conservatives in power: 1979 onwards

Many readers of this chapter will not recall any other government than a Conservative one. However, in eleven out of the fifteen years before Mrs Thatcher first came to power in 1979, Labour had been the governing party. However, few Prime Ministers in Britain's history have left their mark on the nation to the same extent as Margaret Thatcher. Overleaf is a list of some of the main principles and policies of what came to be known as 'Thatcherism', together with some criticisms of them.

THATCHERISM

Principles/practices

The spirit of enterprise — Mrs Thatcher preached the gospel of rich and just rewards for those who work hard and risk their own money. She tried to create the conditions under which capitalism can flourish

Prosperity — The creation of wealth is seen as essential for a good life. In the 1980s, average living standards rose by over 25 per cent. Mrs Thatcher was able to claim that the large majority had become much more prosperous during her period as Prime Minister

Strong government — Mrs Thatcher's style of firm leadership appealed to many of the British voters. Her personal popularity soared after the Falklands War. At home, a tough approach to crime was taken

Criticisms

Greed and selfishness — Not only opposition MPs, but several leading churchmen, including the Bishop of Durham, have argued that Thatcherism encourages greed. The selfishness and disregard for others of 'yobs' and some 'yuppies' is felt to have been made worse by Thatcherism
Growing inequality — The gap between the very rich and the poorest 20 per cent grew considerably. Huge tax cuts for the rich were seen as unfair, given that public services, especially the health service, needed more money. While those in work may have benefited, the unemployed and many elderly people found it increasingly difficult to keep their standard of living
'Jingoism' abroad: rising crime at home — 'Jingoism' refers to a narrow-minded, 'my country, right or wrong' approach. Many critics argue that the Government should have tried harder to reach a compromise over the Falklands. Most crime continued to rise. 'Strong government' has led to growing control of the media, and loss of personal liberties

The wider scene: the Soviet Union

Towards the end of the 1980s, the Russian leader, Mr Gorbachev, began some important changes to Soviet policies at home and abroad. Two Russian words were used to describe this new trend towards 'openness' in the Soviet Union:
Glasnost (openness, liberalisation) — An example of this was that both Soviet and foreign reporters had more

freedom to report events, and to comment on them.
Perestroika (rebuilding, restructuring) — An example of this was the reorganisation of the Communist Party to give greater power to popularly elected bodies. However, these changes proved insufficient to keep Mr Gorbachev in power and the Soviet Union intact.

Stimulus questions

Look at the table and read the extract, then answer the questions which follow.

ITEM A

Figure 15.6. Perceptions of recent change: voters' views on whether there had been an improvement or a deterioration in six matters of concern in the 1987 General Election (%)

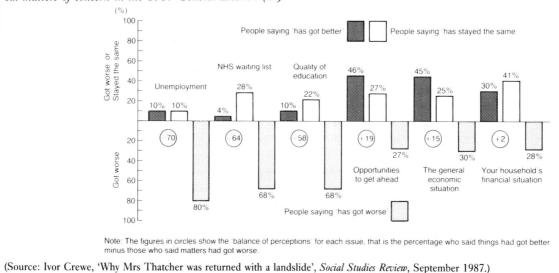

Note: The figures in circles show the 'balance of perceptions' for each issue, that is the percentage who said things had got better minus those who said matters had got worse.

(Source: Ivor Crewe, 'Why Mrs Thatcher was returned with a landslide', *Social Studies Review*, September 1987.)

ITEM B

Private prosperity: the key to the Conservative victory

Whereas a large majority of voters thought that unemployment, the health service and education had got worse, they believed that prosperity (wealth) had improved. The majority of people thought that the economy had got better, their living standards had risen and 'opportunities to get ahead' had increased. It is in this mixture of public poverty and private prosperity that lies the key to Labour's failure.

If electors had voted only on the main issues, Labour would have won. Labour was considered (among people for whom the issue was important) the more capable party on three of the four leading issues — jobs, health and education. Only on defence did Labour lag behind the Conservatives. An election in which voters faithfully supported the party they preferred on the issues they claimed mattered most would have left Labour two per cent ahead of the Conservatives. The final 'balance sheet' favoured Labour.

However, it appears that when answering survey questions on the important issues, respondents think of public problems, but when actually casting their vote, they think of family prosperity. 'Prosperity' is not an issue or a problem, but a blessing. By a decisive 55 per cent to 27 per cent majority, the public regarded the Conservatives as more likely to give it.

(Source: Adapted from Ivor Crewe, 'Why Mrs Thatcher was returned with a landslide', *Social Studies Review*, September 1987.)

Questions

1 What percentage of voters thought that the quality of education had got worse? (Item A) (1 mark)
2 What percentage of voters thought that opportunities to get ahead had got better? (Item A) (1 mark)
3 On which issue did 41 per cent of voters believe that things had 'stayed the same'? (Item A) (1 mark)
4 On which leading issues was Labour a) considered more capable than the Conservatives, and b) lagging behind the Conservatives? (Item B) (2 marks)
5 What would have resulted in a two per cent victory for the Labour Party? (Item B) (2 marks)
6 In your own words, say that you think is meant by 'public poverty' and 'private prosperity'. (4 marks)
7 Discuss the reasons for the differences between Labour's apparent lead over the Conservatives on major issues, and the Conservative election victory. (9 marks)

Structured questions

1 Describe what is meant by a 'democratic society'. (2 marks)
2 Using examples, discuss some of the ways in which pressure groups can try to achieve their aims, saying which methods you think are the most effective, and why. (8 marks)
3 Briefly discuss the factors that may influence the way in which people vote, saying which ones you consider to be the most important. (10 marks)

Project and assignment suggestions

1 *Political beliefs in your own area* — This project should probe deeper than simply asking people which party they support, or which political personalities they admire or dislike. Questions about values and issues, such as those dealt with towards the end of this chapter, should also be asked. This is possibly better as a qualitative, rather than a quantitative, survey, so keep your sample small. To draw out the sociological aspects of the research, you will need to try to find out why your respondents think the way they do. For example, do gender, social class or age appear to have an influence? You will need to think carefully beforehand about the type of information you want, so that you can build in the right sort of questions. Try to make sure that you choose ideas/issues on which your respondents are likely to have an opinion. Will you concentrate on local or national issues, or a mixture of both?
2 *Age and political beliefs* — This is somewhat similar to the project suggested above, except that this time your sample will be carefully chosen with different age bands

in mind. Try not to have too many bands, four or five will be enough: for example, 18–29; 30–44; 45–64; 64+. You might like to add a further band, say, 15–18 year olds, as future voters.
3 *Political opinion and bias in the press* — To be of value, opinion needs to be well supported by evidence. Bias occurs when opinion is found without proper consideration of the facts. There are several ways in which you could study opinion and bias in the press. One way would be to compare the coverage of a long-running political story by two or more different newspapers. You would obviously need to make a file of cuttings. As well as analysing the content of the reports, you could note where the stories were placed in each paper. Try to find examples of the same event (say, an important speech in Parliament, or a visit to a factory) which is reported in such as a way that the words used give very different impressions of the same event. An example of this might be: 'X made a powerful speech outlining his Party's record and achievements, which was enthusiastically

Continued over page . . .

received by the large audience,' together with: 'X made a feeble attempt to defend his Party's record, but the audience, though listening politely, were clearly not taken in.'

4 *Examination of a local political issue* — This chapter has mainly been about national politics, but it is often much easier to research local issues. There is bound to be a local issue in your area at the time you do the project. Perhaps a local school is threatened with closure, a new housing development is planned on what is now open countryside, or the route of a proposed by-pass is causing controversy. Reading the letters page in your local newspaper for a few days will usually allow you to identify what the current local issues are. Your sources of information are likely to include local politicians, the press, business people and community groups, as well as 'ordinary' local people. Remember that all interested groups should be included in your research if it is to do justice to the issue.

5 *The state of the parties* — If you prefer to research a wider issue, the state of the political parties (or, to make it more manageable, just one of them) is a possible topic. At the time of your research, how popular is the party you have chosen? (There are regular opinion polls taken on this issue and widely reported in the press.) What reasons are given for its popularity or lack of it? You will need to do research on published details about recent general elections to find out about the groups of voters whose support the party has been winning or losing, and possibly do some local research to see if this still seems to be the case. There is plenty of material in this chapter to help you make a start, but you must also include some original material.

Key words

Constitution	Ideology
Democracy	Policy
Ethnicity	Power
Government	Pressure groups

CHAPTER *16* Population

Definition of terms

The study of changes in population size, the reasons for the changes and their consequences, is known as *demography*. Demographic information is very important, as it helps governments to predict and plan for the future needs of the society, such as the likely demand for schools, housing, hospitals and old people's homes.

Where do governments get their knowledge of populations from? In Britain, ever since 1837, every birth, marriage and death has had to be registered with a local Registrar, and all this information is carefully stored. In addition to these records, every ten years since 1801 (except in 1941, during the Second World War), there has been a full Census, which counts every person in the population from information filled in on special forms. If demographers want information about the British population before those dates, they have to use other records, such as those kept by churches in their parish registers.

The three things which have the most direct effect on population size are births, deaths and migration. Each of these is, however, itself affected by other things. For example, the number of births is influenced by the average age at marriage in a society, the extent to which contraception is used, and what people of that society think is the 'ideal' family size, while the number of deaths is influenced by the general level of health care and the food supply.

When talking about births and deaths, sociologists look at the birth and death *rate*, rather than the actual number of babies born and people dying. The rate in this case is the number of births or deaths per 1000 people in the population. Using a rate rather than an actual figure allows populations of different sizes to be compared.

One of the most common ways of looking at births is by using the crude birth rate, which is the number of live births per year for every 1000 people in the population. To show why a rate is more helpful than just looking at actual numbers, study the information below, and do the calculations.

Activity (class)

To work out the crude birth rate of a population, take the total number of births, and divide this by the number of *thousands* of people in the population. For example, for a population of 500,000 people, the number of births would be divided by 500.

Country A has a population of 25,000. Last year there were 900 births.

Country B has a population of 56,618,000. Last year there were 755,000 births.

Work out the crude rate for country A and country B. At a guess, before you do the calculations, which one would you say had the higher birth rate?

Were you surprised by your answer? Country B actually represents modern Britain, and Country A has a crude birth rate similar to that of India, although the actual numbers in India's population are, of course, much greater. Another way of looking at birth rates is to look at the number of births for every 1000 women of child-bearing age (usually reckoned as 15–44) in a population. This is known as the *fertility rate*. The fertility rate will be higher than the crude birth rate, as we are dividing the same number of births by a much smaller figure. The fertility rate in Britain in 1986, for example, was 61.6.

The *crude death rate* of a society is worked out in a similar way to the crude birth rate, that is, dividing the total number of deaths in a year by the number of thousands of people in a population.

> **Activity (class)**
>
> In 1986, the population of Britain was approximately 56,618,000, and the number of deaths was approximately 660,800. Using these figures, work out the crude death rate.

Infant and child mortality rates

One death rate which is of particular interest to demographers is the *infant mortality rate*. This rate refers to the number of babies who die before their first birthday, out of every 1000 babies born. As babies are particularly at risk of disease and infection, the infant mortality rate of a society is regarded as a general measure of the overall health and prosperity of that society. There are huge differences in the infant mortality rates of different countries, particularly between the developed and the developing, or 'Third World', countries. The United Nations has calculated that the infant mortality rate in rich countries is about 15, in middle-income countries 25 and in poor countries 129.

The infant mortality rate in Britain in 1987 was 10.3 for male babies and 7.9 for females. (Male infants generally have slightly higher death rates than female babies.) However, within the same country, different groups of people can have different mortality rates, often reflecting different social and environmental factors. In Britain, for example, there is still a noticeable health gap between occupational classes. During the first month of life, a baby from social class V is twice as likely to die as a baby from class I, and this gap widens during the first year of life. For every baby from class I who dies in the first year of life, two will die in class III and four in classes IV and V.

Another clearly demonstrated difference in infant mortality rates between groups in the same country occurs in South Africa. In 1983, the infant mortality rate among white South Africans was 13.4, among Indians 20.7, among Coloureds (people of mixed race) 59.2 and among black South Africans 80.

The difference between the birth and death rates is very important, as it helps to predict the future size of the population. In Britain, for example, the birth and death rates are fairly similar, though the population is actually growing slightly in size because people are generally staying alive for longer than they used to.

Life expectancy

The average expectation of life, or *life expectancy*, is the age to which the people of a population can be *expected* to live. Obviously, because it is an average, some people will die before reaching this age, while others will live beyond it. In the last 100 years, the average life expectancy of new-born babies in Britain has risen from 54 years to 77 years. Much of this increase has been achieved by the fall in infant and child deaths, which keeps more of the population alive for much longer. Even with our current low death rates, only about three in every 100 of us will be around to celebrate our 100th birthday!

Look carefully at Figure 16.1, which shows how average life expectancy in Britain has changed over the years. The life expectancy at age one is higher than life expectancy at birth because so many babies used to die in their first year. Those who survived to their first birthday were obviously a bit stronger and had a better chance of surviving to adult life. Note how the fall in the infant mortality rate has caused this gap to get smaller.

Figure 16.1. Changing life expectancy in Britain

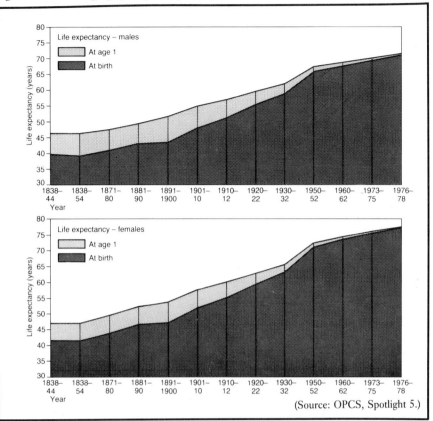

(Source: OPCS, Spotlight 5.)

Activity (class)

1 What reasons might there be for females having a higher expectation of life than males?
2 How would we expect this difference between males and famales to be shown in the elderly age groups in the population?

Stages in Britain's population growth

There have been four main stages in Britain's population growth.

Stage one — before 1750

The rate of growth was slow, with both birth and death rates high. The population was kept in check by a low standard of living, wars, famine and outbreaks of disease, including plague.

Stage two — 1750–1870

This was a period of enormous increase in population. The birth rate was still high, but the death rate fell steadily, although it was still high among infants and young children. Improvements in agriculture and imports of food helped to support a bigger population with a higher standard of living for many.

Stage three — 1870–1920

The rate of population growth was slowed down by falling birth rates. There were further improvements in diet, and important advances in private and public hygiene and sanitation. The purification of water supplies gradually brought to an end the great epidemics of cholera which had killed so many people, especially babies and young children. This period was also important for the start of family planning, although there was so much opposition to this that it had very little effect on the birth rates of the period.

Stage four — 1920 onwards

This period has both low birth rates and low death rates. Infant mortality rates have fallen, and life expectancy increased. There have been still more improvements in the general standard of health, especially noticeable after the introduction of the welfare state at the end of the 1940s. Better medical techniques and new drugs have also played a part in keeping the death rate low and increasing life expectancy. Birth rates have been kept low by the development of more sophisticated and reliable contraceptive techniques, such as 'the pill' and vasectomy. It appears, however, that the rate of growth (the speed at which the population grows) has slowed down in recent years (see Figure 16.2).

Figure 16.2. Population growth in England and Wales

Population present on census night

1801	8,892,536
1811	10,164,256
1821	12,000,236
1831	13,896,797
1841	15,914,148
1851	17,927,609
1861	20,066,224
1871	22,712,266
1881	25,974,439
1891	29,002,525
1901	32,527,843
1911	36,070,492
1921	37,886,699
1931	39,952,377
1939 estimate	41,460,000
1951	43,757,888
1961	46,104,548
1971	48,593,658
1981	49,011,000

(Source: OPCS, Spotlight 9.)

The early censuses were somewhat basic, providing little more than a head count. Gradually the scope of the census has extended in both content and coverage. The modern census is now an invaluable source of statistical information used by government departments, local authorities, the health service, by industry and commerce, and in academic research.

The birth rate

The fall in the birth rate has been a very important factor in the change in the size and structure of Britain's population. Although the overall trend in the birth rate has been downwards over the last century, the fall has been interrupted by a few 'baby booms'. There was one following the end of each of the two World Wars, as family life which had been disrupted by war continued, and marriages took place which had been postponed because of the war. There was also a 'baby boom' in the mid-1960s. These temporary increases in the birth rates show marked effects on other aspects of society, such as the number of children in education, the number of young workers, future numbers of pensioners, etc. The effects on the number of households in Britain can be seen in Figure 16.3.

Figure 16.3. The annual increase in the number of households

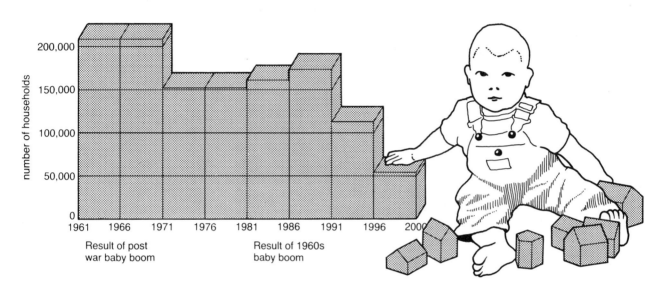

Result of post war baby boom

Result of 1960s baby boom

(Source: *Sunday Times*, 10 January 1988.)

A number of factors have influenced the fall in the birth rate in Britain (Figure 16.4).

Figure 16.4. 'Influences on the falling birth rate'

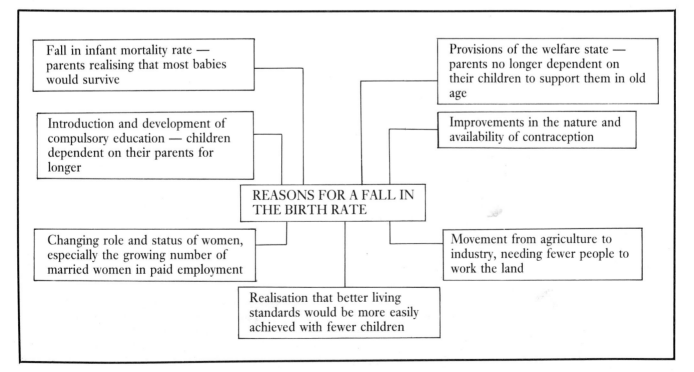

Fall in infant mortality rate — parents realising that most babies would survive

Introduction and development of compulsory education — children dependent on their parents for longer

Changing role and status of women, especially the growing number of married women in paid employment

REASONS FOR A FALL IN THE BIRTH RATE

Realisation that better living standards would be more easily achieved with fewer children

Provisions of the welfare state — parents no longer dependent on their children to support them in old age

Improvements in the nature and availability of contraception

Movement from agriculture to industry, needing fewer people to work the land

---

Activity (class/outside class)

Crude birth rates in selected years in Great Britain

1850	33.4	1947	20.5	1977	11.7
1900	28.7	1951	15.9	1980	13.3
1914	23.8	1956	16.1	1981	13.0
1918	17.7	1961	17.9	1982	12.6
1920	25.5	1966	17.9	1985	13.3
1939	14.8	1971	16.1	1986	13.3
1945	15.9	1976	12.0	1987	13.6

Above are details of the crude birth rate in Britain in selected years. To get an impression of the overall pattern, draw a graph, using the information supplied. There are two important things to note: one is that the years given are not the same distance apart — how will you show this on your graph? The other point is that the birth rates in the years between the years shown would not have followed a steady trend, so you should really mark the birth rate for the years shown with a cross on the graph, and join the crosses with a dotted line. Why do you think that the birth rate was relatively low in 1939? What was happening in Britain during the 1930s which might have had an effect on the number of children people had?

Reasons for the fall in the death rate

Despite the importance of medicine and medical techniques in our society, the major fall in Britain's death rate took place largely because of improvements in hygiene, sanitation and diet, rather than because of medical improvements. Death rates from the biggest 'killer diseases' had already fallen very steeply before the development of immunisations and antibiotics. The one important medical factor was the use of the smallpox vaccination from 1863.

Figure 16.5. Measles death rates of children under 15, England and Wales

The decline in deaths through measles before immunisation began was typical of what happened in the case of most infectious diseases.

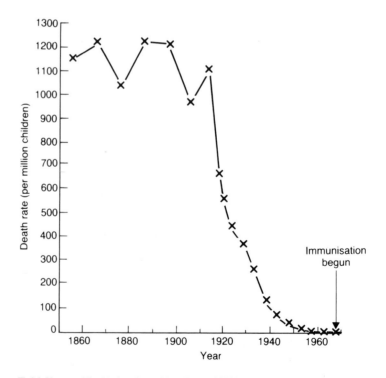

(Source: T. McKeown, *The Modern Rise of Population*, 1976.)

From the 1940s, the infant mortality rate was reduced partly with the help of new drugs, antibiotics, immunisations and improvements in the delivery and care of new babies. However, the fact that the infant mortality rate still varies significantly with social class suggests that level of income, housing and general standard of living are still more important than medicine alone.

Some consequences of changes in birth and death rates

Changes in birth and death rates have important consequences for individuals, for families and for society as a whole. In terms of society, the effects of lower birth rates and increased life expectancy have resulted in Britain's having an *ageing population*, in common with many other industrial societies. An ageing population is one in which an increasing proportion of the total population is found in the upper age groups. It is estimated that the number of pensioners in England and Wales will go up by 2.5 million in the next 40 years. There is also a growing number of people over the age of 75 (Table 16.1).

Table 16.1. The changing age structure of Britain

Year	Under 16s (millions)	Pensioners (millions)
1951	11.6	6.7
1961	12.6	7.6
1971	13.7	8.8
1981	12.1	9.7

(Source: People in Britain, OPCS, HMSO, 1983.)

Activity (class/outside class)

Draw out Table 16.1 as a bar chart. Which arrangement of the data would best show the narrowing gap between the number of under-sixteens and the number of pensioners?

Ethnic minorities

Not all groups in Britain show the same 'population profile'. Families whose head is from the New Commonwealth (the West Indies, India and parts of Africa) or Pakistan show a different population profile from the native British population. Immigrants to a country tend to be in the younger age groups, so the proportion of elderly people among ethnic minority groups is at present smaller than in the population at large. For example, people of pensionable age account for 17.4 per cent of the population of England and Wales, but less than four per cent of people in households whose head is from the New Commonwealth or Pakistan.

The age profile of recent immigrant groups tends to be relatively youthful.

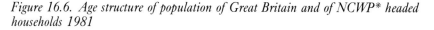

Figure 16.6. Age structure of population of Great Britain and of NCWP* headed households 1981

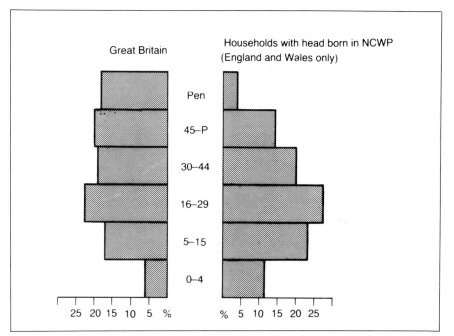

* New Commonwealth or Pakistan

(Source: OPCS Census 1981, 'An Ageing Population', reproduced in Family Policy Studies Centre fact sheet.)

Questions

1 Looking at the population of Great Britain, in which age group was the largest percentage of people found?
2 Which age group in the British population contained the smallest percentage of people?
3 Looking at households whose head was born in the New Commonwealth or Pakistan, in which age group was the largest percentage of people found?
4 Which of the two populations shown in Figure 16.6 had the most even numbers of people in different age groups?

The dependency ratio

The age structure of the population also affects the *dependency ratio*, which is the ratio of young and aged dependents to the producers, i.e. people of working age. In 1983, there were 65 dependents for every 100 people of working age, or 'producers'. Of these 65 dependents, 35 were children under sixteen and 30 were pensioners. It is estimated that by the year 2020, there will be 71 dependents for every 100 producers; 35 children under sixteen and 36 pensioners.

This means that those in work will need to produce enough wealth to provide for a growing number of dependents. Before you decide that we ought perhaps to pass laws to 'do away' with people when they reach the age of 60, it is important to remember two things. Firstly, young dependents will themselves become producers, and, secondly, elderly dependents have already 'done their stint' as producers, working to provide for the current working population when these were still children!

Stimulus question

Look at the information in the charts and tables and then
answer the questions which follow.

ITEM A

Figure 16.7. Marital status of (usually resident) population of pensionable age, Great Britain, 1981

ITEM B

Figure 16.8. Who the elderly live with, 1980

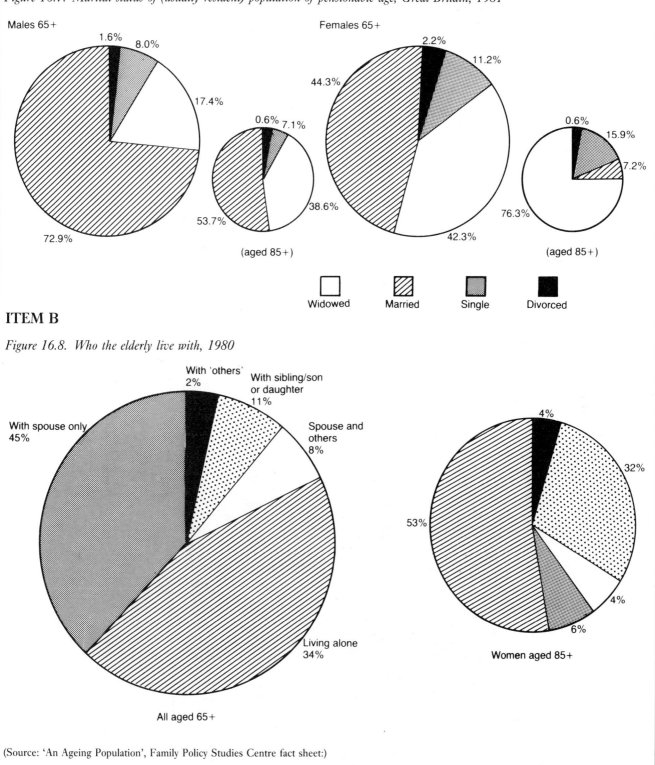

(Source: 'An Ageing Population', Family Policy Studies Centre fact sheet:)

Continued over page . . .

ITEM C

Table 16.2. The elderly population: past, present and future

	1901	1931	1981	2001	2021
000s					
65+	1734	3316	7985	8656	9956
75+	507	920	3052	4082	4401
85+	57	108	552	1047	1230
%					
65+	4.7	7.4	15.0	15.3	17.2
75+	1.4	2.1	5.7	7.2	7.6
85+	0.15	0.14	1.03	1.9	2.1

(Source: 1971 and 1981 Census, and population projections by the Government Actuary Mid-1981 based principal projections 1981–2021.)

Questions

1 What percentage of (a) males and (b) females aged 65+ are married? (Item A) (1 mark)
2 How do you account for the difference in the two figures? (Item A) (2 marks)
3 What is the most common marital status (widowed, married, single or divorced) of both males and females aged 85+? (Item A) (1 mark)
4 What percentage of women aged 85+ live alone? (Item B) (1 mark)
5 How many people aged 65+ were there in the population in 1901? (Item C) (1 mark)
6 Briefly describe two reasons for the increase in life expectancy in Britain. (4 marks)
7 Briefly describe two reasons for the fall in the birth rate in Britain during the past century. (4 marks)
8 Discuss one effect on *each* of following which could arise from an ageing population: a) individuals b) families c) society as a whole. (6 marks)

Population and society

Population pyramids (population structure)

One way of showing population statistics in diagrammatic form is to draw a *population pyramid*. This shows the percentage of people in various age groups (i.e. the structure of the population), divided into males and females, as 'blocks' placed one on top of the other. As you can see, the population structure of a society can change. In a society with a high birth rate and a high death rate, the resulting shape looks like a pyramid, such as Britain in 1901 in Figure 16.9. As birth and death rates change, and alter the numbers of people in the different age groups, so the shape of the 'pyramid' changes.

Figure 16.9. An ageing population

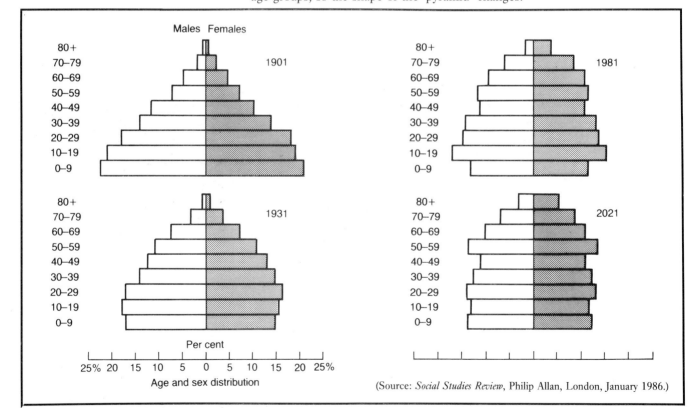

(Source: *Social Studies Review*, Philip Allan, London, January 1986.)

Changes in birth and death rates also lead to changes in the way in which resources are allocated. For example, our present pattern means that there will be a need for fewer maternity hospitals, nurseries, schools and teachers, and a growing need for home helps, sheltered housing and wards and hospitals to provide for the treatment of the elderly ('geriatric medicine'). Of course, not all retired people need such things — there will also be an increasing demand for leisure activities for the retired, many of whom are still very active indeed. Many holiday camps and hotels, including some abroad, have extended their seasons to provide budget holidays for pensioners, and the enthusiastic use by 'senior citizens' of special rail and bus passes has proved very profitable for local transport companies and British Rail. Retired people are much in demand for this reason, as they can travel 'off-peak' and take their holidays out of season, away from the peak school summer holiday time.

Changes in age structure also have an effect on government expenditure. For example, there has been a change in the relative costs of child benefit and old age pensions.

The balance of the sexes

Although women's higher life expectancy has meant that they have always outnumbered men in the upper age groups, they used to do so in the younger age groups as well. However, this pattern is now changing.

Stimulus question

Use the information in the graph and extract to answer the questions which follow.

ITEM A

Figure 16.10.   The balance of the sexes

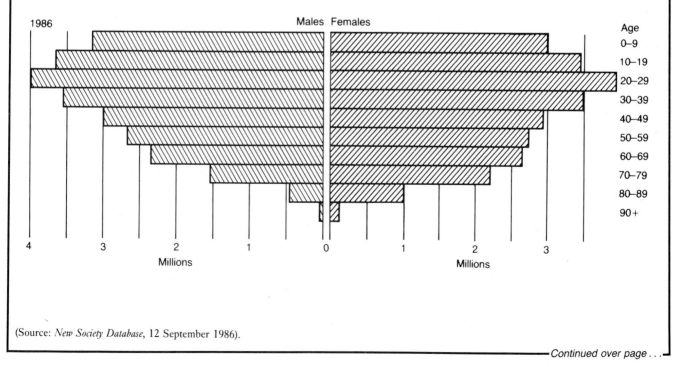

(Source: *New Society Database*, 12 September 1986).

Continued over page . . .

ITEM B

Advantage to girls in mixed doubles

Women will be able to pick and choose their husbands more carefully in future, because men now outnumber women in the marriageable age groups by 3 per cent.

Researchers are predicting that the change will alter the power balance between the sexes and lead to men taking more trouble to attract women, to ensure they are not left on the shelf.

New figures to be released by the Office of Population, Censuses and Surveys next month will show that the trend is becoming more pronounced and that, by the year 2025, the imbalance could reach as much as 5 per cent (105 men to every 100 women).

Traditionally, women have been in the weaker position because they have outnumbered men in the normal marriage years as a result of wars, emigration and a higher death rate among boys. In consequence, many women never married and the phenomenon of the maiden aunt was common.

With lower infant mortality rates and a prolonged period of peace, however, the preponderance of boys at birth is continuing into later years. Boys outnumber girls at birth by more than 5 per cent and, if present trends continue, the disparity could still be evident into the twenty-first century, when today's children are reaching their twenties.

Men now outnumber women in the 16–35 age group by 212,000 and in the peak marriage years of 20–24 by 59,000, or 3 per cent. By contrast, in the census year of 1921, women outnumbered men in the 20–24 age group by 15 per cent, and still outnumbered them by 5 per cent in the 1951 census year.

Melanie Henwood, research officer in the Family Policy Studies Centre, an independent research body, said: 'There is always a time lag between reality and people's attitudes and behaviour. But things will change.

'In the past, with an excess of women, the men have had the pick. Men are now likely to spend longer as bachelors and women will have a stronger hand. They will be doing the picking and choosing.

'Men are likely to marry later — and that is already happening. The average age of first marriage for men was 25 in 1961 and is now 26. In 1985, some 37 per cent of men marrying in the 30–54 age group were bachelors.

'We could see the phenomenon of the maiden uncle develop. The female spinster has had a traditional role of caring for parents in their old age. It is possible that men might move into that area, though I am not optimistic.'

'It could also lead to men looking for mates among older women. The toy boy phenomenon could make sense.'

Although reduced rates of infant mortality have resulted in more boy babies surviving to adulthood, deaths from accidents are still higher among boys.

In 1986, in the under-15 age group, 484 boys died in accidents, compared with 309 girls; in the 15–24 age group, 2,159 young men died from accidental causes, including road accidents, compared with 566 women.

'Men have to look their very best now,' said agony aunt Claire Rayner. 'They simply cannot go round looking like slobs while women are in the minority.'

So the men are stocking up with an array of weapons designed to put the fear of God into the most formidable of opponents: face packs, moisturising lotions, hair restorers, and bronzing face creams...

Boots estimates the male cosmetics market is worth a seductive £250 million a year and it's still an expanding market.

by Annabel Ferriman and Tim Walker

(Source: the *Observer*, 10 July 1988.)

Questions

1 In which age group are there four million males? (Item A)
(1 mark)
2 How many 0–9-year-old females are there? (Item A)
(1 mark)
3 Give two reasons why women have traditionally outnumbered men in the normal marriage years. (Item B)
(2 marks)
4 Why should lower infant mortality rates change the balance of the sexes? (Item B)   (3 marks)

5 By what percentage did women in the 20–24 age group outnumber men in a) 1921, b) 1951, c) 1988? (Item B)
(3 marks)
6 Describe and discuss some of the possible changes in society resulting from the changes in the proportions of younger men and women (Some suggestions are made in Item B, but you should try to think of others for youself.)   (10 marks)

Population and the labour force

Another important social effect of the fall in the birth rate (which also affects individual families) is that smaller families have released a growing number of women into the labour market, which has been important to the economy, and has also enabled many families to improve their standard of living.

The sharp fall in the birth rate which took place in the 1970s meant that for the first time in many years, the late 1980s saw a sharp fall in the number of young people leaving school and coming on to the job market. This has quite significant effects, particularly in those occupations, such as nursing, which traditionally rely on large numbers of young workers.

Stimulus questions

Read the following extract and graphs and then answer the questions.

ITEM A

Firms face contest for teenagers

Strong signs emerged this week that the rapid fall in the number of school-leavers will give rise to conflict in industry and education. Unions as well as employers were warned that they will have to struggle to win the allegiance of increasingly scarce young workers.

The decline in the number of young people coming on to the labour market, together with the upturn in the economy, has already had dramatic effects on youth unemployment. There is now the prospect of a complete turnround in the youth labour market as numbers fall more sharply over the next six years, making school-leavers the group of workers with the biggest potential bargaining power.

Ministers, who for years have been telling young people that they are pricing themselves out of jobs, are now warning employers that they will have to find ways of attracting school-leavers.

A report from the economic committee of the TUC warns unions that it will be up to them to make sure that young people are able to take advantage of their stranger position in the labour market, and they must be encouraged to join unions. A union adviser said: 'At present, young people are being told that they have to choose between pay and training. In future they should be able to insist on both.'

ITEM B

Figure 16.11. Labour force projections 1987–1995

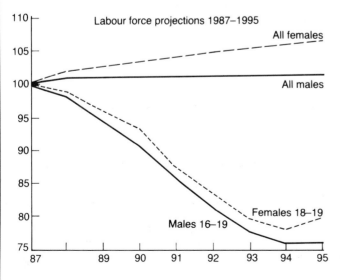

Item C

Figure 16.12. Youth labour supply 1980–2000

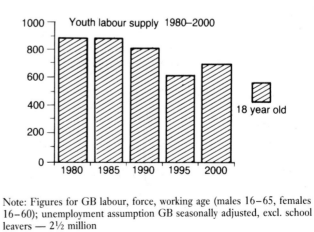

Note: Figures for GB labour, force, working age (males 16–65, females 16–60); unemployment assumption GB seasonally adjusted, excl. school leavers — 2½ million

(Source: Adapted from the *Times Educational Supplement*, 6 May 1988.)

Continued over page...

Questions

1 Which year contained the greatest number of eighteen year olds? (Item C) (1 mark)
2 Which year is estimated to have the smallest number of eighteen year olds? (Item C) (1 mark)
3 What is the projected number of eighteen year olds for the year 2000? (Item C) (1 mark)
4 Which group of workers is expected to show the biggest increase between 1987 and 1995? (Item B) (1 mark)

5 Which two groups will have to try to win the loyalty and support (allegiance) of young workers? (Item A) (2 marks)
6 Which two factors are reported to have had dramatic effects on youth unemployment? (Item A) (2 marks)
7 What is meant by the statement that school-leavers will be the group of workers with the 'biggest potential bargaining power'? (Item A) (3 marks)
8 Why do you think that the TUC considers that it would benefit young workers to join trade unions? (Item A) (4 marks)

With regard to the effects on individuals and individual families of changes in the birth and death rates, the increased number of women in the labour market has already been mentioned. The effects on individuals of increased life expectancy can be both positive, in that people can usually look forward to a long and reasonably active retirement after their years at work, but sometimes negative, as when increasing age is combined with poor health, poverty or loneliness.

As far as families are concerned, the increase in elderly dependents has led to many families (or usually the female members) having to take responsibility for an elderly parent or parent-in-law. This problem has been aggravated by cuts in social services, which have led to the closure of many state-run homes for the elderly and a reduction in geriatric wards. However, many families also benefit from having older relatives, with grandparents acting as baby-sitters or child minders, and often helping out financially.

Activity (class)

On a sheet of blank paper put the heading 'Effects of the changing age structure'. Down the left-hand side make a series of headings of changes which have occurred. Opposite each of these headings, on the right-hand side, write a few words of explanation.

A few headings are given below to get you started. You will need to look back through this section to get your information:

Pensions	Young workers
Recreation and leisure	Dependency ratio

Migration

Migration refers to the movement of people between countries, or within a country. International migration can have an important effect on a country's population size and growth, while internal migration patterns may also have important social consequences.

Activity (class)

In a sentence or two, write down what comes to your mind when you hear the word 'immigrant'. What kind of person do you think of? What do they look like? Where do they come from? We will come back to this description later.

Immigration to Britain

In our society, we hear and read rather a lot in the mass media about 'immigrants'.

The term 'net migration' refers to the difference between the number of people coming into a country (immigrants) and those leaving (emigrants). The difference between these two figures will result in an overall population gain (+) or loss (−).

Table 16.3. Migrant flows: UK 1971–1986

Year	Into UK	Out of UK	Net migration
1971	200,000	240,000	−40,000
1976	191,000	210,000	
1981	153,000	233,000	
1985	232,000	174,000	
1986	250,000	213,000	

(Source: *Social Trends*, 1988.)

Activity (class)

Copy out Table 16.3 and complete the 'net migration' column.

Overall, *natural increase* (more births than deaths) has played a much greater part in the pattern of Britain's population growth than migration. However, the fact that Britain has often been a net exporter of people took considerable pressure off Britain's 'population explosion' of the eighteenth and nineteenth centuries, and also reduced population pressure in the twentieth century.

1879–1931 Over two million Britons emigrated

1901–1951 Over seven million Britons emigrated

Britain has often been an exporter of people. i) Emigrants leaving Britain for Australia in 1852 (right).
ii) Emigrants leaving Britain for Australia in 1947 (left).

Although people from the New Commonwealth (the West Indies, India and parts of Africa) and Pakistan have not made up the majority of immigrants to Britain, most political concern has centred on them, which has been expressed in various Acts designed to control immigration, especially of 'black' people (Figure 16.14). Most blacks consider this to have been unfair (see Chapter Twelve.)

Figure 16.14. Migrant flows into the UK 1986 (thousands)

British	Old Commonwealth	New Commonwealth & Pakistan	Other	EEC	Other Foreign	All
120	16	18	16	35	46	250

(Source: *OPCS Monitor.*)

Questions

1 How many people migrated to the UK in 1986 from the New Commonwealth and Pakistan?
2 Of what nationality were the greatest number of immigrants?
3 How many *more* immigrants came from European Common Market (EEC) countries than from the New Commonwealth and Pakistan?
4 What was the total number of immigrants to the UK in 1986?

Activity (class)

In the light of what Table 16.14 has shown you, go back and read your description of the 'typical immigrant'. How accurate was it? If it was inaccurate, why do you think that you were mistaken? Discuss this as a class.

Internal migration

As well as migration between countries, there is also the movement of population within a country — internal migration. There was a great deal of internal migration in Britain in the eighteenth and nineteenth centuries, as large numbers of people left the land and moved into the new industrial towns.

In the twentieth century, especially since the end of the Second World War, there has been a movement out of the old established towns and cities and into the suburbs, countryside or new towns. This movement of people was shown by the 1981 Census as having a marked regional pattern. Whereas the overall population growth in England and Wales was very small (+0.5%), there were quite marked population changes between regions, as Figure 16.15 shows (see also Chapter Eight).

As far as individual areas are concerned, the 'fastest grower' between 1971 and 1981 was the 'new town' of Milton Keynes, which increased its population by an amazing 85 per cent, while the 'fastest loser' was the Inner London borough of Kensington and Chelsea, which had lost over a quarter (26 per cent) of its population.

Remember that we are looking at percentage changes in population which, although they can show us the overall pattern, can still be misleading. For example, Derbyshire gained 0.3 per cent population, and Greater London lost 0.4 per cent. On the face of it, a similar picture. However, Derbyshire actually gained 2,400 people, whereas Greater London lost 30,500. Similarly. Clwyd's 1.5 per cent gain represented 6,000 people, whereas West Midlands' 1.5 per cent loss represented 40,900 people.

Figure 16.15. Regional population change 1971–1981

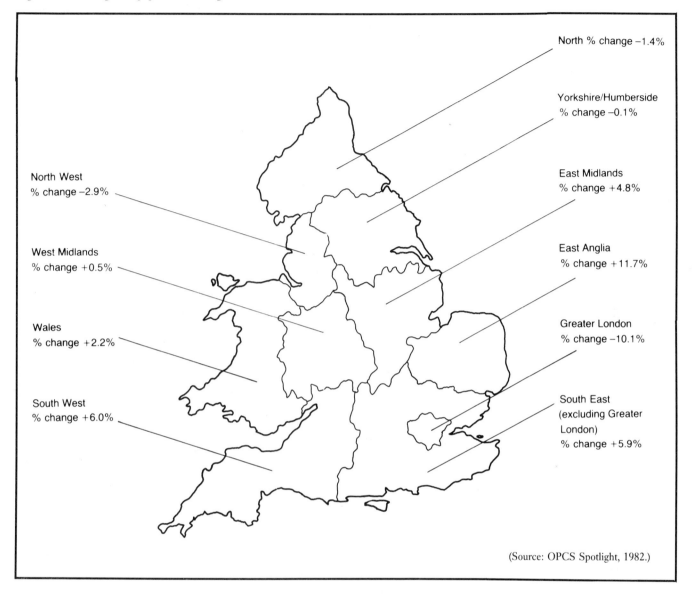

North % change –1.4%

Yorkshire/Humberside % change –0.1%

North West % change –2.9%

East Midlands % change +4.8%

West Midlands % change +0.5%

East Anglia % change +11.7%

Wales % change +2.2%

Greater London % change –10.1%

South West % change +6.0%

South East (excluding Greater London) % change +5.9%

(Source: OPCS Spotlight, 1982.)

Some effects of internal migration

These population movements have had noticeable effects. Large areas of countryside within commuting (travel-to-work) distance of city centres have become 'dormitory towns', with many people only living there at evenings and weekends. As many people's incomes have risen, an increasing number have bought rural properties as weekend or holiday homes. This sort of demand for country housing (especially noticeable in parts of Wales) has pushed up the price of much rural housing to the point at which the 'locals', with their much lower incomes, can't afford to buy houses themselves.

As more and more jobs are in the service or 'sun-rise' electronics industries, which do not need large industrial factories, there is a growing trend for companies to locate themselves in 'green-site' locations, which means in rural areas near open countryside and pleasant market towns.

However, in the mid-1980s, the flow of population out of large urban areas slowed and in Greater London even slightly reversed. Both wealthy professional and city people and Northerners moving South for work partly accounted for this.

Stimulus questions

Read the following article and answer the questions.

More flee cities to rural retreat

Increasing numbers of people are deserting Britain's cities in search of the 'good life' in the country.

The exodus, particularly from London, now far exceeds the natural trend of rural depopulation in many places, research findings show.

Mr David Cross, of King's College, London, used census information and the Registrar General's annual estimates of population to determine how much of the population growth in rural parts was caused by long-distance migration.

He told the annual conference of the Institute of British Geographers at Loughborough University yesterday that, of the 529,000 rise of population between 1971 and 1986 in the 'top 33' rural-growth areas, 97 per cent was due to migration. Between 60 and 70 per cent of the gains were due to long-distance migration between regions.

Leading the list of favourite destinations were: Wimborne in Dorset, Huntingdon, Caradon near Plymouth, north Cornwall, Radnor, Forest Heath and Bambergh, in Suffolk, Breckland in Norfolk, Ryedale and Selby in North Yorkshire, and Holderness, in Lincolnshire.

The main trend, Mr Cross said, was that while the more remote rural parts were often losing population through 'natural' change as old people died and younger people left for the cities, it was far outstripped by the new gains.

More than a quarter of the new arrivals were in the 15-to-29 key-worker age-group.

Mr Cross put the exodus down to an increasing deconcentration of employment opportunity, the improvement of travel facilities — particularly high-speed railway links between East Anglia and London — and the retirement of Londoners, who were able to sell their homes at a significant profit and head for the hills or the coast.

However, another speaker painted a more complex picture of population movements affecting the capital. Dr Tony Champion, of Newcastle University, the author of a study of London's population, said that 1988 would be a crunch year.

There were many uncertain factors affecting the picture. Although more people were looking to live outside of the capital, the big population drop of the seventies had slowed. More people are moving into the capital from overseas, particularly Europe and the Far East, and moving south from unemployment areas in Britain. Added to that was an increase in the birthrate.

'There are trends both in and out of the city,' said Dr Champion.

(Source: the *Guardian*, 1 January 1988.)

Questions

1 Which two sources were used by Mr Cross to see how much rural population growth was caused by long-distance migration? (2 marks)
2 What percentage of growth in the 'top 33' rural growth areas was caused by long-distance migration? (1 mark)
3 Name three reasons which are given in the article for the move to rural areas. (3 marks)
4 What aspect of population had been studied by Dr Champion? (1 mark)
5 From which three areas are people moving into London? (3 marks)
6 Describe and discuss the possible effect of population movement into rural areas on the rural environment and local rural communities. (4 marks)
7 Describe and discuss some of the major differences between living in a large town and living in the countryside. (6 marks)

The global picture

Although many industrialised countries now have relatively slow population growth, the world population is increasing rapidly.

Figure 16.16. The Earth itself isn't getting any bigger!

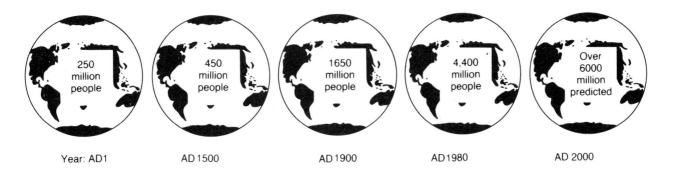

(Source: Nance Fyson, 'Population', Cartoon Sheet 7, Centre for World Development Education.)

It wasn't until 1830 that the world population reached 1000 million, but 2000 million was reached only 100 years after that, 3000 million in another 30 years, and 4000 million in 1975. The United Nations estimates that the world population will reach 10,500 million by the year 2110.

Figure 16.17. The global village AD 2000

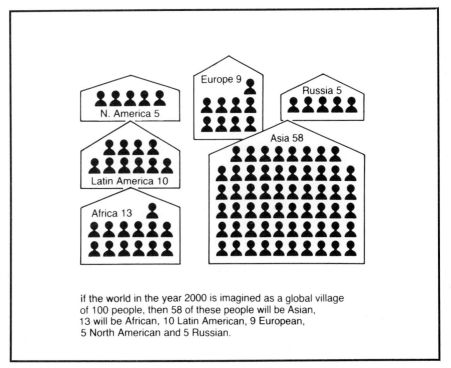

if the world in the year 2000 is imagined as a global village of 100 people, then 58 of these people will be Asian, 13 will be African, 10 Latin American, 9 European, 5 North American and 5 Russian.

(Source: Eric McGraw, 'The Shape of Things to Come', *Population Concern*, June 1982.)

With so many people already under-nourished and even starving, this level of population increase is obviously a cause for concern. It is important to remember, however, the political aspect of the relationship between 'rich' and 'poor' countries. Many of the countries in which there is real hunger and poverty do, in fact, grow enough food to support their populations — but they export it to the wealthier nations instead, often to help pay off the loans which have been made to them. Another problem is that often 'cash crops', such as tea, coffee and tobacco, wanted by the richer nations, are grown rather than the corn or vegetables which would feed the native population. Remember that when Britain had a surplus population, it was able to export millions of people to countries in our Empire, and later the Commonwealth. That option is not available to many 'Third World' countries. Perhaps we in the richer countries might have to stop having an ever-increasing standard of living in order that all of the world's population might have a fairer chance of survival. What do you think?

Stimulus questions

Use the information in the graphs to answer the questions which follow.

ITEM A

Figure 16.18. Changes in the dependency population

Dependent population as a percentage of poulation of working age (males 14–65, females 14–60)

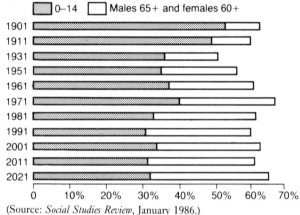

(Source: *Social Studies Review*, January 1986.)

ITEM C

Figure 16.20. British population aged 16–19

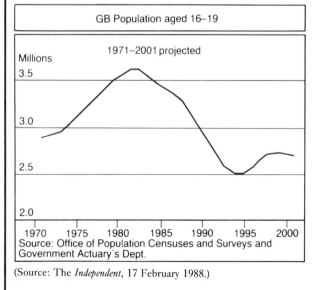

(Source: The *Independent*, 17 February 1988.)

ITEM B

Figure 16.19. An ageing population

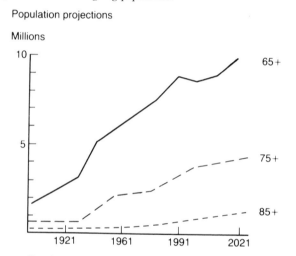

(Source: Population projections by the Government Actuary. Mid-1981 based principal projection 1981–2021.)

Questions

1 In which year did young dependents equal about 50 per cent of the population of working age? (Item A) (1 mark)
2 Which year had a) the lowest and b) the highest number of all dependents? (Item A) (2 marks)
3 What is meant by the phrase 'the dependency ratio'? (2 marks)
4 In approximately which year is the number of people aged 65+ expected to fall slightly? (Item B) (1 mark)
5 By about how many is the number of sixteen–nineteen year olds expected to fall between 1985 and 1995? (Item C) (1 mark)
6 What is meant by the term 'net migration'? (3 marks)
7 Give two probable effects on society of the fall in the number of sixteen–nineteen year olds. (4 marks)
8 Outline three changes in internal population movements in Britain in the last 30 years, giving a reason for each change. (6 marks)

Structured questions

1 Name *four* factors which can affect the size and rate of growth of a population.
2 Discuss the various factors which have an influence on the birth rate.
3 Describe the main changes to Britain's population size, structure and location which have taken place this century.

Project and assignment suggestions

1 *Undertake a study of population changes in your area* — Obtain the census information for your county in two different census years, preferably some time apart, e.g. 1851 and 1981. For each year, draw up a population pyramid. What differences can you see? How could these differences be explained? An important part of your project will be describing how you obtained the census material on which your project is based.
2 *Carry out a survey designed to look at the extent of internal migration into your neighbourhood* — Choose a clearly bounded area, such as a village, a small parish or a housing estate, and choose a sample of households to survey. Design a questionnaire to find out how long the families have been living in the neighbourhood, and where they lived before they moved in. If they have moved in from elsewhere, you could also ask questions about their reasons for choosing your area. As well as working out the percentage of people who are newcomers to the area, you could work out the distances between your town and where they came from, to see how many were long-range and how many were short-range migrants. For purposes of comparison, you could also try to get hold of data about migration into and out of the region as a whole — your local county council might have information on this.
3 *Do a comparative study of birth, marriage and death rates in your area over a period of time* — As well as census material, you might be lucky enough to have a local church whose parish registers go back over a period of time. Such parish records are now often stored on microfiche in the local library. Try to find out what might have caused sudden changes in the rates. For example, a big increase in the death rate is often linked to an epidemic of typhoid or cholera.
4 *Carry out a study of the different population profiles of different countries* — The easiest way of seeing similarities and differences is by drawing up population pyramids. It's not enough simply to get the data and draw the pyramids — you will have to do some analysis. For example, some countries clearly show the effects of past wars on the population — the Soviet Union is a good example of this. Under-developed ('Third World') countries with high birth and death rates show a similar shape. The effects of a very sharp fall in the birth rate in a short space of time in a country such as Sweden is also very noticeable in a population pyramid. Don't forget to include details of where and how you obtained the information.

Key words

Ageing population	Infant mortality rate
Crude birth rate	Life expectancy
Crude death rate	Migration
Dependency ratio	Net migration
Fertility rate	

CHAPTER 17 The Welfare State and Poverty

Description and development of the welfare state

What is the welfare state?

The welfare state consists of those government departments and organisations concerned with the well-being, security and, in some respects, control of the nation's citizens. Figure 17.1 shows a list of the main areas of welfare provision with examples.

Figure 17.1

Service	Example
Health	Free consultation with a doctor
Education	A free state education
Social Security	Unemployment and sick pay
	Income support for those otherwise insufficiently provided for
Housing	Local authority houses and flats
Environment	'Green belts' — where industrial development is banned
Social Services	Social workers, home helps, meals on wheels

Who pays for the welfare state?

The simple answer to this question is that 'we', the citizens of Britain, pay for the welfare state. We do so by providing central and local government with funds raised as follows:

- Tax — Mainly income tax and value added tax (VAT), which is a tax on certain goods and services.
- Rates — These are taxes on property and land raised by local authorities, which are to be replaced by the community tax which is a tax on individuals.
- National Insurance — This is partly taken out of wages to pay for unemployment and sick pay and the state old age pension, so these are called *contributory benefits*. Other benefits, such as income support, which recipients do not directly contribute to are called *non-contributory* benefits.

Figure 17.2. How Britain compares — taxes and social security contributions as percentage of GDP, 1985

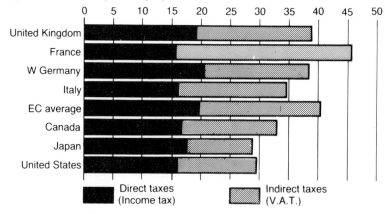

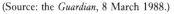

Direct taxes (Income tax)   Indirect taxes (V.A.T.)

(Source: the *Guardian*, 8 March 1988.)

Question

Do Britons pay more or less in taxes and social security contributions than the EC average?

The voluntary sector

In addition to the services provided by the welfare state, there are hundreds of voluntary organisations in Britain concerned with various aspects of welfare. These are financed mainly through government grants and private donations. A well-known voluntary organisation is the National Society for the Prevention of Cruelty to Children whose work has come into even greater prominence as concern over child abuse has increased. Two organisations involved with the needs of the old are Age Concern and Help the Aged. Most voluntary agencies have a small, paid, full-time staff, but also rely on unpaid help from members of the public. Sometimes, such organisations can 'fill in the cracks' left by the welfare state or respond more flexibly to crises. Thus, in the winter freeze of 1987, Help the Aged opened a free telephone line to give advice on keeping warm and claiming benefit.

The voluntary sector could never raise enough funds to replace the welfare state. Indeed, some voluntary agencies, such as the Child Poverty Action Group, see it as part of their role to act as pressure groups on government to do more for their clients. However, the Conservative governments of the 1980s encouraged charities to meet more of the needs of the poor.

Activity (class)

Make two lists: one of the advantages of voluntary organisations being involved in welfare, and the other of the disadvantages. You could do this as a small group activity followed by class discussion.

The right to welfare

The belief that all citizens have a right to basic social security is a relatively new one and is perhaps not yet fully accepted by everybody. After the Second World War, Thomas Marshall argued that the right to social welfare should be considered the third of the three great rights of modern citizenship: political, civil and social. The main political right is the right to vote. Civil rights are based on equality under the law and freedom of expression (e.g. of speech and writing). Social rights are less easy to define, but Marshall considered that they include health, education and basic social security.

In addition to providing welfare, a second purpose or function of the welfare state is social control of the poor. Providing the poor with a basic standard of living might prevent them from resorting to disorderly or violent protest or, perhaps, crime. Some regarded the training schemes of the 1980s as largely an attempt to keep the unemployed in order by keeping them 'off the streets'.

Questions

1 Briefly describe the welfare state. (3 marks)
2 Who would you say 'owns' the welfare state? (3 marks)
3 What are the purposes or functions of the welfare state? (4 marks)

Attitudes to poverty before the founding of the welfare state

We often refer to the '*modern*' welfare state because, until the recent past, the state did not accept the responsibility of providing the full range of services mentioned above. Of course, people have always faced problems threatening their welfare. In the Middle Ages, the chances of becoming poor, ill, or dying early were much greater than now. In much of the undeveloped world, these dangers remain a daily threat, not only because of lack of welfare, but because many of these countries cannot afford the standards of public hygiene Britons now take for granted.

In pre-industrial Britain, the state was more concerned with keeping the poor in order rather than helping them. In the early nineteenth century, a common attitude among the ruling groups and local rate-payers was that merely giving people money (known as outdoor relief) encouraged people to be idle. The Poor Law Amendment Act of 1834 tried to curb outdoor relief by having the poor put in workhouses which were intended to provide a standard of life lower than could be achieved on the lowest wage. Poverty was generally believed to be a result of people's personal failures, or laziness.

Although such attitudes continued into and beyond the nineteenth century, the view that the state should take more care of the poor also gained strength. Industrialisation, urbanisation and the population explosion created great problems concerning working and living conditions. With some exceptions, businessmen did little to improve these conditions (some critics, such as Marx and Engels, said they were the main cause of them) and it gradually became clear that government would have to take action.

Throughout the nineteenth century, there was no welfare state to cope with the poverty and social problems of the industrial towns. This illustration comes from a book written in 1853 by John Cobden which called for reforms in working conditions.

The Labour Government, 1945–50, the welfare state

The welfare measures of the Labour Government of 1945–50 were the climax of perhaps a century of gradual reform. The party was elected on a tide of popular feeling in favour of a more secure and fairer society following the hardship and sacrifice of war. The mood of change had begun during the war.

In 1942, Sir William Beveridge said in his famous Beveridge Report that modern citizenship gives the right to certain freedoms: freedom from the 'giant evils' of want, disease, ignorance, squalor and idleness. To combat 'want', a system of national insurance was set up to provide unemployment, sickness and other payments. In 1944, the Education Act set up a universal system of compulsory secondary education to combat 'ignorance'. In 1946, the National Health Service was set up to combat 'disease'. These measures are sometimes known as 'the three pillars of the welfare state'.

The 'squalor' of poor housing and neglected environment was also attacked in the early post-war years. The Labour Government encouraged local authorities to build council houses and to let them at subsidised rents. The 1946 New Towns Act gave a fresh start to thousands of people from run-down inner cities and the 1947 Town and Country Planning Act made land development subject to local authority approval. 'Idleness', in the form of the high levels of unemployment familiar in the 1980s, was not a problem in the immediate post-war period. However, governments attempted to manage the economy to maintain near full employment and to revive certain depressed regions and industries.

Figure 17.3. Measures which established the welfare state

Freedom from:	National Insurance Acts	1944 and 1946
Want	National Assistance Act	1948
	(set up a 'safety net' for the uninsured)	
Disease	National Health Act	1946
Ignorance	Education Act	1944
Squalor	New Town Act	1946
	Town and Country Planning Act	1947
Idleness	A variety of policies to achieve near full employment	

Question

Which Acts are referred to as 'the three pillars of the welfare state' and which of the 'giant evils' referred to by Beveridge did they attempt to deal with?

Universal or selective (means-tested) benefits?

Should welfare benefits cover all or just part of the population? Should benefits be income (means) tested? Should those who can afford it be allowed to buy certain services, such as education and health privately, or should there be just one public system? These are among the main questions concerning welfare which have been debated in the post-war years.

One view is that *the main* welfare benefits should be *universal*, i.e. that they should be equally available to everybody. For example, the state pension is available to all who reach the official retirement age. Others take the view that benefits should be *selective*, i.e. that they should go only to those who need them. Thus, in the 1980s, council house rent subsidies were made available only for the most needy, whilst rents were sharply increased for others.

Selective benefits are nearly always *means tested* i.e. the person applying for them has to show need by providing information on income and savings. The Labour Party favours a more universalist approach and the Conservative Party a more selective one, which partly explains why the British welfare state has developed as a mix of both types of benefit. In the 1980s, the term 'targeting benefits' was used with the intention of making them more selective.

The universalist approach is based on the view that the welfare state helps promote common and equal citizenship — in education, health and even in the provision of public leisure and cultural facilities. The selectivist approach reflects the view that the welfare state is a 'safety net' for the poor, who may not be able to afford anything else.

Universalism versus selectivity: for and against

	Universalism	*Selectivity*

Universalism

For
1 Everybody is entitled to the service — so nobody is missed out
2 A range of basic services are provided for all as a matter of *citizen's rights*
3 Universalism helps to create a sense of equal membership of the national community

Against
1 Universal services are expensive
2 People may abuse services because they are free and may become dependent on them
3 The welfare state is large and impersonal

Selectivity

For
Services are consumed only by those in 'real' need

The welfare state is smaller and less bureaucratic (i.e. there are fewer forms and officals)
The welfare state is cheaper

Against
Many who are entitled to benefits do not in fact get them
Selective benefits are means tested risking humiliation and stigma (a mark of public disgrace)
Selectivity divides the community into 'winners' and 'losers'

Activity (class/outside class)

1 Draw up a list of five important welfare needs.
2 Construct a questionnaire to find out peoples' opinion about these needs, and particularly whether they think the state should provide for them fully, in part only, or not at all. Here are some ideas for questions:

On health:

• Do you consider that prescription charges should be removed and prescriptions made free for all?
• Do you consider that private health care should be abolished?

On child benefit:

• Do you consider that child benefit should be means tested? (At the moment, child benefit is paid directly to all mothers or guardians of children.)

Comment: You will need to make sure that your wording of questions enables you to get precisely the kind of information (data) you require.

You may find that this activity gives you ideas and information which you can use in your project.

The wider scene: Child benefit for a mother of three

France	*£257*
Luxembourg	*£198*
West Germany	*£125*
Britain	*£ 87*

(1988 figures)

Conservative Party welfare policy in the 1980s

The Conservative Party was in office throughout the decade. Therefore, it was Conservative policies on welfare that passed into law during this period.

The main welfare measure during this period was the Social Security Act which came into force in 1988.

The Social Security Act, 1988: main terms

Income Support

Income support replaced supplementary benefit. It became the main means-tested benefit. Income support is much more simply organised than supplementary benefit, which had become very complicated.

Family Credit

Family Credit supplements ('tops up') the income of low-paid workers. Less money is directly available for rent and rate rebates under Family Credit, which may be one reason why more people had difficulty in paying them in 1987 than in 1988.

The Social Fund

This provides grants and (mainly) loans for particular needs. It replaces a system of one-off single grant payments. Because it replaces a grant with a loan system, this measure has caused a lot of argument. The Government has also recommended those who administer the Social Fund to refer clients more often to voluntary charities. Some see this as an attempt by the Government to pass on its responsibilities for the poor.

There were gainers and losers in the changes introduced by the 1988 Act. Figure 17.4 shows an example of each.

Figure 17.4

Gainer	Loser
Married couple with 2 children aged 6–8 receiving no additional weekly payments or single payment	Single parent mother with 1 child under 5
Old £72.45 New £76.30	Old £57.10 New £51.20
Gain of £3.85 a week	**Loss** of 5.90 a week

The main points of Conservative welfare policy

1 *Selection* — The Conservatives came out strongly in favour of selectivity or 'targeting' the very needy.

2 *Cost-cutting* — The Government was determined to reduce public expenditure, including, as far as possible, welfare spending. However, because of the very high numbers of unemployed, social security expenditure rose rapidly between 1979 and 1987, when the increase began to level off as the numbers of unemployed began to fall. Nevertheless, cuts were made and certain groups suffered. For instance, the 1988 Act resulted in a loss for young, single unemployed people under 25 without children, as well as for many single parents. Over the long term, expenditure on housing was the most severely cut, being reduced by 41 per cent between 1978 and 1988.

3 *Privatisation* — of welfare services means that private enterprise provides them rather than government. For instance, some mainly Conservative-held local authorities privatised a number of old people's homes. Critics of this policy argued that these homes were not always properly inspected and that the principle of 'care for profit' could lead to taking advantage of the elderly.

4 *De-institutionalisation* — means that people housed in large state institutions, such as mental hospitals, are returned to 'the community', provided they are judged to be able to cope. The two criticisms of this policy are that some people have been pushed out even when they could not cope and that, often, 'the community' was not adequately prepared to care for them.

Another approach to welfare: combining the old and new?

The private provision of education, health and social security (pensions) has increased during the Conservatives' period in government. A universalist approach would discourage this trend and instead develop strong, efficient basic welfare, equally for all. However, even with good basic services available, there would still be some people suffering poverty. At the moment, most of the benefits available to the poor are means (incomes/savings) tested. A way to avoid or reduce the need for means testing would be to set a minimum wage or negative income tax (i.e. people below a certain level of income would receive money from the state instead of being taxed). Such proposals would be complicated to work out but have some support.

Perhaps a combination of a universalist approach to basic services and the provision of a minimum wage would provide the basis of a new approach to welfare.

Waiting for change...claimants seeking advice on social security changes at an unemployment centre.

The future of welfare: the 1990s and beyond

By looking at the facts and trends we already know about welfare, we can see roughly what problems and issues are likely to occur in the future.

Cost

Social security, health and education together account for about half of government spending (and remember the Government spends *our money*). However, these are not the areas in which there was the biggest increase in expenditure between 1978 and 1988.

Table 17.1. Spending changes 1978–88

Increases %		Decreases %	
Employment and training	73	Overseas aid	−5
Law and order	58	Environment	−10
Social Security	39	Transport	−11
Health and social		Housing	−41
services	30	Industry, trade	
Defence	24	and energy	−64
Agriculture	21		
Education	9		
Other	6		

Questions

1 Name two welfare services for which spending increased (1978–88) and by what percentage.
2 Name *one* welfare service for which spending decreased (1978–88) and by what percentage.

An ageing population

Britain has one of the oldest populations in the world. About ten million out of a total population of 55 million are retired. The importance of this is discussed in Chapter Sixteen, but one result of having an older population is that more money needs to be spent on health care.

The future of welfare in a richer society

What kind of welfare will the nation want as nearly everybody gets better off? Will more people want to buy education, health and pensions privately, or will there still be majority support for strong state systems in these areas? Another question — will a very rich society seek to abolish poverty, or will it perhaps ignore it?

Welfare and a successful economy

The nation cannot spend what it hasn't got. All the major parties have emphasised the need for a successful economy to create the wealth on which welfare spending depends.

Stimulus questions

Read the article and answer the questions on the next page.

Three of the main welfare services — education, health and social security — reflect more closely the universalist rather than the selectivist view, i.e. they are available to all and used by the great majority. Nevertheless, since the 1950s, there has been a slow drift away from universalism in these services, which has become more marked under the Thatcher governments. For instance, the 1944 Education Act did not seek to abolish private schools and no Labour Government has yet done so. Applications to private schools increased in the mid-1980s when the state system was affected by reorganisation and dispute.

Similarly, a totally free health system did not last long and prescription charges were soon introduced. In 1989, these were as much as £2.60 each, and although there were many exemptions, some people may have chosen to go untreated rather than pay the charge.

The right to unemployment and sick pay and to a state old age pension remain intact as part of the fundamentals of the welfare state. However, in 1988, the Conservative Party made it possible for individuals to 'opt out' of the state old age pension system (including discontinuing contributions) in favour of privately run pension schemes. The Act also sought to 'target' *non-contributory* benefits more precisely partly by more accurate means testing.

Continued over page...

Questions

1 Define what is meant by a *universal* service. (1 mark)
2 Define what is meant by a *selective* service. (1 mark)
3 Give *one* argument in favour and *one* against the existence of private schools. (4 marks)
4 Define what is meant by a non-contributory benefit. Give *two* examples. (4 marks)
5 Give arguments for and against the existence of private medicine in Britain. Explain *your own* view on the matter. (5 marks)

Activity (class/outside class)

Read the following extract before doing the activity.

Caring pub gets award

A Shoebury pub has become the first in Britain to be tested by a group of handicapped people to see if it qualifies for a special award.

The Parsons Barn in Frobisher Way has been given the disabled facilities symbol by the Brewers Society after being surveyed by Southend Committee on Access for the Handicapped.

It means the family pub has got all the requirements that a handicapped person or somebody in a wheelchair needs when they are out.

Access committee chairman Mr. Eric Cohen said: 'I think it is a splendid idea because it is very important that people who build bars think about the problems for disabled people.

'I was very impressed with the pub; it is very suitable for disabled people because it has got level access and lots of room inside,' he said.

Mr. Keith Hall, manager of Parsons Barn since November, said: 'We have had the facilities for the past three years but have only recently been assessed.'

(Source: *Standard Recorder*, 22 April 1988.)

The purpose of this activity is to find out something about the quality of facilities for the disabled in your area. The following could be on your checklist:

- your school
- disco
- pub
- library
- swimming pool
- hospital

Divide the class up in the most convenient way to do the research. Discuss your findings as a class. Does it seem that efforts are being made to enable the disabled to 'mainstream', i.e. to share things with others?

Poverty

Absolute poverty

In parts of the world, people still die or suffer extreme ill-health as a result of poverty. About 40 million people die each year from hunger, almost half of them children. Poverty of this kind is still widespread in many less-developed countries. Warfare and lack of rainfall caused widespread and acute poverty in Ethiopia in 1985 and in the Sudan in 1988, but some other sub-Saharan African countries suffer almost as badly. Poverty which seriously undermines health or threatens life is known as *absolute* poverty.

Activity (class)

We would all agree that poverty such as that experienced by Ethiopia and the Sudan is not a common feature of modern Britain. However, this does not mean that poverty does not exist.
Working in small groups make *two* lists:

1 Write down the things you think would cause a person or family to be ' in poverty'. For example, if you think not owning a TV set makes people 'poor', write down 'no TV'.

2 Write down the groups of people you think are most likely to be 'at risk' from poverty. For instance, if you think homeless people are at risk, write 'the homeless' and so on.

Absolute poverty threatens life.

Seebohm Rowntree, a British expert on poverty, was among the first to define absolute poverty in the late nineteenth and early twentieth centuries. He saw it as a condition in which a healthy life is impossible. His research into the London poor showed a pattern of low pay or unemployment, bad housing, ill-health and poor sanitation. Rowntree wanted to establish a poverty line on the basis of absolute need to decide who was and who was not in poverty. He wrote that to be eligible for state help:

> The children must have no pocket money for dolls, marbles or sweets. The father must smoke no tobacco and drink no beer. The mother must never buy any pretty clothes for herself or her children, the character of the family wardrobe as for the family diet being governed by the regulation 'nothing must be bought but that which is absolutely necessary for the maintenance of physical health and what is bought must be of the plainest and most economical description'.

Ever since, government has tied assistance to the concept of a 'poverty line', although, in fact, the line has moved upwards.

Absolute poverty in Britain?

Can we still speak of 'the poor' and 'poverty' in modern Britain? Sometimes the view is expressed, especially by some who remember 'harder times', that 'real' poverty is now virtually non-existent. But should we judge the present by the standards of the past? How do we decide what poverty is in the late 1980s?

Relative poverty

Most sociologists argue that those who cannot achieve a standard of living comparable to those around them suffer *relative* poverty. Peter Townsend has argued that those who have 'resources so seriously below those commanded by the average individual or family that they are, in effect, excluded from ordinary living patterns, customs and activities' are relatively poor. So, a family in England who could not afford a TV set would be relatively poor, whereas a family in Ethiopia in this position would not be. Not to be able to afford a TV in England might cut off family members from experience normal to their community and prevent them taking part in conversations about, say, 'East-Enders' or 'Top of the Pops'. It might also cause feelings of inferiority or awkwardness, particularly among children, in their relationships with their peers.

Measuring poverty

Various attempts have been made to establish a measure to divide the poor from the non-poor. Victorian researchers, Charles Booth and Seebohm Rowntree, Sir William Beveridge in the 1940s and governments since then have considered such a measure necessary in order to establish elegibility for (who is entitled to receive) what we now call income support. Levels of elegibility have tended to be based on a subsistence view of poverty (i.e. just enough to survive), although they have edged upwards as the country has become wealthier. However, Peter Townsend considers that a measure based merely on subsistence criteria is inadequate. He and Brian Abel-Smith argue for a relative definition of poverty, as explained above. They estimate that the Government's basic allowance plus 40 per cent would be required to meet most people's relative needs. This extra income would provide the means for the poor to meet their social as well as their material commitments.

```
Activity (class)                                   Social commitments
                                                   Giving a birthday present to a close family member
Opposite is a list of some 'social commitments' which most   Owning (or renting) a TV
people in Britain today feel they should meet. For each one  Sending your child on a school trip
say:                                               Buying 'your round' of drinks in a pub
                                                   Sending Christmas cards
1  whether you think all people should be able to afford it,  Having a holiday
2  what the consequences might be for people not able to.    Buying new (rather than second-hand) clothes
                                                   Giving a little money to charity
                                                   'Chipping in' for a friend's wedding present
                                                   Having a night out with friends
```

Relative poverty in the 1980s

What, in terms of practical cases, is relative poverty in modern Britain? Joanna Mack and Stewart Lansley's social survey, *Poor Britain* (1985), asked a sample of 1,174 people what they considered to be the necessities required to maintain 'a minimum standard of living on socially established criteria and not just the criteria of survival or subsistence'. Respondents were given a list of 35 items (see Table 17.2) which had been drawn up after consultation with both the poor and experts on poverty. Twenty-six items were agreed as 'necessary' (as defined above) by a majority of respondents. These items then became the basis of Mack and Lansley's poverty measure. The depth of poverty is indicated by the number of necessities lacked (see Table 17.3).

Table 17.2. The public's perception of necessities

Standard-of-living items in rank order	% classing item as necessity	Standard-of-living items in rank order	% classing item as necessity
1 Heating to warm living areas of the home if it's cold	97	19 A hobby or leisure activity	64
2 Indoor toilet (not shared with another household)	96	20 Two hot meals a day (for adults)	64
3 Damp-free home	96	21 Meat or fish every other day	63
4 Bath (not shared with another household)	94	22 Presents for friends or family once a year	63
5 Beds for everyone in the household	94	23 A holiday away from home for one week a year, not with relatives	63
6 Public transport for one's needs	88	24 Leisure equipment for children, e.g. sports equipment or a bicycle[a]	57
7 A warm water-proof coat	87	25 A garden	55
8 Three meals a day for children[a]	82	26 A television	51
9 Self-contained accommodation	79	27 A 'best outfit' for special occasions	48
10 Two pairs of all-weather shoes	78	28 A telephone	43
11 Enough bedrooms for every child over ten of different sex to have his/her own[a]	77	29 An outing for children once a week[a]	40
12 Refrigerator	77	30 A dressing gown	38
13 Toys for children[a]	71	31 Children's friends round for tea/a snack once a fortnight[a]	37
14 Carpets in living rooms and bedrooms	70	32 A night out once a fortnight (adults)	36
15 Celebrations on special occasions such as Christmas	69	33 Friends/family round for a meal once a month	32
16 A roast meat joint or its equivalent once a week	67	34 A car	22
17 A washing machine	67	35 A packet of cigarettes every other day	14
18 New, not second-hand, clothes	64		

Average of all 35 items = 64.1

[a]For families with children only.
(Source: Joanna Mack and Stewart Lansley, *Poor Britain*, George Allen and Unwin, 1985.)

Questions

1 What percentage of respondents to the survey classify 'a garden' as 'a necessity'?
2 What number in the rank order of items classified as necessary does 'two pairs of all-weather shoes' come?
3 Are there any items you would
 a add to the list
 b take away from the list
 c put in a different place on the list?
Say why, in each case.

Mack and Lansley drew up a chart by which they assessed the degree to which groups were in poverty on the basis of the number of necessities they lack (as defined by a majority of the sample.) They found almost a quarter (22.2 per cent) of the population in or on the margins of poverty and almost one twentieth (4.8 per cent) in intense poverty. Clearly, the situation of the latter group is much worse than those on the margin of poverty, but what is perhaps most surprising is the large number who are struggling to share in 'modern prosperity', the 'other Britain', as the survey refers to them.

Table 17.3. The depths of poverty (in millions)

	In or on the margins	In poverty	Sinking deeper	In intense poverty
Adults	7.9	5.0	3.3	1.7
Children	4.2	2.5	1.4	0.9
Total (millions)	12.1	7.5	4.7	2.6
Percentage of the population	22.2	13.8	8.6	4.8
Lack of necessities (number of)	1–2	3	5–6	7+

Question

According to Table 17.3, how many millions are in intense poverty and what percentage of the population are they?

Activity (class)

Do you agree with the concept of relative poverty as used by Mack and Lansley? Do you have any doubts about it? Discuss.

Who are the poor?

Who, then, are the poor, those on the margin of poverty in contemporary Britain? They are: 1) the unemployed; 2) the low-paid; 3) single parents, 4) the sick and disabled, and 5) some pensioners. Were these the groups you put in the list you made earlier? Clearly, some of these groups overlap. Numerically, the working and non-working poor divide into three groups of roughly equal size:

a those where the head of household is in work (mainly the *low-paid*),
b those where he or she is *unemployed* and available for work,
c those where he or she is *not working and unavailable for work.*

The relative size of the various groups in poverty changes with circumstances. Figure 17.5 shows changes in the lowest fifth group of income between 1971 and 1985 by family type. We can relate the information in the figure to the points made in the previous paragraph.

Figure 17.5. Composition of the lowest fifth group of income: by family type, 1971 and 1985

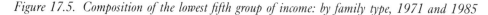

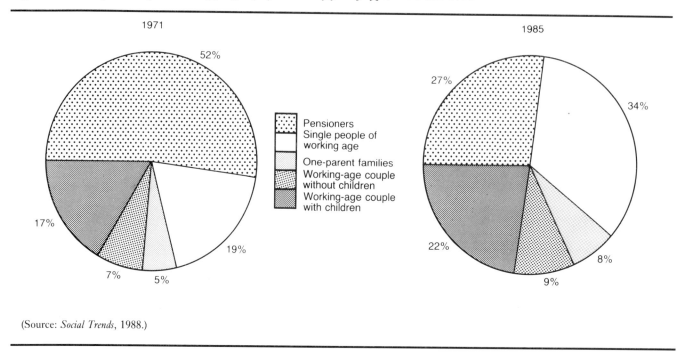

(Source: *Social Trends*, 1988.)

Very roughly, the lowest fifth group of income is approximately those to whom Mack and Lansley refer to as 'in or on the margins of poverty'. By far the biggest increase has been among single people of working age. This is mainly because of the much higher rate of unemployment among young people. The increased percentage of couples, especially with children, is due to unemployment, low pay and the reduction of many social security benefits. The increase in one-parent families in the lowest quintile (fifth) group reflects their increase as a proportion of all families. The great reduction in the percentage of the old in the lowest quintile group of income reflects their improved pension over the period. In turn, this reflects 'grey power', the fact that the number of older voters has greatly increased and the parties depend on them more for votes.

Questions

1. What was the percentage increase of single people of working age in the lowest fifth group of income betwen 1971 and 1985?
2. Select any *two* groups in Figure 17.5. In each case give one explanation for the percentage change in its position in the lowest fifth group of income.

We will now look in more detail at the main groups in or on the margins of poverty.

Groups in poverty

The unemployed, the low-paid, pensioners, one-parent families and the disabled make up most of the poor in modern Britain. It needs to be stressed that not all, or perhaps, even the majority, of the people in these groups are in poverty. However, compared with the general population, a large proportion of these groups are poor.

Figure 17.6. Unemployment 1921–85

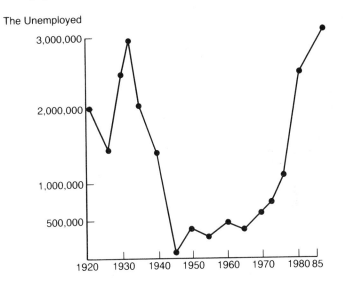

(Source: A. H. Halsey, *Change in British Society*, Oxford University Press, 1986.)

The unemployed

Figure 17.6 shows that between 1920 and 1985 there was a large variation in the numbers unemployed — one of the most disadvantaged groups in society. This was due mainly to changes in the number of jobs available over the period. In addition to material deprivation, research links unemployment to loss of self-respect, decline in status, ill-health and disruption of daily routine and family relationships. The worst hit are the long-term unemployed (just under one million in July 1988). Unemployment can also be experienced by communities as well as by individuals. In parts of Liverpool and the county of Cleveland, high local levels of unemployment tend to be associated with a decaying and depressed environment. Traditionally, work has been the basis on which community is built, and, with the decline of work, whole areas can be threatened with a 'cycle of poverty' which reduces the standard and quality of life.

Activity

Discuss with your teacher which groups are most likely to be unemployed in your area. Why are they more likely to be unemployed than others?

The low-paid

Between 1975 and 1985, the low-paid increased as a percentage of the poor. Between 1976 and 1983, the pre-tax income of the bottom 40 per cent fell from 10.2 per cent to 7 per cent of total income (while that of the top 20 per cent rose from 44.4 per cent to 48 per cent). So the relative position of the low-paid got worse. Using the Government and European index as a basis for calculation, the Low Pay Unit showed that 26.2 per cent of the work force

275

were low paid (nearly four million people), of whom 60 per cent were women. The unit also established that about the same number of part-time workers (four million) were low paid, of whom over 80 per cent were women

The tendency for women to make up a larger proportion of the poor is sometimes referred to as 'the feminisation of poverty', and the increase in low-paying work contributes to this. Most women working in hairdressing, shops, catering and as cleaners, domestics and textile workers are low paid. Routine office work, sometimes involving 'low-tech' skills, is often little better paid than factory work. Because so many married women are in part-time or temporary work, their wages, though often much needed, do not always greatly increase family income. Although female-headed single-parent families are particularly at risk of poverty, the vast majority of families in poverty are two-parent.

Activity (class)

Discuss with your teacher which jobs are low paid in your area. Does low pay in your area result in poverty or not?

Pensioners

The improvement in the position of pensioners has been one of the recent success of welfare state policy. As Figure 17.5 shows, in 1971, pensioners made up just over half (52 per cent) of all families in the bottom fifth of income, whereas, in 1985, they made up just over a quarter (27 per cent). This development has helped to change the face of poverty in Britain.

The improved position of pensioners reflects the consistent commitment of governments of both parties during this period to maintain the purchasing power of the state pension. In fact, the value of the pension increased in real terms. However, there is no guarantee that the gains made by the elderly will be maintained or improved upon. Along with children, the old are the most *dependent* group in society. Between 1971 and 1985, an average 88 per cent of their income came from social security benefits. Perhaps sheer numbers — there are over nine millon pensioners in Britain — could provide their best weapon. They have enough votes to bargain with politicians to maintain their standard of living.

Figure 17.7. Life expectancy of men aged 65 in different countries. By comparison, life expectancy in Britain is shorter. Why?

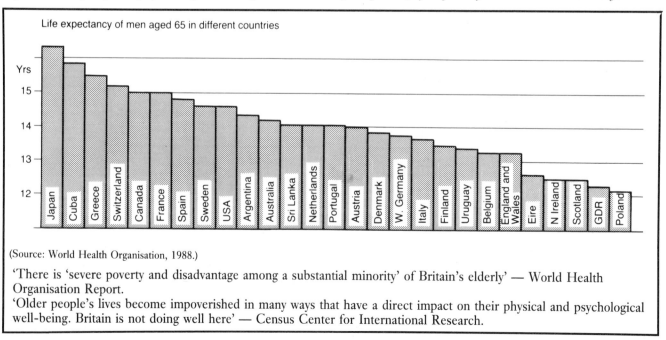

(Source: World Health Organisation, 1988.)

'There is 'severe poverty and disadvantage among a substantial minority' of Britain's elderly' — World Health Organisation Report.
'Older people's lives become impoverished in many ways that have a direct impact on their physical and psychological well-being. Britain is not doing well here' — Census Center for International Research.

However, poverty among the elderly can be particularly harsh and dangerous. The poorer old people often eat inadequately and live in unmodernised housing conditions, sometimes lacking hot water, a bath or even an inside lavatory. For those who live alone, the threat of ill-health or winter cold is particularly frightening. Sheltered housing offers a secure alternative for those who can afford it, but most cannot.

Activity (class)

Discuss with your teacher how widespread poverty among the old is in your area (it may be partly hidden). What is being, or could be, done about it?

One-parent families

Between 1971 and 1985, one-parent families increased from five per cent to eight per cent of the lowest fifth income group. Given that about one in seven families in Britain is now headed by a lone parent, this seems a relatively low figure. It is partly explained by the rapid rate at which married couples and single people have been entering the ranks of the poor. However, one-parent families in the lowest fifth income group are often *very* short of independent resources. In 1971, benefits formed, on average, 77 per cent of their total income and, in 1982, 84 per cent. The vast majority of single parents are female, and the increase in their number contributes to the 'feminisation' of poverty mentioned above.

The disabled

In 1988, an official report estimated the number of people with *some* degree of disability in Britain as six million. This large number is partly due to an increase in the disabled elderly. The report says that over 60 per cent of the disabled are living on or below the poverty line. Disabled people of working age are twice as likely to be on or below the poverty line as their able-bodied peers.

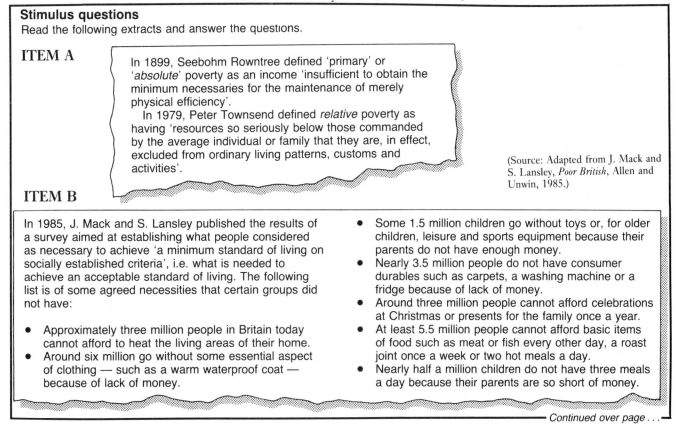

Stimulus questions

Read the following extracts and answer the questions.

ITEM A

In 1899, Seebohm Rowntree defined 'primary' or 'absolute' poverty as an income 'insufficient to obtain the minimum necessaries for the maintenance of merely physical efficiency'.

In 1979, Peter Townsend defined *relative* poverty as having 'resources so seriously below those commanded by the average individual or family that they are, in effect, excluded from ordinary living patterns, customs and activities'.

(Source: Adapted from J. Mack and S. Lansley, *Poor British*, Allen and Unwin, 1985.)

ITEM B

In 1985, J. Mack and S. Lansley published the results of a survey aimed at establishing what people considered as necessary to achieve 'a minimum standard of living on socially established criteria', i.e. what is needed to achieve an acceptable standard of living. The following list is of some agreed necessities that certain groups did not have:

- Approximately three million people in Britain today cannot afford to heat the living areas of their home.
- Around six million go without some essential aspect of clothing — such as a warm waterproof coat — because of lack of money.
- Some 1.5 million children go without toys or, for older children, leisure and sports equipment because their parents do not have enough money.
- Nearly 3.5 million people do not have consumer durables such as carpets, a washing machine or a fridge because of lack of money.
- Around three million people cannot afford celebrations at Christmas or presents for the family once a year.
- At least 5.5 million people cannot afford basic items of food such as meat or fish every other day, a roast joint once a week or two hot meals a day.
- Nearly half a million children do not have three meals a day because their parents are so short of money.

Continued over page . . .

ITEM C

Two ways of measuring poverty

In July 1988, the House of Commons Select Committee on Social Services reported that the number claiming means-tested state benefits had risen from 4.4 million in 1979 to 8.2 million.

However, the Department of Health and Social Security stated that the way the committee had measured poverty could be misleading. First, using the numbers receiving means-tested benefits as a measure made it *seem* that more become poor when benefits were increased — because more became eligible for them. Second, the actual spending power of the poor had risen considerably since 1979 — as had that of the non-poor.

Questions

1 Look at the list of missing necessities (Item B). Why do nearly 500,000 children not have three meals a day? (1 mark)
2 Examine the definitions of relative and absolute poverty (Item A). Is a lack of consumer items, such as carpets, a washing machine or a fridge, an example of absolute or relative poverty? (1 mark)
3 In Item C, which group is using a relative definition of poverty and which is using an absolute definition? (2 marks)
4 Using your own words, define what is meant by 'relative poverty' and give *two* examples of relative poverty from modern Britain. (4 marks)
5 Give *one* argument for and *one* against relative definitions of poverty. (2 marks)
6 Chose *one* group of the poor and give reasons why people in that group are likely to be in poverty. (6 marks)

Activity (class/outside class)

You will need to refer to Table 17.2 to carry out this activity.

1 Make a list of ten items, each of which you consider necessary for you and your family to maintain 'a minimum standard of living on socially established criteria'.
2 Check with someone to see if they agree with your list. You may decide to change it.
3 How many items on your list would you have to be without before you considered yourself 'in poverty'? Does your number agree with Mack and Lansley's number of 'missing necessities' for indicating 'in poverty' (see Table 17.3)?

Explanations of poverty

The following explanations of poverty move from the small scale to the large scale (or social structural), and include individual, cultural and (social) structural explanations.

Individual
There are three main ways in which poverty is seen as an individual problem.

First, there is the view that the poor are responsible for their own situation, that somehow, they deserve to be poor. In some cases, this explanation may be partly correct. Most would agree that habitual criminals who cannot get a job or gamblers who fritter their money away, at least partly, 'get what they deserve' if they fall on hard times. As a general explanation of poverty, however, 'blaming the poor' is weak. For instance, the great increase in the numbers of the poor unemployed in the early and mid-1980s was due to changes in British industry, not to an increase in laziness! (see Figure 17.6)

(Source: *New Internationalist*, No. 115, September 1982.)

Second, some people believe that poverty is justified (and inevitable) because some people are less talented and able than others, and therefore earn less. The problem with this explanation is that researchers generally agree that intelligence is fairly evenly distributed across the social classes. The stereotype of the 'thick labourer' is no more accurate than that of the 'upper-class twit'. Intelligence, or the lack of it, does not explain much about wealth or poverty.

Slipping through the welfare 'safety net'. Who's to 'blame' — the poor or the system? The 'dosser haunt supreme' in the extensive subways of Charing Cross, where home is a four-foot box, carried around or carefully stored away during the day.

Activity (class/outside class)

Some people live in, or on the fringes of, absolute poverty even in modern Britain. These include 'down and outs', the poorest of pensioners and one-parent families.

1 Make suggestions as to what social function the policeman in the photograph might be performing.
2 What does the man on the right of the picture appear to be doing?
3 Where do the homeless sleep in your area?
4 Is there any form of free sleeping accommodation for the homeless in your area?
5 Do you think there should, or should not, be such accommodation?

Third, there is the view that individuals can sometimes be unlucky or unfortunate. Some are physically or mentally handicapped and are dependent on the state from birth. However, accident or disease can strike anyone, and for those who survive, old age can bring its own problems. In 1984, about a third of the poor fell into this category. Few would think a society fair which failed to make adequate provision for this group, by general agreement 'the deserving poor'.

Cultural

The view is often put forward that it is the way the poor live, their culture, which explains their poverty. This is a group rather than an individual explanation of poverty, but it still tends to lay responsibility for poverty on the poor themselves.

In his book *The Heavenly City Revisited*, Edward Banfield argued that the poor create the vicious circle of poverty from which they suffer. He claimed that they are often work-shy and lazy, and lack the pride or motivation to keep themselves or their houses in decent order; even small repairs don't get done.

What makes this theory a cultural rather than an individual one is that the poor *learn* their 'lower-class' behaviour from each other. There is an important generational aspect to this: children learn their cultural values and behaviour mainly from their parents. Thus, the 'cycle of poverty' or 'deprivation' is passed on from generation to generation. It is not *only* through the family that the 'culture of poverty' is learnt. The peer group is another powerful socialising institution. Truancy and unemployment tend to be higher among youth in poorer areas. Time spent on 'the streets' can lead to an alternative 'education' of delinquency involving theft, drugs and violence.

The main criticism of culture as an explanation for poverty is that it does not consider the effect of social conditions on culture. For instance, theft and other forms of crime tend to go up in times of high unemployment. Do you blame culture or social conditions for this? You may feel better able to answer this question after reading the next section.

Structural

Sometimes individuals or groups are affected by changes in society over which they have no control. For instance, many argue that the high levels of unemployment in the mid-1980s (13 per cent in 1986) were due to major changes in technology and in increased competitiveness from Britain's trading 'rivals'. Both the coal industry and the car industry were affected by these factors. Many employees in these industries were made redundant, and in some cases 'fell' into poverty.

Structural changes, then, are major social and economic changes beyond people's personal control. It can be argued that much, if not most, poverty in contemporary Britain can be explained in terms of structural change.

Sometimes jobs are available — even in times of high unemployment — but the people with the skills to do them are not. To some extent this happened in Britain in 1987–8 — especially in computing and engineering. There are times when lack of training is due to the individual, but, in general, the quality of training depends on government planning (see p. 96).

Activity (class)

1 Explain in your own words what is meant by poverty due to the following reasons:
   a individual
   b cultural
   c structural
2 Discuss with your teacher the reasons for poverty in your area. Arrange the list in order of importance. Are the main reasons individual, cultural or structural?

Poverty in the 1990s: a return of the five giant evils?

Earlier, we discussed William Beveridge's desire to defeat the 'five giant evils' of want, disease, ignorance, squalor and idleness. The modern welfare state was an historic attempt to establish freedom from these evils.

In 1985, Jeremy Seabrook wrote an article arguing that the five giant evils had returned, even though, in some cases, in a somewhat different form. His is only one point of view, but it provided an interesting basis for discussion. Seabrook is a socialist and considers that capitalism is concerned with making profits but not with the social problems that can result from profit making. The following is a summary of his argument that the five evils have returned:

Want	There are over eight million on supplementary benefit. Poverty amid well-advertised plenty hurts more
Disease	Drug abuse, 'epidemics' of crime
Ignorance	The booming 'misinformation' industry, e.g. advertising — 'the business of creating...ignorance'
Squalor	'Cultural sewage', e.g. violent and pornographic entertainment, graffiti-daubed estates
Idleness	High unemployment

Jeremy Seabrook observes new kinds of squalor — but the old kind remains. In 1987,

- 100,000 were classed as homeless,
- 160,000 were living in bed and breakfast,
- 1,000,000 houses were sub-standard,
- 4,000,000 houses were unfit to live in.

(Source: figures quoted *New Statesman*, 9 January 1987.)

The problem continues to escalate:

- in 1979, 56,750 were homeless,
- in 1988, 112,730 were homeless.

(Source: The *Observer*, 6 October 1988.)

Housing 'squalor' in modern Britain

Health, poverty and class

Poor health and earlier death is perhaps the highest price to be paid for poverty. That price is paid in full by many of the poor, particularly those in semi or unskilled work.

Figure 17.8 shows the strong tendency for the death rate to be higher among lower socio-economic groups at all ages up to 64. This reflects the higher rate of major illnesses among lower socio-economic groups, including heart disease, cancer and circulatory diseases.

Figure 17.8. Relative mortality of social class

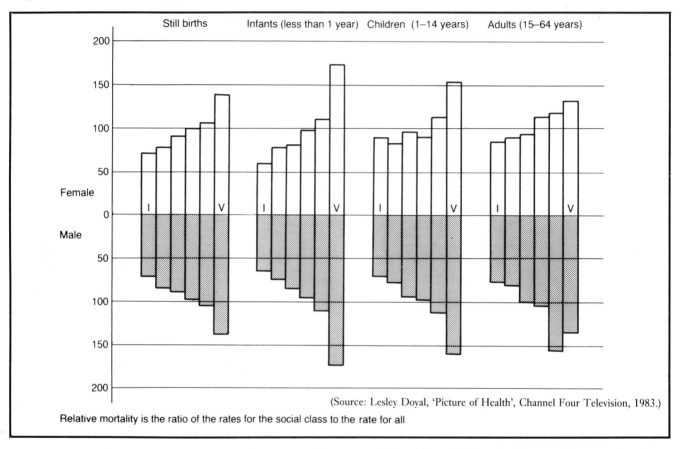

(Source: Lesley Doyal, 'Picture of Health', Channel Four Television, 1983.)

Relative mortality is the ratio of the rates for the social class to the rate for all

The causes of the greater ill-health and higher death rate of the working class are well known and are summarised in Figure 17.9.

Figure 17.9. Causes of ill-health

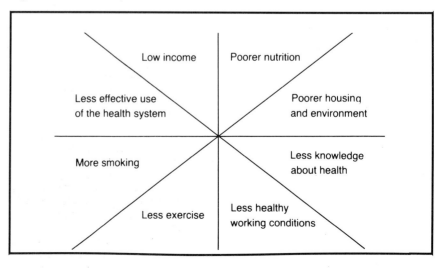

Activity (class/outside class)

1 What are the most important causes in the 'chain of ill-health? List the factors in Figure 17.9 in what you think is their order of importance.
2 Which of the factors would you classify as mainly *cultural* and which *material*? Make two lists under each of these headings.
3 Compare your lists with those of another student or with the group.

Stimulus questions

Read the following extract and the table then answer the questions.

ITEM A

In Britain, certain social groups are more likely to have wealth and health than others. Wealth and health, for example, are both closely related to sexual and racial divisions. For women living alone, poverty and the death of their children are more common experiences than for married women; they are more common, too, among black than white parents. Patterns of wealth and health similarly highlight the existence of class differences in living standards and life chances. Families in social class five have weekly incomes one third of those in social class one. Their health is correspondingly worse. Children born into social class five are more than twice as likely to die in the first year of life as those born into social class one.

(Source: Adapted from Hilary Graham, *Health and Welfare*, Macmillan, 1985.)

Questions

1 How much more likely to die in their first year of life are children born into social class V than those born into social class I? (Item A) (1 mark)
2 How many more ounces of sugar per week does a person in income group D consume than a person in income group A, and how many ounces less of fruit? (Item B) (2 marks)

ITEM B

Table 17.4. Income and nutrition

Income group	white bread	sugar	potatoes	fruit
		Food (ounces consumed per person per week)		
A	18	9.3	29	33
B	25	11	39	24
C	28	13	49	20
D	31	15	52	17

(Source: From 'Inequalities in Health', DHSS report, reprinted in Anna Coote, 'Death to the Working Class', *New Statesman*, 12 September 1980.)

3 Give two reasons for the relationship between income and food consumption shown in Table 17.4. (Item B) (4 marks)
4 Why are a) the children of women living alone, and b) the children of black parents generally at greater risk of death and illness? (Item A) (6 marks)
5 The National Health Service was intended to provide an equal service for all. Why is it, then, that some social groups are generally less healthy than others? (7 marks)

Structured questions

1 Describe what is meant by a 'welfare state'. (2 marks)
2 What reasons are there for some groups of people being more 'at risk' of poverty than others? (6 marks)
3 Some people argue that making benefits easily available to people creates a 'dependency culture' in which people automatically turn towards state 'hand-outs' rather than try to improve matters for themselves. What evidence would you use to try to convince someone that this was for too simple a view? (12 marks)

Project and assignment suggestions

1   *A study of poverty in your own neighbourhood/area or a part (even a street) in your own area* — The wider your area of study, the more you will need *statistics* on matters such as unemployment and poor housing. You will need to request these from the relevant central or local government office. You may also want to interview a social worker or housing officer to improve the personal quality of your data.

    You may want to relate poverty in your area to the national context. Is your area a traditional industrial region of high unemployment, or a better-off area of service employment?

2   *A small-scale* study of the poor — This could involve in-depth interviews or close observation (backed by notes/audio or video recordings). Do not research in a way likely to cause offence.

3   *A study of welfare policy* — This could be a study of national policy drawn mainly from secondary sources, or of how the welfare system works in your area. The latter would involve acquiring data from the relevant offices, including the Department of Health and Social Security.

Key words

Benefits — selective universal	Poverty — absolute relative
De-institutionalisation	Privatisation
Humanistic	Voluntary organisations
Policy	Welfare state

CHAPTER 18 Course Work: Problems and Assessment

Chapter One 'threw you in at the deep end' by suggesting that you do a 'mini-project' right at the beginning of your GCSE course, and introduced the various research methods. This chapter will not repeat that material, but you should look again at Chapter One for guidance on what methods to use in your main piece of course work — usually known as a project or enquiry — and for help and suggestions for shorter assignments.

This chapter is intended to show you how your project will be assessed, what to do to get marks and how to avoid losing them. The chapter follows, in outline, the marking scheme used by your teachers for the Southern Examining Group (SEG) project, but the requirements of other examining boards are also considered. The following are the seven main points assessed by the SEG marking scheme:

1 Aim/hypothesis
2 Methodology
3 Sources
4 Content
5 Presentation
6 Evaluation
7 Individual initiative

Notice that the assessment headings roughly correspond to those used in describing the 'stages of research' given in Chapter One (p. 2). The 'stages' describe how to do research, and how your research will be assessed is explained.

Aim/hypothesis

A piece of research involves finding someting out. So make sure you ask a *clear* question about your topic, e.g. a) Why are there more males than females in senior positions in the teaching profession?, or b) Do members of a particular ethnic minority (in your area) consider they are treated equally? We will follow through these examples in the rest of the chapter.

Don't make your topic and question too broad, e.g. 'Race in Britain', or too narrow, e.g. 'Why my Uncle voted Conservative in the 1987 election'.

In fact, you can ask a question about *any* area of social life — but try to make it a question that will be interesting to others as well as yourself!

A hypothesis is a guess at the answer to your question and you will *test* how accurate it is by your research. You should base your hypothesis on reading into the subject, not on your own 'common sense' which could easily mislead you. For instance, hypotheses to the questions asked in the examples above might be: a) Because women are socialised to accept inferior positions to men, because women often lose several years of their careers producing and bringing up children, both of these points, and/or others; b) Most do, but a large number of young black people feel they are discriminated against.

Your main hypothesis — 'Most do' — is *qualified* by the suggestion that young people may be an exception. You will have to make sure your research *tests* both the main hypothesis and the qualification by researching both groups.

In fact, the point of the hypothesis or guess is to test it. The hypothesis gives focus and direction to the research; it gives something to support or reject. The most rigorous (toughest) test of a hypothesis is to try to disprove it. If you can't, you know it is quite likely to be along the right lines.

Whilst a question or curiosity about something is always part of research, a hypothesis or guess at the answer is not absolutely necessary. Sometimes a researcher may simply want to gather information without a clear idea of what it will show.

It is very important to get the first stage of your research right — and that means a clear idea of what you intend to research. If you don't, the rest of your project will be more or less a mess. You should write down your aims clearly *before* you actually start doing your research, and then use them to help you shape the research.

Methodology

The main point here is to choose a method or methods that will provide information to answer the question you have asked. Many students produce poor projects because they have used sloppy or 'easy' methods which don't enable them to demonstrate anything. Here are examples of both bad and good approaches to research — again, using the 'running' example:

Bad practice

a Researching the position of women in teaching. Asking your parents what they think about the matter.
b Racial discrimination. Asking five or six of your friends whether they think members of a particular minority are treated equally (asking a few friends what they think about something is *not* sociological research).

Good practice

a Use your own school as a *case study* of gender equality in the teaching profession. Draw up a chart of the teaching positions — broken down by gender. Interview or give questionnaires to *properly selected* samples of, say, five male and five female teachers. Try to find out what the picture is nationally so you can do a comparison.
b Given that your topic is whether members of a particular minority feel they are treated equally, *their* opinion and experience must be sought. Again, well-devised interviews or questionnaires of a well-chosen sample of ethnic minority members are required. A sub-sample of young members of the group would also be needed.

Once you have carried out your research, you can evaluate it (draw conclusions from it) — see below.

Sources

In most cases, your main source of information will be your own research. However, whatever your area of research, it is almost certain that somebody else has already done work on it. You might get some ideas or information that support(s) your own project from this *secondary* material. It is important to acknowledge (state) when you are using secondary material in your project.

In some pieces of research, you will be able to use a wide variety of secondary sources (for instance, there is a lot of work on gender and education). However, you will only get marks for doing so if you *relate* the secondary source material to your own work. For example, figures which show gender inequality in teaching appointments would be very relevant to the first of our running examples.

Content

The project content is what you present to your teacher (and external examiner) for assessment — the project itself. There are two main points to remember about content: it must be *relevant* and *thorough*.

'Relevant' means related to the point. In this case, the point is the question or hypothesis that you are researching. So, if you are trying to find out why there are more males than females in senior positions in teaching, a discussion of the position of women in other professions is *only* likely to be useful as a comparison (so you should not get 'bogged down' in it). All content should be relevant to the subject of your research.

'Thorough' means that the content is i) the product of using methods *properly*, and ii) that relevant content is *fully* included. For instance, in a sample survey, you should decide what information you need to include about respondents and include the same information for them all in the project. If you have used a questionnaire to obtain information, a copy of the questionnaire should be included.

Presentation

Presentation is closely related to content. Content is *what* is in the project; presentation is *how* it is organised and laid out.

The following is a good framework for presenting your project — though you might want to vary it after consultation with your teacher, or because of the particular requirements of your examination board:

Title — Put this on a separate page; keep it as short and exact (in describing the project) as possible.

Summary — A *summary* of the project should follow the title page. This should just be a few sentences — perhaps just one sentence each on: the area covered by the project, the aims, the research done, the main findings, and the main conclusions.

Contents page — This should include the main chapter headings.

Main content/report — This should include:

- introduction,
- primary and secondary sources/methods used,
- main findings (results),
- analysis (i.e. working out) or results,
- interpretation/evaluation (i.e. assessing the importance/meaning of results),
- conclusions,
- list of sources/bibliography.

Some presentation tips

Language — Above all express yourself clearly. Don't try to use words you don't understand; the examiner won't be impressed. It is no use producing good content if you can't make yourself understood.

Style — Avoid 'I did this...', 'I think that...' Use impersonal forms of expression such as: 'the results showed', 'the findings suggest', 'it is clear that'.

Neatness — Be as neat as possible. A project written on a typewriter or word processor will look good, but make sure your examination board does not insist on handwritten projects before using one of these.

Illustrations and diagrams — These often make or develop a point better than words can, but make sure they are *relevant* to the main text.

Evaluation

Evaluation is deciding what your findings mean. Again, relevance is the key. Your conclusions must be *relevant* to your findings. Your findings may *confirm* (support) your hypothesis or not (if not, you should *re-evaluate* your hypothesis in the light of your findings). For example, suppose your hypothesis was that women are generally in inferior positions in teaching because of the way they are socialised. However, your findings might suggest that the main reason is the years women lose from teaching because of having children. In re-evaluating your hypothesis, you would have to include consideration of this finding. So, if you *restated* (put into new words) your hypothesis after your research, it could be very different from the original hypothesis.

Try to be as *perceptive* as possible in evaluating your project. This means carefully and thoughtfully drawing out the conclusions that are actually there. However, don't try to be too clever and read more into your information than it really supports. Otherwise, you will tie yourself in knots!

Individual initiative

Individual initiative is about your *personal* contribution to the project. How much effort and creativity have you put into it?

You can show initiative in any aspect of your project, but three areas stand out:

- use of sources,
- use of methods,
- evaluating findings.

It often requires a real effort to go to a library and look up books or newspaper clippings on your project area. However, such trips often provide the stimulus that fires the project into life and the results are well rewarded by examiners.

Again, there is a temptation for students to be lazy or sloppy in using the methods chosen for their primary research. Make sure you take your sample properly, be careful to observe precisely and to record observations. Don't assume that 'a survey' is *always* the best research method.

Evaluation is what *you* make of your findings. However, it would show real initiative to ask others (perhaps fellow students) to evaluate your results, and to take their comments into consideration where relevant.

Conclusion

The above advice should help you not only to produce a good project, but to enjoy doing so. Try to plan ahead and to give yourself enough time to do your project thoroughly. As you will probably have several projects to do, from a variety of subjects, it is worth noting down as early as possible all the different deadlines so that you can plan your project work properly. The quality of your own project is the best measure you have of your ability as a social scientist.

Glossary

Afro-Caribbean is a description of people of African ancestry and heritage who have cultural or kinship links with a Caribbean country

Age stage refers to the different ways societies create the way of life of a given age group

Ageing population (an) is a population in which there is an increasing proportion of people in the upper age brackets.

Alienation at work means that the worker's abilities are hardly used or developed — perhaps resulting in severe boredom.

Amplification (the) *of deviance* is an increase in deviant behaviour due to increased public concern (especially expressed through the media)

Assimilate (to) means one ethnic group being absorbed by (become a part of) another ethnic group

Belief (a) is an acceptance of something as true with or without proof

Benefits — selective benefits are available only to a particular group of people — eligibility is usually means tested
— universal benefits (or services) are available to everybody

Capitalist economy (a) is an economic system in which people produce goods and services for profit in competition with others

Censorship is use of the power to control the content of a medium, e.g. of newspapers

Class — There are various definitions of class. The most common definition bases a person's class mainly on his or her occupation. Marxists define class on the basis of relations to the means of production (the capitalist class owns the means of production, e.g. factories, and the working class 'works' them)

Clique (a) consists of from two to at most six, peers (see below) who are close friends

Cohabitation refers to partnerships in which an adult male and female live together without being married

Community (a) is a group of people sharing strong relationships and usually living in the same area, such as a neighbourhood, village or part of a town

Comprehensive school (a) is one which takes pupils across the full (or a very wide) ability range without a test or examination. The comprehensive secondary system has largely replaced the tripartite system (see below)

Conglomerate (a) is a number of companies (businesses) owned by a major shareholder, e.g. Rupert Murdoch's media conglomerate

Conjugal roles are the social roles of husbands and wives within marriage

Consciousness (class) refers to the awareness (or lack of awareness) a person or group has of the class to which they belong

Constitution (a) is a written statement of the form of government of a particular government, organisation or society

Consumer (a) is a person who buys or uses the goods and/or services which are produced

Control group (a) is as similar as possible to the experimental group but not exposed to the experimental stimulus (see 'Experimental group')

Core labour force (a) is the generally skilled, permanent body of employees, which in return for secure work is expected to be co-operative and flexible.

Correlation study (a) is research into the connection between two factors (things)

Crowd (a) consists of several cliques (see above) — the sort of grouping who might get together for a teenage party

Crude birth rate (the) is expressed as the number of babies born in a society per year per thousand of the population

Crude death rate (the) is expressed as the number of deaths in a society per year per thousand of the population

Culture is the way of life of a particular group. It includes media, literature, fashion, style and the way people live their everyday lives

Data are the information collected and/or used by social scientists in their research

De-institutionalisation is the policy of returning back to the community people housed in state institutions, e.g. hospitals for the mentally handicapped

Democracy is a form of government in which the people have control

Dependency refers to any part of the population supported by others, e.g. children, some elderly people

Dependency ratio is the ratio of young and aged dependants to the number of people of working age in a population

De-urbanisation is the movement of people out of cities and large towns, particularly inner-city areas, to the suburbs or countryside

Deviance is behaviour which is considered to break the norm

Discrimination refers to the treatment of a person or group in an unequal and usually (though not necessarily) unfair manner

Division of labour (the) refers to the way work is shared out in an economy — who does what

Economy (the) is the part of society concerned with the production (making), distribution (making available) and consumption (buying and use) of goods and services

Ethnic group (an) is a group which shares a common origin (e.g. history) and culture

Experimental group (an) is the group which is the subject of an experiment (see 'Control group')

Extended family (an) is a family unit which either lives together or keeps very close contact and which includes a wider range of kin (relations) than the nuclear family (see below), e.g. grandparents, aunts, uncles, cousins

Family functions refer to the contributions made by the family, both to its members and to society as a whole, e.g. reproduction, socialisation

Fertility rate (the) refers to the number of births in a population per year per thousand women of child-bearing age

Gender roles are the different characteristics and patterns of behaviour which are associated with males and females. Gender roles are learned during the socialisation process

Generation (a) refers to those people born at approximately the same time.

Government (a) is the group of people (e.g. Ministers) who administer ('run') a country or an area

Grammar school (a) is a school which restricts entry to those pupils who have passed the eleven-plus examination

Humanism is the belief that the most important thing in human life is the welfare and development of human beings

Hypothesis (an) is the researcher's guess or suggested answer to the question(s) posed by the research. It is an unproven theory

Ideology is a term used to describe ideas and beliefs about life or some aspect of life. It is a broad framework of ideas, values and beliefs

Infant mortality rate (the) is the number of babies out of every thousand born who die before their first birthday

Interview (an) is a method of obtaining information by asking questions

Label (to) someone means publicly to treat them as belonging to a certain group, e.g. criminals, usually on the basis of appearance, such as wearing rough clothes

Leisure is the time when people do as they choose — their 'own time'

Libel (a) is an untrue and damaging statement published about somebody

Life expectancy refers to the age to which the people of a population can be expected to live

Life-style is the way a person lives, e.g. the type of possessions, habits and friends he or she has

Life cycle (a) is made up of the age stages (see above) between life and death

Longitudinal study (a) is a study of a particular matter over a period of time, e.g. a group of pupils from five to sixteen years of age

Lumpenproletariat refers to those people — nearly all poor — who are not in regular work and so are not part of the organised working class

Net migration is the difference between the number of people coming into a country (immigrants) and the number of people leaving that country (emigrants) in a given period, usually a year

Norm (a) is any kind of social 'rule', written or unwritten

Nuclear family (a) is an adult couple and their child or children

Obligated time is time spent doing necessary things in relation to home, work or bodily functioning, e.g. cleaning, travelling to work, shaving

Marketable wealth is the part of a person's wealth that they can spend as they choose

Means tested refers to those benefits which are only given after a person's income and savings are checked to make sure that he or she is entitled to receive them

Media (the) are the means by which it is possible to communicate with large numbers of people, e.g. TV, newspapers

Migration refers to the movement of people between countries (external) or within a country (internal)

Mixed economy (a) is one which is partly (usually mainly) capitalist and partly socialist

Observation is a sociological method based on looking at something and recording the information

Participant observation is a sociological method in which the researcher both participates (joins in) and observes the subject of research

Participation (political) refers to people taking part in the decisions which affect their lives, e.g. as members of tenants' associations

Patriarchy is the power and control exercised by men simply because they are men

Peer group (the) consists of people of about the same age who provide each other with support and identity.

Pluralism (ethnic) is the view that some differences will remain between ethnic groups even though they are all citizens of the same country

Policy refers to the main general plans (e.g. in education, defence) of governments

Politics is the study of power, especially in relation to governments

Poverty — absolute poverty is the lack of the means (such as food and shelter) to survive properly
— relative poverty is the lack of the means to live at a level which compares with that of the community or society at large

Power is having the means to do what you want to do, and also to make other people do what you want them to do

Pressure groups are organisations of citizens which seek to influence politicans to act in a certain way

Private sector (the) is the capitalist (privately owned) part of an economy

Privatisation (the) of welfare or other services means that private enterprise provides them or carries them out, rather than the state

Privatised family (the) is a family unit whose members spend a great deal of time (especially leisure time) together, i.e. they are 'home centred'

Producer (a) is a person who creates goods and services

Public sector (the) is the nationally owned part of an economy

Questionnaire (a) is a list of questions used to obtain research data, usually as part of a social survey (see below)

Racism is believing or behaving as though an individual or group is/are inferior on the grounds of race, ethnicity or both

Reconstituted family (a) is a family in which one or both parents have been married before, i.e. there are step-parents and step-children

Reserve army of labour (the) consists of workers who are usually semi-skilled or unskilled and can be easily hired when business expands and fired when it contracts

Role (a) is a part the individual plays in society or in a social group

Role models are people whose ideas and behaviour we consciously or unconsciously try to copy

Sample (a) is a group which has been systematically selected from a larger group in such a way that it is representative of the larger group

Sanction (a) is a way of trying to make people conform, e.g. a punishment

Satisfaction (work) — intrinsic satisfaction is a feeling that results from liking a job or some part of a job for its own sake
— extrinsic satisfaction is a feeling that results from liking something outside of, but related to, the job, e.g. the wages

Secularisation refers to the decline in religious beliefs and practices, and in the power and influence of the church and organised religion

Sexist refers to language, ideas or behaviour which treat females in an unfavourable way compared with males

Sexual division of labour (the) is the way in which work (both domestic and paid employment) is divided between males and females

Socialisation is learning to become a member of society

Social control is the process by which members of a group or society are encouraged or made to conform (behave in a certain way)

Social mobility is movement up or down the social scale, usually measured by a person's occupation

Social order occurs when people generally act according to the norms of a society

Socialist economy (a) is one which is publicly owned. Democratic involvement in socialist economies varies

Society is the way in which people, individually and in groups, organise their lives together

Status is the amount of prestige or importance a person has in the view of other members of society

Stereotype (to) is to label somebody as a 'type' without properly considering them as an individual

Subculture (a) is a group of people within a larger group who have their own distinctive ideas, beliefs and life-style

Subsystem (of society) (a) is one of the ways developed to meet the needs of the people of a society. The main subsystems are the economic, the family, the political and the cultural

Survey (a) involves the collection of information about a particular group of people, usually by interviewing or questioning members of the group

Symmetrical family (the) is a small, nuclear unit with both parents as breadwinners and sharing many domestic tasks

System (social) (the) refers to the ways people organise to meet their social needs, which are mainly economic, family, political and cultural

Tripartite system (the) is the system of secondary education which divides schools into three types — grammar, technical and secondary modern. Pupils are allocated to one of the three types, usually on the basis of the eleven-plus examination

Uncommitted income is 'free' income, i.e. it does not have to be spent on necessities such as food, mortgages, etc

Underclass (the) is a term which generally refers to the long-term poor who are 'cut off' from the rest of society by circumstances such as unemployment or low pay

Urban movement (an) occurs when a large number of people organise in support of a cause, over a long period of time

Urbanisation is an increase in the number and size of towns and cities and the proportion of the population who live in them

Value (a) is a principle or standard, such as honesty, self-interest or caring for others

Voluntary organisations are private bodies which try to deal with social problems and issues

Welfare state (the) is a system in which the state accepts responsibility for the well-being of its people. It consists of those government departments concerned with the well-being, security and, in certain respects, control of the nation's citizens

Women's movement (the) refers to groups of women throughout the world who are trying, often in different ways, to fight against discrimination and injustice to women in all areas of life

*I*ndex